Strategic Human Resource Development

Lyle Yorks

COLUMBIA UNIVERSITY, TEACHERS COLLEGE

THOMSON

™

SOUTH-WESTERN

THOMSON

──────✦──────™

SOUTH-WESTERN

Strategic Human Resource Development, 1e

Lyle Yorks

VP/Editorial Director:
Jack W. Calhoun

VP/Editor-in-Chief:
Michael P. Roche

Executive Editor:
Joe Sabatino

Senior Developmental Editor:
Mardell Toomey

Marketing Manager:
Jacquelyn Carrillo

Production Editor:
Stephanie Blydenburgh

Technology Project Editor:
Kristen Meere

Media Editor:
Karen Schaffer

Manufacturing Coordinator:
Diane Lohman

Production House:
Argosy Publishing

Printer:
Quebecor World
Kingsport, TN

Internal Designer:
Rik Moore

Cover Designer:
Lisa Albonetti

Cover Designer:
Rik Moore

For permission to use material from this
text or product, submit a request online
at http://www.thomsonrights.com.

For more information
contact South-Western,
5191 Natorp Boulevard,
Mason, Ohio 45040.
Or you can visit our Internet site at:
http://www.swlearning.com

To our granddaughter Maya Claire Yorks,
who brings energy and enthusiasm to her learning
and into our lives.

Contents

Introduction

Human resource development (HRD) has emerged, in part, out of training and development that has traditionally been recognized as the function of overall human resource management (HRM), which has included recruitment, selection, and compensation. HRD reflects both a growing awareness of the strategic implications of human resources and linkages to other HRM functions, like performance management. The terminology of HRD also reflects the awareness that much learning and development (as opposed to training and development) takes place *outside of the classroom*. HRD, however, is rooted in the training classroom and focuses on the individual learner developing skills and competencies.

My goal in this book is to address the learning objectives and the questions implied in comments such as these, from students in a recent HRD class:

> "I am on study leave from the University of Asia and the Pacific. My last position included HRM-related oversight responsibility . . . I want to more deeply understand the link between HRM/HRD and overall corporate strategy."

> "I am a manager of education and training at [a television network]. I want a clear understanding of the interplay and differences between HRD, HRM, and OD [organizational development], along with a theoretical understanding of my work and of organizations."

> "My human resources manager and I would like to learn more about the HR/organizational issues facing organizations and how they are being dealt with. I would also like to learn more about HRD trends."

> "I am fairly new to the field of HR—a little over one and a half years into my first HR position as an HR specialist. I want to understand more fully the strategic issues around HRD and how to think about them more critically."

> "I am a technical recruiter. Since I really should find a niche to concentrate on, I hope this course will help me decide if I would like to venture into training."

These questions are similar to questions HRD executives are asking themselves, such as:

- What kinds of learning initiatives make sense for our company?
- How far do we go with "shared services" (sharing learning resources across the corporate organization as opposed to dedicating learning resources to specific business lines)?
- How much HRD work should we outsource?
- What are the implications of our using distance learning?

Questions like these are critical for organizations; this book provides a strategic context for addressing them. Accordingly, it has a dual purpose. Its first, and primary, purpose is to serve as a text in graduate courses in HRD. To meet this purpose, we address core and emerging issues in HRD practice, including 1) HRD as a professional field of practice; 2) HRD's relationship to OD and HRM; 3) organization of the HRD function; 4) theoretical foundations of HRD practice; 5) design of learning experiences; 6) the rapid movement to Web-based learning; and 7) assessing results.

The book's secondary purpose is to offer a specific perspective on HRD, one that links HRD to enhancing organizational strategy and to developing performance capability through learning interventions that meet strategic needs. We begin by strategically viewing the organization from a general management perspective as a driver for the HRD function—specifically creating a focus on strategic learning and developing performance throughout the organization. This text is, therefore, very well suited for human resource practitioners and other business professionals.

The book's two purposes are linked by a belief in the value, to graduate students who are being introduced to formal study in the field and to the various roles and competencies that are foundational to HRD practice, of framing HRD practice from the perspective of the strategic imperatives of organizations. The purposes are also linked by the belief that it is important to stimulate debate about the role of HRD in organizations.

In our Adult Learning and Leadership Program at Teachers College, Columbia University, "Human Resource Development in Organizations" is one of a cluster of courses that comprise the workplace learning concentration for our students. This particular course examines HRD from the perspective of organizing and managing the HRD function: one of the course objectives is to present models that can inform the kinds of questions and points students need to raise in their conversations with managers when seeking to add value to organizations through assessing, designing, and implementing HRD interventions. Ideas, constructs, and models are presented as core tools for thinking about the possibilities for effective HRD practice; that mindset is at the heart of the phrase "theory to practice." In this text I have drawn heavily on the writing and thinking of scholars and practitioners whose work is central to the field; writing and thinking that has proven extraordinarily useful in my own thinking about the profession and in informing my own research and consulting. As in my practice, I have relied on those models and constructs that, in my experience, provide frameworks helpful for taking action.

The book is organized into three parts. Part One—*Strategy Making as Learning: Positioning the Role of HRD in Strategic Management*—begins with an introduction to HRD as an emergent profession with its own foundations in theory and practice. The evolution of HRD is framed along with key points of debates and discourse in the literature. At the heart of the first chapter are the unique questions, from a practice perspective, that HRD, OD, and HRM ask and answer in the service of providing value to the organization. The questions are important, the lines dividing these fields of practice that are not HRD and HRM practices need to be aligned, and HRD and OD, while coming from different foundations, are increasingly overlapping as fields of practice. The next two chapters look at the strategy literature, first from a traditional management perspective (Chapter Two) and then by framing strategy development as a learning process (Chapter Three). Chapter Four addresses HRD leadership and the organization of the HRD function, with special attention given to advocacy, political action, and questions of power. Chapter Five reviews key empirical literature on the relationship between strategy, HR systems, and organizational performance. It concludes with a political-economy model that integrates the various themes in Part One.

Part Two—*Putting HRD into Practice*—begins in Chapter Six with the theoretical foundations of HRD practice. These include adult learning theory, team learning, and organizational learning and performance improvement as well the implications of adult development. Chapter Seven discusses the design of learning programs, with special attention to the lessons of models and the research on learning transfer as part of program design. Chapter Eight extends the design discussion to core issues in the development of e-learning. Program assessment, with special attention to research on and critique of the most widely known taxonomy of evaluation—the Kirkpatrick four-level evaluation framework—is covered in Chapter Nine, where we give considerable attention to return-on-investment calculations (ROI) and describe and discuss evaluative inquiry and other more systemic approaches to assessment. Chapter Ten is an integrative chapter that links learning to performance and seeks to reinforce the perspective of the text. Chapter Eleven examines trends and emergent issues that are likely to shape HRD practice in the coming decade.

Part Three—*From Theory to Practice*—is a set of cases written by HRD professionals working in the field. Each case captures primary and secondary themes that run through the book. The cases are arranged to reinforce the general flow of the book, but each case reflects a combination of issues found in the world of practice that doesn't conveniently reduce itself to one set of problems at a time. Each case is followed by a set of questions that can facilitate its analysis through various concepts that have been presented.

ACKNOWLEDGMENTS

The theories and research of my colleagues in the field have provided the stimulation and source of ideas that inform my courses, my own research and practice, and, subsequently, the content of this book. My colleagues, of course, bear no responsibility either for how I have chosen to integrate their diverse ideas and models or for how I have added to them. Since my colleagues are an eclectic lot, I imagine some will be amused and a few, appalled, at the results. I find the intellectual fun in the tensions among the various positions in the field. All I can say is these interpretations have worked and continue to work for me in both my academic research and professional practice, and I thank you all. Also thanks to many doctoral students who have provided support through their critiques, both in class and in papers. At the risk of exclusion, Denise Williams, Lucia Alcantara, Janet Reid-Hector, Charles Stull, Art Shirk, Tina Luddy, and Maxim Voronov have all influenced my thinking, and I thank them for their expertise. They are among many students who make it enjoyable to be at Teachers College, Columbia University. Special thanks go to Angie Sites, our program secretary, and Rika Wilcox, a master's student in organizational psychology, who also works in the program office. Both were generous with time and ideas, helping me solve various technical problems by importing files, locating sources, and helping with creative designs as I moved between various computer systems. Rika kept track of permissions and repeatedly kept the project from slipping into chaos. Thanks also to Russell Yorks for his expertise with computers that proved invaluable at times. The comments of the following reviewers were particularly helpful in working towards the final manuscript, and they were very generous with their thoughts on how to improve the first draft manuscript: Bradford S. Bell, Cornell University; Joan F. Brett, Arizona State University; Lisa Burke, Louisiana State University; Robert Cardy, University of Arizona; Derek E. Crews, Seminole Community College; Diana Deadrick, Old Dominion University; Satish P. Deshpande, Ph.D., Western Michigan University; Paul N. Keaton; University of Wisconsin; Douglas M. McCabe, Georgetown University; Karen Overfield, Carnegie-Mellon University; Robert K. Prescott, Rollins College; and Suzanne Zivnuska, University of North Florida.

Also, I thank Mardell Toomey, senior developmental editor at South-Western, for her patience in seeing this project through to completion, and Stephanie Blydenburgh, who was responsible for production of this text.

I especially thank my wife Joanne whose support helped me to maintain my sanity while in the midst of engaging in this particular form of madness as I spent days revising and working toward deadlines.

INSTRUCTOR RESOURCES

The Instructor's Resource CD (ISBN 0-324-071790-5) includes an instructor's manual with a chapter overview, chapter outline, instructor's notes, suggestions for additional readings, experiential exercises, and discussion questions and answers. Also included are possible essay questions for testing purposes and notes on the cases included at the end of the text.

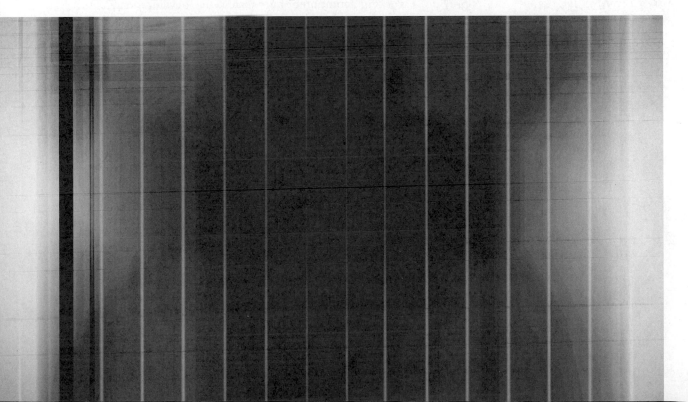

part I

Strategy Making as Learning: Positioning the Role of HRD in Strategic Management

1

This chapter

- introduces the various ways in which human resource development has been conceptualized and defined by scholars and practitioners in the field;

- relates human resource development (HRD) to human resource management and organizational development;

- discusses two perspectives on the fundamental purpose of human resource development in organizations: 1) the performance improvement perspective and 2) the learning perspective;

- reviews the historical and theoretical foundations of operational effectiveness; and

- provides a working definition of human resource development.

Key terms:

human resource development	**organization development**	**Training Within Industry Project**
human resource management	**performance improvement**	

Defining the Scope of Human Resource Development Practice

The old Chinese adage, May you live in interesting times, seems very appropriate for the field of human resource development in the early years of the 21st century. Informed and influenced by fields such as adult education, adult development, organizational psychology, economics, and organizational theory, HRD practitioners are experimenting with and adopting a broad view of learning: how it can be facilitated and its impact on individual and organizational performance. Concepts such as informal and incidental learning,[1] reflection-in-action and reflection-on-action,[2] tacit knowing,[3] transformative learning,[4] and learning from experience[5] have become increasingly influential in the field, supplementing the orientation toward behaviorism that has provided the theoretical foundation for many training courses. These concepts have been especially influential in professional and executive development. Approaches such as action learning[6] and work-based learning,[7] which, in the early 1990s, were often met with resistance by training departments wedded to traditional classroom based training, were being widely diffused by 2000.

At the same time, technology has opened up new possibilities for delivering, in more convenient and economical ways, traditional training topics to people at all levels of the workforce. Companies are establishing their own "corporate universities" and "learning management systems"—some located in physical facilities and, increasingly, others con-

sisting of virtual Web-based learning offerings—as well as "knowledge management" and "experience library" networks to provide training and education to their employees.[8] The notion of "learning organizations"[9] has made learning a topic of discussion at the senior levels of organizations, with some business school scholars suggesting (not without controversy) that organizational learning itself constitutes an important element of corporate strategy.

As an academic discipline, HRD has emerged as a field in its own right, differentiated from human resource management (HRM). The establishment of the Academy of Human Resource Development (www.ahrd.org) in 1993 and the refereed journals it sponsors, Human Resource Development Quarterly, Human Resource Development International, Advances in Human Resource Development, *and* Human Research Development Review, *marked important points in the evolution of HRD as a field of study, standing for the value of practice informed by theory-based research. A growing body of theory and research is guiding responsible practice in areas such as performance improvement,[10] transfer of learning,[11] and results assessment.[12]*

As HRD matures as a field of practice, these advances in theory and research that guide it need to be accompanied by a focus on learning programs that impact performance; this will continue to enhance HRD's credibility with senior management. Dilworth, McClernon, and Redding identify actions that will move the field of HRD closer to being part of the business, including several that reach the heart of this book, namely:

- *become knowledgeable about the core issues of the business in which HRD professionals practice;*
- *align HRD's purpose and activities with the outcomes valued by senior management; and*
- *demonstrate the value of HRD from a managerial perspective.[13]*

Although "strategically-driven HRD" is a phrase that has popular currency in the literature, much that has been written on the subject focuses more on strategically positioning HRD within organizations, in contrast to demonstrating how HRD is an integral part of the strategic and tactical activities of the business.

The perspective of this book is straightforward: it examines the role of HRD expertise as an integral element in the successful implementation of organizational strategy. Three premises underlie this perspective: first, that HRD professionals in organizations have to focus their efforts on learning as a critical link between strategic intent and organizational performance; second, that successfully making this linkage requires effective political action on the part of HRD leadership; and third, that effective strategically-linked HRD interventions need to be coordinated with other human resource management-driven changes in staffing, compensation, and performance management. Together these three premises provide a subtext to the book—learning, when skillfully promoted within the political economy of an organization's internal power structure and external strategic niche, is a potential force for leveraging individual and organizational performance.

For example, Shillaber has described how, when the senior executive team at the pharmaceutical company Berlex adopted opportunism and flexibility as strategic imperatives for guiding their business, they needed to make trans-

formational changes in the company's functionally oriented organization and bureaucratic culture.[14] This strategic shift, which placed an emphasis on identifying and seizing emerging product opportunities and quickly forming alliances and partnerships, required organizing a massive organizational learning effort around the theme of "relationship." Learning interventions, which took the form of a series of workshops directed at such skills as risk analysis and risk taking, relationship management, flexibility, and team development, were necessary both to give substance to the business model and to support the required changes in organizational culture; these learning interventions needed to be reinforced by changes in the performance management system and in compensation practices.

Conner and Smith report that when the consumer products company Colgate-Palmolive began aggressively pursuing a strategy of global geographic expansion, over time senior management began to question whether the company's management-succession pipeline, which was based on a time-honored notion in the company that "somehow, the cream always rises to the top" would be sufficient to support the planned growth.[15] At the initiative of CEO and Chairman Ruben Mark, Bob Joy, Vice President of Human Resources, traveled extensively throughout Colgate's global business documenting that many of Colgate's leaders considered the most critical human resource issue facing the company to be expanding the general management pool, which would require building support throughout the company for a widespread, experience-based development program. HR built support for a process of executive development that would systematically identify and move high-potential managers through varied and challenging job assignments. Realizing the company's cultural mindset, that to be successful a manager had both to understand how the company really operated and to learn business competencies like marketing and finance on the job, HR eschewed traditional educational approaches and put priority on developing a systemic focus on development through on-the-job experience. A strong emphasis was placed on coaching and career development through job rotation.

In both Berlex and Colgate-Palmolive, HRD initiatives were necessary to support the strategic direction of the company. To provide this support, senior HR executives had to have the confidence of senior leadership. Equally important, HRD linked their initiatives and recommendations to the strategic requirements of the business. Making these connections visible to management in a compelling way was itself a process of facilitating organizational learning. HRD's success also involved creating alliances with executives throughout their respective organizations.

The effectiveness and ultimate success of HRD in an organization depends on making a pervasive case for link-ages between learning and development in the particular organizational context. For example, the Colgate-Palmolive HRD group realized that on-the-job development would be most accepted in the organization. Aware also of research that supported work-based learning, they tailored their approach to developing executive talent to fit the organization.

Chapter Two begins framing HRD practice within the context of strategy development. Chapter One provides a backdrop, both of the history of HRD and the critical conversations that are currently taking place in the field—conversations fundamental for the subsequent development of the perspective of this book. We begin with a fundamental question—What is HRD?

WHAT IS HUMAN RESOURCE DEVELOPMENT?

Human resource development is emerging from its early roots in training and development, becoming a sophisticated academic discipline and field of practice centered on learning and performance in organizations. The change in language from *training* to *learning* is more than a semantic one. Rather, this change in terminology reflects a new understanding of the potential for facilitating individual learning and development, encompassing a wide range of learning platforms, including traditional training as well as development and leveraging opportunities for learning from actual experience in order to improve organizational performance.

This new understanding perhaps finds its most complete expression with the popularity of the "learning organization." The idea of a learning organization has raised the discussion around learning to the level of considering the source of sustainable competitive advantage through developing unique organizational core competencies, fostering capacity for rapid organizational change, developing human and intellectual capital, and knowledge management. This expanded focus, however, has been accompanied by debates within the field about the scope and focus of HRD practice. These debates are, to a certain extent, reflected in different definitions offered by various writers.

Definitions of Human Resource Development, and Their Implications

The term "human resource development" was first introduced in 1969, by Leonard Nadler at the annual conference of the American Society for Training and

Development (ASTD). A year later Nadler offered a formal definition that he and his wife, Zeace, have continued to use during the decades that followed;[16] they define HRD as "organized learning experiences in a definite time period to increase the possibility of improving job performance growth."[17]

Implicit in Nadler and Nadler's definition is a view of HRD that involves the initiation, design, and delivery of formal learning events with the intention of improving job performance. This focus on job performance suggests HRD involves individual learning, as opposed to organizational-level learning, an approach that differentiates HRD interventions from team or organizational-level interventions such as organizational development (OD, discussed below). Nadler and Nadler's definition leaves open the possibility that HRD can play a role in supporting team or organizational interventions.

Most important, perhaps, is that Nadler and Nadler step back from *promising* improvements in job performance: they caution that HRD professionals cannot promise improved performance on the job, because not only do skills learned in training influence performance levels, but also personal and organizational factors impact the transfer of learning. All an HRD professional can promise is to design learning activities that will provide the competencies necessary for an individual to improve his or her job performance. Translating this capacity into actual performance is ultimately determined by the motivation and ability of the individual to do so, and is often strongly influenced by other variables in the workplace, such as supportive supervision and the work processes themselves.

Alternative definitions of HRD have proliferated as various scholar/practitioners have brought new perspectives to the field. A representative sample of these definitions are found in Box 1.A.[18] Consider each definition carefully, focusing on how they differ from Nadler and Nadler and from one another.

Differing Perspectives on the Field   The various definitions in Box 1.A contain some subtle but important variations in various authors' approaches to the field. Swanson, in contrast to Nadler and Nadler, is more definitive in the emphasis he places on performance improvement. In his view, performance improvement is the raison d'etre of HRD practice. He takes a performance-improvement systems perspective, one that goes beyond the design of learning events themselves. His ideas on performance improvement expand the scope of HRD practice to include working within the organization in order to impact on systemic and process factors that in turn impact on job performance.

Watkins' definition emphasizes HRD as a long-term development activity that focuses on facilitating learning at multiple levels of the organization and involving individuals, teams, and organizational-level interventions. Inherent in her definition is an integrated concept of HRD that broadens the focus on learning and moves it toward the practices of organizational development. Watkins' definition speaks of developing learning *capacity* at each of these levels—individual, team, and organization. This shifts the focus of HRD from a direct link to an indirect link to performance, implying that HRD practice creates a resource for the organization that may or may not be effectively utilized by its leaders.

BOX 1.A   **Representative Definitions of Human Resource Development**

Human Resource Development is:

- The integrated use of training and development, career development, and organizational development to improve individual and organizational effectiveness (McLagan and Suhadolnik, 1989).
- The field of study and practice responsible for the fostering of a long-term, work related learning capacity at the individual, group, and organizational level of organizations (Watkins, 1989).
- The study and practice of increasing the learning capacity of individuals, groups, collectives, and organizations through the development and application of learning based interventions for the purpose of optimizing human and organizational growth and effectiveness (Chalofsky, 1992).
- About enhancing and widening these skills by training, by helping people to grow within the organization, and by enabling them to make better use of their skills and abilities (Armstrong, 1992).
- A proactive, system-wide intervention, linked to strategic planning and cultural change. This contrasts with the traditional view of training and development as consisting of reactive, piecemeal interventions in response to specific problems (Beer and Spector, 1989).
- Process of developing and/or unleashing human expertise through organization development and personnel training and development for the purpose of improving performance (Swanson, 1995).
- Encompasses activities and processes that are intended to have impact on organizational and individual learning (Stewart and McGoldrick, 1996).

Chalofsky's definition presents a perspective very similar to Watkins, as does Stewart and McGoldrick's. Each of their definitions suggests an *enabling* rationale for the HRD function. Armstrong's definition also seems to suggest this rationale, although his definition specifically focuses on training and places HRD in a more tightly prescribed role.

If Watkins definition moves HRD toward OD, McLagan and Suhadolnik's definition includes functions beyond the role of designing learning events per se as envisioned by the Nadlers. McLagan and Suhadolnik clearly place HRD as a management function, distinct from and equal to HRM functions. Finally, Beer and Spector present a definition that seems to equate HRD with a system-level approach, suggesting HRD is virtually synonymous with organizational development and, similar to McLagan and Suhadolnik, that it must be treated as an important management function, albeit at the strategic level.

Some Key Commonalities in Understanding HRD   Although there are clear differences in perspective reflected in the definitions offered by these writers, the definitions share certain key commonalties as well. *Learning* is clearly central to the notion of HRD; it is either explicitly mentioned or implicitly assumed by all of the definitions (raising the need for us to define learning, an issue we shall deal with in Chapter Six). Whether one focuses on training or system-level interventions, on individual, team, or organizational level activities, on strategic or job level performance, ultimately HRD is centered on fostering learning.

Also evident in these definitions is that learning is intended to enhance the efficacy of the learner in terms of his or her performance in the organizational setting and, ultimately, the organization's performance. Beyond these points of basic agreement are nuances that reflect different points of view within the field.

Over time, HRD theory and practice seems to be evolving toward certain centers of gravity, with tensions and controversies that currently serve to infuse vigor into the discourse. We need to address two of these controversies before offering our own definition of HRD for purposes of this book: 1) the relationship of HRD to organizational development and human resource management (HRM) and 2) the primary focus of HRD—serving the development needs of the learner with an indirect impact on performance improvement or a direct impact on improving performance.

Human Resource Development and Human Resource Management

In the early 1980s, the field of personnel management shifted its emphasis as personnel departments renamed themselves "human resources departments." In some instances this change was cosmetic, but in many cases the change in language marked a subtle shift, from a function that essentially handled staffing and related administrative activities to a function that focused on the development of people as a resource to the organization.

This shift in roles put into practice what Miles had, much earlier, described as the distinction between a *human relations* perspective and a *human resources* perspective.[19] In a precursor to the idea of empowerment (before many organizational practices managed to turn "empowerment" into a pejorative word), Miles argued that most employees are capable of contributing more to the organization than traditional management practices allow. Management's task is to create work situations that permit employees to contribute as broad a range of their talents as possible to the organization's goals. Work should be developmental. Following this line of reasoning, training and development, and especially management and organization development, become in many ways the standard barriers of the new HR department.

As organizations confronted new challenges of global quality and cost competition, human resource management became increasingly defined as a line management responsibility, with the human resource department a generalist support function. These changes paralleled the emergence of HRD as a field of study and practice. The emergence of HRD as a function distinct from HRM reflects both a growing awareness of the strategic implications of human resources and linkages to other HRM functions, like performance management. The terminology of HRD also reflects the awareness that much learning and development (as opposed to training and development) takes place outside of the classroom. Although the term HRD is rarely found in companies, titles such as Director of Employee and Organizational Development, or Vice President of Learning and Performance Solutions are increasingly common along with the informal designation of chief learning officer. Occasionally reporting directly to the CEO, most individuals serving in this role, have, at minimum, regular direct access to the chairperson or president of the organization.

As previously mentioned, HRD has its roots in training and development, which in turn has traditionally been one of several HRM functions that include recruitment, selection, and compensation. HRD practice has extended beyond relying largely on classroom and structured teaching material to facilitating learning throughout the organization. HRD practitioners organize problem- and issue-focused conferences among executives to identify various best practices; they explore in detail how these practices work in different business settings, creating communities-of-practice for the purpose of sharing experiences and learning among professionals who work in similar functions yet are often isolated from each other. These kinds of interventions are designed to develop networks of participants who are sharing real experiences for purposes of learning. As learning has taken on strategic implications, the activities that HRD scholars identify as part of their field are often grouped together and elevated to equal other functions of organizational management. Although HRD is still an overall HR activity, making the distinction between HRD and HRM helps to clarify the focus of each.

McLagan and Suhadolnik define HRD as a management function, distinct from and equal to HRM functions. Wilson reinforces this notion in his metaphor of the Human Resource compass (Figure 1.1) adapted from the Human Resources wheel proposed by McLagan and Suhadolnik.[20]

As with any academic topology, the distinctions among sectors of the wheel are somewhat arbitrary and artificial. For our purposes, such distinctions point out the need for coordination among various HR functions within a comprehensive HR strategy that is integral to the competitive focus of the organization. Labels, however, are less important than the clear way in which the various functions on the wheel are organized and coordinated with one another.

The guiding principle of HRM can be expressed as *positioning the right people to achieve the highest possible performance in order to meet strategic goals.* Successfully putting this principle into practice involves continually raising and then answering questions such as "What kinds of people do we need, that is, what abilities and motivations do we seek? How many people do we need? Where and how do we find them? How do we best position them in the organization once they are employed? How do we motivate and retain these employees? What systems will manage them effectively?"

The guiding principle of HRD can be expressed as *preparing and continually developing people and learning systems to achieve the highest possible performance in order to meet strategic goals.* Successfully executing this principle in practice involves continually answering questions such as "What kind of learning and development do members of the organization need? How do we allocate learning opportunities among employees? How do we keep track of our employees' various and individual competencies and capabilities? How do we recognize and utilize the tacit knowledge held by members of the organization? How do we capture and document what employees are learning from their experience as members of the organization? How do we manage the knowledge and the social and intellectual capital of the organization?"

A moment's reflection reveals that these HRM and HRD questions are highly interdependent. The answer to questions like "What kind of people do we need?" and "Can we successfully recruit such people?" influences what kind of training and

FIGURE 1.1   **Wilson's Human Resources Wheel**

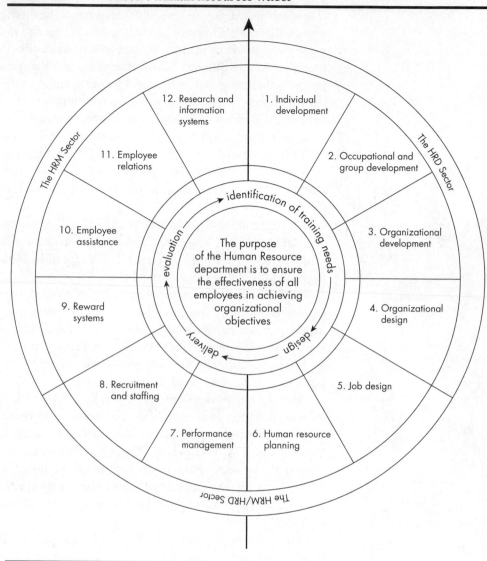

development is required. Often retaining highly talented people depends on how we allocate learning and development opportunities. In short, coordination and synchronization of HRM and HRD activities are necessary, regardless of how an organization structures its HR functions.

When John Gumpert moved from General Electric to become the Chief Learning Officer at Union Carbide Corporation, he also assumed the title Director of

Workforce Acquisition and Development, along with responsibility for all the HR functions that directly touched the people and the composition of the workforce. His counterpart, the director of human resources, was responsible for administrative HR functions, such as compensation and benefits. Gumpert was able to comprehensively manage the organization's talent pool as well as its human resource development. Because his responsibilities included overseeing safety training, supervisory and management development, executive development, career planning and development, organizational development, recruitment and selection, succession planning, and performance management, he could easily coordinate the interrelated challenges of positioning people and developing them. For example, supervisory and management training objectives could be framed in a manner consistent both with the selection and succession needs of the organization and with the career development opportunities in the organization. This resulted in maximum coordination among the overlapping sectors of HRD and HRM functions.

HRD and Organizational Development

Grieves and Redman have described human resource development as searching for identity while living in the shadow of OD.[21] In their analysis of the history of HRD, they conclude that the concept of the knowledge-centered company that views personal and organizational learning as critical for competitive growth is the driving force behind HRD; the HRD function is "partisan" to the goals and objectives of the organization. In this view, HRD is an organizational strategy for aligning the organizational objectives of knowledge-centered companies with the competencies and capabilities of their employees.

Accomplishing this alignment, of course, often requires using methods pioneered in OD practice such as team building, survey feedback, and structural design. We can express the guiding principle of OD as *aligning processes and systems for organization effectiveness, growth, and development.* This places OD in the context of the competitive organization and reflects much OD work in practice. It is important, however, to note the strong vein of normative OD literature that is embedded with humanistic values and charges OD with developing psychologically healthy organizational environments.

The social system is the entry point for discussions about interventions for the OD professional; for the HRD professional the entry point is often the learning and development needs of individuals. These two different entry points reflect the historical differences between the two disciplines. OD has its roots in the applied behavioral and social sciences; HRD, in the practice of training and development. The paradigmatic values of OD have been humanistic psychology; HRD's paradigmatic values rest in behaviorism, human capital theory, and performance engineering. A major focus of OD has been social system effectiveness, while HRD's focus has been largely defined in terms of skill development and performance; consequently the intervention strategies of each have differed. OD interventions have focused on interpersonal processes, team building, and large system change, while

HRD interventions have focused on facilitating individual development through training programs, educational experiences, and coaching. OD interventions center on facilitative consultation, while HRD interventions center on designing learning events and experiences (see Box 1.B).

The lines between HRD and OD are becoming increasingly blurred within organizations, especially at the strategic level of practice where, as is the case with the various HRM/HRD functions, a coordinated effort is required that takes into account both the need for social system development and alignment and the development of performance competencies of individuals, teams, and larger organizational groupings.

The increased blending of OD and HRD initiatives is reflected in The Beer and Spector definition (Box 1.A), which virtually eliminates the distinction between them. With increasing emphasis both on developing learning organizations and on understanding how learning transfers across organizational boundaries, the two disciplines are coming together. The growing recognition of non-classroom learning experiences, such as action reflection learning programs, increasingly blurs their boundaries. An example of the blending of HRD and OD learning interventions can be found in Grace Cocoa's strategic transition from a multinational corporation of largely autonomous business units to a fully integrated global corporation.[22] This transition required the development of both global management competencies among executives and managers and the realignment of organizational units and systems. This story is summarized in Box 1.C.

At the level of individual practitioners, especially entry-level professionals, the core competencies of HRD and OD remain relatively distinct. OD professionals develop group process competencies, survey feedback skills, and organizational diagnostic strategies. Many HRD professionals begin their careers with expertise in needs analysis, instructional design, classroom facilitation, and skills assessment. Managing a comprehensive HRD/OD function requires not only experience in both sets of skills but also the ability to properly allocate OD and instructional resources to match development needs with any particular situation.

BOX 1.B   **Comparison of the Early Foundations of Organization Development and Human Resource Development**

	OD	HRD
Roots:	Applied Social Psychology and Sociology	Training and Development Practice
Dominant Paradigmatic Values:	Humanistic	Behaviorist, Pragmatism, Human Capital Theory, Performance Engineering
Focus:	Social System Effectiveness	Performance Centered Individual Effectiveness
Intervention Strategy:	Interpersonal Process/Consultant Facilitation	Designing Learning Programs and Experiences

BOX 1.C

In 1989 Grace Cocoa was the world's largest producer of industrial chocolate, with operations in 14 locations in 10 countries on 5 continents. Assembled by acquisitions, the various operating companies that comprised the business functioned autonomously with little or no cooperation among them. CEO Pedro Mata believed that the future success of Grace Cocoa depended on the company becoming a fully integrated global organization with a single profit-and-loss–statement mentality. This would, among other things, both position the company to better serve its corporate customers, who were increasingly becoming global organizations, and leverage Grace Cocoa's advantage in size and worldwide reach.

Realizing this strategic vision would require the commitment of the strong-willed division presidents to meld the robust individual cultures and identities of the operating companies. In 1990 Mata hired Christopher Dennis as Grace Cocoa's vice president of human resources and organizational development. Dennis became a member of the company's executive committee, charged with devising a strategy for bringing the organization together.

As a first step Dennis, with the help of Marvin Weisbord, the seminal writer on future search methodology, organized a four-and-one-half-day future search conference among the top 50 managers from across the company. The conference revealed considerable support for the global strategy within this critical tier of the organization, but the participants expressed considerable cynical frustration over the lack of cooperation among Grace Cocoa's divisions.

One tangible outcome of the conference was the formation of a marketing/communication task force, which organized joint presentations at key industry trade shows. In all, the search conference was a solid step in seeding the vision of Grace Cocoa as a global player in the cocoa and chocolate industry. But more follow-up was needed to maintain the momentum for the kind of structural and cultural change needed for Grace Cocoa to become a global company.

Next, Dennis established a company-wide organization development task force consisting of himself, another member of the executive committee, and four upper-level managers from the three operating divisions.

Systematically-gathered data by the task force revealed that people in the organization believed that, because of how the autonomous operating companies functioned, Grace Cocoa was suboptimizing its performance by not taking advantage of global opportunities. The data also revealed significant gaps in the managerial competencies the organization would need to become a global organization. Specifically and prominently, the data indicated the need for developing 1) a global perspective, 2) interpersonal communication, 3) teamwork, 4) trust, 5) conflict management, 6) leadership, and 7) innovation and change. The future search conference and the organization development task force supplemented the strategic discussions, within the executive committee, on globalization and began building commitment among the senior team for the globalization strategy. However, it was clear that considerable executive development would be needed to support the change.

Dennis could have proposed a traditional management development program organized around courses and guest speakers, or he could have initiated team-building efforts in parts of the organization. Neither approach, however, would provide the simultaneous strategic realignment and competency development he believed was necessary for realizing the kind of transformative changes that the globalization strategy required. Dennis believed that to successfully implement the strategy would require a change in how people understood their roles in the organization.

He proposed an intensive action-learning program that would build competencies, challenge assumptions about roles, and produce meaningful answers to questions that would arise as the organization changed to a global structure. Over two years, three such programs were conducted; each program included 20 upper-level managers drawn from around the world and consisted of four six-day meetings, spaced five to six weeks apart and held in different locations. Each group of 20 participants functioned as a learning community-of-practice and was divided into four teams. Each team was sponsored by a member of Grace Cocoa's executive committee, and each team worked on a significant question related to globalization, such as "How should we organize a global logistics system?" and "How should

(continues)

BOX 1.C   [CONTINUED]

the executive committee be organized to support glob-alization?" Participants also engaged in numerous learn-ing and development activities.

The results of the action-learning program projects pro-vided the initial groundwork for Grace Cocoa's success-ful transition to a global organization while also estab-lishing a network of managers who had developed both strong working relationships and new competencies.

PERFORMANCE VERSUS LEARNING: TWO VIEWS OF THE PURPOSE OF HRD

Perhaps the most fundamental division in HRD centers on the purpose of HRD practice: 1) improving organizational performance versus 2) development of the learner. This divide is often referred to as the performance versus learning debate,[23] which can also be framed as

- production-centered (i.e., behaviorism or libertarianism), developing people as human capital both to increase performance (as defined by the organization) and to achieve its goals; versus

- person-centered, i.e., developing people as self-authoring individuals willing to contribute productively to those groups of which they are a part.

Swanson and Arnold straightforwardly articulate the performance (production-centered) position stating "that the purpose of HRD is improved performance. . . . when practiced in productive organizations, [HRD] should strive to contribute directly to the organization's goals."[24] This view, which is highly influential in the field, couples HRD practice with performance improvement theory.[25]

Advocates of the performance-improvement perspective take the pragmatic stance: to be taken seriously by management and to legitimately demand resources for their work, HRD professionals must demonstrate the results of their efforts in terms of measurable performance improvements. Swanson and Arnold directly state this view, maintaining that performance is the dependent variable in any model of HRD effectiveness.

While virtually all HRD professionals agree that their work must benefit the organizations in which it is practiced, those holding the learning (person-centered) perspective resist the notion that the purpose of HRD practice is *directly* linked to measurable improvement in performance.[26] This view parallels Watkins' definition (Box 1.A): HRD professionals work to develop a capacity for learning in individuals, teams, and organizations, a capacity that will translate into improved performance; but the relationship between learning and performance improvement is indirect, and is a function of an enhanced capacity for performance.

Bierema is even more explicit regarding the development of the learner as the primary responsibility of HRD practitioners. She writes of the need for a holistic approach to the development of individuals, leading to a more productive workplace.

She argues that this approach is fundamental for overcoming the fragmentation that results from taking a narrow mechanistic approach to learning, an approach that is no longer appropriate for a global world in which the challenges that confront organizations are fluid and change rapidly.[27]

Essentially, the argument made by advocates for a learning perspective is that HRD creates the potential for improved performance, but learning is the outcome that should matter most for HRD practice. Learning not only potentially impacts performance but also brings about other desirable outcomes that are critical, but not likely to be championed by any other function within the organization.

Historical Foundations of HRD and the Performance versus Learning Debate

The performance versus learning debate has its roots in the distinct traditions that provide the foundations of HRD. Improving performance was the early rationale for training and development; an example is the Training Within Industry Project during World War II. Behaviorism and, more recently, social-learning theory have also reinforced this perspective. Human-capital theory and human-competence theory have also strongly influenced the link between training and performance. The learning side of the debate in large part reflects the influence of adult educators in workplace learning; adult education has a strong normative tradition of democratic values, social justice, and social change, and within this tradition education is a vehicle for increasing the capacity of individuals and groups for actively engaging and participating in the institutions of society. Learning should be in the service of society and organizations, making people think more critically about their institutions and the interests they support, rather than in the service of predetermined organizational goals and interests.

Foundations of the Performance-Improvement Perspective

Proponents of the performance perspective trace its history to the work of a United States government agency formed to support industrial production in World War II, the *Training Within Industry Project* (TWI). The TWI was established as an emergency service to America's war contractors to assist them in meeting their manpower needs through training workers to maximize use of their skills; Ruona calls it "one of the most pivotal turning points in the history of training and in the emergence of Human Resource Development."[28] The TWI established performance requirements that were used to systematically help workers gain needed knowledge and expertise, with success measured by whether a training program improved production, efficiency, and cost-effectiveness.

If the TWI was a practical demonstration of the connection between training and performance improvement, Becker's human capital theory provided a more scholarly foundation.[29] Becker's work has been widely influential in the field of human resource management, reinforcing the concept of people as a potential economic resource and spurring efforts toward financial analysis of human resource practices.[30]

Behaviorism, especially as it is formulated in the work of B. F. Skinner, became influential in the field of training and development in the early 1970s. The emphasis on specific behaviors, as opposed to cognitive development, was consistent with the epistemic assumptions of performance measurement. Having trainees practice specific observable behaviors linked to the job with feedback measures—either direct, through results, or indirect, through the assessment of others—provided visible evidence of learning associated with performance. Behavioral modeling, with learners observing "displays" of behavior and focusing on previously identified learning points also became integrated into behaviorally based learning events.[31] Assertiveness training programs that provide learners with specific alternative behaviors for acting assertively or supervisory training courses on how to respond to a disgruntled employee during a performance counseling discussion typically rely heavily on behavior-based learning theory.

Another important foundation for the performance improvement perspective is the seminal writing of Gilbert on human performance technology.[32] His work on measuring human competence and its potential for improving performance made significant contributions to the theory of human capital. Gilbert's behavior engineering model focuses on events that can be constructively manipulated in the scientific sense, and he made important distinctions between performance engineering and behavior modification theory as formulated by Skinner; one of the most significant of these distinctions was recognition that the meaning of behavior is a function of values—behavior is not "value neutral." Accordingly, Gilbert systematically incorporated values into his framework. While focusing on competencies and individual development, Gilbert's work took into account the fact that businesses are cultures and performance engineering involved changing the cultural context. He was one of the first theorists to include different levels (i.e., philosophical, cultural, policy, strategic, tactical, and logistic) in defining accomplishment variables in his performance matrix.

Although the performance improvement perspective traces some of its roots to training and development, most organizations have failed to pursue any significant efforts toward systematic assessment of the results of their training practices. Hence (and ironically), while the performance improvement perspective is arguably the dominant voice in HRD theory, its proponents continue to face a daunting challenge that many practitioners are resisting financial assessment of their interventions.

HRD and the Learning Perspective

In contrast to the performance improvement school, proponents of the learning perspective generally come from the field of adult education, with its focus on learning through experience and fostering human autonomy through critical reflection. Foundations of this perspective are seated in the philosophical pragmatism of William James and John Dewey; in the humanistic psychology of Carl Rodgers and Abraham Maslow; in Jungian psychology; in critical social theory, including the work of Paulo Feire and Jurgan Habermas; and in feminist informed theory such as the work of Carol Gilligan, Mary Belenky, Blythe Clinchy, Nancy Goldberger, and Jill Tarule.

Champions of the learning perspective by and large occupy an uneasy space, balancing a concern for creating educative and developmental workplaces with a broader commitment to adult education. A diverse group in terms of the foundational theories that inform their practice, these adult educators are united by the idea that organizations that have to be flexible and responsive to rapid changes in both their markets and the world will require more informed employees who are self-authoring and capable of thinking critically about their organization's practices.

Laura Bierema, Karen Watkins, Victoria Marsick, and John Dirkx, all influential researchers and practitioners of workplace and/or organizational learning, have come to HRD as adult educators who understand the workplace as an important arena for adult learning and development.[33] Accordingly, they bring to their work in HRD a tradition of adult education that is supportive of democratic values; they share the values of the early organizational development practitioners who focused on developing highly participative organizations. As Dirkx has written, while the motto of traditional HRD practice tends to be the market economy and the slogan "It's the economy, stupid," an appropriate motto for the adult education perspective would be "It's the democracy, stupid."[34] Another way to illustrate the difference between performance improvement and learning perspectives is to notice how each perspective uses the term "resource"—should people be resources for the organization (the performance-improvement perspective)? Or should organizations be resources for people, who in turn reciprocate, adding value to the organization (the learning perspective)? In addition to behavior and action, the learning perspective emphasizes developing peoples' capacity to learn by critically reflecting not only on their experience but also on the premises that form the lens through which they interpret that experience. These premises may relate to their tasks or to the processes and actions they engage in while pursuing their tasks.

The learning perspective also views people in a socially holistic context, as having a life outside the organization who, one way or another, have to integrate their work life with other adult roles. Adult educators working in HRD would argue that, ultimately, organizations and society are best served by developing employees who are constructively critical of their experiences in organizations and who make informed choices regarding their careers and work.

Learning events that deal with content of a nontechnical nature (such as organizational change and restructuring) are particularly valuable opportunities for facilitating this kind of informed choice; examples are training and development programs that encourage participants to examine their own needs and goals as well as the extent to which these personal goals fit with the direction of the organization, so that, for example, they might decide what career decisions are in their best interest during a downsizing. The willingness of an organization to facilitate a conversation between its managers and employees about where the organization is going and what the managers and employees can realistically anticipate (as opposed to attempting to sell the organizational "line") rests on the assumption that the organization will have a stronger and more motivated workforce if people are encouraged to make informed choices about career decisions.

Many HRD theorists championing the learning perspective might also point to the recent experiences of companies like Enron, Arthur Andersen, and WorldCom and ask whether these companies would have been better served by a more open culture of learning that encouraged divergent thinking rather than focused almost exclusively on predetermined performance matrixes and faith in the senior leaders of the company.

Ironically, as these HRD/adult educators seek to infuse values of learning and democracy into the field of HRD, they come under attack from many adult educators who decry the encroachment of what they view as "vocationalism" into adult education's traditional focus on issues of social justice and the defense of civil society, as separate from economic interests.[35]

BEYOND THE PERFORMANCE VERSUS LEARNING DEBATE

Kuchinke has argued for moving beyond the dichotomy of performance versus learning, arguing that "dualistic viewpoints are inherently problematic because they ignore the continuity present in reality and because they prevent us from recognizing the promise of synthesis."[36] Drawing on the literature from organizational theory and administrative science, Kuchinke observes that organizations are created for achieving certain goals and objectives, and regardless of the nature of HRD interventions, the ultimate value of those interventions is the degree to which they contribute to the overall purposes of the organization. HRD activities might be a means to a number of ends, some of which are short-term and immediate, such as providing instruction in specific technical skills needed by employees. Other HRD practices might be long-term in their focus, although equally important, and broader, such as providing development opportunities that help to maintain an organization's ability to sustain its position as the employer of choice in a particular labor market, or raising questions for open discussion about certain values that are emerging in the organization's culture and philosophy.

These latter kinds of interventions are not easily measured in terms of traditional cost-benefit analysis. Kuchinke observes that in contemporary organizations the kind of knowledge that needs to be developed in terms of social and intellectual capital is multi-dimensional and often focused on competitive capacity-building. There is a need for a view of the relationship between learning and performance improvement that is richer and more comprehensive "than the often unidimensional notions of performance as advanced by Swanson . . . ."[37]

Such a multidimensional view requires that HRD take into account the long-term needs of strategic performance as well as the performance improvement. Long-term strategic performance requires a sustainable position in the market place in the context of changing values, attitudes, and customer needs. It is also often linked to the quality of organizational citizenship. The debate that has engulfed companies, such as Nike, in the use of low paid, child labor overseas is an example of how companies can find themselves on the defensive when management practices are perceived as violating social values.

In the literature, discussions of strategically integrated HRD tend quickly to gravitate toward shorter-term operational practices of system diagnosis and method. For example, Swanson calls attention to the need for HRD practitioners to build theory that addresses three performance levels: organization, process, and individual performance.[38] He argues for a total-system–theory perspective, linking performance and strategy, along with theory- and research-driven practice. Holton identifies domains of performance including mission, process and critical performance subsystems, and individuals, distinguishing between outcomes and drivers for each level.[39]

Although the arguments made by these theorists have implications for generative, strategic learning, their tone and focus is on problem solving. Holton writes, "HRD professionals should be gatekeepers for performance improvement, using [their] expertise to analyze performance problems, identify the best interventions, and evaluate outcomes."[40] Similarly, Swanson writes:

> Performance may be identified within missions, goals, and strategies, but not always. *Performance is the valued productive output of a system in the form of goods and services.* The actual fulfillment of the goods and services requirement is thought of in terms of *units of performance.* These goods or services units of performance are usually *measured* in terms of quality, time, and quality features measures.[41]

The focus is on system fixing, not system creation: the nexus of the discussion is on the operational level of the organization. At present, HRD theory is most thoroughly developed at the operational level of careful analysis and improvement. Significant advances have been made during the past couple of decades in providing a foundation for sound professional practice serving the needs of organizations. However, this foundation is directed toward the concerns of middle management and limits senior management's perception of HRD practitioners to a constrained, and variably important, operational role. Breaking this perception will require recognizing the taken-for-granted assumptions inherent in the language of performance *improvement*, which by definition suggests working on an existing system. However unintentional, it is a perspective of incremental instrumental learning, not learning of a generative strategic kind. Performance improvement needs to be pursued within context of strategic performance development.

The importance of linking HRD to strategic concerns is embedded in the discourse on performance improvement even though, as argued above, the premises of much of this writing tends to move back to operational concerns. Long-term strategic performance requires an educative focus on developing executive talent, fostering spirited critical debate about an organization's direction and the opportunities that may be presenting themselves, and connecting to strategy-nascent trends in society as well working on system improvements.

As a result of the restructuring that has taken place in many organizations over the past decade, the need to develop high-potential talent has presented new challenges that impact long-term strategic performance. Organizations that have flattened their structures are finding themselves having to pay increasing attention to the development of general management and executive talent to fill future senior-level positions. Where such development used to take place incrementally, as managers moved up the organizational hierarchy, now promotions often mean major leaps in responsibility. Moving from managing a functional department, such as engineering, to managing a significantly-sized profit center business unit has few, if any, intermediate steps.

Keeping management open to new trends in technology and customer preferences presents another challenge in sustaining long-term strategic performance. Both scenario planning and future search conferences can open up the conversation within the organization about changes in its markets and task environment, while, at the same time, develop executive talent.

Walton makes a useful distinction between "piecemeal HRD strategies or ways of doing things which collectively might contribute to the SHRD [Strategic HRD, sic] effort, but fall short of a holistic approach [entailing, sic.] the search for, and intention to implement, a coherent set of subsidiary strategies in accordance with a set of guiding principles that will contribute to an overall organizational 'grand design' or sense of direction."[42] His argument explicitly builds on Rothwell and Kazanas' admonishment that, despite the pressures of having to market HRD, the HRD leader's ultimate responsibility is to lead the formulation and implementation of a coherent plan for guiding learning in an organization.[43]

Any coherent organization-wide learning plan needs to target both the long-term requirements for strategic performance *and* the more immediate needs of performance improvement; it also must take into account the need for developing people and organizational systems. This multiple focus will be emphasized in the metaphor of the HRD learning pyramid, which we will introduce in Chapter Two. At the strategic level, facilitating learning is not always a linear rational process. Walton has observed that emergent writing on strategic human resource development has tended to produce models that stress how planned learning can contribute to organizational performance. These models "have largely adopted a rational-structuralist approach [and focus on] cementing the link with what is nowadays being deemed as old-style business and human resource planning."[44] This condition parallels the tendency for strategy text-books to continue to present linear step-by-step models of strategic planning despite growing evidence of wide divergence in how effective strategy emerges in practice. These issues will be addressed in more detail in Chapters Two and Three. The practice of HRD is an evolving field with the ability to contribute significantly at both the strategic and operational levels of organizational performance.

HRD DEFINED

In this text HRD is conceptualized and defined as *both an organizational role and a field of professional practice. The fundamental purpose of HRD is to contribute to both long-term strategic performance and more immediate performance improvement through ensuring that organizational members have access to resources for developing their capacity for performance and for making meaning of their experience in the context of the organization's strategic needs and the requirements of their jobs.*

Advocating for and justifying these resources for development is a fundamental responsibility of senior HRD professionals. At the center of the HRD organizational role is the responsibility for facilitating learning at the individual, team, and organizational levels, respectively.

There is a strategic and operational dimension to this role. To be effective, the HRD practitioner has to advocate learning needs consistent with organizational strategy, and this includes helping senior members understand both the development of strategy as a learning issue and how the HRD role should be structured in support of strategy. At the operational level, the HRD role involves asking questions toward identifying the learning needs that support strategic direction and workforce performance at all three levels—individual, team, and organization. This is a porous role, overlapping or aligning with various HRM and OD concerns. As a field of professional practice, it requires competence in classroom and group facilitation, learning methods, program development, performance management, and change management.

SUMMARY

HRD is maturing rapidly, as both an academic and a practice-based profession. Although a number of definitions of HRD exist, learning is central to all of them. These definitions vary in the degree to which they emphasize how definitive HRD professionals should be in promising specific performance-improvement outcomes and in terms of the scope of activities that HRD should embrace. A central debate in the literature is whether the primary focus of HRD should be on performance or on the learner. From a pragmatic stance, the field is moving toward a multifaceted view of its work that goes beyond the performance versus learner dichotomy.

HRD is most effective when it is focused on leveraging the strategic initiatives of the business. Accomplishing this requires making a targeted case for learning both at various levels of the organization and in various formats—workshops; experienced-based development; and organizational development interventions, such as survey feedback methods. Further, these interventions typically require support from other components of the human resource function, such as performance management and compensation.

Questions for Discussion

1. Given the discussion in this chapter, and your current understanding of the role human resource development can play in organizations, either identify the definition that most closely fits how you would define the field, modify one, or write your own.

   ▌ Describe the rationale for your definition.

   ▌ What assumptions are you making in your definition?

   ▌ How does your definition relate HRD to aspects of HRM practice and OD?

   ▌ What would have to be true of senior management's beliefs about the role of learning for your definition to be acceptable in an organization?

   At the end of the course refer back to your definition.

   ▌ How, if at all, might you modify your definition based on your learning? What is your reasoning?

2. What is your position on the "learning" versus "performance" debate? What assumptions are you making in adopting this position?

3. Considering the various issues raised by authors in each side of the "learning" versus "performance" debate and your own position on it—what are limitations or "downside" of your position that would have to be guarded against in terms of playing a meaningful role in the organization?

End Notes

1. V. J. Marsick and K. Watkins, *Informal and Incidental Learning in the Workplace* (London: Routledge, 1990); V. J. Marsick and M. Volpe, eds., *Informal Learning on the Job: Advances in Developing Human Resources,* 1 (3) (1999).

2. D. A. Schon, *The Reflective Practitioner: How Professionals Think in Action* (New York: Basic Books, 1983).

3. G. Ryle, *The Concept of Mind* (London: Hutchinson, 1949).

4. J. Mezirow, *Transformative Dimensions of Adult Learning.* (San Francisco: Jossey-Bass, 1991). J. Mezirow and Associates, *Learning as Transformation: Critical Perspectives on a Theory in Progress.* (San Francisco: Jossey-Bass, 2000).

5. D. Boud, R. Cohen, and D. Walker, eds. *Using Experience for Learning* (Buckingham, England: SRHE and The Open University Press, 1993); D. A. Kolb, *Experiential Learning: Experience as the Source of Learning and Development* (Englewood Cliffs, N.J: Prentice-Hall, 1984).

6. R. W. Revans, *The Origin and Growth of Action Learning* (London: Chartwell Bratt, 1982); M. Pedler, *Action Learning for Managers* (London: Lemos and Crane, 1996); M. J. Marquardt, *Action Learning in Action: Transforming Problems and People for World-Class Organizational Learning* (Palo Alto: Davies-Black, 1999); L. Yorks, J. O'Neil, and V. J. Marsick, eds., *Advances In Developing Human Resources* 1 (2) (1999).

7. J. A. Raelin, *Work-based Learning: The New Frontier of Management Development.* (Upper Saddle River, N.J.: Prentice-Hall, 2000).

8. J. C. Meister, *Corporate Universities: Lessons in Building a World-class Work Force,* rev. ed. (New York: McGraw-Hill, 1998).

9. P. M. Senge, *The Fifth Discipline: The Art and Practice of the Learning Organization* (New York: Doubleday/Currency, 1990); K. Watkins and V. J. Marsick, *Sculpting the Learning Organization: Lessons in the Art and Science of Systemic Change* (San Francisco: Jossey-Bass, 1993).

10. R. J. Torraco, ed., *Performance Improvement: Theory and Practice: Advances In Developing Human Resources* 1 (1). (San Francisco: Berrett-Koehler and Academy of Human Resource Development, 1999).

11. E. F. Holton III, T. T. Baldwin, and S. S. Naquin, eds., *Managing and Changing Learning Transfer Systems: Advances In Developing Human Resources,* 2 (2). (2000).

12. R. A. Swanson, "Demonstrating the Financial Benefit of HRD: Status and Update on the Theory and Practice," *Human Resource Development Quarterly,* 9 (1998): 285–95; R. A. Swanson and E. F. Holton III, *Results: How to Assess Performance, Learning, and Perceptions in Organizations* (San Francisco: Berrett-Koehler, 1999); C. M. Sleezer, J. R. Hough, and D. B. Gradous, "Measurement Challenges in Evaluation and Performance Improvement," *Performance Improvement Quarterly,* 11 (4): 62–75 (1998); H. Preskill and R. T. Torres, *Evaluative Inquiry for Learning in Organizations* (San Francisco: Sage, 1999); J. J. Phillips, *Return on Investment in Training and Performance Improvement* (Houston: Gulf Publishing, 1997).

13. R. L. Dilworth, T. R. McClernon, and J. Redding, "No Respect: Bridging the Gap between HRD Practitioners and Senior Management," *A What Works Report* (September, 2000, Alexandria, Va.: American Society for Training and Development).

14. J. B. Shillaber, "Transformation in the Pharmaceutical Industry: HR's Prescription for Success," in *HR to the Rescue: Case Studies of HR Solutions to Business Challenges,* E. M. Mone and M. London, eds. (Houston: Gulf Publishing, 1998): 243–69.

15. J. Conner and C. A. Smith, "Developing the Next Generation of Leaders: A New Strategy for Leadership Development at Colgate-Palmolive," in Mone and London, *HR to the Rescue,* 120–48.

16. L. Nadler and Z. Nadler, eds., *The Handbook of Human Resource Development,* 2nd ed. (New York: John Wiley & Sons, 1990).

17. *ibid.,* Ch. 1:3.

18. P. A. McLagan and D. Suhadolnik, *Models for HRD Practice: The Research Report* (Alexandria, Va.: American Society for Training and Development, 1989); K. Watkins, "Business and Industry," in *Handbook of Adult and Continuing Education,* S. Merriam and P. Cunningham, eds., (San Francisco: Jossey-Bass, 1989); N. Chalofsky, "A Unifying Definition for the Human Resource Profession," *Human Resource Development Quarterly,* 3 (2) (1992): 175–82; M. Armstrong, *Employee Reward* (London: IPD, 1996); M. Beer and B. Spector, "Corporate-wide Transformations in Human Resource Management," in R. E.

Walton and P. R. Lawrence, *Human Resource Management: Trends and Challenges* (Boston: Harvard Business School Press, 1989); R. A. Swanson, "Human Resource Development: Performance Is the Key." *Human Resource Development Quarterly,* 6 (1995): 207–13; J. Stewart and J. McGoldrick, eds., *Human Resource Development: Perspectives, Strategies and Practice* (London: Pitman, 1996).

19. R. Miles, "Human Relations or Human Resources?" *Harvard Business Review* (July–August, 1965): 148–63.

20. J. P. Wilson, "Human Resource Development," in *Human Resource Development: Learning and Training for Individuals and Organizations,* J. P. Wilson, ed. (London: Kogan Page, 1999): 16; P. A. McLagan and D. Suhadolnik, *Models for HRD Practice.*

21. J. Grieves and T. Redman, "Living in the Shadow of OD: HRD and the Search for Identity," *Human Resource Development International,* 2 (1999): 81–102.

22. C. Dennis, L. Cederholm, and L. Yorks, "Learning Your Way to a Learning Organization," in *In Action.* Watkins and Marsick, eds.

23. Swanson, "Human Resource Development, 207–13; R. A. Swanson, "In Praise of the Dependent Variable," *ibid.* 7 (1996): 203–7; K. Watkins and V. J. Marsick, "The Case for Learning," in *Proceedings of the 1995 Academy of Human Resource Development Annual Conference,* E. F. Holton III, ed., (Baton Rouge, La.: Academy of Human Resource Development, 1995); R. A. Swanson and D. E. Arnold, "The Purpose of HRD Is To Improve Performance," in *Workplace Learning: Debating Five Critical Questions of Theory and Practice: New Directions for Adult and Continuing Education,* R. W. Rowden, ed., (Winter, 1997): 13–9; J. Barrie and R. W. Pace, "Learning for Organizational Effectiveness: Philosophy of Education and Human Resource Development," *Human Resource Development Quarterly,* 9 (1998): 39–54; K. P. Kuchinke, "Moving Beyond the Dualism of Performance Versus Learning: A Response to Barrie and Pace," *ibid.* 9 (1998): 377–84; J. Barrie and R. W. Pace, *ibid.* "Learning and Performance: Just the End of the Beginning—A Rejoinder to Kuchinke," *ibid.* 10 (1998): 293–6.

24. Swanson and Arnold, *The Purpose of HRD,* 13.

25. R. J. Torraco, *Performance Improvement.*

26. L. L. Bierema, "Development of the Individual Leads to a More Productive Workplace," in Rowden, *Workplace Learning,* 21–8; J. M. Dirkx, "Human Resource Development as Adult Education: Fostering the Educative Workplace," in Rowden, *Workplace Learning,* 41–7; Watkins and Marsick, *In Action.*

27. Bierema, "Development of the Individual."

28. W. E. A. Ruona, "Foundational Impact of the Training Within Industry Project on the Human Resource Development Profession," in *Origins of Contemporary Human Resource Development:* R. A. Swanson, ed., *Advances In Developing Human Resources,* 3 (2) (2001): 119.

29. G. S. Becker, *Human Capital: A Theoretical and Empirical Analysis with Special Reference to Education.* 3rd ed., (Chicago: University of Chicago Press, 1993).

30. B. E. Becker and M. Huselid, "HR as a Source of Shareholder Value: Research and Recommendations," *Human Resource Management,* 31 (2) 1–27; L. Harris, "A Theory of Intellectual Capital," in *Strategic Perspectives on Knowledge, Competence, and Expertise,* R. W. Herling and J. M. Provo, eds., (San Francisco: Berrett-Koehler) 22–37; M. E. Smith, "Another Road to Evaluating Knowledge Assets," *Human Resource Development Review* (March, 2003): 6–25.

31. Wexley and Latham, *Developing and Training Human Resources in Organizations,* 3rd ed. (Upper Saddle River, N.J.: Prentice-Hall).

32. T. F. Gilbert, *Human Competence: Engineering Worthy Performance,* Tribute Ed. (Amherst, Ma.: HRD Press, 1996).

33. Bierema, "Development of the Individual"; Watkins and Marsick, "Sculpting the Learning Organization"; Dirkx, "Human Resource Development."

34. Dirkx, "Human Resource Development," 46.

35. M. Collins, *Adult Education as Vocation* (New York: Routledge, 1991); M. Newman, *Defining the Enemy: Adult Education in Social Action* (Sydney: Stewart Victor Publishing, 1994); T.J. Fenwick, "Sleeping With the Enemy: Toward a Critical HRD." *Proceedings of the 44th Annual Adult Education Research Conference* (San Francisco State University, 2003).

36. Kuchinke, *"Moving Beyond the Dualism,* 377.

37. *ibid.,* 380.

38. R. A. Swanson, "The Foundations of Performance Improvement for Practice," in Torraco, *Performance Improvement,* 1–25.

39. E. F. Holton III, "Performance Domains and Their Boundaries," in Torraco, *Performance Improvement,* 26–46.

40. *ibid.,* 36.

41. R. A. Swanson, "The Foundations of Performance Improvement and Implication for Practice," Opt. Cit, 5.

42. J. Walton, *Strategic Human Resource Development* (Essex, England: Pearson Education, Ltd, 1999), 81.

43. W. J. Rothwell and H. C. Kasanas, *Improving On-the-Job Training: How to Establish and Operate a Comprehensive OJT Program* (San Francisco, Ca: 1994).

44. Walton, *Strategic Human Resource Development,* 83.

This chapter

- provides an introduction to the concepts of strategy, strategic thinking, strategic intent, and strategic management;

- defines organizational strategy;

- differentiates an emergent strategy that makes process a learning journey, from highly formalized and analytically linear models of strategic planning;

- discusses the importance of the business model, or livelihood scheme, and winning proposition;

- defines operational effectiveness;

- differentiates strategy and operational effectiveness;

- introduces the HRD pyramid; and

- relates strategy, tactics, and operations to the HRD pyramid.

Key terms:

strategy	organizational strategy	winning proposition
strategic thinking	tactics	operational effectiveness
strategic intent	business model	HRD pyramid
strategic management	livelihood scheme	imaginal learning

Strategy, Tactics, and Operational Effectiveness

Despite the diversity of perspectives on the scope of Human Resource Development, the field has been characterized by a gradual but persistent evolution in the focus of HRD practice—from classroom training to performance improvement to building strategic capability. This evolution reflects the growing sophistication of the field of Human Resource Development as it has extended its theoretical base by drawing on the full spectrum of behavioral and social sciences and more closely aligning itself with management perspectives.

The development of HRD theory has paralleled the development of both management theory and human resource management theory. As strategy emerged as an important field of management study, interest in strategic HRD followed. The focus on strategic HRD also increased with the belief that the ways that people work together to blend their knowledge and abilities for performance are themselves a resource of strategic importance. In a global economy increasingly driven by knowledge assets, the capabilities of organizational members can be a source of distinct competitive advantage not easily duplicated by competitors.

Despite the almost intuitive logic of this position, there is an obvious gap between this assertion and how people are managed in most organizations. Indeed, HRD practitioners acknowledge that they are often afforded less respect than other functional areas held to be of strategic importance.[1] This chapter examines the implications of strategy, tactics, and operational effectiveness for human resource development. The metaphor of an HRD pyramid can be used to link each of these key areas of organizational learning and action with the organization of HRD practice. In Chapter Three we will examine specific frameworks of strategy analysis from the perspective of learning and discuss methods for facilitating strategic thinking that link them to the pyramid.

STRATEGY, TACTICS, OPERATIONAL EFFECTIVENESS, AND THE METAPHOR OF THE HRD PYRAMID

The literature on strategy makes a distinction between strategy and tactics and describes the success of each as being dependent on operational execution. Learning is generally involved at each of these three levels of organizational performance. The metaphor of an HRD pyramid is a way of organizing our thinking about how these three levels of organizational action involve learning and how they are all interrelated and of exploring their implications for HRD practice.

Figure 2.1 illustrates this pyramid in general terms. Learning at the strategic level involves identifying the strategic pattern of events, including trends in the external environment, the consequences of existing strategic initiatives, and the emergent strategy of the organization. Strategy evolves from this process of learning. Developing strategic thinkers at various levels within the organization is a challenge for corporations and not-for-profits alike.

Learning at the tactical level involves experience, drawing lessons especially from initiatives such as the after-action reviews developed by the United States Army. Much traditional training and development activity has taken place through operational-level learning, such as sales training, training in process improvement methods (e.g., total quality management and six sigma), basic management development, and job skill training throughout the organization.

We will begin this chapter, then, with an introduction to the basic concepts of strategy and strategic management and their relationship to tactics and operational effectiveness. We will then return to the HRD pyramid to frame an HRD agenda for linking different levels of HRD practice to the learning challenges presented by strategy and organizational performance.

FIGURE 2.1   The HRD Pyramid

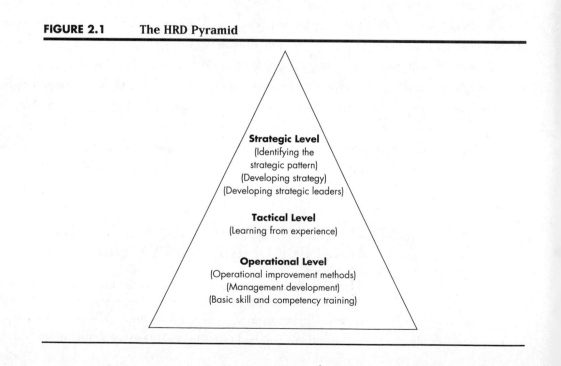

FOUNDATIONAL IDEAS ABOUT STRATEGY AND STRATEGIC THINKING

The concept of strategy has a long history and is rooted in the practice of war and diplomacy. Derived from the Greek words *strategia,* meaning "generalship," and *strategos,* meaning "a general set of maneuvers carried out to overcome an enemy," strategy refers to an overall framework for action. A strategic framework consists of a plan for a general set of maneuvers, in contrast to tactics, which are the specific actions taken by those charged with translating a strategic framework into operational effectiveness. In military terms, strategy is the framework for winning the war; tactics are the initiatives and actions taken to win specific battles once the strategy is put into play.

Despite the strong association between strategy and military science, strategy relates to diplomacy as well. In fact, contemporary political science considers war, or its threat, to be an instrument of diplomacy and statesmanship. *Merriam-Webster's 11th Collegiate Dictionary* broadly defines strategy as: "the science and art of employing the political, economic, psychological, and military forces of a nation or group of nations to afford the maximum support to adopted policies in peace or war" (2003, p. 1233).

Strategic thinking is ubiquitous in modern life. Coaches think strategically in putting together game plans for their players. Politicians strategically think through their election campaigns and legislative initiatives. Professors, who in their academic governance roles must perform as amateur politicians, think strategically about how to get curriculum changes through committee. Parents are strategic in trying to influence their children's behavior. Children are strategic in seeking to influence their parents. One of the great mysteries of life is how children's truly impressive ability to think and act strategically atrophies when they become parents. (One suspects this is linked to one of the fundamental inhibitors of good strategic thought—ego involvement—resulting in the inability to realistically assess the abilities of one's opponents.) And of course, organizational executives must think strategically about how to position their organization for success in uncertain environments where they must compete for scarce resources.

Strategic thinking assumes

▪ a set of needs or objectives that are considered important and are potentially contested by others;

▪ these others can be conceptualized as opponents who are either competitors for scarce resources or wish to achieve objectives different from and contrary to one's own objectives; and

▪ these opponents typically have their own strategy and are also going to react to the perceived strategy and tactics that one puts into play to achieve one's objectives.

HRD can make a significant contribution to organizational performance by developing organizational members' capability for strategic thinking and creating social spaces in the organization where strategic conversations can take place.

The Meaning of Organizational Strategy

Although the term *strategy* is widely used, its meaning in practice is not well understood. Its complexity defies simple, one-sentence description;[2] however, there is wide agreement on its basic parameters. In terms of organizational strategy, De Kluyver provides one of the clearest statements:

> Strategy is about *positioning* an organization for *sustainable competitive advantage*. It involves making *choices* about *which industries to participate in*, what *products and services to offer*, and how to *allocate corporate resources* to achieve such a sustainable advantage.[3]

It is also important to note that in a complex organization organizational strategy exists at different levels: one can think of corporate-level strategy, business-unit strategy, and functional, or operational, strategy. The extent to which the strategic levels are aligned will depend on the diversity of the organization and how tightly coupled the various levels are in contributing to its overall success. Achieving this integration requires an additional competence that is closely related to strategic thinking yet distinct from it: systems thinking on the part of key members at various levels of the organization.

De Kluyver's description provides an important foundation for thinking about the strategic role of HRD. Before building on this foundation, however, we must consider some other, equally important concepts and ideas.

Strategic Intent

Core ideas often drive strategic alignment in organizations, and one of these is the notion of strategic intent, as advanced by Hamel and Prahalad.[4] Strategic intent refers to a leadership position envisioned relative to one's competitors and establishes a focused criterion against which the organization can chart its progress. Said another way, strategic intent is a core idea that guides the organization over the long term, providing the basis for making decisions in the face of emerging opportunities and threats. Typically, strategic intent focuses on a specific competitor or group of competitors and expresses ambitions out of proportion with available resources and capabilities.

Hamel and Prahalad give the examples of the Japanese company Komatsu, which set out to "encircle Caterpillar"; Canon Copiers, which sought to "beat Xerox"; and Coca-Cola, which intended to "put a Coke within arms reach" of every consumer world-wide.[5] Each of these examples captures, in a simple phrase, the organization's strategic intent. These statements of strategic intent invoke a vision that challenges members of the organization vis-à-vis their major competitor and provides a rallying point for action. At the same time that vision is concrete enough to provide a guideline for managers in devising competitive tactics. Managers at the operational level of the business can ask themselves, In what ways do my plans and actions contribute to our "encircling Caterpillar," "beating Xerox" or "putting a Coke in arms reach of consumers world-wide"? Strategic intent has power when it becomes an obsession that provides a context for creative strategizing and tactical moves in business units throughout the organization, when it motivates people, and when it serves as a guide for resource allocation. Simple statements, when well crafted, become potent mechanisms for focusing and coordinating activity across a geographically dispersed and decentralized organization.

Alas, in social affairs, every advantage carries within it a potential disadvantage. Too narrow a focus on strategic intent can blind an executive management team to the emergence of new competitors or disruptive technologies.[6] Not every organization has a clear statement of strategic intent, and there is no empirical evidence that demonstrates that such a focus is a prerequisite for strategic success. However, inherent in the concept of strategy is a concise idea of what the organization is trying to achieve, an idea that can direct the actions of people throughout the organization.[7]

Miller and Dess posit a "hierarchy of strategic intentions" as an alternate to this specificially defined form of strategic intent.[8] They propose determining 1) a broad vision of what the organization should be; 2) the organization's mission; 3) a set of specific goals; and 4) measurable strategic objectives as a sequence comprising the hierarchy of setting strategic direction. Their framework is not incompatible with the concept of strategic intent, but places it within the broader context of a formalized and analytical strategic management process.

The Strategically Focused Organization

Kaplan and Norton argue for their concept of "the balanced scorecard" for creating a strategy-focused organization.[9] The balance scorecard consists of four perspectives of organizational performance: one is the traditional financial perspective of measures, which are lagging indicators of performance. The other three perspectives—the customer perspective, the internal business-processes perspective, and the learning and growth perspective—are business drivers, measures of which are leading indicators that predict future performance. These four perspectives are generic categories that Kaplan and Norton offer as an organizing framework for a strategic management system. Translating strategy into concrete descriptions and measures of each category provides an organizing framework for a strategic management system (Figure 2.2). Based on the balanced-scorecard strategy, maps can be created for each organizational function at multiple levels of the organization, aligning and focusing the entire organization around the strategy.

Because strategies will differ from company to company, the specifics of the scorecard and maps will vary. Figure 2.3 presents the scorecard for Mobil North America Marketing and Refining (NAM&R). Mobil NAM&R used the scorecard to align and focus the organization around a shift to a two-pronged strategy of reducing costs and increasing productivity across the value chain while generating increased volume on premium-priced products and services. Believing that low cost alone was not a viable long-term strategic differentiator, because the industry as a whole was focused on cost reduction, the second part of this strategy was critical— fostering long-term growth by attracting customers who were likely to purchase

FIGURE 2.2   To a Strategic Management System

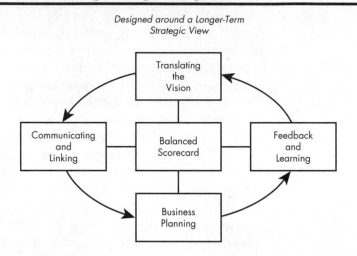

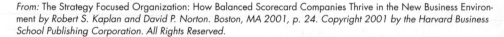

premium products and services, to buy more gasoline than average, and to make other purchases in the retail station.

Strategic Management

Wheelen and Hunger define strategic management as "that set of managerial decisions and actions that determines the long-run performance of a corporation . . . . Originally called business policy, strategic management incorporates such topics as long range planning and strategy."[10] However it is formulated, strategic management involves the following:

- Scanning both the external and internal environment. The external task environment involves potential and actual opportunities and threats coming from the actions of customers, competitors, allies, and other stakeholders who provide the organization with necessary resources and support. Broadly conceptualized, the task-external environment consists of general social and political forces and the specific industry or industries in which the organization operates. The internal environment includes the organization's culture, structure, political dynamics, and resources.

- Strategy formation, beginning with a core strategic insight that provides the basis for articulating a compelling vision and mission, strategic frameworks or plans, and policies.

- Strategy implementation including tactical initiatives, programs, allocation of resources, and deployment of people.

FIGURE 2.3   **Mobil NAM&R's Balanced Scorecard**

	STRATEGIC THEMES	STRATEGIC OBJECTIVES	STRATEGIC MEASURES
Financial	Financial Growth	F1 Return on Capital Employed	• ROCE
		F2 Existing Asset Utilization	• Cash Flow
		F3 Profitability	• Net Margin Rank (vs. Competition)
		F4 Industry Cost Leader	• Full Cost per Gallon Delivered (vs. Competition)
		F5 Profitable Growth	• Volume Growth Rate vs. Industry
			• Premium Ratio
			• Non-gasoline Revenue and Margin
Customer	Delight the Consumer	C1 Continually Delight the Targeted Consumer	• Share of Segment in Selected Key Markets
			• Mystery Shopper Rating
	Win-Win Dealer Relations	C2 Build Win-Win Relations with Dealer	• Dealer Gross Profit Growth
			• Dealer Survey
Internal	Build the Franchise	I1 Innovative Products and Services	• New Product ROI
			• New Product Acceptance Rate
		I2 Best-in-Class Franchise Teams	• Dealer Quality Score
	Safe and Reliable	I3 Refinery Performance	• Yield Gap
			• Unplanned Downtime
	Competitive Supplier	I4 Inventory Management	• Inventory Levels
			• Run-out Rate
		I5 Industry Cost Leader	• Activity Cost vs. Competition
	Quality	I6 On Spec. on Time	• Perfect Orders
	Good Neighbor	I7 Improve EHS	• Number of Environmental Incidents
			• Days Away from Work Rate
Learning and Growth	Motivated and Prepared Workforce	L1 Climate for Action	• Employee Survey
		L2 Core Competencies and Skills	• Personal Balanced Scorecard (%)
		L3 Access to Strategic Information	• Strategic Competency Availability
			• Strategic Information Availability

The Strategy Focused Organization: How Balanced Scorecard Companies Thrive in the New Business Environment, *by Robert S. Kaplan & David P. Norton. Boston, MA 2001, page 41. Copyright 2001 by The Harvard Business School Publishing Corporation. All Rights Reserved.*

    ■ Evaluation and control involving the assessment of performance for purposes of learning and arriving at new insights.

    Varied opinions exist in the literature on how decision making occurs within this process of strategic management. Mintzberg has characterized strategy making as a craft, arguing that there is no one pattern or approach to the process of strategy formation. Strategies, he argues, have a grass-roots character, growing like weeds in a garden. "They take root in all kinds of places, wherever people have the capacity to learn (because they are in touch with the situation) and the resources to support that capacity. These strategies become organizational when they become collective, that is, when they proliferate to guide the behavior of the organization at large."[11] Admitting that "this view is overstated," Mintzberg argues it is no more extreme than conventional views of strategic planning.

A similar view is expressed by Quinn, who describes the process of strategic decision making as "logical incrementalism."[12] In Quinn's model, senior management may have a reasonably clear idea of the organization's mission and objectives; however, the process of formulating strategies is a highly interactive one, with a task environment in which management probes and learns from partial (incremental) commitments rather than from formulations of total strategies. Eden and Ackermann see all strategy making as emergent, arguing that effective strategy is socially constructed through a process that involves many stakeholders in an organization.[13]

Although the understanding of strategic management as an emergent process is gaining ground among those who study the process, many, if not most, formal textbooks on the subject continue to offer highly linear and rationalistic approaches to it. Regardless of how strategic management is conceptualized, feedback and learning have emerged as critical. For example, Wheelen and Hunger write:

> Good arguments can be made for using either the entrepreneurial . . . (or logical incrementalism) in certain situations. . . . in most situations the planning mode . . . is a more rational and thus better way of making strategic decisions. The planning mode is not only more analytical and less political than are the other modes, but it is also more appropriate for dealing with complex, changing environments. We therefore propose the following eight-step **strategic decision making process** . . . [14]

Although we believe Wheelen and Hunger to be overly optimistic about the extent to which such eight-step models apply in practice, we do agree with another point they make, namely:

> As it takes less and less time for one product or technology to replace another, companies are finding that there is no such thing as permanent competitive advantage. . . . This means that corporations must develop strategic flexibility—the ability to shift from one dominant strategy to another. Strategic flexibility demands a long-term commitment to the development and nurturing of critical resources. It also demands that the company become a learning organization—an organization skilled at creating, acquiring, and transferring knowledge, and at modifying its behavior to reflect new knowledge and insights.[15]

Even in their highly structured model of the strategic management process, feedback and learning are fundamental processes.

The Business Model, or Livelihood Scheme, and the Winning Proposition

The outcome of a successful strategy-development process is a statement of a core strategic idea that is widely agreed upon among key organizational members and that makes explicit the basis on which the organization will do business. As Eden and Ackermann express it:

> For the private sector this is an expression of the "business model"—the idea that will convert purposeful activity into revenue and profit—and in the public or not-for-profit sectors the "livelihood scheme"—the *rightful* purpose of its existence as a public or charitable organization.[16]

At the center of an organization's business model or livelihood scheme has to be what Pietersen calls the organization's winning proposition.[17] Simply stated, the winning proposition is the answer to the question, What will we do differently or better than our competitors?[18] The answer to this question focuses the organization on paying attention to those few things that will make the biggest difference in "winning the game."

Analysis of such strategic factors as an organization's *distinctive or core competency,*[19] its *intellectual capital,*[20] and the *value chain*[21] needs to be considered to bring into focus the business model or livelihood scheme and to articulate the winning proposition. In practice, strategic thinkers must engage in a continuing reflective conversation around how changing conditions impact both the organization's strategy and the concepts that support it. This conversation highlights the role of learning in the strategic decision-making process, a topic we will consider in detail in Chapter Three.

Tactics

Although the distinctions between strategy and tactics are clear at the extremes, the line between them is often blurred.[22] Strategies are very broad, and, compared to tactics, strategies have fewer details; there is typically a wide range of alternatives among which managers must choose in making strategic decisions, and strategy is developed with much greater uncertainty than are tactics. Tactics are the specific steps taken to implement strategy; they are the link between strategy development and operational processes and practices. Strategic decisions posit a gap between where the organization is and where it needs to be. Tactics are moves that close the gap and/or sustain the organization's dominance in its market.

Some strategic tactics fall within the purview of senior management; these include major capital investments, financial and/or organizational restructuring, acquisitions and/or divestitures, new product or service lines, and overall allocation of resources. Other tactics are more operational, more within the domain of upper middle-management; these include staffing changes, pricing changes, reorganization of facilities, advertising and promotions, and resource allocation.

Formal tactics are codified in plans and policies spelling out the time and scope of actions to be taken and the resources to be provided. These plans may be offensive in nature, seeking to exploit weaknesses in a competitor's position; or defensive, trying to strengthen or offset the organization's vulnerabilities. Going head-to-head with competitors, such as Wal-Mart has done with Kmart, Target, Ames, and other discount retailers, is an example of an offensive tactic. For this confrontational tactic to work, management is betting that it has sufficient resources and that its value proposition is appealing enough to customers to overpower the established position of competitors and build a new sustainable market position. When MCI and Sprint tried to compete head-to-head with AT&T, they only succeeded in driving down profits for all three service providers, weakening AT&T, but failing to build their own superior presence in the marketplace.

Other offensive tactics include bypassing competitors or outflanking them. Instead of going head-to-head with Intel, Cyrix developed a math co-processor for Intel's 386 chip that ran 20 times faster than Intel's microprocessor.

Defensive tactics can include raising structural barriers to entry to the marketplace through exclusive agreements with suppliers; filing for patent extensions; or lobbying for legislation creating favorable trade policies. Farm subsidies—the product of industry lobbying, both in the United States and Europe—are examples of legislation designed to protect local agricultural producers. A corporation, like United Technologies, with a significant stake in defense contracts might locate facilities in various states, because each state provides it additional votes from senators and representatives eager to produce jobs in their states and districts. Boeing may contract with suppliers from around the world, partly for lower costs and partly to build support for aircraft purchases from overseas governments.

As the embodiment of strategy, tactics put strategy into play. As a result, tactics provoke responses from competitors, adversaries, and adversely affected stakeholders; these responses must be countered. Some tactics provoke unanticipated consequences: a retailer may be forced to pull certain advertising because of adverse reactions from parents, as happened several years ago to Calvin Klein with its use of young adolescent girls in provocative poses. In each instance, sense or meaning must be made of the reaction to tactics and taken into account going forward.

Strategic and Tactical Effectiveness

Ultimately, the test of any strategy and of the tactics that are adopted to implement it is results. However, the relationship between strategy and results is not linear. It is not apparent whether poor results reflect poor strategy or poor implementation of strategy because of bad tactical decisions or the weak execution of tactical decisions. Charan and Colvin, writing in *Fortune* magazine in 1999,[23] estimated from their study of CEO failures that in 70 percent of the cases the problem wasn't strategy but bad execution.

In his seminal study of the emergence of the modern corporate structure, Chandler revealed how strategic decisions by DuPont, General Motors, Sears, and Standard Oil initially failed because organizational structures did not support the strategy.[24] Aligning structure with strategy is a key implementation issue; other implementation factors, such as allocation of resources, organizational culture, and management programs that pull people in different directions, are all examples of factors that can defeat strategy. Creating alignment and focus is the point of the aforementioned ideas of strategic intent and the balanced scorecard.

Tactical learning can eventually result in the reframing of a poor strategic idea. Pascale reports how Honda motorcycles were introduced into the United States market, beginning in the late 1950s.[25] With a start up inventory evenly divided among the company's four products, the 50cc Super Cub, and the larger 125cc, 250cc, and 305cc bikes, Honda intended to compete with established American manufacturer Harley-Davidson by featuring Honda's big bikes, particularly their 250cc and 305cc machines. The 50cc Super Cub, popular in Japan, was deemed inappropriate for the United States, where everything was larger and more luxurious and where the image of bike riders was one of macho, hard-riding, adventure-seeking rowdies. However, these large bikes, designed for road conditions in Japan, were a flop in the United States, where Honda was striving to compete head-to-head with Harley-Davidson.

However, in America, a geographically larger country with an expansive highway system, traditional motorcyclists rode their large bikes much further and faster than in Japan. The Japanese bikes, not designed for this heavy usage, soon developed problems, leaking oil and experiencing clutch failures.

While featuring the big bikes, Honda managers and employees rode the Super Cubs around town on short errands, because they were convenient and cost effective. The Super Cubs attracted a lot of attention, even generating a call from a Sears buyer who had repeatedly noticed the Honda employees riding them. Inquiries from retailers interested in selling them were coming from sporting goods stores, not from the traditional motorcycle outlets.

Selling small bikes through such retailers would be a significant departure from traditional practice in the motorcycle industry. Further, promoting Honda as a manufacturer of small bikes would require a marketing program and sales campaign that was virtually the exact opposite of motorcycle marketing in North America. However, with the large bikes breaking down, Honda had no choice but to focus on moving the small bikes. Contentious discussions ensued within Honda about a new marketing slogan, "You meet the nicest people on a Honda" (developed by a University of California Los Angeles advertising major who, with encouragement from his professor, sold it to an advertising firm that was soliciting the Honda account), as the centerpiece for a promotional effort that defined Honda in way completely at odds with the rest of industry in the United States. The president of The American Honda Motor Company and its treasurer as well opposed the move, which was strongly supported by the director of sales. A decision was made to try out the approach in a limited market and then expand incrementally. By 1964, one out of every two bikes sold was a Honda as "the nicest people" campaign drove sales in a new market, medium-income leisure riders. The resulting success of the strategy opened the American market for Honda and redefined the image of motorcycling; it even changed the nature of available financing—banks and finance companies began offering financing, where previously dealer credit was virtually the only source.

The Honda example illustrates the essence of many strategic breakthroughs—they change the game by fundamentally redefining the business model of the industry. Pascale makes the point that strategic thinking often involves dealing with initial miscalculations and taking note of serendipitous responses, such as the inquiries from the Sears buyer and from sporting goods stores, that are typically outside management's initial field of strategic vision.

Operational Effectiveness

Porter makes a clear distinction between strategy and operational effectiveness.[26] Strategy involves creating a unique, sustainable position of providing value by performing activities in a distinctive pattern that cannot be easily duplicated or imitated by competitors without compromising their existing strategic position. Operational effectiveness involves performing activities better, that is, faster and/or with better quality and cost effectiveness than competitors; increasing operational effectiveness involves process improvement.

The success of Southwest Airlines rests on the strategic bet that providing no-frills service would be attractive to a large segment of the flying public if the service were reliably on time, offered at a significantly lower cost than competitors charge, and delivered in a good-natured, humorous way. The foundation of Southwest's strategic idea lay in organizing its activities in a substantially different way than its brand-name competitors had organized theirs. Instead of operating from hubs, Southwest scheduled flights point-to-point, and the airline uses only one model of aircraft, thus making all of its cockpit crews interchangeable, reducing the training required for all of its employees, and simplifying maintenance and inventories—all practices that ran counter to prevailing industry practice and conventional wisdom. Of course, to effectively deliver the airline's value proposition to its customers, employees had to perform their operational tasks in a highly efficient way, and both strategy and tactics had to be supported by a high level of operational effectiveness.

An important part of Southwest's strategic idea was that its established competitors would not be able to imitate its strategy and tactics because of fixed costs and prevailing organizational cultures. The bet has paid off. To date, Southwest's competitors have failed to imitate its strategy even when they have established a subsidiary airline, in part because they lack the corporate core competencies (core competencies are discussed in detail in Chapter Three) necessary for managing this new alignment of activities. It is not easy to mix strategies such as creating a low cost subsidiary that is part of a larger, traditional airline. Indeed, only new entrants to the market, like Jet Blue, pose a potential competitive threat to Southwest Airlines.

Porter argues that operational effectiveness and strategy are complementary in that both are required for sustained superior performance. However, Porter's main point is that focusing on operational effectiveness alone is no substitute for broad, innovative strategy, because over time most advances in operational effectiveness are imitated, leading to convergence in practices that erode the early competitive advantages the practices originally provided. An example is the ability of some American companies to catch up with their Japanese competitors in quality. The aforementioned example of Mobil NAM&R's strategy—competing through growth and differentiation, based on attracting a certain customer segment with different purchasing habits, reflects management's belief that cost and productivity improvements achieved largely through process efficiencies would not constitute a long-term strategic differentiator. Mobil's competitors had access to low-cost crude, and process efficiencies were the focus of companies throughout the industry—all leading to a convergence in cost structures.

For the past several decades, training in various total quality management methods combined with an increased emphasis on performance management and improvement has created a strong demand for HRD activity at the operational level of organizations. Training activity—including statistical process control (SPC), continuous improvement, six-sigma, re-engineering, reliability control, and similar techniques—created a bonanza for external consultants, university continuing education departments, and internal trainers alike, placing HRD practitioners in the important mediating role of providing training programs directed toward developing in the workforce both the skills and the mental perspectives essential to these techniques.

Managing how this training unfolds in an organization is a critical HRD responsibility. Ideally, HRD's role is that of an enabler, working in concert with various levels of management and with other staff functions to develop a coherent approach to learning and development that focuses on operational performance while avoiding a random, almost cafeteria-style delivery of programs that unintentionally reinforce a "flavor-of-the-month" mentality among workers.

For example, Cole has documented how, initially, the general high quality of Japanese products challenged American companies to invest heavily in sending their supervisors and employees to workshops on quality techniques.[27] However, the philosophy behind these techniques and methods was divorced from the dominant mindset in company management; at the time, American business strongly held that managing quality and productivity levels involved a tradeoff—increasing one meant sacrificing the other. This was at odds with the basic premise of the new understanding of quality management promulgated by experts such as the seminal writers on statistical quality control Deming and Juran—that high quality and productivity are consistent with one another when both are properly conceptualized and measured.

Consequently, when supervisors and employees attending the quality workshops returned to the workplace, they were unable to use what they had learned. Effective application of the total-quality management techniques required management to reframe how they thought about the relationship between quality and productivity. In many companies, employees became cynical when each new initiative and its accompanying training program—such as statistical process control and quality circles—were announced as the key to moving the organization forward.

The haphazard implementation of training, divorced from a more comprehensive change in operational philosophy, probably prolonged the competitive advantage enjoyed by the Japanese companies that adopted these methods and aligned them with their broader operational philosophy. According to a report issued in July, 2003, by J. D. Power and Associates, who closely follow and analyze the performance of the auto industry, Japanese automakers still maintain a quality advantage over their American competitors, although American cars have demonstrated significant gains in dependability as American automakers align quality management philosophy and methods into their ways of doing business in the industry. The J. D. Power report is important because most consumers consider dependability the most important consideration in buying a vehicle.

By using a mechanism such as the balanced scorecard, which tracks the strategic perspectives of learning and growth as leading indicators, learning interventions at the operational level are more likely to be aligned with strategic needs across the organization. This is especially true if regular strategic management review meetings are scheduled. Kaplan and Norton report "that 85 percent of management teams spend less than an hour per month discussing strategy."[28] When this is the case, especially under conditions of strategic shift and new competitive challenges, it is little wonder that operational training becomes uncoupled from strategic needs.

THE HRD PYRAMID: MIRRORING THE STRATEGIC, TACTICAL, AND OPERATIONAL NEEDS OF THE ORGANIZATION

The HRD pyramid we presented at the beginning of this chapter mirrors the conceptual framework of strategic, tactical, and operations management. Watkins and Marsick use a learning pyramid to demonstrate the interdependence of organizational, team, and individual learning domains,[29] and Holton provides a taxonomy of learning domains and drivers that include mission, processes, subsystems, and individuals.[30] While both Watkins and Marsick's pyramid and Holton's taxonomy are useful frameworks for understanding the various foci of HRD practice, each has, as its starting point, domains of HRD practice: the HRD pyramid focuses on the domains of organizational action in which HRD professionals have to link learning to the organizational strategy, tactics, and operational processes; the pyramid also assumes that strategic HRD must begin within the framework of broader organizational action.

Strategic and Tactical Learning

At the strategic level, management must answer the question, *How are we going to differentiate ourselves in a way that will produce both value for our customers and other stakeholders that is greater than the value our competitors are providing and one that is not easily copied or imitated?* Or framed another way, *What is our winning value proposition?*[31] Answering this question requires noting the changes both in the domain that the organization claims for itself and in its broader task environment. Managers and others need forums for discussing to what extent these trends and changes threaten to erode its current strategy and market position and/or provide new opportunities. Once the strategic question is answered, the core tactical question is *What actions do we need to take to make our strategy work?*

Answering these questions is a learning challenge in itself; in practice, making strategy is an emergent process. It is the nature of strategic questions that reasonable, thoughtful, and well-intended people may disagree about the answers. Answering strategic questions involves what can be called *imaginal* learning, because it requires challenging one's suppositions and premises and making sense of the world in a new way, so learning of this kind has also been called transformative.[32] When addressing strategic questions, the challenge is freeing one's self from the bonds of past experience.

As mentioned earlier, the ideal in strategy making is "changing the game" to position the organization in a way that cannot be easily duplicated. Southwest Airlines, Honda Motorcycles, and Wal-Mart all changed the game in their industries, creating a major problem for more established brand-name competitors. Organizations that have established their dominance or have what appears to be a secure place in their market, rarely "change the game," because their perspective is what Pietersen calls "inside-out."[33] They engage in strategic planning that extends what they are currently doing and typically focuses on the services or products they want to provide and how they want to provide them rather than what might be new ways of meeting needs. Pietersen argues that making strategy is a process of working "outside-in," looking at trends, not data points, and asking what, if it were possible for it to be provided, the customer would like.

The essences of strategic thinking are ideas and insight, requiring making sense of a changing and challenging environment. It is clear that domains and task environments of organizations are changing in fundamental ways; for example, marketing distribution channels have changed. The roles of middlemen mediating businesses are being threatened as an increasing number of producers are selling direct to their customers through the Internet. Insurance companies, as one example, are increasingly bypassing the independent agency system. Understanding the implication of these changes for the strategic positioning of a specific business or organization, however, is often less clear.

The kind of learning involved in strategy making is similar to what Revans has called "Q learning," or *questioning insight*.[34] Revans differentiates this kind of learning from "P learning," or programmed learning, which refers to learning knowledge that has been codified in books, lectures, or analytical techniques. "P learning" is very appropriate for what Revans calls "puzzles," or problems for which a correct solution exists even if it is hard to find, such as the best way of reducing the time or cost of some specific manufacturing operation, or the answer to a make versus buy decision in cost accounting. P learning is appropriate for addressing problems of operational effectiveness.

Strategic questions correspond to Revans' notion of Q learning because they typically represent "quandaries," difficulties or opportunities to which no solution clearly exists. Strategic decision making involves quandaries because

▪ the validity or value of the course of action eventually chosen cannot be determined until the action is implemented, lived with, and the results reflected upon; and

▪ even if the chosen course of action proves successful in that it meets or exceeds expectations, the opportunity costs of alternative courses of action—the roads not taken—cannot be accessed.

Gaining strategic insight requires first asking discriminating questions and then combining data analysis with past experience and intuitive judgment in answering them. The dilemma is how much of each—analysis, experience, and judgment—is required by the strategic quandary at hand.

HRD practitioners can facilitate this kind of learning through designing meetings that help executives to reframe their experience, to reinterpret the meaning of emerging-trends, and to challenge their assumptions. Future search conferences, action learning programs, scenario planning, and dedicating management meetings to critical discussion around alternative futures and opportunities are all ways of opening space for strategic learning.

Tactical learning takes place through assessment and reflection on what has happened. The aforementioned after-action reviews are one way of structuring this learning. More than simply debriefing experiences, after-action reviews require the suspension of rank and privilege so that open dialogue and discourse can take place. They are one way of putting the feedback and learning cell in Kaplan and Norton's concept of a strategic management system into operation (refer back to Figure 2.2).

We will say more about these issues in subsequent chapters. Here we note the dual role of HRD: first, using an understanding of the relationship between learning and decision-making to frame and facilitate the conversation about the content of strategy and tactics; second, working with senior management and other human resource management functions to clarify the implications of the conversation, that is, for positioning and enabling people, if strategy is going to be effectively implemented.

Important questions to consider are:

▪ What are the critical human resource linkages in the implementation path?
▪ To what extent do these linkages involve new meaning schemes, new working relationships, new competencies, and new knowledge on the part of managers and employees?
▪ What evidence do we have that as an organization we have the knowledge and expertise to ensure that these linkages are executed with a high level of effectiveness?
▪ What learning initiatives can enhance the probability of success?
▪ Which of these issues needs to be addressed? What are the consequences of not addressing them or of postponing addressing them?
▪ How is power involved in addressing these issues?

While addressing the strategic and tactical learning needs of the organization, HRD practitioners are simultaneously developing capable strategic and tactical leaders. For our purposes, capability is defined as *the ability to successfully interact with one's business environment.*

Capability requires a unique melding of competencies and expertise, tacit knowledge and experience, reflective capacity, and personal attitude. It is a way of thinking about the business environment and challenging strategic quandaries, sometimes utilizing prior expertise and at other times jettisoning it in the process of generating novel ideas and solutions.

Developing capable business leaders is an important HRD responsibility. To borrow a term from Kegan, the learning challenge is to prepare learners to deal with the "hidden curriculum" of their business environment.[35] Not only does engaging executives and high-potential managers in the kind of learning situations described above facilitate strategy development, but also participating in these kinds of learning events is itself developmental for them as strategic thinkers.

The Operational Level

The operational level of HRD practice involves enhancing and improving organizational performance through process and individual effectiveness. Competency and skill development, knowledge management, many kinds of best practices, and statistical process control are all examples of ways to increase organizational effectiveness through operational-level learning, which is foundational to the execution of strategy and basic to performance improvement. Operational-level learning primarily involves behavior skills, although, often, using skills effectively also requires a shift in meaning schemes in order for learners to accept the validity of what is being taught. As previously noted in this chapter in our discussion of total quality management, during the early days of quality improvement efforts in the United States, managers had to learn to reframe their thinking about productivity and quality.

A Final Word on "Levels"

Although our HRD pyramid suggests a traditional organizational hierarchy, it is important to remember that the hierarchy it pictures relates to learning challenges and to the kind of learning embodied in each level. These levels do not map strictly onto the levels of the managerial hierarchy, although, in general, there will be a loose correspondence between the two.

Although organizational structures are flatter and have broader spans of control than in the past, strategy and tactics are typically the responsibility of more senior management, while operational improvements involve less senior employees. This is true even in those organizations in which work occurs through networks of relationships. However, depending on the organization and industry, strategic learning may involve employees across many levels; senior managers often need operational training in the form of new competencies. Getting learning to the right people at the right time is part of the HRD challenge.

SUMMARY

Strategy is basically how a person or a group of people will accomplish a difficult goal that is contested by others. In an organization, strategic thinking is about positioning the organization, within its competitive context, to win through a unique value proposition that cannot be easily imitated and is sustainable over the long term. Successful strategic initiatives change the game on the competition. Learning, in particular, transformative learning, is at the core of strategic thinking.

Strategy involves making choices about not only what the organization is going to do but also what it is not going to do. Often the latter are the most difficult. Making choices is important, because clear strategic direction provides the basis for resource allocation and for guidance to business-level managers and supervisors in tactical and operational decision-making. Expressions of strategic intent reinforce this guidance and are motivational as well. While strategic management is often described in linear models as a logical, sequential process of analysis, in practice, strategy is typically more emergent, involving reaction to trends and growing out of intense conversations.

A clear distinction needs to be made between strategy and operational effectiveness. Both are necessary, but operational effectiveness is more easily imitated and doesn't provide the long-term advantage of the unique, winning proposition at the heart of a successful business or livelihood model. Much traditional HRD work has been done at the operational level of the organization. The HRD pyramid structures the HRD agenda around strategic, tactical, and operational learning needs. At the strategic level, organizational members must answer the question, How are we going to differentiate ourselves in a way that will produce greater value than our competitors' value stakeholder resources? Senior HRD professionals need to be proactive in organizing the conversations that address that question. HRD professionals also need to structure learning events that develop capable strategic and tactical leaders in the organization—executives and managers with the ability to successfully interact with the dynamic business environment. Additionally, HRD professionals need to ensure that the potential lessons from tactical actions are indeed learned by the organization. At the operational level, HRD needs to focus on giving members of the organization the competencies necessary for meeting performance expectations and implementing strategy and tactics. Essentially, HRD executives need to ask, Where are the critical linkages required for executing strategy, and what, if any, unmet learning and development needs are demanded by these linkages?

Questions for Discussion

1. Think of a highly successful business that seems to hold a unique strategy niche that competitors have not been able to imitate.

   ▍ How would you describe the essence of this business' strategy?

   ▍ What, in your opinion, is its winning value proposition?

   ▍ What learning needs would be required for the business to sustain this advantage?

   ▍ What trends (consider technology, demographics, social attitudes, economics) might threaten this strategy?

2. How would you differentiate strategic thinking from tactical or operational thinking? Could you recognize the difference in practice? Give examples of these different kinds of thinking from current business or international news—perhaps, for example, in a political campaign.

3. Give an example, from your experience, of operational-level training. How would learning events required for developing capable strategic leaders be different from operational-level training?

4. Can you think of a long-term goal that you have in your life, one that will be difficult to achieve? Describe the elements of a strategy for achieving this goal. What value proposition might drive your strategy? What choices will you have to make? How can you position yourself, what tactical actions might be required, and what "operational" skills will you need to implement the strategy?

End Notes

1. R. L. Dilworth, T. R. McClernon, and J. Redding, "No Respect: Bridging the Gap Between HRD Practitioners and Senior Management," *A What Works Report* (September, 2000 Alexandria, Va.: American Society for Training and Development).

2. C. A. DeKluyver, *Strategic Thinking: An Executive Perspective* (Upper Saddle River, N.J.: Prentice-Hall, 2000).

3. *ibid.*, 3.

4. G. Hamel and C. K. Prahalad, "Strategic Intent," *Harvard Business Review* (May–June, 1989): 63–76.

5. *ibid.*

6. C. M. Christensen, *The Innovator's Dilemma: When New Technologies Cause Great Firms to Fail* (Boston, Ma.: Harvard Business School Press, 1997).

7. J. Walton, *Strategic Human Resource Development* (Edinburgh Gate, Harlow Essex, England: Pearson Education Limited and Associated Companies around the World, Financial Times and Prentice Hall, 1999).

8. A. Miller and G. G. Dess, *Strategic Management,* 2nd ed. (New York: McGraw-Hill, 1996).

9. R. S. Kaplan and D. P. Norton, *The Strategy Focused Organization: How Balanced Score-card Companies Thrive in the New Business Environment* (Boston: Harvard Business School Press, 2001).

10. T. L. Wheelen and J. D. Hunger, *Strategic Management Business Policy,* 7th ed. (Upper Saddle River, N.J.: Prentice-Hall, 2000): 3.

11. H. Mintzberg, "Crafting Strategy," *Harvard Business Review* (July–August, 1987): 70.

12. J. B. Quinn, *Strategies for Change: Logical Incrementalism* (Homewood, Ill.: Irwin, 1980).

13. C. Eden and F. Ackermann, *Making Strategy: The Journey of Strategic Management* (London and Thousand Oaks, Ca.: Sage, 1998).

14. Wheelen and Hunger, *Strategic Management,* 19.

15. *ibid.,* 8.

16. Eden and Ackermann, *Making Strategy,* 4–5.

17. W. Pietersen, *Reinventing Strategy: Using Strategic Learning to Create and Sustain Breakthrough Performance.* (New York: John Wiley & Sons, 2002).

18. *ibid.,* 62.

19. C. K. Prahalad and G. Hamel, "The Core Competence of the Corporation," *Harvard Business Review* (March–April, 1993), 80–91.

20. T. A. Stewart, *Intellectual Capital: The New Wealth of Organizations* (Garden City, N. Y.: Doubleday, 1997).

21. M. E. Porter, *Competitive Advantage: Creating and Sustaining Superior Performance* (New York: Free Press, 1985).

22. G. A. Steiner, J. B. Miner, and E. R. Gray, *Management Policy and Strategy: Text, Readings, and Cases,* 3rd ed. (New York: Macmillan Publishing, 1986).

23. R. Charan and G. Colvin, "Why CEOs Fail," *Fortune* (June, 1999). Reported in Kaplan and Norton, *The Strategy-focused Organization,* 1.

24. A. D. Chandler, *Strategy and Structure* (New York: Doubleday, 1962).

25. R. T. Pascale, "Perspective on Strategy: The Real Story behind Honda's Success," *California Management Review* (Spring, 1984): 47–72.

26. M. E. Porter, "What is Strategy?" *Harvard Business Review* (Nov–Dec, 1996): 61–79.

27. R. Cole, "Learning from the Quality Movement: What Did and Didn't Happen and Why," *California Management Review* (Fall, 1998): 43–73.

28. Kaplan and Norton, *The Strategy Focused Organization,* 13–4.

29. K. Watkins and V. J. Marsick, *Sculpting the Learning Organization: Lessons in the Art and Science of Systemic Change* (San Francisco: Jossey-Bass, 1993).

30. E. F. Holton III, "Performance Domains and Their Boundaries," in *Performance Improvement: Theory and Practice. Advances in Developing Human Resources,* R. J. Torraco, ed., (San Francisco: Berrett-Koehler and Academy of Human Resource Development, 1999): 26–46.

31. Pietersen, *Reinventing Strategy.*

32. J. Mezirow, *Transformative Dimensions of Adult Learning.* (San Francisco: Jossey-Bass, 1991); J. Mezirow and Associates, *Learning as Transformation: Critical Perspectives on a Theory in Progress* (San Francisco: Jossey-Bass, 2000).

33. Pietersen, *Reinventing Strategy.* (This summary of the Honda story adapted from this article copyright © 1984 by the Regents of the University of California, reprinted from *The California Management Review,* Vol. 26, No. 3. By permission of the Regents.)

34. R. W. Revans, *The Origin and Growth of Action Learning* (London: Chartwell Bratt, 1982).

35. R. Kegan, *In Over Our Heads* (Cambridge, Ma: Harvard University Press, 1994).

chapter 3

This chapter

- examines how learning has evolved to become central to strategy development;

- differentiates between the strategic fit and leveraging resources view of strategy development;

- discusses some influential ideas in strategy development that involve learning, including the Boston Consulting Group's growth share matrix and portfolio management, the experience curve, the five-factor model of industry structure, core competencies, and emergent strategy;

- presents the strategy-making process as a series of conversations;

- introduces situation analysis for generating questioning insight;

- summarizes the strategic learning cycle; and

- introduces the role of the Senior HRD executive or Chief Learning Officer (CLO).

Key terms:

strategy as learning	five-factor model	learning window
strategic fit	core competencies	situation analysis
leveraged resources	strategy as craftsmanship	strategic learning cycle
portfolio management	emergent strategy	chief learning officer
experience curve	strategic conversations	

Strategy Making as Learning

In Chapter One, we discussed how the HRD literature has increasingly emphasized the role of strategy for HRD practice. But the concept of learning has become increasingly important in this literature as well:[1] a convergence of disciplinary thinking offers great opportunities for HRD practitioners. In this chapter, we examine more deeply how *learning is central to the seminal literature on organizational strategy. We consider various models for thinking about strategy development and then ask what tradeoffs, in terms of learning, they make and what the implications of these tradeoffs might be for both strategic learning and the practice of HRD.*

FOUNDATIONAL STRATEGIC CONCEPTS, TOOLS, AND LEARNING: THE ANALYTICAL STRATEGIC-POSITIONING APPROACH

Although learning was always implied in the strategy literature, it became explicit with the development of the "experience curve" (originally called the "learning curve") by the Boston Consulting Group (BCG) in the 1970s.[2] BCG's model was based on research that demonstrated a predictable and exponential inverse relationship between costs and a company's experience producing a particular product. The model postulates that this "economy of experience" provides a significant competitive advantage to any company with a new product line that can establish itself as the early market leader, because of the superior ability to control pricing and margins based on experience.

Although the experience curve has proven more effective in some instances than others,[3] it remains an influential concept, compatible with a more formal and analytical view of strategic learning, and it underlies the BCG "growth share matrix," with its emphasis on success being linked to the highest market share. The BCG growth share matrix popularized the portfolio-analysis approach to corporate strategy, treating the various businesses of a diversified company as a portfolio of business units. The dimensions of the matrix are 1) relative competitive position against the market leader and 2) industry attractiveness, expressed as the business growth rate (see

Figure 3.1). Based on an assessment of each business in the organization's portfolio, businesses are placed in one of four cells:[4]

■ *Stars,* market leaders that are at the peak of their product life cycle and are able to generate sufficient cash to sustain their position. When their market growth rate slows, stars turn into *cash cows.*

■ *Cash cows,* businesses that bring in more money than they need to maintain their share of the market. Cash cows generate resources for *question marks.*

■ *Question marks,* new products with potential for turning into stars. Their future is still a risk that must be funded with money from more mature products, typically cash cows.

■ *Dogs,* cash cows that are in a declining market, or businesses with low market share. Either these businesses should be divested, or their cash flow, carefully managed.

The BCG matrix implies ongoing learning and assessment based on market share analysis. Although easy to understand, BCG analysis has been criticized as too simplistic, focusing only on comparison with one competitor—the market-share leader—and using a simple dichotomy of high and low. Additionally, the empirical link between profitability and market share is weak—low market share businesses can be highly profitable—and market share is only one aspect of an organization's

FIGURE 3.1   **The BCG Growth Share Matrix**

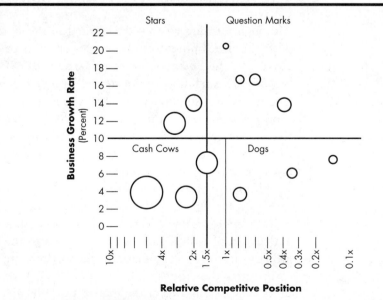

Reprinted from Long Range Planning, *Vol. 10, Hedley, B. Strategy and the Business Portfolio, page 12. Copyright February 1977. With permission from Elsevier.*

competitive position.[5] Many organizations have developed a more complex matrix for their own use, adding considerations other than market share in the industry attractiveness/business growth rate dimension of the matrix and also adding other considerations in the business strength/competitive position dimension, leading to a more tailored and nuanced model.

Perhaps the most influential analytical tool for strategic thinking is Porter's five-forces model of strategic positioning (Figure 3.2).[6] Porter posits five competitive forces that shape competitive strategy: 1) industry competitors, 2) suppliers, 3) buyers, 4) potential new competitive entrants, and 5) substitute products. These five structural forces interact with one another to comprise a framework for analyzing the strategic position and opportunities for a company. Porter advocates using the framework to rapidly identify and focus management's attention on the forces that determine the nature of competition in an industry.

In his later work, Porter identifies learning as an important element in executing successful strategy in diversified companies. Porter's explanation for the generally poor track record of diversified corporations is that in following portfolio models such as the BCG matrix, management is thinking more like a corporate banker making decisions about the distribution of capital to strategic business units (SBUs), rather than searching for strategic opportunities. Assuming efficient external capital

FIGURE 3.2   Porter's Five-Forces Model

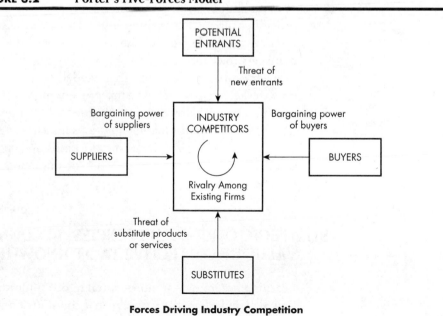

Forces Driving Industry Competition

markets, this corporate-banker approach fails to add value. Porter argues that value can be added to the business through the synergies produced when learning and expertise are shared across the businesses. Strategy, according to Porter, involves performing activities differently from competitors, an action that requires a unique fit among the various components of an organization's activity system linked to a specific strategic position in the market. Achieving this fit requires making tradeoffs in activities performed and market positions pursued, which, in turn, implies generative learning. However, the basis of Porter's model remains analysis and strategic fit.

Both Porter's five-forces model and the portfolio analysis of the BCG matrix have grown out of the early formal school of strategic planning,[7] which framed strategic problems as what Revans calls "puzzles" (see Chapter Two) for which a solution clearly exists, even if finding it requires considerable analytical skill.

Initially, formal models of strategic planning gave impetus to the creation of corporate planning staff functions in large organizations. Beginning in the 1980s many companies reconsidered the value of these functions, downsizing many staffs and moving the responsibility of planning down to business units. The role of corporate planning concurrently shifted to providing technical input and analysis in support of strategy as opposed to formulating strategy, a trend that continues as organizations strive to become more entrepreneurial by putting less emphasis on operating through vertically integrated organizations and working toward functioning as internal market economies rather than planned economies. Mintzberg has characterized this evolution of the planning function as the "fall and rise of strategic planning."[8]

This shift in management's understanding of the role of strategic planning—as providing supporting analysis rather than creating strategy—holds the potential for HRD practitioners to facilitate the strategic thinking increasingly required of line managers, by supplementing the data provided by financial planning staffs with a broader process for sensemaking. Models such as Porter's five forces and the BCG growth share matrix provide conceptual frameworks that can point managers toward relevant analysis. However, as we argued in Chapter Two, the answers are not in the data but in the discriminating questions managers ask of the data, questions that lead to insight. As we will argue below, the kinds of conversations managers hold around the data and the questions they ask of one another are the core of the strategy-making process.

STRATEGIC CORE-COMPETENCIES: RECOGNIZING THE STRATEGIC VALUE OF COLLECTIVE TACIT KNOW-HOW

Learning becomes even more central to our understanding of effective strategy with Prahalad and Hamel's argument that the source of competitiveness lies in an organization's core competencies.[9] Distinguishing between an organization viewing itself as a portfolio of competencies, and its viewing itself as a portfolio of businesses, Prahalad and Hamel vigorously argue against the dominance of the latter over the former.

Prahalad and Hamel identify core competencies as the collective learning embedded in the organization's culture, particularly, knowing how to coordinate diverse sets of skills, blend technologies into new streams for product innovation, and organize work. Using Casio as an example, they note that producing a miniature radio the size of a business card requires more than knowing how to put a radio on a computer chip. Know-how in miniaturization, in the design of microprocessors, in material science, and in ultra-thin precision casting must all be harmonized. *Harmonizing* these *streams of know-how* is the same *core competence* used in Casio's miniature televisions, card calculators, and watches. Prahalad and Hamel offer Citicorp's core competence in systems that provide a cutting edge, 24-hour-a-day operating system for participating in world markets as another example.

Developing these kinds of core competencies requires a strong commitment to the authentic involvement of many levels of people working together across functional and other organizational boundaries. Marketing, engineering, and technical specialists must forge a deep understanding of technological possibilities and how they might mesh with potential customer needs and wants. This kind of competence cannot be easily imitated; rather, it must be developed over time. Core competencies are tacit organizational knowledge, the kind of organizational learning that is only visible in its execution—it can't be stored in an organizational database.

Prahalad and Hamel agree that diversified corporations, in addition to being portfolios of competencies, are portfolios of businesses and products. They maintain, however, that a primary focus on strategic business units (SBUs) as the strategic frame of reference creates a mindset that undermines long-term innovation and, by extension, excludes the organization from potential new markets. In the short run, SBU competitiveness derives from the price/performance attributes of current products. However, through the prism of traditional SBU-based portfolio matrixes, markets are judged "mature," and companies exit them prematurely.

The decision to exit the color television business by Motorola, GTE, and GE are examples of companies judging a business mature and selling off competencies germane to competing in the nascent, but high-potential high-definition television market in the future. If the organization is viewed as a set of business units, each positioned in the context of a particular industrial structure, the ability to work across business units can be lost as SBUs focus on keeping their current products competitive. Core competencies are lost when organizations pursue tactics such as outsourcing manufacturing of key component parts. In outsourcing a significant proportion of its Mitsubishi and Hyundai engine and power train components to Mitsubishi and Hyundai, Chrysler also outsourced a critical core competency; these components were the "physical embodiments of core competencies."[10]

This analysis is consistent with Porter's explanation, which we presented above, for the poor performance of many diversified corporations. When management focuses only on the performance of each business unit the organization fails to develop core competency in cultivating synergies across business unit boundaries. One obstacle to developing this kind of core competency is competition for human resources among business units. This competition can be intensified when strategic thinking in an organization focuses solely on SBU performance in a portfolio of diverse businesses, leading to a tendency for SBU general managers to resist sharing key people for work on joint projects, collaborations that are critical for developing and understanding core competencies. Developing core competencies, then, requires both coordinated HRM, OD, and HRD initiatives and senior management support.

Not-for-profits have core competencies as well. The School for International Training in Brattleboro, Vermont, for example, has a core competence in building learning communities composed of highly diverse student populations, a process that requires cooperation among core faculty in developing their courses and interacting with students.

EMERGENT STRATEGY: THE FOCAL POINT OF STRATEGIC LEARNING

As we discussed in Chapter Two, Mintzberg has put forward an alternative to the traditional description of strategy making as a highly linear and formalized process of planning, positing instead an emergent view of strategy making as a craft and rejecting any one pattern or approach as foundational.[11] An enriched view of learning is central to this alternative view of strategy formation.

Descriptions of the strategy-formation process by writers like Mintzberg and Quinn[12] are consistent with notions of strategy growing out of conversation, trial and error experimentation, and even retroactive sensemaking, as managers make meaning out of emergent patterns of strategic action. They are also consistent with a view of the learning challenge that inheres in the idea of strategy formation as a quandary, a dilemma for which no one correct answer—only relatively better or worse courses of actions—can be established.[13]

If the concept of an experience curve has made the importance of learning more visible in the strategy literature, a debate between Mintzberg and Ansoff invigorated it.[14] Their debate is perhaps theoretical for strategy scholars, but it is important for HRD executives seeking to advocate a learning approach to strategy making for their organization. Mintzberg framed the difference between the emergent approach he describes and the more conventional, formal analytical approach as "strategy-as-planning" versus "strategy-as-learning."[15] Ansoff challenged Mintzberg, arguing that the differences instead lie in two contrasting views of strategy as learning, an argument that brings the processes of learning implied in the planning models to the foreground.

Ansoff called Mintzberg's emergent strategy approach the inductive "existential model," and his own planning oriented approach the deductive cognitive model which he further developed into a "cognition-trial–cognition-trial" approach to strategic learning. Their debate can be likened to the "grand tension" between theoretical physics ("think-then-do") and experimental physics ("do-then-think") or between strategy as a process of learning through hypothesis generation and revision, and strategy as a process of learning through exploration and discovery.[16]

Ansoff's argument essentially makes strategy formation at the organizational level analogous to learning styles in individuals, but this analogy fails to clarify the processes through which the "think-then-do" approach translates from an individual level to an organizational level learning pattern. Simply bringing highly intelligent individuals together is insufficient for organizational learning to occur;[17] it requires consensual agreement among a critical mass of organizational members that becomes institutionalized either in policy and procedures or informally in the organization's culture (see the discussion of Popper and Lipshitz's analysis of organizational learning in Chapter Six).

For his part, Mintzberg describes the dichotomy between planning and strategic thinking in extreme terms in order to call attention to the emergent character of much strategy formation, but he does not exclude the value of formal planning. Arguing that strategic planning is analysis, as opposed to strategic thinking, Mintzberg maintains that planners should support strategy making by supplying the analyses and the hard data that strategic thinking requires. These data need to be provided to broaden the range of issues considered during strategy discussions rather than to discover the right answer. Strategy making is not done in isolation from the work of the organization. It involves the synthesis that grows out of involvement with the business, a digging for ideas. Hard data are valuable as long as they don't blind people to possibilities.

This is analogous to Revans' learning of formula, $L = P + Q$ (Learning = Programmed Instruction + Questioning Insight) (P and Q were both presented in Chapter Two) which can be modified here slightly to $SL = SA + Q$ (Strategic Learning = Strategic Analysis + Questioning Insight).

Pietersen builds on Mintzberg, explicitly defining strategy formation as a process of learning and making a clear distinction between strategic thinking as a form of learning and strategic planning (Table 3.1).

Strategic Learning

Writing normative literature for business and other organizations about the keys to success is obviously a risky proposition. In the same way that companies like General Motors, Motorola, AT&T, Xerox, Hewlett-Packard, and McDonald's have been hailed at one time as exemplars of excellence but at other times have been characterized as exemplars of strategically struggling organizations, proponents of one approach to

TABLE 3.1

Strategic Thinking is about:	Strategic Planning is about:
Ideas and Insight	Numbers and Analysis
Outside-in	Numbers and Analysis
Divergent Perspectives	Convergent Thinking
Learning and Leadership	Management

Adapted from Reinventing Strategy: Using Strategic Learning to Create and Sustain Breakthrough Performance, *W. G. Pietersen. Copyright 2003, William G. Pietersen. This material is used by permission of John Wiley & Sons, Inc.*

strategy can use their approach to point to some companies as examples of success, while using other companies as illustrations of the limitation of other approaches.

3M built its portfolio of businesses around its core competence with sticky tape, in contrast to GE, which focused on acquiring a mix of businesses that were No. 1 or No. 2 in their markets and strategically shifted to services. IBM was revitalized with a strategic move to providing integrated solutions. All three companies represent corporate success stories, and for all three, learning played a significant role in their success, although each used learning in a different way. Understanding the nuances—in how each company used learning, how this learning was based on a creative balance of cultural legacy and leadership, and how this understanding can be adapted to another situation—is the fundamental challenge facing the HRD practitioner seeking to help his or her organization achieve similar success. Lack of such understanding is what confounds imitators who simply borrow obvious best practices without understanding the critical cultural success factors that made them work in certain settings. Many companies are struggling while trying to imitate GE's success with action-learning programs and its education center in Crotonville, New York, or IBM's success as a provider of business solutions. But a company cannot imitate its way to strategic excellence any more than a person can imitate his or her way to success through blindly copying another.

A company cannot imitate its way to strategic success, but that does not mean that an organization can't learn vicariously. However, vicarious learning through methods such as best practices must be blended into the unique qualities of the adopting organization in order to achieve successful strategic positioning.

Achieving strategic success is less a matter of theoretical purity than it is of finding a successful strategic model and executing it with purpose and discipline. Professors and consultants use some cases, such as Honda motorbikes, to illustrate both a strategic positioning approach and the leveraging of core competencies, demonstrating that successful strategy is often a unique blend of various approaches. In such cases, different lenses reveal different lessons. What is important is forging a strategy and the learning mechanism to support it, one that is purposeful, coherent, and difficult to imitate.

Learning is increasingly recognized as the fundamental element of the strategy-making process, whether this learning takes place at the individual, group, or organizational level. Strategic planning can support strategy learning, but the data strategic planning provides doesn't provide insight. Pietersen goes to the heart of strategic learning when he quotes Nobel Prize-winning biochemist Albert Szent-Gyorgyi, "Discovery consists of seeing what everybody has seen and thinking what nobody has thought," and Cyberpunk Novelist William Gibson, "The future is already here. It's just not evenly distributed yet."[18] Strategic learning is about generating insight, seeing previously unseen truth by making new sense out of a changing business or organizational environment.

The McDonald Brothers did exactly these things when, in the 1950s, they closed their very successful drive-up, car-hop restaurant for nine months while they literally reengineered it into the one of the first fast-food outlets in America, an operation that violated every rule of the food business—they offered only a very limited, preset menu with no variation, and required that customers get out of their cars to walk to the window for service. Later Ray Kroc saw their hamburger stand as an idea that could work anywhere in the country; he realized the value of franchising their formula (although it took his financial executive to figure out that the real profit would be in collecting real estate rental fees from franchisees, and not from the narrow percentage of his share of the margins on the food). Decades later, similar insight—seeing what others didn't see when looking at computer software as opposed to computer hardware, and the Internet's potential for a new form of retailing—led to new companies like Microsoft and Amazon.com. Of course not all insights prove viable; strategic thinking is not a science.

Strategy Making as Learning Conversations

Questioning insight occurs through conversation with others that focuses on a broader context—what is happening outside the organization and the adaptive patterns that are taking place within the organization.[19] Ideas and insight are part of a creative process; they need to be carefully cultivated, not manufactured. Cultivating insight involves asking the right questions; listening for and challenging assumptions and premises of others while having others challenge one's own assumptions; and encouraging thinking that is inclusive of diverse perspectives.

Ideas, of course, must be tested against alternative scenarios and the core competencies of the organization. If new ideas require new core competencies, consideration must be given to how these core competencies can be developed as opposed to simply bought. The synergistic integration of particular functional competencies constitute core competencies. These kinds of synergies, like ideas, must also be cultivated.

Eden and Ackermann characterize this creative process as the "journey" of strategy making—*JO*intly *U*nderstanding, *R*eflecting, and *NE*gotiating strateg*Y*.[20] This journey can be conceptualized as a series of conversations, as depicted in Box 3.1.

Working at the Top of the HRD Pyramid—Designing and Facilitating Strategic Conversations

Strategic conversations can be structured in various ways—for example, 1) a series of off-site "game changer" meetings comprising the top fifty or so executives from across the organization, or within the context of an action-learning program designed to arrive at new strategic insights while simultaneously developing managers; or 2) as part of a series of senior team meetings and upper management development initiatives. In practice, these sets of conversations overlap with one another, so that conversations one and two may cycle between one another, as may conversations two and three, and three and four, in a process of learning (Figure 3.3).

Facilitating Strategic Conversations   Various methods can be employed for structuring and facilitating these conversations. Planning and strategic analysis documents can provide useful data that can inform strategic conversations. In using these data

BOX 3.1   The "Journey" of Strategy Making as a Series of Conversations

1st Set of Conversations clarifying

- What we have been doing
- Our implied aspirations

2nd Set of Conversations

- What are we capable of doing (core competencies)?
- What is the foundation of our success?
- How are we positioned?—Situation Analysis
- What is our winning value proposition?
- What should be our strategic intent, our focus?

3rd Set of Conversations

- Testing our strategy against
  — our core competencies
  — political realities—external and internal
  — alternative futures—scenarios

4th Set of Conversations

- Allocation of resources
- Implications for alignment of HRM, OD, and HRD actions

the starting point is outside the organization, with a focus on trends, not specific data points.[21] Cognitive mapping (discussed more specifically in Chapter Seven) can be used to surface the participants' thinking in order to detect emergent strategy in the organization.[22] Formal dialogue can be used for surfacing premises and assumptions, for subsequent critical reflection, and for reframing (also discussed further in Chapter Seven).[23]

The author has sent small teams of executives out into various communities with specific questions that can only be answered if they interact with customers, distributors, or demographic groups with whom they seldom interact. Sometimes the team assignment is to come back and present its findings in the form of a skit, the purpose of which is to find more expressive ways of communicating, ways that often open up new insights that would not likely arise if teams simply put their findings into a PowerPoint® presentation. This kind of experience often results in a very stimulating dialogue session.

These methods surface diverse perspectives for sharing among people engaged in the strategic conversation and collective sensemaking. They facilitate the process of looking for new and emergent linkages in the broader environment as sources for strategic insight.

FIGURE 3.3   **The Journey of Strategy Making as a Circle of Interactive
                    Conversations**

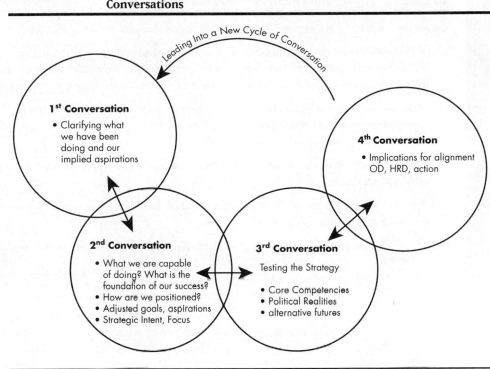

Situation Analysis   The methods and activities described above do not provide answers; they stimulate the process of generating strategic possibilities during the first and second conversations. The data and perspectives they produce can become part of a more comprehensive situation analysis that looks at customers, competitors, the organization's own realities, industry dynamics, and the broader socio-economic-technological context (Box 3.2).[24] Notice that the questions raised in a situation analysis are designed to initially foster divergent thinking that leads to questioning insight.

As the questioning moves toward insight and strategic ideas, the premises on which this thinking is based must be tested. There are no tests that provide absolute guarantees; ultimately, the viability of a strategic idea is demonstrated by its eventual success or lack of success. Unfortunately, although ideas can be market tested, there is no conclusive quasi-experimental design that verifies strategy; strategic learning is the ultimate in learning through experience. Even initial miscalculations can lead to better insights, if managers and employees are vigilant, noticing the unexpected consequences of early strategic initiatives and drawing lessons from them. The saga of Honda motorbikes that we described in Chapter Two is an example of a company learning from the consequences of an initially misconceived strategy.

BOX 3.2   Situation Analysis for Questioning Insight

Customers—What underlying trends are reflected in their actions, markets, and problems?

Competitors—What are their distinctive core competencies and performance trends? How do they make money? What is their business or livelihood model? How do customers perceive them? What are the underlying trends impacting their business or livelihood model, and what do these trends suggest about emergent needs?

Our Realities—When, where, and how do we make money (or achieve the most impact)? How do the answers to our customer and competitor analysis compare with our own distinctive core competencies, and what are the implications for our business or livelihood model?

Industry Dynamics—What trends are apparent in the industry, and what forces are driving these trends? What might disrupt these dynamics?

The Broader Context—What are the economic, social, and technological trends? What trends exist in social attitudes and underlying cultural dynamics?

Derived from: Reinventing Strategy: Using Strategic Learning to Create and Sustain Breakthrough Performance, W. G. Pietersen, Copyright 2003, William G. Pietersen. This material is used by permission of John Wiley & Sons, Inc.

Since strategic decisions are always judgments of calculated risks, it is important for executives to be clear about what they know, what they think they know, and what they know they don't know. The learning window is a tool for testing these ideas (Table 3.2).

To meet the test of "what we know" the data or evidence on which a claim is based needs to be explicitly stated, with consensual agreement about its interpretation. Otherwise the claim is "what we think we know" and needs to be either tested further or accepted as an attribution. Through this process, the conversation often surfaces additional unknowns that are brought into the strategy-making group's awareness. Whether or not the explicit tool is used, asking the questions is important.

As a strategic idea comes into focus, testing it against the core competencies of the organization becomes important. The best strategy in the world is useless if the organization lacks the capability for executing it. Scenario planning is another process that can be used to assess the robustness of a strategy under different conditions.[25] Scenarios can also be used early in the second conversation, to help open up the thinking of those engaged in strategic thinking (or to lay the groundwork for future thinking).

TABLE 3.2   Learning Window

What We Know	What We Think We Know
What We Know We Don't Know	?

Based on Intellectual Capital: The New Wealth of Organizations, Thomas A. Stewart. Copyright 1997 by Thomas A. Stewart. Used by permission of Doubleday, a division of Random House, Inc.

We have highlighted the above methods to illustrate how strategy making is, at its core, all about learning. Fostering and facilitating learning is the central competency of HRD. Making this link visible to others in the organization is the responsibility of the "chief learning officer" and his or her staff.

THE CORE RESPONSIBILITY OF THE "CHIEF LEARNING OFFICER"

Although titles vary, the senior HRD executive typically carries the title of Vice President or Director, with a formal reporting relationship to the organization's senior human resources executive and a line of direct communication open to the chief executive officer. This is the role that in recent literature has been dubbed the chief learning officer. The core responsibility of the chief learning officer is ensuring that the learning needs of the organization are identified and met. In addition to providing managerial oversight to the various learning initiatives in the organization, the Chief Learning Officer is the executive who must make explicit where to find the meaningful links among the particular organization's strategy and its performance requirements.

It falls to this person and his or her key associates to ensure that the strategic conversations taking place in the organization include the consideration of

- the extent to which both learning that has taken place within the organization and the tacit knowing and formal knowledge this learning has produced are potential sources of strategic advantage, and
- the learning implications of the strategic decisions that are made, including alignment, ongoing assessment of results, development of core competencies, and skills required for operational effectiveness.

Chapter Two suggested some of the questions that this responsibility entails. Carrying out these responsibilities involves leadership along two dimensions of organizational action:

1. Organizing and overseeing implementation of the organization's learning agenda (through)
2. The effective use of influence and power.

Despite the exhortations of the literature on the learning organization, learning, from a management perspective, is not a corporate strategy. Rather, it is a requirement for devising and executing "game changing" strategy. "Learning" begs the question, Learning what? The product of the strategic learning process provides strategic advantage; however, establishing a culture that facilitates this learning can be a mediating source of strategic advantage.

Strategic thinking always involves learning, and in many organizational settings a frantic focus on immediate tasks drives out learning to the detriment of performance. In other organizations, strategic learning has been informal, incidental, and tacit. HRD practices propose capturing and formalizing these learning processes. In bringing this proposal to the table, HRD professionals have to be prepared to facilitate processes that add value to the informal learning that has traditionally taken place.

An ability to appropriately leverage learning can be a strategic advantage as has been postulated by Porter, who argues that sharing knowledge and skills across diversified product lines can add value through creating new product applications. Theorists such as Prahalad and Hamel, who emphasize the value of framing strategic thinking in terms of a portfolio of core competencies, as do more explicit learning-oriented theorists, such as Mintzberg and Pietersen. Leveraging learning requires HRD professionals to recognize that theirs is not an open-ended mandate that requires continually seeking additional resources and promoting new learning initiatives. Neither does the ability to "sell" or "market" a learning program mean that the program is necessary or adds value to the organization.

Pietersen conceptualizes the entire process of strategy as a strategic learning cycle (Figure 3.4). Keeping a broad perspective on how this cycle is playing out in practice, raising challenging questions, and initiating opportunities for learning at the various points in the cycle of strategic learning are all useful ways of seeing opportunities for HRD to add value in the organization. This cycle is also a useful way of educating senior executives about the role of learning in a way that has relevance to their world. Over time, sustained success for the HRD function requires increasing the awareness of the line executives as to the linkages between strategy, learning, and performance. Executives with this awareness become key allies for building a meaningful learning capability in the organization.

FIGURE 3.4   **The Strategic Learning Process**

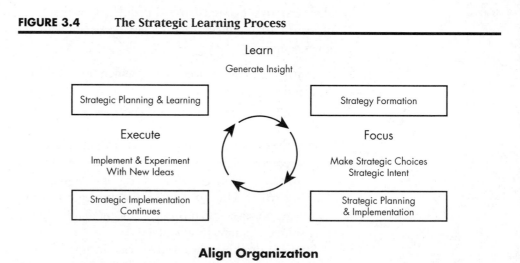

Adapted from W. Pietersen, Reinventing Strategy: Using Strategic Learning to Create and Sustain Breakthrough Performance *(New York: John Wiley & Sons, Inc. 2002).*

SUMMARY

Learning's role in strategy is becoming more and more explicit in the literature, capturing an important aspect of the strategy-making process. The concept of the experience curve, the process of assessing industry dynamics using such frameworks as the five-forces model, and the idea of core competencies all imply that learning is a critical part of the strategy-making equation. Mintzberg has made the role of learning explicit in his research, demonstrating the emergent character of much of the realized strategy of organizations.

Making strategy requires divergent thinking, looking at trends in the data in new ways, and reframing the possibilities that exist for the organization. This process involves a series of conversations that, at least initially, largely focus on trends happening outside the organization, testing assumptions, and confirming ideas with data. Thorough situation analysis is a critical part of this process. Later conversations test both converging strategic ideas against the core competencies of the organization and possible, if highly improbable, scenarios.

The entire strategic process can be conceptualized as a cycle of organizational learning. The role of the senior HRD executive is to establish and build the credibility of leveraging learning for sustaining long-term strategic performance. Successfully carrying out this role requires political action that builds the connection between learning and the economic realities that confront the organization, shaping performance. Chapter Four frames this role in terms of the political economy of the organization.

Questions for Discussion

1. Think of a setting in which a group with which you were involved was trying to carry out a strategic plan.

   ▌ How did the strategy evolve, or was it adjusted over time as new opportunities arose (that is, was it an emergent strategy)?

   ▌ What were the advantages and disadvantages of emergent strategy in terms of consequences?

2. Think of a highly successful organization with a successful strategy. How would you describe its core competencies?

3. What factors make it difficult to align an organization around a strategic idea?

4. The idea of strategic learning requires continually remaining open to trends that threaten existing strategic advantage. Think of an organization that was highly successful and dominant in its market but lost its strategic advantage. What do you think hindered its learning? What does this suggest about the challenges that a senior HRD executive might face in facilitating strategic learning?

End Notes

1. B. Leavy, "The Concept of Learning in the Strategy Field: Review and Outlook," *Management Learning,* 29 (1998): 447–66.

2. T. L. Wheelen and J. D. Hunger, *Strategic Management Business Policy,* 7th ed. (Upper Saddle River, N. J.: Prentice-Hall 2000), 97.

3. Leavy, *The Concept of Learning;* P. Ghemawat, "Building Strategy on the Experience Curve," *Harvard Business Review*, (March-April): 143–9.

4. B. Hedley, "Strategy and the Business Portfolio," *Long Range Planning* (February, 1977).

5. Wheelen and Hunger, *Strategic Management.*

6. M. E. Porter, *Competitive Strategy: Techniques for Analyzing Industries and Competitors* (New York: The Free Press, 1980); M. E. Porter, *Competitive Advantage* (New York: The Free Press, 1985).

7. H. I. Ansoff, *Corporate Strategy,* (New York: McGraw-Hill, 1965).

8. H. Mintzberg, "The Fall and Rise of Strategic Planning," *Harvard Business Review* (January–February, 1994): 107–14.

9. C. K. Prahalad and G. Hamel, "The Core Competence of the Corporation," *Harvard Business Review* (March–April, 1993): 80–91.

10. *ibid.,* 82.

11. H. Mintzberg, "Crafting Strategy," *Harvard Business Review* (July–August, 1987): 66–75.

12. J. B. Quinn, *Strategies for Change: Logical Incrementalism* (Homewood, Ill.: Irwin, 1980).

13. R. W. Revans, *The Origin and Growth of Action Learning* (London: Chartwell Bratt, 1982).

14. H. Mintzberg, "Rethinking Strategic Planning, Part I: Pitfalls and Fallacies," *Long Range Planning* (June, 1994): 12–21; H. Mintzberg, "Rethinking Strategic Planning, Part II: New Roles for Planners," *Long Range Planning* (June, 1994): 22–30; H. I. Ansoff, "Comments, Henry Mintzberg Rethinking Strategic Planning," *Long Range Planning* (June, 1994): 31–2; H. Mintzberg, "The Design School: Reconsidering the Basic Premises of Strategic Management," *Strategic Management Journal* (March–April, 1990): 171–95; H. I. Ansoff, "Critique of Henry Mintzberg's 'The Design School: Reconsidering the Basic Premises of Strategy Management,'" *Strategic Management Journal* (September, 1991) 449–61; H. Mintzberg, "Learning 1, Planning 0—Reply to Igor Ansoff," *Strategic Management Journal* (September, 1991): 463–66. Also, many of the issues of the Honda case were explored in a review forum, with contributions from H. Mintzberg, M. Pascale, M. Goold, and R. Rumelt, "The Honda Effect Revisited," *California Management Review* (Summer, 1996): 78–117.

15. Leavy, *The Concept of Learning.*

16. *ibid,* 458.

17. S. D. N. Cook and D. Yanow, "Culture and Organizational Learning," *Journal of Management Inquiry,* 2 (1993): 373–90.

18. W. Pietersen, *Reinventing Strategy: Using Breakthrough Learning to Create and Sustain Breakthrough Performance* (New York: John Wiley & Sons): 81 and 71, respectively.

19. The metaphor of strategic conversations has been advanced by J. M. Liedtaka and J. W. Rosenblum in "Shaping Conversations: Making Strategy, Managing Change," *California Management Review* (Fall, 1996): 141–57.

20. C. Eden and R. Ackermann, *Making Strategy: The Journey of Strategic Management* (London and Thousand Oaks, Ca.: Sage, 1998).

21. Pietersen, *Reinventing Strategy.*

22. A. S. Huff and M. Jenkins, *Mapping Strategic Knowledge* (London and Thousand Oaks, Ca.: Sage, 2002); also Eden and Ackermann, *Making Strategy.*

23. W. N. Isaacs, "Taking Flight: Dialogue, Collective Thinking, and Organizational Learning," *Organization Dynamics* (1993): 24–39; E. H. Schein "On Dialogue, Culture, and Organization," *Organization Dynamics* (1993): 40–51.

24. Pietersen, *Reinventing Strategy.*

25. L. Fahey and R. M. Randall, eds., *Learning From The Future: Competitive Foresight Scenarios* (New York: John Wiley & Sons, 1998).

chapter 4

This chapter

- frames the challenges facing HRD leadership;

- explores the implications of the concept "human resources";

- discusses HRD strategy and the organization of HRD resources;

- examines the relationship between corporate level and field level development programs;

- discusses how the "corporate university" contributes to the organization of HRD resources;

- describes key competencies for HRD professionals; and

- discusses key competencies for political advocacy.

Key terms:

leadership of HRD in the organization and within the HRD function	midlevel development	political advocacy
leveraging of human resources	entry and maintenance programs	currencies
leading and strategic thinking	corporate universities	mapping the political territory
corporate oversight and signature programs	the three Cs of corporate curriculum	creditability path
shared services	HRD credibility gap	challenging assumptions
	HRD competencies	alliance building

The Role of HRD Leadership in the Organization

The advocacy role that we described in Chapter Three is a form of leadership that takes the initiative in positioning learning within the value chain of an organization's performance. This chapter examines in more detail the leadership initiatives necessary for aligning various learning functions and activities throughout the organization. Accomplishing this alignment within the learning function also requires advocacy and political savvy.

While various theorists hold different perspectives on the distinction between leadership and management[1] it is generally agreed that leadership is especially critical during times of change and turbulence and that leadership is required for creating new social order.[2] These are clearly times of change and turbulence in the HRD function; a strong case can be made that, more than ever, working in HRD requires as much leadership as it does management or administration.

Not the least part of this change has been widespread corporate downsizing, resulting in less time available for remaining employees to engage in learning activities, increased competitive pressure for productivity, and the emergence of the Web as a platform for delivering learning content. These trends are intensifying in the first decade of the 21st century, while, concurrently, corporations are coping with a global slowdown in economic growth. Soft markets in most industries have led to intense pressure to cut

costs in organizations. Under these circumstances, the HRD function needs leadership that provides strategic direction to the learning and development function and maintains the morale of those working in the learning organization.

Ironically, the same competitive and economic factors that are putting pressure on HRD organizations are creating emergent learning needs in the broader organizations they serve. Changing strategic directions, globalization, restructuring, consolidations, and mergers and acquisitions often carry with them implications for workforce and management development. While the context varies from one management team to another, regardless of the setting, this educative role calls for continuing diligently to seek champions within the management ranks of the organization. Senior HRD leaders have to maintain a dual focus, providing 1) leadership in the broader organization that supports relevant HRD practice as to high performance, and 2) leadership in the HRD function itself. In practice, the two are inextricably linked.

Although we use the term "chief learning officer (CLO)" throughout this chapter, meeting these leadership challenges is not limited to the senior managers of the learning and development function. Certainly the ability of the CLO to provide leadership is crucial, especially in making connections with the senior executive team of the organization and in building the capacity of the HRD function. However, leadership is also distributed throughout groups.[3] All members of the HRD function have an obligation to contribute to HRD leadership within the organization.

In smaller organizations, a managerial-level professional has to play this leadership role, which particularly requires facilitating targeted learning at key operational level positions in the value chain and brokering with outside resources to provide necessary expertise. Often alliances with community colleges are an excellent way to provide necessary training.

THE STRATEGIC POSITIONING AND THE ORGANIZATION OF THE HRD FUNCTION

Leadership often requires reframing the way others think about their world.[4] In practice, the context in which HRD professionals function is less than ideal. The often-heard saying—that people are the organization's most important asset—to the contrary, people are often the first resource jettisoned during market downturns and economic retrenchments. This is partly because human resources are more easily divested and reacquired than fixed capital commitments, and partly because many line executives are impervious to the strategic value of their people, despite research data and anecdotal experience suggesting that impulsive cost-cutting through layoffs can cripple an organization's ability to respond to strategic threats, triggering a downward performance spiral. Pfeffer[5] describes how Kaiser, having lost its position as a low-cost provider of medical services, reacted with layoffs and restructuring to cut costs instead of implementing systems that would have generated skills and behaviors necessary for competitive success through service improvements. The result was low motivation, and additional turnovers that crippled the company's ability to respond. Not only does this kind of cost cutting create motivational problems, but it can also result in the loss of core competencies as an organization's culture is disrupted.

Pfeffer details how Apple Computer's troubles, admittedly largely stemming from a number of poor strategic decisions, were compounded by cost-cutting moves, similar to Kaiser's, that made it increasingly difficult for the company to turn itself around. Crudely-handled layoffs along with other cost-cutting measures occurred in waves over time, with little advance warning and no open communication.

As many writers have observed, HRD professionals have to function in a complex environment where management's actions with regard to people run counter to what research would suggest is the best policy. Regardless of whether the HRD practitioner's philosophy favors the performance perspective or the learning perspective (see Chapter One), supporting and enhancing organizational performance provides the only firm justification for investment in HRD initiatives, especially in times of economic difficulties. The author interviewed several corporate chief learning officers in early 2003, and all reported that their focus was on demonstrating the "business case" in terms of contributing to performance improvement for their programs and initiatives.

Leading the HRD Function through Strategic Thinking

The HRD literature consistently talks about marketing strategy as crucial for the development of a vigorous learning function in an organization.[6] Market-segmentation strategies, such as targeted marketing, customized marketing, and product marketing, have all been presented as strategies for the HRD function to market itself within organizations.[7] The caution is that marketing is often about what can be sold, as opposed to what is needed, unintentionally resulting in a perception of HRD being non-core to the success of the business. A marketing orientation is important, and admittedly has a place in the HRD function, but it needs also to take into account a more fundamental set of constraints that define the context in which HRD practice is advocated.

Two such constraining factors that drive strategic decision making in the HRD function are 1) the changing management philosophy of senior management, and 2) changes in the external political and economic forces that converge on the organization; both may result in new learning needs in the organization as well as possible threats to the HRD function. Management may centralize the HRD function, along with other staff services, into a corporate level community-of-practice in order to bring discipline and comprehensive oversight to the business enterprise. In this situation, senior HRD managers have considerable control over the learning agenda in the organization. In another scenario, perhaps in the same organization but a decade later, corporate oversight becomes more limited as senior corporate management decentralizes staff functions and gives operating divisions more control—perhaps in reaction to corporate staff that have become too rigid and divorced from the discipline imposed by a dynamic, competitive environment—and corporate HRD has less control.

Many times HRD operates in what is essentially a mixture of the two scenarios we just described, with more generic learning needs centralized in a shared services or "corporate university" model, while operating units retain the right to make decisions regarding how to meet their business-specific learning needs.

Key members of the senior management team are often skeptical of the importance of learning and development as a business imperative, hampering, rather than effectively positioning the HRD function. Consequently, learning officers have to function in an environment where they are perceived as tangential to financial performance and only tenuously connected to the strategic initiatives of the business. HRD finds itself *in* the business, but not *of* the business.

Under these conditions, HRD leadership has to construct a separate "business model" for the HRD organization, one that increasingly establishes the value added for "internal customers" in the business units while establishing a "mental model" in the HRD organization, of functioning either as a service provider within the business or as a broker linking needs with outside venders. This model needs to express a theme that essentially reflects the strategic intent of the HRD function—for example, *first-choice provider of HR solutions*. This is especially the case in organizations with no legacy of learning and development, with training managers reporting in lower in the organization than CLOs.

Regardless of the form of the HRD organization, contemporary internal learning staff are few in number, increasingly conducting needs analysis and making decisions about the most effective and economical forms of delivery, building the case for their budget lines, and identifying and vetting external vendors who provide content and delivery. The key to this approach is a vision of building a learning architecture that grows business capability and meets basic organizational maintenance needs.

A Generic Structure of HRD Organization

How various learning units are organized varies from company to company. However centralized or decentralized the learning function, and whatever the budget situation, we can identify three generic levels of learning needs in organizations. The first is technical-support training, targeted at operators and nonexempt employees and new entry professionals; the second is more advanced technical training and supervisory and management development, directed at the specific needs of business units; the third is corporate-level education and development. Figure 4.1 illustrates these general levels and their domains of learning along with the administrative dynamics between them.

Generally speaking, business units maintain a small group of training and development specialists who organize the delivery of technical support training at the first level, and the technical/functional training that is either very generic and requires only slight tailoring, or is very industry specific. These programs can include training in basic business functions, such as marketing and finance, first-line supervisory skills, and basic human relations. Much of this training seeks either to tailor the basic concepts learned in university degree programs to the particular business setting or to provide basic business competencies to employees who have not received such training elsewhere. The second level of training and development may be provided either by business unit or corporate level HRD specialists. These are more advanced learning programs. At the third level, corporate learning and development has the responsibility for meeting the learning needs identified for the top layers of corporate management—high-potential young managers—new company-wide initiatives connected to the philosophy of the CEO or other influential senior operating executives and corporate citizenship training. Aligning the distribution of the learning challenges described by the HRD pyramid throughout the levels is an important task of HRD leadership.

An elaborate dance of coordination and turf protection often unfolds within this general framework. It falls to the CLO to choreograph this dance. At Praxair Corporation, an engineering-focused company and a global leader in industrial gas production, John Gumpert, CLO, along with his manager, the vice president of human resources, is in dialogue with the learning and development professionals throughout the corporation about the establishment of entry-level programs that will not only provide necessary learning but also permit informed early decisions about which people to retain. These dialogues provide Praxair with solid development plans that

FIGURE 4.1   **Generic Architecture of HRD Organization**

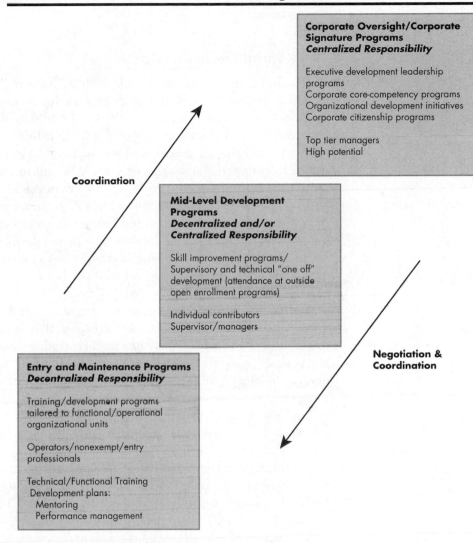

will maximize the contribution of newly hired professionals in both the short and long term. Gumpert believes such programs should be marked by consistency, including job rotation among the operating companies, mentoring that provides learners exposure to senior management, performance management assessment, and basic training and development tailored to the various business functions such as marketing and finance. In coordination with corporate management, these programs can both feed into a company's need for early identification of the fit between the organization and recent hires and provide better information on the talent already available in the organization.

Three Variations in Practice

In visits to the author's classes, Harold Hillman, former chief learning officer at Prudential Financial Services, talked about how his function, formally called talent development and performance solutions (TD&PS), had to train its staff members how to talk about the value their corporate unit brings to the table. In 2002, the office of the chairman created very specific boundaries around what could be controlled by corporate staffs versus what could be controlled by the operating business units; this changed the way that Hillman's unit operated. The various business units select corporate policy and oversight programs, but are otherwise essentially clients of TD&PS and control which, if any, learning programs (offered by TD&PS) are initiated or sustained. TD&PS operates on a shared-services model and has to justify its curriculum offerings by their utilization by business units. Business units can look outside the organization if they feel their needs are not being met by TD&PS. The office of the chairman implemented this change in order to "infuse a business mindset and rigor around various corporate functions, including human resources."[8] The system also reflects the changing cost structure of an insurance firm that has transitioned from a mutual company to a publicly traded stock company.

As part of corporate policy and oversight, Hillman controlled leadership development for the top 400 executives in the company, including vice presidents (and above) in the business units. In addition, his function has responsibility for defining technical standards for system-based learning platforms, so that platforms can be shared across business units, and for the succession-planning process. Beyond these areas, as he puts it, "the business units call the shots."

Operating in an environment where "the business units must be willing to bring us in," Hillman's people provided "just-in-time" learning solutions to the units. He has a select number of HRD professionals who have "the skill set" to sit with the business leaders, talk about their business unit strategy, and design learning opportunities that are both relevant to their clients' articulated needs and can contribute to their success. These learning professionals have to be able to define tangible metrics and demonstrate to the client "exactly how the learning contributes to their success, what they are getting for their money, and the impact beyond the learning initiative itself." Hillman and his staff monitored how business units utilize the courses in the curriculum provided by TD&LS, "fixing" or dropping those courses that are not utilized in proportion to their potential internal market.

In addition to the program development professionals charged with the above responsibilities, Hillman had a small number of development associates, who functioned as consultants to the generalist HR consultants in the business units. These development associates support the HR generalists in the field organization with interventions such as team building, work restructuring, and change management. Overall Hillman's people work in a "demand-driven" situation—gone is the mindset of "Build it and they will come." Four years ago there were 142 people in his learning organization; now Hillman's unit has 27 professionals. We discuss the core competencies needed by both the HRD professionals and the development associates in Hillman's organization later in this chapter.

Bettina Kelly, CLO of Chubb Corporation (see the Chubb case in Part Three of this book), has two responsibilities: addressing the "leadership transition points" in the careers of executives, and sales training. The first responsibility involves developing the leadership "pipeline" for the corporation, and both involve skill sets and competencies that are common across the company.

Leadership transition points are new job assignments that involve a significant expansion of responsibilities, such as becoming a department head or a regional manager of a line of business. Programs preparing people for these career moves are designated as corporate "signature" programs. Because the sales-and-marketing approach is essentially the same across regions, training in core sales competencies is also considered a corporate signature program.

Each of the major business regions maintains a training curriculum for management and supervisory development between these transitional moves, for example, basic supervisory, listening, and influencing skills, as well as technical training within the functions. While the training designs in these regional programs may vary between the regions, the basic topics and content are similar although adapted to local needs.

A similar structure is found in Praxair Corporation, where entry-level training programs are closely linked to the staffing process and are tailored to the needs of local functional areas such as engineering, finance and information technology, research and development, and human resources. These training and development programs are administered by the field organization, which also administers professional, management, and leadership training programs designed to strengthen both interpersonal skills and basic technical skills.

Corporate responsibility focuses on selection and development of high-potential leaders. Those identified as high-potential managers go through a series of three programs, beginning with initial identification early in their careers; the capstone program targets at seasoned performers with significant senior-level responsibilities. The first program in this sequence is the Corporate Development Program; it is followed by the Global Manager Program; and the third is the Global Leadership Program. Each program is increasingly more selective; participation in the sequence is linked to advancement in the managerial hierarchy.

In the final analysis, the HRD function is justified by its contribution to maintaining the well-being of the organization as a social entity and its support and enhancement of the organization's performance as an economic entity. The first of these involves what Harold Hillman calls corporate citizenship programs (such as affirmative action); corporate citizenship also requires that employees are knowledgeable about human resource policies. In the second category are business competencies and practices driving performance. In the long run, these two contributions, social and economic, must be congruent with one another. Many times, in the short term, the actions of management place them in conflict with one another. Advocating for an acceptable balance of both is a key HRD leadership responsibly.

THE CORPORATE UNIVERSITY

The concept of a corporate university has gained in popularity over the past two decades. Disney Institute, Harley-Davidson University, and Intel University are among corporate learning centers popularly associated with the establishment of strong corporate cultures and strategic change. To a great extent this popularity is linked to the visibility in the literature of Motorola University and GE's Crotonville Leadership Center.

However, these two corporate learning initiatives had scopes of coverage very different from each other. Motorola University was a comprehensive workforce development center, fostering the development of basic language and math skills needed by its workforce as well as quality and management development activities. Products from the center were distributed throughout Motorola's worldwide organization. Crotonville, too, offered a wide range of programs, but focused on professional and managerial leadership populations. Many of these programs were revised and utilized as part of former CEO Jack Welch's effort to remake the corporation and drive continuous change. The target audience was, and is, high-potential corporate talent, with a large variation in the rest of the training and development activity in GE's various companies.

Both Motorola's and GE's corporate universities came to be symbolic of the role learning should play in the strategic thrust of the company.[9] In addition to providing skills and knowledge, these corporate universities became centralized forces in socializing employees into the organization's culture as well as focal points for shaping the attitudes of a critical mass of human resources in the organization. In many respects, they are analogous to the command and staff colleges and war colleges of the United States military. Indeed, Meister identifies Air University in Montgomery, Alabama, as a corporate university.[10]

Air University has a long tradition, as have a number of corporate learning centers that long preceded the idea of a "corporate university." The now-defunct Arthur Andersen Center for Professional Development in St. Charles, Illinois, was ahead of its time as a campus-based center. McDonald's Hamburger U was among the first to borrow the designation "university." GE's Crotonville first opened in 1955. These, among many others, were corporate learning centers before the metaphor of the university became popular.

Now the idea of a corporate university is used, more loosely, for the organization of corporate-level oversight and signature programs. In response to both costs and the impact of the Web, corporate universities are now increasingly virtual, with residential courses held in conference centers and hotels. The emergence of e-learning technology, along with the need to make learning accessible to employees in remote locations scattered across the globe has expanded the definition of the corporate university to include "provider of learning that is delivered over the Web (something colleges and universities are also doing. The University of Phoenix, which has "strategically changed the game" for many regional universities; Duke University, also, offers an on-line MBA). Not surprisingly, Dell University, Sun U (Sun Microsystems), and Verifone University are virtual corporate universities.

The Corporate University as Metaphor

Essentially the idea of the corporate university is a metaphor that conjures up expectations consistent with the goals of a knowledge-based strategy. By suggesting a parallel between the corporate education center and traditional universities, such initiatives seek to provide a vision of learning and development that is based on cutting-edge ideas and instills a sense of professionalism throughout the organization. When CEOs utilize their learning centers in the way that GE has, learning centers also become an instrument of strategic change, putting into practice an insight long understood by political leadership in many countries: control of the education system is a critical leverage point for the creation and transmission of shared values and belief systems and, by extension, a leverage point for control.

Additionally, the metaphor of the corporate university provides a strategic umbrella for systematizing the training and development effort. It centralizes the design, development, and administration of learning in the organization and provides a language for (educationally) justifying the cost efficiencies of a shared services model. In this regard, the corporate university metaphor provides richness to the discourse about how learning should be organized and delivered, drawing on the idea of satellite campuses for offering local programs, with corporate oversight and input regarding the selection of venders and suppliers—in other words, a multi-tiered educational system.

The metaphor of the corporate university also suggests experimenting with new ways for employees to learn. The corporate universities may do better than their traditional counterparts in this area. It is telling that corporate universities were at the forefront of action learning in executive development, abandoning the traditional reliance on lecture and case studies, which are still the mainstays of many business and other professional schools. And perhaps corporate universities, in their various manifestations, will be on the cutting edge of distance learning pedagogies, finding new ways of using e-learning—although this is only speculation, at this point.

It's the Process That Is Important

Each organization has to balance the strategic value of its mix of learning initiatives. The core of the corporate university concept is a centralized and strategically purposeful learning initiative linked to the needs of the organization. This requires a coherent philosophy of learning, with consistent design, development, and delivery criteria for each development opportunity. The corporate university can also take responsibility for knowledge sharing and transfer within the organization through establishing communities-of-practice and coordinating knowledge-creation and management strategies. Corporate university staff can also seek opportunities for learning and development across the value chain, which includes suppliers and distributors. Jeanne Meister,[10] who has chronicled the evolution of corporate universities, identifies what she calls the three Cs of the core curriculum:

- Corporate citizenship—building the values and principles that are intended to sustain the organization's culture and that provide intrinsic guidance for behavior
- Contextual framework—providing an understanding of both the business environment in which the company functions and its dynamics
- Core workplace competencies—developing the skills and capabilities, both behavioral and conceptual, necessary for performance

Meister argues that these three Cs represent the framework around which a corporate university should develop its learning architecture and programs. This implies a group of learning professionals, including executive-level managers, to provide direction and governance; organization development/HRD specialists interfacing with various user groups; and curriculum designers/administrators working together to provide a tailored set of learning experiences that add value to the organization.

Of course, many of the companies that have established corporate universities have not sustained growth or performance, a fact that serves as a reminder that success depends upon the quality of corporate strategy and operations and on making sure people are properly trained, motivated, and positioned to perform that determine success, not simply on the establishment of a learning center.

BUILDING CREDIBILITY WITH SENIOR MANAGEMENT

The effectiveness of any HRD organization depends on the relationship between the leaders of the learning function and senior operating management. Three themes were identified by senior executives and HRD professionals who participated in a project that explored the basis for establishing credibility:[11]

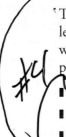

- understanding the business,
- taking the initiative, and
- developing a broad range of skills.

Each has important implications for putting the phrase, often-heard from HRD professionals, "being a business partner" into practice.

Understanding the Business

Understanding the business is a critical issue for chief learning officers, who are not likely to survive if they cannot engage senior management on topics related to the business model of the organization. However, this ability is equally important for all HRD professionals. If HRD work is defined in terms of facilitating learning, then asking questions that start people thinking and that change the conversation within the organization is as important as anything that takes place within the context of formal programs.

Knowledge key to understanding the business includes the specifics of the industry and the basis for the organization's competitive advantage, including its value proposition and how it makes money. Basic financial literacy, including understanding the financial matrixes used in the business and what factors drive them, is fundamental to this knowledge base. Bettina Kelly at Chubb requires her staff to understand how to compute valuation of the business and expects them to keep abreast of the financial news in the press.

In addition to benchmarking the HRD initiatives of key competitors, HRD professionals need to pay attention to the trends and forces that might impact the industry and the organization, and they need to develop executive summaries highlighting the key HRD-related issues that need to be considered in strategic conversations. Additionally, HRD can initiate learning processes that stimulate conversation among managers about the possible impact of scenarios that, while unlikely, are not as implausible as conventional wisdom would argue, and that could have significant implications for the organization.

Developing a Broad Range of Skills   The field of HRD is becoming more complex, and in many cases the HRD professional will need to significantly broaden his or her skill sets in order to contribute to the performance of the organization in a meaningful way. One executive interviewed in the ASTD research committee study by Dilworth and his colleagues stated, "Most of the HRD professionals in our company found their way into the field without any training or background in learning theory or program development. They have either had to invent what they do or have understudied someone who knew a little more than they did."[12]

Although there are various ways in which HRD competencies can be grouped and defined, generally the skill sets required for HRD work fall into two categories: program development and consulting. Moving into more senior HRD roles requires a broad understanding of both, although, generally, the expertise of an HRD professional is more soundly grounded in one or the other. Figure 4.2, based on Harold Hillman's corporate-level Talent Development and Performance Solutions group described earlier in this chapter, provides one example of these skills sets.

Figure 4.2 is a good summary of the range of skills and competencies that HRD professionals need if they are going to be adaptable to the changing needs of their organizations and provide HRD leadership to the strategically driven organization.

Taking the Initiative   HRD is often seen as a reactive, service role, implementing strategy rather than being instrumental in shaping it. These role limitations are often self-imposed. If HRD professionals are knowledgeable about the strategic and operational drivers of the business, senior management often supports personal initiatives on the part of HRD professionals. This is especially true when the caliber of the organization's workforce is a key competitive issue for top management. Depending on whether the focus of the learning need is developmental, issue-linked, and/or

FIGURE 4.2　　**Examples of Program Development and HR Consulting Competencies based on Prudential Financial Services' Talent Development and Performance Solutions Group**

Learning and Leadership Development Competencies (Program Development):

- Classroom facilitation and presentation capabilities
- Knowledge and application of adult learning theory, including learning styles, learning contexts, and a variety of learning methods such as accelerated learning and action learning
- Needs analysis and program assessment
- Curriculum design

HR Consultant Competencies Supporting HR Generalists and Business Unit Managers:

- Understanding and executing the consulting process
- HR "literacy" in the various HR disciplines, including learning and development, organizational development and effectiveness, compensation, staffing, policy and strategy, executive sourcing and succession planning, and diversity and affirmative action
- Business/product knowledge
- Project management team dynamics, including the capability of building a cohesive team
- Coaching and development
- Diagnosis and problem solving

strategic, HRD professionals may need assistance with linking learning initiatives to organizational issues; this is the relationship-building aspect of HRD work. Involving managers in decision-making and implementation of HRD initiatives is an important aspect of the HRD role.

POLITICAL LEADERSHIP IN HRD

When considering an innovative learning program that will be a departure from past practices in the organization and likely to meet with resistance from some key executives, it is often helpful to map the political territory. The mapping process proposed by Deluca[13] centers on the key decision-makers around the proposal in question and can become a focal point for strategizing on the part of HRD leaders (see Figure 4.3). Producing the map, which can be easily done in an office, can be part of a strategizing process among key HRD staff.

The starting point for creating the map is developing a list of key decision-makers and stakeholders, along with an assessment of: a) on a scale of 1 (low) to 10 (high), their level of influence in the organization; b) on a scale of -10 to $+10$ (0 = neutral), their likely initial reactions to the proposal; c) how firm they are likely to be in their opposition or support; and d) the significant relationships that exist among the decision-makers and stakeholders, either negative or positive. These are, of course, relative judgments made only for purposes of discussion. The numbers are a way of classifying the political territory and should be the result of consensual agreement among those participating in the mapping process. Mapping the political territory is a learning process. When developing the map, HRD leaders need to employ the same tests of the learning window (see Chapters Three and Seven) that they would require of other executives in learning situations, being clear on the *what they know they know*, the *what they think they know*, and the *what they know they don't know*. Attributions about others have to be tested.

When this discussion is mapped onto Figure 4.3, the political territory is presented as a whole, and, quite often, opportunities that would otherwise be overlooked in the strategy discussion become visible. The ensuing discussion about strategizing can seek to link agendas with other executives and to discuss what currencies these executives will find useful.

Bradford and Cohen describe several types of currencies that managers use when exercising influence without authority.[14] Currencies are resources that are useful to others in the organization and therefore have exchange value in terms of, and can be used in, building and sustaining alliances. Some currencies are relatively tangible, such as information, time, or task support. Other currencies are more intangible, but

FIGURE 4.3   Sample Power Map from J. Deluca, *Political Savvy* (1999)

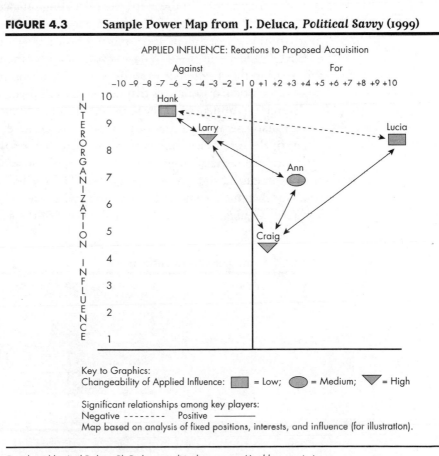

Developed by Joel Deluca Ph.D./www.politicalsavvy.com. Used by permission.

often just as valuable, such as lending personal support, recognition, or visibility to others. HRD professionals need to build reservoirs of currencies that can become the lifeblood of their work within the organization.

The relationships among the key players on the political map provide insight into the "credibility path."[15] The credibility path rests on the principle that influencing someone on a decision about a learning program often turns on who is the messenger making the proposal. Therefore, convincing others of the value of a proposed intervention frequently depends on who communicates the idea. Effective influencers "follow the credibility path," often letting whoever has the most credibility carry an idea forward.

When discussing the sources of opposition, especially the concerns of those who are only moderately opposed, a key question is, "What assumptions are they holding that are the basis for their opposition, and how might they be encouraged to reflect on them?" Influencing is often an educative process. Figure 4.4 summarizes some approaches for exercising influence.

The map is simply a tool that raises questions for thinking about how to exercise leadership through opportunistic advocacy. The most effective executives intuitively consider the variables in the map when deciding on a course of influencing action. In the case of very important initiatives, making the process explicit can lead to a more thorough assessment and a more robust strategy making process. In the case of HRD leaders, they need to have several maps in their heads—one that indicates the position that key senior executives hold regarding HRD in general, and others linked to particular initiatives that are being proposed.

Exercising influence is a key leadership responsibility. Little of importance, good or bad, happens in organizations without the exercise of political influence. And, often, in the case of leadership, what happens behind the scenes is as important as the more visible behaviors of leadership. It is, of course, important to exercise influence in an ethical and responsible manner; Deluca defines ethical political action as behavior that one is comfortable defending whenever the agenda becomes visible and known.[16] Generally, this means that the goals of the actors are beneficial to others

FIGURE 4.4   **Exercising Influence**

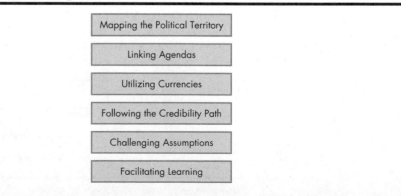

Mapping the Political Territory

Linking Agendas

Utilizing Currencies

Following the Credibility Path

Challenging Assumptions

Facilitating Learning

and to the organization; they are not simply self-serving. In the final analysis, the personal reputation of HRD leaders is their most important asset.

SUMMARY

Today's organizations find themselves having to negotiate chaotic and complex task environments. Strategic learning is an imperative capacity for the organization as is the ability to place and develop those human resources that leverage performance. In this dynamic context, HRD leaders have an important role to play, both in focusing the larger organization on those learning needs that are important to its performance and in marshalling and organizing the capabilities of the HRD function so it is positioned to meet those needs. While the effective organization of learning activities will vary from organization to organization, an important function of HRD leadership is facilitating a dialogue among the various learning providers throughout the organization, identifying what initiatives should be corporate oversight programs and what learning is best provided on a decentralized basis. Generally, corporate oversight programs will focus on leadership development, driving corporate strategic change and corporate citizenship programs. Functional, supervisory, and product training is often provided locally. However, opportunities for shared services and coordinated learning objectives still exist. The emergence of e-based learning has created the need for shared platforms across business units.

The organization of the learning function around the metaphor of the corporate university can give further coherence to the organization of HRD practice. Developing and implementing the corporate university idea requires decisions around scope, the extent to which the university will be a physical facility, pedagogical assumptions, and content. The key to making these decisions is having the university reflect, both symbolically and in substance, the leadership ethos of the CEO and the key members of his or her team.

Putting any of these ideas into practice demands business acumen that bridges the gap between HR and the senior leadership of the organization, translating ideas on how targeted development of the organization's human resources is necessary for strategic success and sustained performance.

Exercising influence is an important part of HRD leadership. When considering new learning initiatives that are beyond the experience of what has historically been done in the organization, HRD leaders must cultivate allies. It is helpful to map the political territory as part of the process of deciding on a course of influencing action.

Questions for Discussion

1. What criteria do you consider most important in determining what learning activities and initiatives should be centralized and decentralized?

2. In what ways does the concept of the corporate university contribute to HRD practice?

3. What are the pros and cons of having a "brick and mortar" corporate university?

4. How can HRD leaders prepare themselves to effectively partner with senior management?

End Notes

1. J. M. Kouzes and B. Z Posner, *The Leadership Challenge: How to Get Extraordinary Things Done in Organizations* (San Francisco: Jossey-Bass, 1991); J. G. Hunt, *Leadership: A New Synthesis* (Newbury Park, Ca.: Sage, 1991); Max DePree, *Leadership Is an Art* (New York: Doubleday, 1989); A. Zaleznick, "Managers and Leaders: Are they Different?" *Harvard Business Review,* 55 (September–October, 1977): 67–78.

2. Kouzes and Posner, *The Leadership Challenge;* M. J. Wheatley, *Leadership and the New Science: Discovering Order in a Chaotic World* (San Francisco: Jossey-Bass, 1996).

3. W. Drath, *The Deep Blue Sea: Rethinking the Source of Leadership* (San Francisco: Jossey-Bass, 2001); DePree, *Leadership Is an Art.*

4. Kouzes and Posner, *The Leadership Challenge.*

5. J. Pfeffer, *The Human Equation: Building Profits by Putting People First* (Boston: Harvard Business School Press, 1998).

6. J. W. Gilley and S. A. Eggland, *Principles of HRD* (Reading, Ma.: Addison-Wesley, 1989); J. Walton, *Strategic Human Resource Development* (Edinburgh Gate, Harlow Essex, England: Pearson Education Limited and Associated Companies around the World, Financial Times and Prentice Hall, 1999).

7. Walton, *Strategic Human Resource Development.*

8. All quotations from H. Hillman were personally communicated to the author during the spring of 2003.

9. R. Slater, *Jack Welch and the GE Way* (New York: McGraw-Hill, 1999).

10. J. C. Meister, *Corporate Universities: Lessons in Building a World-Class Work Force,* 2nd ed. (New York: McGraw-Hill, 1998).

11. R. L. Dilworth, T. R. McClernon, and J. Redding, "No Respect: Bridging the Gap Between HRD Practitioners and Senior Management, *A What Works Report,* September, 2000 (Alexandria, Va.: American Society for Training and Development).

12. *ibid.*

13. J. Deluca, *Political Savvy: Systematic Approaches to Leadership Behind the Scenes,* 2nd ed. (Berwyn, Pa.: The Evergreen Business Group).

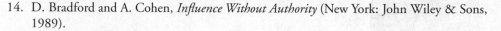

14. D. Bradford and A. Cohen, *Influence Without Authority* (New York: John Wiley & Sons, 1989).

15. J. Deluca, *Political Savvy.*

16. M. Voronov and P. T. Coleman, "Beyond the Ivory Towers: Organizational Power Practices and a 'Practical' Critical Postmodernism," *The Journal of Applied Behavioral Science,* 39 (2003): 169–85.

17. J. Deluca, *Political Savvy.*

This chapter

- examines prominent empirical research on the relationship between strategic fit, HR systems, and organizational performance;

- introduces a political economy framework as a basis for comparative analysis of strategic action;

- reviews research linking industrial fit models and human resource interventions in a political economy perspective; and

- develops opportunistic advocacy as a key element of the chief learning officer role within a political economy context.

Key terms:

advocacy	cultural superstructure	analyzers
polity	defenders	control-oriented HR system
economy	prospectors	high-commitment HR system

Strategic Positioning
and Human Resource Development

Chapter Three introduced the concept that the chief learning officer—the senior HRD executive—is responsible for ensuring that the learning needs of the organization are met and its development resources are properly leveraged for the benefit of the organization and its members. Chapter Four provided an overview of positioning HRD in organizations: it argued the importance of advocacy and negotiation, supplemented by sound knowledge of business fundamentals, for effective positioning of the HRD function, and it highlighted practices for taking political action.

This chapter examines, in more detail, arguments for aligning HRD practices with corporate strategy. We begin with the general debate in the literature regarding what is called "the best strategic fit versus the main effect," or the argument for best practices in organizing HR systems. Next, we examine the implications of this argument for HRD practice. We conclude with the political economy model as an integrative framework for the literature on strategy, HRD, and leadership issues.

---

⑥

STRATEGY AND HR SYSTEMS, AND PERFORMANCE—EMPIRICAL RELATIONSHIPS AND POSSIBLE IMPLICATIONS

The HR management literature generally makes the argument that a fit between strategy and HR practices improves organizational performance. Despite the intuitive logic of this position, research evidence at the industry level provides no support for the hypothesis that performance is better in those organizations that achieve best fit between their HR practices and business strategies.[1] Instead, the data suggest that the main effects of investing in employees through high-involvement–high-commitment human resource systems are higher productivity, financial gains, and a positive influence on HR-related factors, for instance, a reduction in absenteeism.

Assessing the Empirical Data Framing the Argument

By studying a national sample of nearly 1,000 companies, Huselid evaluated the links between high-performance work practices—including extensive employee involvement and training—and firm performance; his results indicate that high-performance practices have a statistically significant impact on both intermediate employee outcomes, such as turnover and productivity, and short- and long-term measures of corporate financial performance.[2] He found limited support for the argument that the impact of high-performance practices is contingent on their fit with competitive strategy.

In an empirical study of ten firms, Tsui, Pearce, Porter, and Tripoli found that, in general, employees performed better on core tasks, demonstrated better citizenship behavior, and expressed a higher level of affective commitment to the organization when their relationship to their employer was one of overinvestment by the employer or one of mutual investment by both employer and employee than when the relationship was a quasi-spot contract or underinvested.[3] While the measures of the study don't specifically map onto high-commitment management systems, the general nature of the overinvestment and mutual investment relationships reflect that philosophy. The overinvestment relationship is sustained by a work setting in which "the employer offers open-ended and broad-ranging rewards, including training and a commitment to provide the employee with career opportunities, while the employee performs only a well-specified set of job-focused activities."[4]A number of government jobs and many jobs governed by labor contracts fit into this category. A mutual-investment relationship is sustained when the employer's inducement offers go beyond short-term monetary rewards to the employer's investing in the employee's career; the employee's responsibilities in a mutual-investment relationship include working outside the core task responsibilities (such as assisting colleagues), accepting job transfers, and, in general, serving the organization's overall interests. This is the historical professional contributor relationship and the high-quality-of-work–life approach. Quasi-spot-contract employer-employee relationships involve short-term, purely economic inducements in exchange for well-specified contributions by the employee; neither party has an obligation for maintaining a long-term relationship. Stockbroker jobs are an example; rewards are tied to specific outcomes, and brokers are not expected to assist others in the firm. Finally, underinvested relationships involve situations where the "the employer reciprocates with short-term and specified monetary rewards with no commitment to a long-term relationship or investment in the employee's training or career."[5]

In a sweeping review of studies encompassing a wide range of industries, Pfeffer finds overwhelming evidence that managing people through high-commitment, high-involvement practices is the key to superior levels of organizational performance. Quoting Huselid, Pfeffer writes that "the existing research literature clearly shows that 'prior empirical work has consistently found that use of effective human resource management practices enhances firm performance.'"[6]

Despite the results of these studies, the issue is far from settled and probably requires a more integrated perspective. While finding that mutual investment, closely followed by overinvestment to be the most effective relationships in terms of individual level performance, Tsui et al. also note that establishing such relationships may be problematic for those employers who are in a highly cost-competitive situation or who lack resources. They conclude with the observation that "although firms may need to rely upon under-investment as a temporary means of weathering severe economic downturns . . . they should consider moving back toward the mutual investment approach in the long term to remain viable."[7]

This, of course, leaves open the definition of "the long term" in an environment where financial results are reported on a quarterly basis. Generally, the constraints placed on an organization's practices reflect the general political-economic context, especially constraints created by the business practices of the competition. Large retail chains are under assault from the low-cost strategy of Wal-Mart and its increasing control of the larger supply chain. Pfeffer cites Wal-Mart as an example of a company that has "many features consistent with virtually all descriptions of high commitment work systems,"[8] a strange choice, given that the company's "sales clerks made less on average than the federal poverty level,"[9] and many store managers stand accused of requiring employees to continue working "off the clock" without pay after they punch out of their shift, which is, perhaps, evidence of the Wal-Mart employee's high level of commitment. The company's "hard line on costs has forced many factories to move overseas [and] its labor costs are 20 percent less than those at unionized supermarkets."[10] At times, Pfeffer's examples of application of high-commitment HR systems seem to stretch the definition so much as to approach a strategic-fit model.

Although he found only modest evidence that better fit between external competitive strategy and internal practices will increase firm performance, Huselid cautions that the theoretical arguments for internal and external fit remain compelling, and require research based on refined theoretical and psychometric measures of constructs. This should not deflect attention from the central findings of the study but instead call attention to the need for more research on the issues. Mabey, Salaman, and Storey have noted that the rather global measures of HR practices used by Huselid and others, such as a company having a formal appraisal system, may mask the more important question as to the form and content of these practices and how they are implemented.[11] Referring to Huselid's work, Mabey et al. noted that "the reported results are, if taken at face value, good news for HR directors battling in their boardrooms for resources and recognition. . . . [I]t has to be said that . . . some of the questionnaire items connoting high performance work practices are still highly instrumental. In other words, *the way in which* various HR policies are derived and managed *is* probably a more accurate gauge of their effectiveness than the fact that . . . employment tests are used in requirement as an indication of enlightened 'employee skills and organizational structures,' or the proportion of the workforce participating in formal appraisals as a measure of 'employee motivation.'"[12]

Arthur has argued for a more nuanced analysis in studying the relationship between HR practices and strategy; he notes that a more finely-grained comparative analysis raises new questions.[13] His study of steel minimills in the United States demonstrated that for the overall industry, it was more effective to pursue a high-commitment HR system rather than a control-oriented HR system. This raises the question, Why don't all firms in the industry adopt a high-commitment system? One answer, Arthur suggests, is that managers are just not knowledgeable about the advantages of such a system. Another explanation, of course, is that they are not willing to change their management practices or adopt such a high-commitment system, preferring to exercise more direct power over employees and, in the case of middle managers, to work under such direct management. A third explanation could be that managers lack the competencies necessary for making such a system work.[14]

All three explanations are reasonable; all three might be offered by an HRD practitioner, aware of Arthur's general findings for the industry or benchmarking the best practices of a highly successful competitor. The three explanations suggest an argument for putting together an education program that engages managers with the results from the research and/or benchmarking studies. Perhaps leadership development labs that enable managers to confront their use of power would be useful. Competency training for managers might prepare them for functioning in a high-commitment environment.

However, Arthur's subsequent research shows the difficulties involved in proposing HR policy on the basis of such initial interpretations without taking into account the strategy of the organization. He proposes yet a further explanation for why all companies do not try to adopt a high-commitment work system:

> although having a Commitment-type [high-commitment] HR system is beneficial to all mills, the economic benefits for an investment in the type of HR system is much smaller for mills following a Low-Cost business strategy than for mills following a Differentiation strategy. If the costs for a Commitment-type HR system exceeded the benefits from these investments in Low-Cost mills but not in the Differentiation mills, then the fit patterns that exist in mills may be seen as rational from an economic perspective.[15]

Control-type HR systems are marked by highly standardized jobs and require less worker participation and fewer formal training programs. While investing in these areas might not hurt worker performance, the payback on the investment for firms pursuing a "Low-Cost" strategy will probably be insignificant, in contrast to those situations where the success of the business strategy depends on either producing higher quality product or switching production among a variety of products. In such an environment, workers must be more broadly trained, more highly skilled, and more committed to the organization's objectives than with the low-cost producers.

Although directly testing this alternative argument is not possible because of the lack of cost data associated with each of the HR systems, Arthur did make comparisons between fit and performance, in terms of productivity, quality, and employee turnover, for mills pursuing different strategies. He found a much stronger and statistically significant relationship between fit and performance for the subsample that followed a differentiation strategy. The relative costs of turnover were also higher for these firms than for those following a low-cost strategy, suggesting a greater payback, in terms of a reduction in turnover, for HR systems in firms that follow a differentiation strategy.

Implications for HRD Practice

The research we have discussed focuses on HR practices in general; HRD is one component of those practices. In any case, Arthur's work demonstrates that the relationship between HR practices in general (and HRD in particular) and performance, is complex and, like the learning versus performance improvement debate we presented in Chapter One, in practice settings, it transcends the theoretical dichotomy of fit versus best practices. Even while they advocate for certain practices that they believe will be in the best interest of the company and its employees, HR and HRD professionals have to work with the constraints of the strategic and operational thinking of the management team. What is important is that HRD practitioners critically assess the organization's strategic learning needs that involve the relationship between its cost structure, market competitiveness, financial evaluation, and long-term development in terms of the demographics of the firm's labor market and that they be prepared to engage in a dialogue with other members of management about the implications of this assessment for performance.

To quote Pfeffer, "Success comes from implementing strategy, not just from having one."[16] This idea is at the core of his proscribed alignment diagnosis process, which begins with determining the organization's business strategy, and then asks what skills and behaviors are necessary for implementing the strategy; for purposes of feasibility, he focuses on five to eight skills and behaviors that are perceived to be most critical. Ideally, this is done as part of the strategic learning process we described in Chapter Three. Alternatively, clarifying existing strategic direction and reaching consensus as to what skills and behaviors are needed can itself be an educative and developmental process for members of management.

Once consensus is obtained on the organization's strategic direction and the skills and behaviors it requires, a list of key management practices around recruiting and selection; compensation policies; learning and development activities, including career management, forms of work, and organizational structure can be compiled. The process of compiling this list is also likely to be the subject of a lively and educative discussion. If the previously identified skills and behaviors are placed on one dimension of a matrix and the management practices on the other, we can ask a very simple, yet provocative, question: "To what extent can we expect each management practice or program to produce or fail to produce each of the skills we identified as critical?"[17] Pfeffer suggests letting each person participate in the exercise by using a simple scale of +1 to −1 to rate each program or practice in terms of producing each skill, and then working as a group to resolve differences of opinion. Such an exercise can surface misalignments between business requirements and management practices, providing a framework for determining the necessary changes for implementing strategy.

A similar exercise can be used both to build support for changes in management and HR practices and to prioritize learning initiatives. The resulting matrixes and analyses can also be monitored over time to see how well experience validates the judgments that have been made. Similar analysis at a more detailed level look at the alignment between learning and development practices and at the extent to which critical competencies are being demonstrated at the operational level of the HRD pyramid.

Whether it is labeled "fit" or "alignment" (Pfeffer's term), the idea that the specifics of how people are selected, developed, and managed has a connection to strategic requirements. People *are* important to the execution of strategy. The dilemma facing HRD practitioners is that they cannot wait for industry specific research to clarify the specific linkage and development needs for their industry in general and, perhaps, for their organization's strategic challenges in particular. HRD practitioners have to use methods and practices that help the managers in their organization connect learning and training needs to their particular business model.

ALIGNING STRATEGY, MANAGEMENT PRACTICES, AND LEARNING NEEDS: WORKING WITH THE POLITICAL ECONOMY OF THE ORGANIZATION

We now describe a political economy framework as a macro-level theory that integrates the literature on strategy and HRD better than do debates around fit, or alignment, and best practices. How do HRD professionals make comparisons between the "best practices" in other organizations and the opportunities and needs of their own? To address these questions, the political economy framework also connects various models in the strategy literature such as strategic fit, strategic types, and resource allocation.

A political economy model is integrative; it points toward the necessary linkages between the pedagogical knowledge of program development and delivery and the positioning of learning initiatives within a broader field of organizational action and how these vary between different strategic situations. In prior chapters we emphasized the importance of advocacy on the part of HRD professionals in establishing these linkages in practice; political economy models make explicit how human agency must operate through power.

Methods of research that extend our knowledge of HRD as an area of leadership practice and that focus on comparative analyses of how learning is organized in various settings are equally important research initiatives. The political economy framework is intended as a guide for comparative institutional analysis for these and other research initiatives.

A Political Economy Framework for Comparative Analysis of Strategic HRD Practices

The concept of political economy (P-E) is not new to the analysis of social affairs; Zald uses it in his analysis of organizational change in the YMCA. He describes his system as a "middle-range, integrative, theoretical framework for the comparative study of organizations."[18] Wamsley and Zald applied it in an analysis of the institutional behavior of public agencies,[19] and Yorks and Whitsett utilized it in their analysis of advocacy and the diffusion of job redesign initiatives in corporations.[20] Additionally, Zald's framework has been employed for theory development in marketing.[21] More broadly, Benson has used a political economy approach in his analysis of interorganizational networks,[22] Van Houten adopted a political economy perspective in his research on work humanization efforts in Sweden,[23] and Cole brought a political economy perspective to his research into the spread of small group activities in companies.[24]

An essential characteristic of political economy thinking is the simultaneous focus on the interdependencies between "the polity" and "the economy" of the organization.[25] Additionally, this dual focus explicitly considers the relationship between external and internal polities and economies. Such an approach departs from the individual and psychological emphasis that has quite naturally been the focus of learning theory, incorporates Swanson's argument that economics is one of the theoretical foundations of HRD theory,[26] and brings issues of power and influence onto center stage as part of the discourse in HRD theory. (HRD writers—with the exception of those with a strong adult education background, such as Brooks, Cervero, and Garrick—have largely overlooked issues of power and influence.)[27] The dual focus also provides linkages to seminal strategy literature that is essentially framed in a political economy context.

Strategy and the Political Economy of the Organization

An organization's economy involves external relationships, including its capital, product, and labor markets and the characteristics of each. Porter's five-factor model (see Chapter Three), arguably the most influential of the strategic positioning frameworks, is essentially situated within political economy thinking. The dynamics of industry competition and the threat of new entrants manifest themselves in the economic dimension, although they are often addressed through political action, such as industry associations lobbying for protective legislation. Economies of scale, the experience curve, industry growth rates, access to capital, switching costs, and access to distribution channels are some of the barriers to entry in an industry. Although economic variables, such as switching costs, profit levels, and level of concentration in the industries involved, shape the competitive landscape of buyers and suppliers, these factors manifest themselves in the bargaining power of these groups, which is essentially a power-dependency or political relationship. According to Business Week "Wal-Mart homes [sic] in on every aspect of a supplier's operation—which products get developed, what they're made of, how to price them."[28] This bargaining is often mediated by more overtly political variables, such as government regulations and subsidies that are also important factors influencing industry competition and are themselves a product of political action by organizational lobbyists and industry associations. Again, Wal-Mart often extracts tax breaks from local communities, even though for every Wal-Mart Supercenter that opens over the next five years, it is estimated that two other supermarkets will close, resulting, as some economists argue, in no net increase in jobs and tax revenue.

An organization's internal economy comprises the productive exchange system of the organization, including division of labor arrangements; the allocation of resources for accomplishing work; managerial accounting systems; and compensation and incentive systems. MacDuffie's research in the automobile industry illustrates the linkage between the internal and external economy and the alignment of HR practices; he concluded that "at least for assembly plants, the flexible production approach consistently leads to better performance than the mass production approach."[29] Further, a particular "bundle" of HR practices were predictors of effectiveness. Flexible production systems required workers with multiple skills and conceptual knowledge, but these skills are of little value to the organization unless the workforce is motivated to perform, contributing both mental as well as physical effort. This requires that workers see their interests aligned with the organization and that they believe the company is committed to their well-being through practices common to a high-commitment human resource system. MacDuffie's findings were generated in the context of global change in the competitive political economy of the industry, which created a situation where business strategy required employees to make decisions involving their work.

An organization's polity consists of the patterned use of power and influence within it, the structures and mechanisms that reinforce these patterns, and, as discussed above, the patterns of influence between the organization and other social institutions in its task environment that sustain its economic form.[30] Goal structures [both official and operative],[31] the composition of the organization's dominant coalition,[32] many boundary spanning roles, and taken-for-granted norms of authority embedded in an organization's culture[33] comprise an organization's inner polity.

Miles and Snow[34] provide a typology of strategies that describes the alignment that, they argue, must be achieved between an organization's internal economy and its polity. Miles and Snow argue that organizations must establish a fit between their entrepreneurial business, or livelihood model, their technological systems for production of goods and/or services, and their administrative processes. In effect, the technological system must be aligned with the entrepreneurial model to form one part of the economy of the organization, while administrative processes form another part of the organization's economy, linking it to the polity. One of the central components of Miles and Snow's framework is the concept of a politically dominant coalition that emerges as the organization achieves fit between its business model, its technological system, and its administrative processes. For example, one of their strategic types—defenders—stake out a domain, or niche, and focus on protecting that position (the entrepreneurial problem); make investments in upgrading and maintaining the technological methods of production; and generally have centralized, administrative control structures and processes. Over time, achieving this fit among entrepreneurial strategy, technological systems, and administrative systems and processes results in the emergence of highly developed specialized engineering and financial capabilities in the organization. Representatives of these functions become the most influential members of the dominant coalition of managers leading the company; these coalition members have frames of reference that shape future strategic conversations in the organization and the lessons derived from its experience.

Where models of strategic positioning, such as Porter's model that we discussed in Chapter Three, provide tools for analyzing a competitive industry, Miles and Snow provide a model linking strategic type to the internal organizational economy. Their model also provides explanations for both the emergent power bases in the organization and how these power bases facilitate and constrain subsequent strategic choices. This points the way toward addressing a question not explained by strategic positioning models such as Porter's—why, or how, some organizations adopt effective strategy while others fail.

Miles and Snow organize their work around a typology of strategic types—what they call defender, prospector, and analyzer strategies. Defenders maintain a limited, stable product line, competing through a particular core competence in cost efficiency achieved by economies of scale. Prospectors have a broad, changing product line and seek to be first to market with new products and technologies. Analyzers combine stable and changing product lines with particular competence in imitation and improvement, seeking to be second to market with improved products, effectively transferring to efficiencies of production. Miles and Snow argue that while prospectors reap the advantage of being first to market with significant branding opportunities, they also suffer the liability of newness in creating a new market. The particular core competence of prospectors lies in innovation, and often they are not as good as defenders and analyzers in efficient operations. Consequently, prospectors fail to realize the marginal returns that defenders and analyzers reap by essentially learning from the experience curve. More recently, Miles and Snow have extended their analysis, incorporating the emergence of networked organizations, distinguishing among 1) stable networks operating in mostly predicable markets, 2) dynamic networks in faster paced competitive environments, and 3) internal networks in which a market is created within the company itself, with various units selling goods and services among themselves. These networks introduce another level of complexity into the core competencies.

The strategic categories in the Miles and Snow typology only loosely map onto to Porter's theory. Defenders are essentially focused competitors who compete on cost. Prospectors seek product differentiation through the creation of new markets; the markets they create may make existing product lines obsolete. The current competition between movie rental and movies-on-demand through cable services provide an example. In addition to their three strategic types, Miles and Snow also describe a reactor-type organization, which fails to develop a set strategic direction and loosely corresponds to Porter's "stuck in the middle" position.

Less a theoretical framework for understanding the dynamics of competitive strategy than an anchor for a model of organizations, the power of the model for understanding the internal dynamics of organizational adaptation (or lack of adaptation) adds to our understanding of the strategic learning challenges facing organizations. Although not framed in terms of core competence, and expressed at a higher level of generality than Prahalad and Hamel's[35] seminal concept (which we discussed in Chapter Three), a core dynamic of Miles and Snow's model is the idea that strategic type evolves a core competence that supports its strategic posture. For example, defenders maintain a limited, stable product line, competing through a particular core competence in cost efficiency achieved by economies of scale; whereas the particular core competence of prospectors lies in innovation; and analyzers combine stable and changing product lines with particular competence in imitation and improvement, seeking to be second to market with improved product and effective transfer to efficiencies of production.

The idea of core competencies links effectiveness to organizational learning. However, much of this learning is informal or incidental and, like other core competencies, not always recognized by the organizations that depend on them. Further, as the larger external economy evolves through various phases of development, both the changes required in organizational form and the ideological challenges that are demanded for organizational adaptation are themselves major organizational learning challenges. Managing power dependency relationships and the symbolic forms of power and authority are what Voronov and Coleman call "secondary power"—the exercise of power in the conventional sense of the ability to attain goals.[36]

Voronov and Coleman introduce the concept of organizational power practices (OPPs) to differentiate this source of imbedded power from overt political behavior like opportunistic advocacy. OPPs are the taken-for-granted practices that *"serve to position individuals in relation to other organizational members . . . that are most central to . . . sustaining and perpetuation of various—frequently unnoticed—hierarchies"[37]* and sets of power relations.

Secondary power is exercised through manipulating dependency relationships. This is in contrast to what Voronov and Coleman call primary power, which is the product of socio-historical processes of reality construction. Primary power underlies the ideological structures within which both the political economy is embedded and certain actions are legitimatized. Miles and Snow, in extending their analysis to the various forms of network organizations that have emerged from changes in the external global economy, provide an analysis of how ideology, a core component of a political economic system, has evolved through various economic epochs, each of which necessitated new strategy and, consequently, new forms of organizational structure and processes. Ideology, we suggest, is the DNA of strategic invention, transforming not only ideas, but people, and their organizations as well. In other words, it is the foundation of organizational learning:

> [L]eading-edge firms respond to new environmental demands by inventing new strategies and developing the structures and processes required to make them work. Such new organizational forms work best when managers have a wide and deep understanding of the operating logic that guides the use of the form. However, even with an organizational form and its operating logic in place, one essential element for the successful functioning of a company is missing. That element is managerial ideology—a value system that defines and

explains how people should be managed in the new form. Unless a new organizational form is supported and energized by an appropriate managerial ideology, its competitive advantages will never be fully realized.[38]

Culture and the Political Economy of the Organization

Variables such as sentiments and values have a complicated relationship to the polity and economic dimensions. These sentiments and values are largely a function of the actions taken by members within the political/economy framework of the organization in interaction with the larger culture of national, and increasingly global, society. Organizational culture is continually being reproduced through the consistent meanings people attach to their daily interactions. Culture is not a "thing"; it is a socially constructed system of meanings. At the same time, the culture supports and stabilizes the exchanges that take place in the organization, rendering life somewhat predictable. Socially constructed and continually reproduced, culture is extraordinarily difficult to change, as a legion of OD, HRD, and management practitioners can attest. Patterns of interaction become habitual, linked to emotional responses and rooted in value-laden presuppositions that become part of the shared life-world of individuals.

A significant part of HRD work seeks to impact an organization's culture, ideally helping people make sense of their experiences and the choices confronting them. Clusters of sentiments, such as *ideological consensus* (the degree of agreement among managers and employees regarding the lifestyle and values that are appropriate for approaching tasks in the organization [Dell employees speak of accomplishing work in "Dell time," and 24/7 has entered the national vocabulary as a reference to the demands of work everywhere]; *positive evaluation* (the judgments workers make about the value of their work and the work of others); and *work coordination* (collaborative or cooperative beliefs),[39] clearly constrain work performance and, following institutional change, are shaped by it.

Garrick has discussed this aspect of the HRD role, focusing on

> discourses of staff development, learning and training which construct and promote certain valued kinds of identity. It would be unusual for staff development and training not to be seen as serving corporate outcomes, but what has changed is that empowerment and self-direction are now seen as necessary to the achievement of corporate outcomes. These *are* now corporate "group norms."[40]

Elaborating his analysis in a way consistent with a political economic understanding of modern organizational environments, Garrick goes on to observe:

> Workers are active in their compliance with an ensemble of disciplinary practices that have significant implications for workplace learning, skill development and knowledge transfer. Experience of workplaces, power relations, "group norms," team-work, shared e-mail systems, performance appraisal mechanisms and so on influence what/how performance knowledge is constructed by the learner.[41]

For HRD practitioners, this is more than a theoretical issue. A significant portion of HRD work involves learning events that, at least in part, involve intentionally influencing the meaning organizational members make of events. The language associated with change management initiatives such as "rightsizing," "empowerment," "globalization," and diversity training is a cursory example of meaning creation. Many strategic initiatives are undercut because of the culturally embedded primary power of specific groups and their connection to the dominant coalition within the organization. Voronov and Yorks[42] argue that the exclusivity of many strategy creation processes (i.e., limiting the conversation to senior management), results in strategy that is blocked in its implementation. In addressing these issues, HRD practitioners have to be aware of the extent to which various stakeholders may be invested in maintaining the existing power relationships. Implementing significant strategic change almost always surfaces organizational power practices during the alignment phase. Political economy thinking positions political action and the advocacy skills we introduced in Chapter Four as central to the HRD role.

Opportunistic Advocacy

Opportunistic advocacy means more than finding a willing manager to establish a pilot effort for some new HRD method. Rather, it involves connecting an HRD agenda to widely ranging trends in the political economy of the organization. Senior HRD professionals must create a *believable conversation* that resonates with others, providing a focus for building unity of effort throughout large segments of the organization. As Garrick has observed, once they are embedded in the organizational culture, such conversations are themselves a mechanism of control through which the professional identities of members of the organization are produced.[43]

Producing such conversations requires that senior HRD executives become a credible source for *interpreting* events in the organization. Building alliances, ascribing meaning to events that become part of the discourse in the organization, working within the context of shifting agendas among senior executives in the organization—each of whom has his or her own perspective on the shifting business interests confronting their part of the organization and the organization as a whole—are as much an act of statesmanship as anything else.

Opportunities for HRD to add value to the organization are created by competitive conditions, technological innovation, and/or compatible strategic and operative goals of members of the dominant coalition and require *obtaining access* to members of the coalition, *defining opportunities*, and *building alliances* by linking agendas among various units. Building effective alliances can itself be a problematic enterprise; alliances must be forged for the long term, since instability of support results in the "flavor of month" perception in employees repeatedly exposed to new HRD initiatives that quickly go away, only to be replaced by new programs.

There is a temporal dimension to advocacy.[44] Over time advocacy, whether effective or ineffective, creates a new political-economic context within which future action takes place. Advocacy is neither tidy nor linear in its processes and involves both planned utilization of existing resources and the skillful manipulation of fortuitous events. Figure 5.1 summarizes the political economy framework and opportunistic advocacy.

CORE QUESTIONS FOR THEORY BUILDING AND FOR ENHANCING PRACTICE

The literature cited in this chapter illustrates the complexities involved in linking strategy with HR models and practices. However, while such models demonstrate the statistical relationships among variables, their variables are acting on variables. These models don't really tells us much about what agency looks like "on the ground," with senior HRD practitioners responding to shifting political economic contexts. We need research that explicates both those questions that highly effective senior learning executives ask of themselves and the perspectives that they develop as they adjust to changing contexts of operation: What patterns emerge? How do these patterns vary among different political economic contexts? What practices, in terms of organizing and positioning the learning function, are most applicable within mature

FIGURE 5.1   A Political Economy Framework of Opportunistic Advocacy

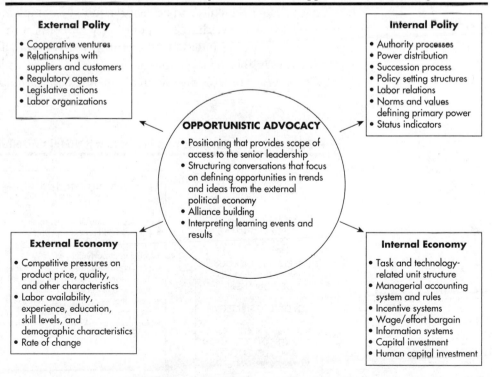

External Polity

- Cooperative ventures
- Relationships with suppliers and customers
- Regulatory agents
- Legislative actions
- Labor organizations

Internal Polity

- Authority processes
- Power distribution
- Succession process
- Policy setting structures
- Labor relations
- Norms and values defining primary power
- Status indicators

OPPORTUNISTIC ADVOCACY

- Positioning that provides scope of access to the senior leadership
- Structuring conversations that focus on defining opportunities in trends and ideas from the external political economy
- Alliance building
- Interpreting learning events and results

External Economy

- Competitive pressures on product price, quality, and other characteristics
- Labor availability, experience, education, skill levels, and demographic characteristics
- Rate of change

Internal Economy

- Task and technology-related unit structure
- Managerial accounting system and rules
- Incentive systems
- Wage/effort bargain
- Information systems
- Capital investment
- Human capital investment

markets versus emergent ones, stable markets versus chaotic ones, centralized control structures versus decentralized ones? Where is the value added through learning in deregulating markets, mature markets, volatile markets, global versus local markets, or networked organizations? Equally important, what are the implications for the competency sets required for effective agency, and how can they best be developed by HRD practitioners?

The answers to these questions can inform HRD practice by providing insight into how effective HRD professionals both bridge the gap between HRD and other strategic value providers in the organization and provide the basis for a strategic decision-making framework of HRD action. Figure 5.2 provides a preliminary illustration of such a framework calling attention to the dimensions that a grounded theory approach would develop.

SUMMARY

Research suggests that high-commitment HR systems have a powerful effect on organizational performance. However, this research may mask the effects of management processes that underlie how these systems are actually used in practice. National level data measures the reported establishment of formal structural and procedural practices in companies, but don't get at the specific content of such practices. However, it is clear that what is critical is creating alignment between strategy and management practices that produce the skills and behavior required for implementing that strategy.

HRD executives have a responsibility for being conversant with a multiplicity of ways of providing and assessing learning interventions. This is the technical, or content dimension, of their role and implies an economic dimension of insuring a *value-added return* on the resources expended on learning. Additionally, senior HRD

FIGURE 5.2   Example of a Preliminary Model of Opportunistic Advocacy

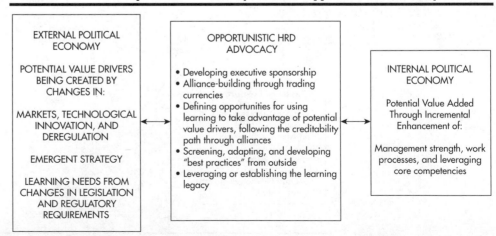

executives have to *position* these learning resources in the organization and link them to strategic initiatives that maximize their effectiveness. Accomplishing this linkage implies a political dimension to the CLO role—influencing, engaging in opportunistic advocacy, and exhibiting political savvy. In practice, the economic and political dimensions of the CLO role are interdependent with one another, making the linkage describable in terms of a political economy framework for action.

A political economy model adds power to our understanding of strategic HRD practice by providing a macro-level framework for integrating various perspectives on strategy and for raising the importance of power and political agency in HRD work. A political economy perspective views organizational change, over the long term, as a product of prevailing external and internal political economic forces, and the pattern of responses to them within the internal polity. Senior HRD practitioners must facilitate the conversations that are shaping this pattern in a way that produces learning. While accepting the interconnectedness of organizational subsystems, a P-E perspective argues for 1) a variety of possible coalitions among functions, 2) the relative diversity and autonomy of political and ideological forces in organizations, and thus 3) an emphasis on human agency rather than laws of systemic balance in explaining the performance of organizational subsystems and, hence, the impact of HRD interventions. In highlighting the role played by advocacy patterns, a political economy perspective makes clear the need for better understanding of how successful HRD executives respond to the various changes and influences that are brought to bear on the organization.

Questions for Discussion

1. Many researchers, such as Huselid and Pfeffer, argue for a "main effects," or best-practices, approach to HR practices, maintaining that the effect of a high-commitment model of managing people is the best way to maximize organizational performance. Do you agree? Justify your position.

2. Pfeffer argues that practices such as guaranteed employment security are an important element of a best-practices HR system. Think of the pros and cons of this position. What are they?

3. What are the implications of a political economy perspective for the strategic fit versus main effects debate? Give examples.

4. Some scholars have observed that performance may be explained not by the HR practices that are reportedly in place, but by the content and the way those practices are used. What do you think? Can you give examples of variation in a performance management system that reflects differences in strategy?

5. How does the distribution of power in the organization affect HRD strategy?

End Notes

1. J. E. Delery and D. H. Doty, "Modes of Theorizing in Strategic Human Resource Management: Tests of Universalistic, Contingency, and Configurational Performance Predictions," *Academy of Management Journal,* 39 (1996): 802–35; M. A Huselid, "The Impact of Human Resource Management Practices on Turnover, Productivity, and Corporate Financial Performance," *Academy of Management Journal,* 38 (1995): 635–72.

2. M. Huselid, "The Impact of Human Resource Management."

3. A. S. Tsui, J. L. Pearce, L. W. Porter, and A. M. Tripoli, "Alternative Approaches to the Employee-Organization Relationship: Does Investment in Employees Pay Off?" *Academy of Management Journal* 40 (October, 1997): 1089–122.

4. *ibid.*

5. *ibid.*

6. J. Pfeffer, *The Human Equation: Building Profits by Putting People First* (Boston: Harvard Business School Press, 1998): 59–60; Huselid, "The Impact of Human Resource Management," 640.

7. Tsui et al., "Alternative Approaches."

8. Pfeffer, *The Human Equation,* 58.

9. A. Bianco and W. Zellner, "Is Wal-Mart Too Powerful?" *Business Week* (October 6, 2003): 103.

10. *ibid.*

11. C. Mabey, G. Salaman, and J. Storey, eds. *Strategic Human Resource Management* (Thousand Oaks, Calif.: Sage, 1998): 101.

12. Mabey et al., *Strategic Human Resource Management,* 101–2.

13. J. B. Arthur, "Explaining Variation in Human Resource Practices in U.S. Steel Minimills," in P. Cappelli, ed., *Employment Practices and Business Strategy* (Oxford, U.K. and New York: Oxford University Press, 1999), 11–41.

14. J. B. Arthur, "The Link between Business Strategy and Industrial Relations Strategies in American Steel Minimills" *Industrial and Labor Relations Review,* 45 (1992): 488–506.

15. *ibid.*, 24

16. Pfeffer, *The Human Equation,* 17.

17. *ibid.,* 110.

18. M. N. Zald, "Political Economy: A Framework for Comparative Analysis," in M. N. Zald, ed., *Power in Organizations* (Nashville, Tenn.: Vanderbilt University Press, 1970), 222.

19. M. N. Zald, *Organizational Change: The Political Economy of the YMCA* (Chicago: University of Chicago Press, 1970).

19. G. L. Wamsley and M. N. Zald, *The Political Economy of Public Organization* (Bloomington, Ind.: Indiana University Press, 1976).

20. L. Yorks and D. A. Whitsett, *Scenarios of Change: Advocacy and the Diffusion of Job Redesign in Organizations* (New York and West Port, Conn.: Praeger, 1989).

21. R. S. Achrol, T. Reve, and L. W. Stern, "The Environment of Marketing Channel Dyads: A Framework for Comparative Analysis," *Journal of Marketing,* 47 (1983): 55–67; J. Arndt, "The Political Economy Paradigm: Foundation for Theory Building in Marketing," *Journal of Marketing,* 47 (1983): 44–54; L. W. Stern and T. Reve, "Distribution Channels as Political Economies: A Framework for Analysis," *Journal of Marketing,* 44 (1980): 52–64.

22. J. K. Benson, "The Interorganizational Network as a Political Economy," *Administrative Science Quarterly* 20 (1975): 229–49.

23. D. R. Van Houten, "The Political Economy and Technical Control of Work Humanization in Sweden During the 1970s and 1980s," *Work and Occupations,* 14 (November, 1987): 483–513.

24. R. E. Cole, "The Macropolitics of Organizational Change: A Comparative Analysis of the Spread of Small Group Activities," *Administrative Science Quarterly,* 30 (1985): 560–85.

25. Arndt, "The Political Economy Paradigm."

26. R. A. Swanson, "The Foundations of Performance Improvement for Practice," in *Performance Improvement Theory and Practice* ed. by R. J. Torraco, *Advances In Developing Human Resources,* 1(1) (San Francisco: Berrett-Koehler Communications and Academy of Human Resource Development, 1999), ch. 1, 1–25.

27. A. Brooks, "Power and the Production of Knowledge: Collective Team Learning in Work Organizations," *Human Resource Development Quarterly,* 5 (1994): 213–35; R. M. Cervaro and A. L. Wilson, *Planning Responsibly for Adult Education: A Guide to Negotiating Power and Interests* (San Francisco: Jossey-Bass, 1994); J. Garrick, *Informal Learning in the Workplace: Unmasking Human Resource Development* (New York: Routledge, 1998).

28. Bianco and Zellner, "Is Wal-Mart Too Powerful?"

29. J. P. MacDuffie, "Human Resource Bundles and Manufacturing Performance: Organizational Logic and Flexible Production Systems in the World Auto Industry," *Industrial and Labor Relations Review,* 48 (1995): 218.

30. Zald, "Political Economy"; O. E. Wililiamson, *The Economic Institutions of Capitalism: Firms, Markets, Relational Contracting* (New York: The Free Press, 1985).

31. C. Perrow, "The Analysis of Goals in Complex Organizations," *American Sociological Review,* 26 (1961): 854–66.

32. R. E. Miles and C. C. Snow, *Organizational Strategy, Structure, and Process* (New York: McGraw-Hill, 1978)

33. M. Voronov and P. T. Coleman, "Beyond the Ivory Towers: Organizational Power Practices and a Practical Critical Postmodernism," *The Journal of Applied Behavioral Science,* 39 (2003): 169–85.

34. Miles and Snow, *Organizational Strategy;* R. E. Miles and C. C. Snow, *Fit, Failure, and the Hall of Fame: How Companies Succeed or Fail* (New York: Free Press, 1994).

35. C. K. Prahalad and G. Hamel, "The Core Competence of the Corporation," *Harvard Business Review* (March–April, 1993): 80-91.

36. Voronov and Coleman, "Beyond the Ivory Towers."

37. *ibid.,* 179.

38. Miles and Snow, *Fit, Failure, and the Hall of Fame,* 41.

39. Benson, "The Interorganizational Network."

40. Garrick, *Informal Learning,* 99

41. *ibid.*

42. M. Voronov and L. Yorks, "Making the Undiscussable Discussable in the Strategic Conversation: Improving Strategic Management through Recognizing the Role of Primary Power," *Strategic Management Society, 23rd Annual International Conference,* Baltimore, Md.: November 9–12, 2003.

43. Garrick, *Informal Learning.*

44. A. Pettigrew. *The Awaking Giant: Continuity and Change in ICI* (Oxford, UK: Basil Blackwell, 1985).

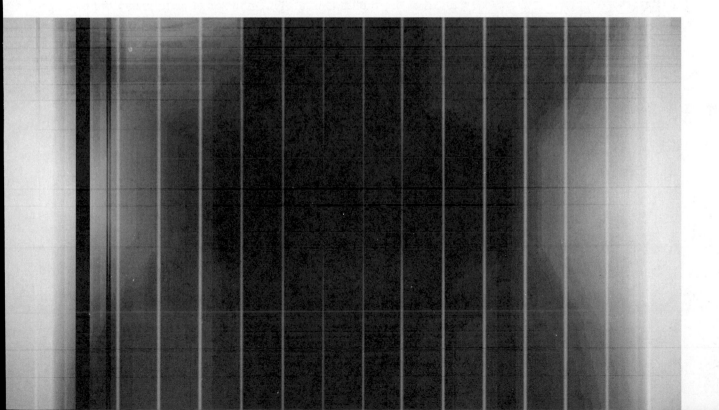

part 2

Putting HRD into Practice

6

chapter

This chapter

- discusses the difficulties in arriving at a definitive definition of learning;

- explores the differences between "learning" as a noun (outcomes) and "learning" as verb (process);

- discusses different frameworks for understanding various types of learning;

- presents two versions of the learning cycle and explains how the learning cycle relates to the task cycle;

- provides key concepts for understanding organizational learning;

- discusses the implications of a system model of performance improvement; and

- illustrates the importance of adult development theory for HRD practice.

Key terms:

know what/know why

know how/care why

tacit knowing

single-loop learning

double-loop learning

transformative learning

response learning

situation learning

transsituation learning

transcendent learning

learning cycle

affective and whole person learning

technician

achiever

strategist

magician

organizational learning mechanism

shared organizational learning values

team learning processes and modes

performance levels and performance domains

Theoretical Foundations
of HRD Practice

As the review of HRD definitions we presented in Chapter One demonstrates, the common denominator that runs through the HRD literature is "learning." Performance improvement theory is another foundational piece of practice. Improving organizational performance is the ultimate goal of HRD practice, regardless of whether the practitioner adheres to the "learning perspective" or the "performance improvement perspective" (see Chapter One) of HRD theory. Systems theories of performance improvement discuss learning at individual, group, and organizational levels, making the concepts of organizational learning another important pillar of HRD practice. Closely related to learning is the developmental level of the learner. Many theorists argue that the learner's level of development plays an influential role in determining what learning is derived from experience.

The foundation of effective practice is a working knowledge of the theories of learning, adult development, and performance improvement, which can be used as a lens for understanding the HRD issues that present themselves in the organizational environment. The concepts that each body of theory provides are tools for thinking about HRD issues. The basic definition of personal capability in HRD practice is "having the ability to draw from these three platforms of practice in meeting the varied and complex organizational challenges that present themselves to the HRD practitioner."

This chapter introduces the core ideas from each of these bodies of theory and research. We begin with learning theory, then performance improvement theory, and then adult development theory.

INTRODUCTION TO LEARNING THEORY AT THE INDIVIDUAL, TEAM, AND ORGANIZATIONAL LEVEL

Learning is the pivotal link between HRD practice, business strategy, operational processes, and the varied experiences of individual organizational units, teams, and members. The latter implies that learning is a process that takes place on several levels of organizational life. For learning to be effective, the river must flow both ways—back and forth between individuals and across organizational groupings and levels, in a continuing conversation. To a great extent, the effectiveness of this conversation determines whether or not HRD professionals are able to implement learning events that can impact individual and organizational performance. Understanding how to foster this conversation requires that we look into a number of issues in detail:

▪ What is learning? What are the various ways it has been understood in the literature?

▪ What are the implications of these various ways of learning for the design and implementation of learning events at different levels of the HRD pyramid?

▪ What is organizational learning? How is it manifested in organizations?

▪ What is the relationship between organizational learning and knowledge creation/management?

We begin with a very basic question, What do we mean by learning?

What Is Learning?

What is learning? How do we understand it to have taken place? Two very basic questions, but more complicated than initial impressions suggest. Gregory Bateson, one of the seminal researchers and theorists in adult learning, writes about levels of learning, but equivocates and declines to define it, writing; "The word *learning* undoubtedly denotes *change* of some kind. To say what *kind* of change is a delicate matter."[1] In declining to define learning per se, Bateson identifies the defining characteristic of learning: it involves personal change, change that is stimulated through reacting to some encounter and not just a function of natural processes of maturation.[2] This change may take place in any of a number of domains, including motor skills, intellectual skills, knowledge content, cognitive strategies, awareness, or attitudes. Management learning specialists have broadly captured these domains as

▪ abstract knowledge, involving *know what* and *know why*, and

▪ knowing in practice, involving *know how* and *care why*.[3]

The distinction between "know what/know why" and "know how/care why" "makes it possible to differentiate 'talking about' from 'talking within' a practice: the former tends to be more descriptive, explanatory, and systematic, whereas the latter more performative and *ad hoc*."[4] Writing in a similar vein, Vaill defines learning as "Changes a person makes in himself or herself that increase the know-why and/or know-what and/or the know-how the person possesses with respect to a given subject."[5] The distinction between practical knowledge and abstract knowledge parallels the differentiation, made a century earlier by the philosopher William James, between *knowledge about* and *knowledge of acquaintance*[6] and has implications for learning program design and assessment.

Learning knowledge *about* requires the effective transfer of information and the integration of that information into conceptual models and frameworks. Knowledge about can be obtained through delivery methods such as classroom lecture, reading, and Web-based material. It is important to recognize, however, that the meaning of information is interpreted through the frames of reference of the learner. As material becomes more complex or addresses issues about which there are diverse viewpoints, the ability to interact with others, to question, and to reframe becomes increasingly important, especially when the context in which the information learned may have to be used is varied and contingent. The meaning of information is socially constructed; for example, information on company policies around diversity and/or attendance policies may appear straightforward, but people may have different understanding of how the policy might be applied in certain situations.

The author once attended the operating committee meeting of a small manufacturing company that was a supplier for several major companies, including Ford Motor Company. The president of the small company, in an attempt to resolve some of its scheduling issues, made a statement about priorities that was followed by very little discussion. Everyone agreed that the statement was clear and that they were in agreement about it, but as the author spent time with members of the committee during the course of the day, it became clear there were at least three different interpretations of the word "priority" from managers who attended the meeting. One interpretation was, roughly, "we continue to do what we are currently doing, but in a crisis, we address the production needs in a certain sequence." The second interpretation was that "we pursue all three sets of production needs but proportion resources according to the priorities." The third interpretation was more sequential: "we do priority one, then the next, and then the third." Most interesting was that none of these executives were trying to play political games or put spin on the information; in fact, all of the executives were sincere in their support of the president and each was interpreting the information honestly, but through his or her preferred frame of reference.

Knowledge of *acquaintance* requires first hand encounters in practice; it is learned through experience, and, although it may find expression in personal mental models, the heart of such knowledge is imbedded in physical and behavioral skill, and in tacit knowledge. Knowledge of acquaintance is what Polanyi has called personal knowledge.[7] Knowledge of acquaintance can only be acquired through intimate first-hand experience of the phenomenon or process in question—through practice, feedback, cycles of action, and reflection. It can be acquired through informal learning, incidentally through experience, and from structured activities, such as action-learning programs, that are intentionally planned.

Although the analytical distinction between knowing what (knowledge about) and know-how (based on knowledge of acquaintance) is a powerful distinction, often the relationship between them is as important to understand as the difference. Knowledge about provides a framework that is then modified in practice and becomes knowledge of acquaintance. Applying decision-making models, interpreting a complex balance sheet in order to make an informed investment decision, and using interviewing methods are all examples that require interaction between formal knowledge about and knowledge of acquaintance.

Learning Frameworks—Levels and Types of Learning

Theorists and researchers, such as Chris Argyris and Donald Schon,[8] Gregory Bateson,[9] Edward Cell,[10] and Jack Mezirow,[11] have advanced our thinking about learning by differentiating among levels or types of learning. The distinctions among types of learning are important when considering the differences between *basic manual skills* training, such as keyboard skills, *interpersonal skills,* such as active listening, and *strategic learning* that often requires significant reframing of past experience.

Edward Cell's Typology of Learning   Cell identifies four types of learning that we can use to organize our thinking about learning beyond the basic distinction between "knowledge about" and "knowledge of acquaintance." The first of these is what he calls "response learning"—a change in the way we are prepared to respond in a particular situation. Response learning is studied by behaviorists in psychology and includes rote learning and what Skinner has called "operant conditioning." Behavioral modeling training, where supervisors learn to respond with a prepared set of answers when disciplining an employee for attendance or lateness, is an example of response learning. Certain kinds of sales and customer service training also involve response learning, such as specific techniques for handling certain customer objections. This kind of learning can also require the learner to apply a sequence of skills, or to match responses to varying complex contingencies in situations such as selecting a certain negotiating tactic from among many possibilities in the midst of a contentious negotiation.

The second kind of learning that Cell identifies is what he calls "situation learning," which involves a change in how a person organizes his or her understanding of a situation, a "change in ability to do response learning."[12] Cell notes that response learning is dependent on situation learning, since how we interpret a situation shapes our response to it. What management views as punishment may be experienced as positive reinforcement by a worker in a workplace where the workforce doesn't respect management. Punishment can enhance a worker's status, reinforcing an adversary role in a labor organizing campaign. Basic employee and management training in topics such as affirmative action and sexual harassment involve situation learning—recognizing or interpreting situations differently and making judgments about how to react appropriately. In some instances, the success of such programs may require what Mezirow describes as transformative learning (discussed below) on the part of some participants. Participants who basically respect other workers but are unaware of how their actions impact others may extend an existing meaning frame or learn a new one as they become aware of and reflect on their assumptions. Other program participants with strongly held racial, gender, or sex-based biases may be unlikely to modify these biases, although they may modify their behavior to avoid disciplinary penalties. In other words, response learning will follow the training experience.

The third kind of learning Cell identifies is transsituation learning—learning how to change our interpretations of a situation. This is what many HRD practitioners and adult educators call learning-to-learn. This kind of learning involves reflecting on our learning processes themselves and identifying and questioning the assumptions that we are making about a situation. What Cell refers to as transsituation learning requires learners to reflect on the processes that characterize their learning, using reflective inquiry practices for critical self-reflection on *how* they have engaged in testing their assumptions and attributions.

Learning to recognize the differences between single-loop and double-loop learning (discussed below), and how to use each effectively involves transsitutional learning. Chapter Seven discusses metaphors such as "the left hand column" and "ladder-of-inference" as ways of helping people to engage in this kind of learning. Employees in a field office of a federal agency participating on an action research team addressing workplace stress and aggression reported that using these and similar methods helped them to become more aware of their learning processes. This awareness made it possible for a highly diverse group of managers and workers to identify and implement change.

Cell's fourth kind of learning is transcendent learning—modifying or creating new concepts. Cell describes this kind of learning as providing "possibilities—new tools—for interpreting individual situations."[13] Terms such as "psychological contract," "servant leadership," "empowerment," and the controversial term "rightsizing" all change how we talk about leadership and management and have opened up new avenues of research and practice. Such concepts become tools for social transactions and are also tools that can facilitate changes in points of view and habits of mind. Managers have long understood the importance of language, and especially new concepts, in seeking to inspire transformative change.

Mezirow's Transformative Dimensions of Adult Learning   While Cell's typology provides a broad framework for thinking about kinds of learning, the seminal work of Jack Mezirow on the transformative dimensions of adult learning is especially useful for thinking about the kind of learning necessary for both strategic learning and supporting transformational organizational change. Mezirow, who among several influences draws in part on Cell's typology, most clearly grounds his work in the pragmatism of John Dewey and William James and the critical social theory of Jurgen Habermas, resulting in what can be considered a critical pragmatic lens on learning from experience.[14]

Drawing on the work of Habermas, Mezirow postulates that learning takes place within two domains, each with its own purpose and logic. The first is the domain of instrumental learning—"learning to manipulate the environment or other people" in the service of accomplishing tasks or solving problems. Response learning is a form of instrumental learning, but so is any "learning what and how" directed toward controlling or acting on the environment. In organizations, this is the domain of performance improvement. The second is the domain of communicative learning—"learning what others mean when others communicate with one another in the service of sensemaking."[15] This is a form of situational learning in which people extend or change their frame of reference. In organizations, sensemaking is the domain in which meaning is attached to instrumental actions and thus provides the contextual framing for performance improvement initiatives.

Each of these two domains has its own standards of validity. Instrumental learning holds to validity tests of facts, measurements, and outcomes. Communicative learning has more nuanced validity tests requiring the assessment that others make of the speaker's and each other's authenticity, truthfulness, and qualifications as they test the meanings of experience. It is heavily influenced by, and in turn, shapes or transforms, the cultural context in which people act. Instrumental learning can be fostered through programmed instruction that involves the transfer of information through lectures and visual presentations, reinforced through practice and coaching. High-quality science, quality management in engineering programs, technical training, and supervisory development programs include these elements, with information followed by laboratory work, simulations, or role-playing. Pedagogical designs that are focused on instrumental learning combine learning methods (see Chapter Seven) that foster a combination of "learning what" and "learning how."

Communicative learning requires dialogue and discussion, often building on experience and making sense of data. This kind of learning most often involves people who socially construct their learning through these processes of meaning-construction. In the absence of open dialogue, learners make judgments about the validity of the message based on their assessment of the trustworthiness of the source. Communicative learning occurs when messages about the intent of corporate policy are communicated or when projects and interventions designed to help employees make sense of organizational changes are implemented. Team-building, for example, involves elements of both instrumental and communicative learning, as participants develop interpersonal skills and competence in group dynamics while also constructing common meaning out of their experiences together.

Mezirow argues that all learning, in a sense, involves situational learning, agreeing with Cell that even changes in response learning are dependent on an elaborated or altered frame of reference. He defines learning as "the process of using a prior interpretation to construe a new or revised interpretation of the meaning of one's experience as a guide to future action."[16] This reinterpretation can occur in one of four ways:

- by elaborating an existing frame of reference,
- by learning new frames of reference,
- by transforming points of view, or
- by transforming habits of mind.

Mezirow defines a frame of reference as a perspective organized by the assumptions and expectations that filter how we perceive the world. Frames of reference have two dimensions: 1) habits of mind comprising a set of assumptions—broad, generalized, predispositions that guide our interpretations of events and experience, and 2) points-of-view, clusters of beliefs, feeling, attitudes, and judgment that commonly operate outside of our awareness but are expressions of our broader habit of mind.[17]

Frames of reference shape our understanding of both the instrumental and communicative domains of our experience. Some learning is basically additive in nature, as when a person elaborates an existing frame of reference or adds a new frame of reference without changing the beliefs and presuppositions of existing ones. However, when a disorienting dilemma or a disconfirming experience challenges people's frames of reference, it can lead them to critically reflect on their beliefs and presuppositions, resulting in either a transformed point of view or a transformed habit of mind.

Transformative learning can occur in either the instrumental or the communicative domain and can be *epochal* in nature—a sudden, reorienting insight—or *incremental*—the result of a progressive series of experiences that transform a person's point of view. At the societal level, fundamental paradigm shifts in science represent transformative changes in instrumental learning. Americans experienced significant cultural transformations during the last third of the 20th century that involved communicative learning, including the civil rights movement and our understanding of race; feminism and changes in understanding the role of women in society; and changes in attitudes toward labor organizations.

In the 1970s and 1980s, American executives experienced transformation in both the instrumental and communicative domains, as they embraced total quality management models that required transformed habits of mind as to how managers understood the meaning of quality in relationship to productivity. Where traditionally the relationship between quality and productivity was understood to involve making a tradeoff—high quality meant sacrificing productivity—the disorienting dilemma of competition from high-quality products imported into the United States started the process of transforming how managers thought about operations management. Today, six sigma programs are essentially elaborations of, or additions to, the existing frames of reference about operations management.

Transformative learning almost always requires placing people in situations that put them outside their comfort zones, belying the notion that learning is always fun. Changes in strategic thinking often require assessing alternative points of view, leading to changed habits of mind as executives and managers have to reframe their view of the market place.

Facilitating Learning-Reflection and Critical Reflection—Single-Loop and Double-loop Learning   Learning involves reflecting on experience and information and incorporating the conclusions into our subsequent thinking, our responses to situations, and our planned actions. Argyris and Schon make essentially the same distinction with their concepts of single-loop and double-loop learning.[18]

Single-loop learning occurs when we detect error; our actions fail to produce the results we desire, and we adjust our tactics or strategies without challenging the assumptions that frame our understanding of the situation. Double-loop learning requires us to question the assumptions, or "governing variables" which guide our actions and inform how we frame or interpret a situation. Double-loop learning is often the key to resolving difficult interpersonal quandaries or formulating strategy that involves a new way of looking at emergent opportunities that are being created by demographic shifts or new technologies. It is also the key to resolving many conflicts. Box 6.1 provides a very basic example of single-loop learning and suggests how the situation it describes might be approached differently through double-loop learning.

Double-loop learning is an integral part of the process of transforming points of view and habits-of-mind. Double-loop learning can be triggered informally by

BOX 6.1 **Unintended Consequences from an Employee-of-the-Month Program—Single-Loop Learning in Action**

This story is based on a term paper written by a student in an organizational behavior class. Subsequent to reading the paper, the author substantiated the basic details of the case. The student was one of a group of young people working part-time in a store in a local shopping mall; several full-time employees also were employed by the store. At one point, the store manager initiated an employee-of-the-month program, in which the selected employee would both receive a gift certificate for shopping elsewhere in the mall and be recognized on a plaque. The employees seemed enthused by the idea; however, over a period of months the part-time people (all students) noticed that only full-time employees received the award. They came to the conclusion that the award was only for full-time workers, even though this was not how the award had been defined. Feeling devalued, they came to view their job as simply an economic transaction, and they increasingly did only the minimum work it required. Noticing the decline in their work, the store manager introduced additional controls on the part-time work force, which led to further declines in performance.

This rather simple story can be analyzed from several perspectives: communication theory, expectancy theory, or just plain human relations. Examining how it unfolded also reveals how responding to perceived error with single-loop learning and making attributions without reflecting on and checking assumptions and presuppositions can produce more error. An unspoken, possibly even unconscious, assumption on the part of the store manager was that the students were primarily interested in making money for school and had little interest in either the award or the general performance of the store. Interpreting the situation this way, he focused on the performance of the full-time employees. The student workers (also without seeking to publicly check their attributions) concluded the store manager wasn't interested in them, and their declining performance seemingly validated the store manager's prior interpretation. He took disciplinary action to shore up the performance of the store, which in turn seemed to validate the prior interpretation made by the students. Two processes of single-loop learning were operating to produce outcomes neither party wanted. Had either party sought to publicly check its assumptions (double-loop learning), it might have opened up a very different conversation. Broader governing values in the store tended to lead both groups to engage in defensive behavior that inhibited this kind of checking until one student made a personal intervention, which, though initially shocking to the manager, led to a more open situation (and a change in the program). The manager later confided that the episode had given him an interesting lesson.

---

traumatic events and experiences that cause people to deeply question their assumptions or through a cumulative series of experiences that incrementally lead to people rethinking their premises. More formally, adult educators and HRD professionals use structured critical reflection dialogues to foster double-loop learning and to help facilitate transformative learning.

The author and his colleagues often work with executives who bring the real challenges they are confronting on the job to management development programs. In groups, each executive takes a turn describing his or her challenge (in action learning terminology, called "holding the space"); this is followed by questions from the other group members. The questions are open-ended and reflective in nature, and they are asked without the questioner giving advice. The executive who is holding the space doesn't respond or answer the questions but just records them for reflection. After the question period, the space holder can request additional elaboration on those questions that stimulate new thinking. At the close of the dialogue session, each member of the group provides additional content for critical reflection by completing the following sentence, "I think I hear you assuming that . . ." The executive holding the space then describes what new course of action he or she might take to test their assumptions. Generally, there are two objectives for this exercise. The first is to facilitate transformative learning by helping the space holder to reflect on the beliefs and presuppositions forming his or her point of view regarding the problem. The second is to train executives in how to engage in this kind of critical reflection and to raise their awareness of how they can think differently about similar situations—in Cell's terms, facilitating transsituational learning.

Transforming organizations requires collective transformative learning on the part of employees. When a new frame of reference becomes part of the organization's culture, organizational learning has taken place. These same concepts of instrumental and communicative transformative learning will become relevant when we discuss team and organizational learning later in this chapter.

The distinctions we have made above among kinds of learning are important to the HRD professional because they both help bring into focus the various dimensions of learning and facilitate thinking about their implications for the design of learning events. What kind of learning is a particular training program or learning intervention seeking to produce? What do we know about the factors that facilitate or inhibit this kind of learning? Different kinds of learning objectives require different training and different educational designs. Certain delivery formats work better than others for meeting some kinds of learning objectives. Response learning can be achieved through very concrete behavior designs, whereas training that involves selecting from among a range of responses based on the specifics of the situation typically requires structured case study designs along with behavioral practices. Conversely, developing the capacity for dealing with rapidly changing, unfamiliar, or new situations requires the development of inquiry practices that often can only be effectively learned through experiential learning designs, such as action learning. Although more conventional language and terminology typically must be used when talking with line managers and others, these basic distinctions become important in doing sophisticated needs analyses and in helping others to understand the limitations of various learning program designs.

Learning as Process

We have been describing learning in terms of the kind of learning a learning program might be intended to produce—a change that may involve acquiring a body of knowledge, a set of skills or competencies, a new attitude, or a reframed perspective. We are, then, essentially treating learning as a noun—as an outcome or a product.

Learning also involves a process, as in *She is learning*. As Knowles observes, learning is a process that is internal to and controlled by the learner.[19] From the perspective of HRD practice, it is important to understand learning as both process and product, both in continuous relationship with each other. Understanding how to work with learning processes to produce a given outcome is as important as being clear about the kind of learning that is needed. Using reflection and critical reflection to facilitate single-loop and double-loop learning involves working with the *process* of learning. These concepts are links between kinds of learning and the processes through which learning occurs.

The Learning Cycle—Kolb and Honey-Mumford   Kolb's learning cycle is an influential theory that highlights learning as a process.[20] Kolb describes experiential learning as a circular process (see Figure 6.1), beginning with a concrete experience and continuing through reflective observation, abstract conceptualization, and active experimentation, which in turn results in additional concrete experience. A variation of Kolb's model has been developed by the British specialist in executive and management development Alan Mumford and his colleague Peter Honey, who see the cycle as a continuous spiral of having an experience, reviewing, concluding, and planning (see Figure 6.2).[21] Both the Kolb and the Honey-Mumford models of experiential learning are relevant to any instrumental or communicative learning situation that goes beyond absorbing information.

FIGURE 6.1   Kolb's Learning Cycle

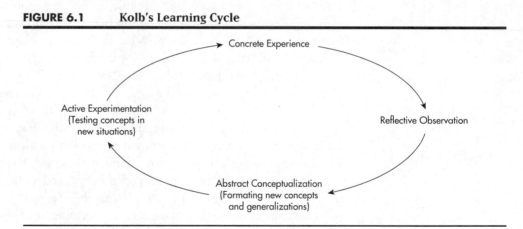

From D. A. Kolb, Experiential Learning: Experience as the Source of Learning and Development *1st Edition,* © 1981 *Reprinted by permission of Pearson Education, Inc., Upper Saddle River, N.J.*

FIGURE 6.2   The Honey-Mumford Learning Cycle

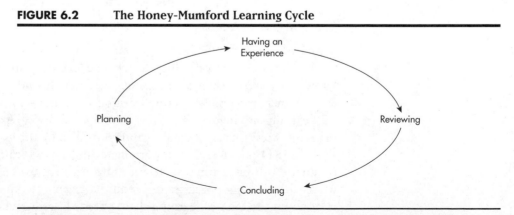

Adapted from P. Honey and A. Mumford (1989) The Manual of Learning Opportunities. *Used with permission.*

Both models describe how people learn, independent of particular situational constraints, such as formal classrooms or informal organizational experience. Learning is understood as a process, not as a one-dimensional act of repetition or memorization of information or as rote repetition of behavior or actions. In workplaces where people are often confronted with uncertainty or ill-defined problems and puzzles, employees as well as HRD professionals need to have an understanding of the learning process. In these settings, employees must repeatedly engage in learning practices, either in groups or individually, to resolve problems that emerge in the course of their work and go beyond their initial training. Both the Kolb and Honey-Mumford models understand learning as a process of creatively resolving issues, continually improving, and, through the integration of thought and action, internalizing knowledge.

Although the entire cycle is involved in the most challenging learning situations, most people favor parts of the cycle over others, giving rise to the notion of learning styles. Kolb identifies four styles (Figure 6.3), each derived from a combination of two of the points of the learning cycle:

- *divergent style*—derived from concrete experience (CE) and reflective observation (RO), with strengths in imaginative abilities and sensitivity to diverse perspectives;

- *assimilation style*—derived from reflective observation and abstract conceptualization (AC), integrating diverse perspectives into explanatory frameworks;

- *convergence style*—derived from abstract conceptualization and active experimentation (AE), with strengths in applying ideas to practice; and

- *accommodator style*—derived from active experimentation, with strengths in doing things and learning through trial and error.

FIGURE 6.3   Kolb's Four Learning Styles

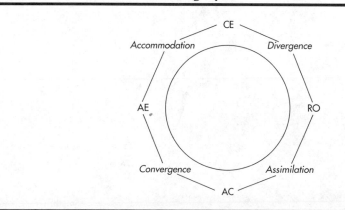

Kolb postulates that, in addition to describing preferred ways of learning, style preferences often produce defensive behavior when there is a mismatch between style and the press of a particular situation. Mumford identifies the styles as activist, reflector, theorist, and pragmatist, consciously choosing to focus on "recognizable managerial behavior, rather than about specifically 'learning' behavior. ("Honey and I thought the sensible starting-point was the *general* behavior in which learning is grounded rather than trying to identify, as David Kolb, *learning* behavior, which in fact managers have rarely thought about.")[22] Apart from the differences in how the two models describe behavior, Kolb's seminal work is a comprehensive theory of learning, explicitly constructed on the premises of Dewey's pragmatism, and has been extended to broader issues of organizational behavior. Mumford's work has focused on the application of theory to practice, aligning learning with other processes of management (see Figure 6.4). These distinctions will become more evident in the discussion that follows.

Implications of the Learning Cycle   The idea of learning styles is powerful in a number of ways. It has implications for the design of learning events that are classroom based, for example, highlighting the need for diverse instructional strategies. Extending this implication, and following Kolb's analysis, when training *content* runs counter to a learner's aptitude and/or self-image of his or her abilities, the "press" of learning can produce counterproductive defensiveness. This mismatch can

FIGURE 6.4   **Mumford Task Cycle (Outer Cycle) Combined with the Learning Cycle (Inner Cycle)**

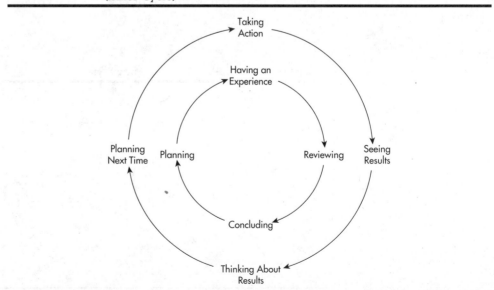

Adapted from P. Honey and A. Mumford (1989), The Manual of Learning Opportunities. *Used with permission.*

be intensified even more if the *design* of the learning event is inconsistent with the style of the learner.

Kolb's research suggests that the learning demands of various professions and occupations tend to lead to certain career choices. The cumulative effect of these choices across a number of people is a correlation between learning styles and certain organizational functions. This effect has implications for team and organizational learning. In essence, such occupational selection can embed certain strengths and limitations in terms of the collective learning of a work group or of an occupation. The advantage of this state of affairs is the fit between learning strengths and occupational demands; the disadvantages are the potential blind spots for learning that inhibit generative team and organizational learning. In contrast, teams composed of diverse learning styles have the potential for arriving at innovative solutions to highly unstructured or very volatile problems, if they know how to take advantage of the diversity of perspectives and views that different styles often produce. When working on strategic learning, where divergent views are an asset (Chapter Three), helping executives to recognize, appreciate, and work effectively together is an important part of the process.

A third implication of the Kolb and Mumford models has been particularly championed by Mumford: the need for intentionally drawing on our understanding of the learning process to bring tacit learning into consciousness and reinforce what learning is taken away from learning events. As previously mentioned, Honey and Mumford have specifically framed their model in terms of managerial behavior. Mumford strives to relate the learning cycle to the more general managerial task cycle (see Figure 6.4) to impress on managers the idea that work provides informal learning opportunities that must be intentionally harvested. He argues that the same explicit focus on harvesting learning should be characteristic of formal learning events, and he decries what he views as the general lack of such harvesting in many development programs. This harvesting can be accomplished through holding a brief reflection and dialogue session at the end of a program.

Periods of reflection and dialogue can be held either in the classroom or in Web-based training with interactive discussion boards. In the case of an extended residential program that meets periodically over several days or weeks, reflection can be done periodically at points throughout the program. This kind of activity, while sometimes resisted at first, is germane to creating a learning community and also to facilitating what Cell refers to as "transsituational learning." Most learners, given the opportunity to reflect on their own learning, come to appreciate the process once they experience the value of hearing what others have taken from the session.

Many corporate learning events explicitly seek a balance among learning methods such as lectures, cases, experiential learning, and simulations. Even so, often the design of these events focuses on the delivery of content and learning objectives, overlooking both the learning process itself and what learners take away from the event. John Gumpert, CLO at Praxair Corporation, uses coaches to encourage participants in the company's management development program to bring tacit learning into conscious awareness and to help participants see the diverse learning that each participant has taken from the experience.

Limitations of the Learning Cycle Models   Kolb's model has significant limitations in terms of capturing the learning process, however. First, it fails to account for the difference between single- and double-loop learning. Taken at face value, it is essentially a single-loop model that postulates simple reflection. Double-loop learning requires what Mezirow describes as "premise reflection," seeking to bring into consciousness one's presuppositions and questioning existing attributions about one's experience. For example, the store manager in Box 6.1 essentially engaged in a process similar to Kolb's or Mumford's learning cycle, even though his learning was dysfunctional. This raises the question of how a learner can test the validity of the conclusions he or she draws from reflective observation. In the Kolb and Mumford models, the validity test is seen in concrete experience. However, as our example of the store manager demonstrates, one may easily draw erroneous conclusions from reflection on the content of one's experience, leading to a closed cycle of dysfunctional learning. Premise reflection and publicly testing one's conclusions with others are specific methods for building double-loop learning, or critical reflection, into the learning process as forms of validity testing. Playing the Devil's advocate and intentionally testing assumptions through direct and open inquiry are two methods for validity testing in practice.

Second, although Kolb acknowledges the role of the affective dimension of human learning, his model is essentially based on the rational dimension of learning. Heron notes that Kolb's model "is really a model of experiential learning derived from scientific inquiry; we reflect on experience, generalize from these reflections, then test the implications of these generalizations through further experience."[23] Acknowledging that this is one valid model for producing learning, Heron adds that it "is a highly intellectual account of experiential learning . . . in the tradition of Dewey, Lewin, Piaget, and Kelly [that makes] the dubious assertion that 'the scientific method provides a means for describing the holistic integration of all human functions.'"[24]

The Role of the Affective in the Learning Process   While most discussions of learning in the literature focus on some combination of assimilating information, cognitive change, and/or behavioral skill, increasingly the emotional aspects of learning[25] and tacit learning[26] are becoming explicitly incorporated into learning theory. Theorists have long recognized that the affective is an important dimension of learning. Bloom et al. included the affective as one of their domains, identifying it as changes in interests, attitudes, values, and adequate adjustment.[27]

Although closely linked to the cognitive, Bloom et al.'s definition of the affective is particularly relevant to new employee assimilation programs in that it raises the question as to what constitutes adequate adjustment. The frequent disconnect between the authentic feelings of people at work and the behaviors required of them in their jobs has been studied as "emotional labor."[28] One example is the customer service representative who has to maintain a positive demeanor when dealing with confrontational customers and resolving problems over which she has little control; another example is the airline service counter representative whose company policy doesn't allow for accommodating people who are stranded because of bad weather or equipment problems. Still another example is the employee at a theme park, such as Disney World, who is trained to be cheerful regardless of the circumstances of his personal life.

An important part of the performance equation is how the dissonance created by training, job requirements, and the job situation manifests itself in stress and aggressive behavior. Helping employees at all levels of the organization deal with emotional labor is an important learning challenge and one that has special importance for managing aggressive behavior in the workplace. The literature increasingly emphasizes emotional intelligence as a dimension of leadership,[29] providing another important learning challenge. This increasing emphasis on the emotional dimension of life makes it difficult to imagine effectively addressing these challenges without incorporating the role of feelings and emotion into the learning process—whole person learning.

The whole person is involved with learning,[30] and so emotions are integral to it. Traditionally, the role of the affective in learning has been viewed either as potentially inhibiting learning through anxiety, leading to an emphasis on creating safe learning environments, or as phenomena that can be brought into conscious awareness as objects for rational analysis. David Boud, writing with various colleagues, has stressed the role of feelings and emotions in learning while noting that they are often treated separately. Boud et al. observe that despite the fact that learning is experienced as a seamless whole, "In contemporary English-speaking society, there is a cultural bias towards the cognitive and conative aspects of learning. The development of affect is inhibited, . . . leading to a lack of emphasis on people as whole persons."[31]

Short and Yorks describe various ways that HRD professionals can take emotions into account in training.[32] These include establishing a climate of learning-within-relationship, creating the right environment for discussing feelings and emotions, and recognizing individuals' different emotional needs. Learning-within-relationship refers to persons who are fully engaged with their own whole-person knowing, as well as the dynamic whole person of their fellow participants in the learning process. This requires creating a climate of learning-within-relationship by the establishing an "empathic field" or "field of mutuality" that allows learners to effectively share and emphatically understand the felt experience of others through methods that are expressive in nature and vary by learning context, such as storytelling, metaphor, and artistic representation. These methods help learners and facilitators to connect to one another by communicating dimensions of experience that are not easily captured linguistically. When established, learning-within-relationship promotes less distorted discourse and dialogue than when learners lack insight into the life experiences of one another. Creating an empathetic field of mutuality helps those in highly diverse groups understand the perspectives of people different from themselves. Without a field of mutuality, "learners very different from the facilitator and very diverse from each other, will not be able to authentically question their deeply held assumptions."[33]

A climate of learning-within-relationship serves as a container for the disclosure of feelings and emotions. HRD professionals should establish a normative context for dialogue, in which participants can surface what they really think and feel, talk about where they stand on issues, notice and explore assumptions, connect with those who have different views, and eventually generate new possibilities—exactly the kind of exchange that is critical for strategic learning.

Summary: Learning as Product and Process

Making the learning process transparent links process and product. What are learners learning? How are the dynamics of the learning process shaping or impacting what is being learned? There is a strong tradition of behaviorism in the training and development field, with some theorists arguing that learning has only occurred when it is visible through changed behavior. This argument has much to recommend it, especially when the goal of the learning event is to teach specific skills or techniques. If a learner cannot execute the desired skills, then learning has not taken place. However, as we have also discussed, being able to effectively apply skills or competencies is a potentially complex issue, especially if appropriate application requires judgment and situational sensitivity. Often timing, as in the use of active listening skills during disciplinary or coaching sessions, or dealing with complexity, as with solving a difficult problem or issue, mediates the effectiveness of application. Formal knowledge must be integrated with tacit knowing, or "a feel" for the situation. Or cognitive knowledge must inform the use of behavior skill. This link between cognitive knowledge and behavioral application is often mediated by tacit knowing. Tacit knowing is itself partly intuitive, and triggered by one's feelings and affective responses. Learners must learn how to continue learning informally and how to formalize their learning in their own learning logs. When the author does certain executive development programs, he distributes blank journals, saying, "This is the text. *You* need to write it and test and revise its ideas on a continuing basis. Memorizing the theories of others, which help you to think about issues and provide you with a theoretical framework for practice, won't help you manage. What you need is to develop *your own* theory-in-use."

We define learning as "a process of change in some combination of behavior, its accompanying frames of reference and/or the capacity for acting differently. This change may or may not involve the acquisition of formal information, skills, or values, but does result in learners who are more effective in their personal context and, possibly, more inclusive in their views of the world." This definition acknowledges the difficulty of defining learning beyond the central fact that it involves change in one or more domains of a person's cognitive, conative, or affective capacities and that this change can be of several types.

FROM INDIVIDUAL TO TEAM AND ORGANIZATIONAL LEARNING

We have been describing learning as individual phenomena, and, when a large number of members of the same community have a similar learning experience, there is a change in the collective frame of reference, or mental model. However, much work in organizations is done in groups, and many group tasks explicitly depend on creativity borne of the collective efforts of team members to learn together.

Organizational behavior researchers have argued that teams or groups that are characterized by effective group process are more effective than individuals working alone in solving unstructured problems,[34] for which not only the answer or solution isn't known, but also it is equally unclear what factors or variables need to be considered in solving the problem. In short, unstructured problems are what Revans calls "quandaries" (see Chapter Two).[35] Groups are more effective in solving unstructured problems, because, in the absence of a structure for resolving the quandary, diverse perspectives and reasoning are more likely to reveal still more aspects of the problem. Strategic learning involves solving unstructured problems. Much of the literature on group process as been focused on helping people to perform effectively in addressing these kinds of unstructured problems so that they can benefit from the thinking of everyone involved.

A Team Learning Model

Scholars have recently come to understand the dynamics of teams as collective learning units.[36] Kasl, Marsick, and Dechant provide an empirically based team learning model that posits four learning modes that describe the extent to which team is learning collectively as a unit.[37] *Fragmented learning* is individual learning that is neither shared by a group nor necessarily shared with or by others. In *pooled learning,* individuals share information and perspectives, and small groups of people learn together, but the group as a whole doesn't learn. *Synergistic learning* occurs when the group as a whole creates knowledge mutually, integrating divergent perspectives in new ways but integrating team knowledge into individual meaning schemes. In *continuous learning* synergistic learning becomes habitual. These modes are phases, rather than linearly progressive steps, and groups may move back and forth between them.

Movement from fragmented learning through the other phases is a learning process identified by Kasl's group as framing, reframing, experimenting, crossing boundaries, and integrating perspectives (see Box 6.2). These processes are the same as those learning processes that are suggested by Mezirow's theory of transformative learning. Facilitating them in the group begins with individual learning and as the group becomes a more cohesive learning unit progresses to become a collective phenomenon, moving the team through the phases. Kasl and her colleagues argue that facilitating learning in groups requires the creation of three general sets of learning conditions: appreciation of teamwork (openness to hearing and considering other's ideas and the extent to which members value playing a team role); individual expression (having the opportunity to give input in forming goals, influencing group operations on an ongoing basis, and expressing objections); and operating principles (extent the group has organized itself for effective operation; established commonly held values, beliefs, and structure, and balances working on tasks and building relationships).

Hackman notes that assuming team members already have all the competencies they need to work well as a team is one of the "trip wires" that can block the establishment of effective teams.[38] HRD professionals can serve as coaches to teams, but

BOX 6.2   Team Learning Process

- Framing—the initial perception of an issue, event, situation, or person based on past experience. In practice, this means spending time surfacing each member's understanding of the problem or challenge that the group is working on and explicitly framing it and testing for common understanding.

- Reframing—transforming the initial perception into a new understanding, or frame. In practice, this suggests periodically reflecting on both the data and the experience of the group to date and stating how the problem might be reframed.

- Experimenting—group action taken to test hypotheses or moves, or to discover and assess impact. Specific action steps are taken with the intention of reviewing, reformulating, and developing new actions based on experience—in effect, collectively engaging in the learning cycle.

- Crossing boundaries—individuals seeking or giving information, views, and ideas through interaction with individuals or units; also, seeking the insights of devil's advocates.

- Integrating perspectives—group members synthesizing their divergent views such that apparent conflicts are resolved through dialectical thinking, not compromise or majority rule.

Kasl, Marsick, and Dechant, Journal of Applied Behavioral Science, vol. 33: 227–46, Copyright © Sage Publications 1997. Reprinted by permission of Sage Publications, Inc.

equally important is developing team leadership skills in managers that will help them coach teams effectively. The research done by Hackman and his colleagues affirmed "that whatever occurs when a team is created—when members first meet and begin to come to terms with one another and the work they will do—has enduring effects."[39] Getting a team off to a good start has enduring effects, and, as Hackman notes, the long-term cost of a poor launch often becomes evident when the team is working against a critical final deadline.

Hackman's work suggests the importance of establishing effective learning conditions when first forming a team. One approach is to have team members brainstorm to identify how they are going to work together and what norms will guide their work, and then discuss each norm individually, for clarification and to ensure that everyone agrees. While the norms will vary across situations, experience suggests the importance of including certain categories—how the team will handle leadership, how they will make decisions, and how they will resolve conflict when there is serious disagreement around decisions. This initial list of norms can be considered a group constitution that can be interpreted and, if necessary, amended with experience.

The list of norms can then be structured into a set of statements with an accompanying five- or seven-point scale. Periodically, the group can reflect on and dialogue around how well it is adhering to its norms, each individual reflecting on the meeting or series of meetings that have taken place and then rating each statement. Then, without discussion, the team creates a frequency distribution for each statement. The group can then have a dialogue around any statement when there is a significant range indicating differences of opinion as to how the group is functioning or around any statement with a relatively low mean. The important question is, What should the group do differently? If this process is followed with reasonable frequency, it can be done efficiently, and issues can be avoided before they become problematic. The process also reinforces learning practices that can facilitate reframing and sensemaking from experimenting with ideas. Box 6.3 provides one example of an instrument developed through the above process for a team who work in a pharmaceutical company.

BOX 6.3   High Performing and Learning (P&L) Team Instrument

Circle the number on the scale from 1 [very little] to 7 [very much] indicating your perception of the team situation. Use "not applicable" [N/A] or "don't know" [DK] where appropriate. Provide examples of the data you are using to derive your ratings.

Disclosure

1. Our conversations are characterized by open sharing of data.
   1   2   3   4   5   6   7   N/A or DK

2. We have access to financial data on the performance of the business.
   1   2   3   4   5   6   7   N/A or DK

Leadership

3. We are sharing leadership responsibilities appropriately.
   1   2   3   4   5   6   7   N/A or DK

Responsibility and Accountability

4. We stay on track and focus on our goals.
   1   2   3   4   5   6   7   N/A or DK

5. We maintain a strategic perspective in our discussions.
   1   2   3   4   5   6   7   N/A or DK

6. We demonstrate responsibility for growing the business.
   1   2   3   4   5   6   7   N/A or DK

7. We all work together and we each accept responsibility for running our parts of the business.
   1   2   3   4   5   6   7   N/A or DK

Open Communication

8. Our conversations take place in a climate in which we each can speak our mind freely and without fear.
   1   2   3   4   5   6   7   N/A or DK

9. We engage in healthy debate marked by a balance of advocacy and inquiry.
   1   2   3   4   5   6   7   N/A or DK

10. Our conversations are characterized by respectful listening.
   1   2   3   4   5   6   7   N/A or DK

Teamwork/Participation

11. We demonstrate teamwork directed toward the success of the total enterprise.
   1   2   3   4   5   6   7   N/A or DK

12. Our conversations are characterized by broad-based participation.
   1   2   3   4   5   6   7   N/A or DK

Support for the Process

13. We meet our commitments to one another.
   1   2   3   4   5   6   7   N/A or DK

14. We demonstrate a collective focus for maintaining effective group process.
   1   2   3   4   5   6   7   N/A or DK

Other

The kind of formal activity described above, which systematically focuses on processes of learning, is most important when teams are launched, after the completion of cycles of complex and critical tasks, or when teams are intended to be organizational learning mechanisms (described in the next section), especially teams dealing with highly unstructured problems such as strategy development. Research suggests that in teams that have good group process, team members routinely engage in informal learning, asking questions of one another, passing information through give-and-take, and sharing useful knowledge through informal conversations. Whether this represents fragmented individual level, pooled, or synergistic learning and whether the learning is leveraged for maximum performance improvement will vary from situation to situation.

There are, of course, different kinds of teams and different teams present distinct challenges in terms of how they learn. Clutterbuck has presented a typology of teams based on two dimensions: task stability and membership stability.[40] Some teams are relatively stable in terms of both task and membership; most production teams fall into this category. Other teams, such as pilot crews and cabin crews in airlines, have stable tasks but new and changing membership as members bid on new routes on a regular, often monthly, basis and are assigned to them by seniority. Other teams have both changing membership and changing tasks. Some consulting firms that do high-end, think tank project work may fall into this category, where new configurations of staff are assigned to work on each unique client engagement. Finally, there are crisis teams and development teams that have stable membership but face changing challenges. The rhythm of learning needs and the challenges one faces in developing a team's capacity for learning will vary with the type of team, and virtual teams add another dimension.

Organizational Learning

Team learning is a form of organizational learning. Senge made the concept "team learning" visible to the general management community, defining it as the pivotal element linking individual and organizational learning by writing "teams, not individuals are the fundamental learning units in modern organizations. This [is] where 'the rubber meets the road'; unless teams can learn the organization cannot learn."[41] Organizations are, of course, federations of groups and of larger units that are more or less tightly coupled and more or less autonomous, depending on the degree of centralization in the organization's structure. Where team learning stops and organizational learning begins is an open question, especially when a team's learning crosses boundaries and is shared with other groups. Just as individual learning processes are the starting point for individual learning, team learning is the cornerstone of organizational learning.

While the idea of the learning organization became popular in the early 1990s,[42] the concept of organizational learning has been part of organizational theory and the subject of considerable discussion and debate for some time.[43] One significant fault line in this discussion is whether organizations can truly learn or if only individuals can learn on behalf of the organization. Organizational sociologists such as March and Olsen argue that learning implies thought and that the concept of organizational learning attributes human characteristics to organizational structures—a problem of anthropomorphism.[44] Other theorists such as Hedberg, Fiol and Lyles, and Shrivastava, have argued that learning takes place at multiple levels of an organization and that organizational learning can be productively conceptualized as embedded in the procedures, systems, and practices of the organization.[45] Ironically, this latter position is not entirely inconsistent with the early theories of March and Simon, who describe organizational rules and procedures as akin to habits in individuals, representing standardized ways of handling routine, reoccurring events or decisions. The distinction being made by theorists such as Simon and March and Olsen is that such organizational practices are the result of the decisions taken by individuals, albeit collectively and driven by experience, and should not be confused with human processes of cognition.

There exists a broad consensus in the current literature that the conceptual distinction between individual and organizational learning is useful for thinking about important issues in organizational adaptation and change. This literature conceptualizes organizational learning as embedded in organizational-level systems, practices and procedures, information technology, routines, the organizational culture, and other sources of institutional memory, but these artifacts of organizational learning must be conceptualized as distinct from the cognitive processes of individual learning.

Popper and Lipshitz, along with various colleagues, have offered a framework for thinking about organizational learning that operationalizes the concept of organizational learning for purposes of research and practice.[46] Agreeing that anthropomorphism is a problem in the organizational learning literature they argue for a distinction between "learning in organization" (LIO) and "learning by organizations" (LBO). Their theoretical framework is empirically based and is very consistent with the model of team learning that we described above. Learning-in-organization occurs when members learn on behalf of the organization; learning-by-organization occurs when this individual-level learning has organizational-level output. Organizational-level outputs are changes that are captured and widely utilized by the organization, including informal norms, or changes that are being codified in formal procedures or practices. This learning takes place through organizational learning mechanisms (OLMs), "institutional structural and procedural arrangements that allow organizations to systematically collect, analyze, store, disseminate, and use information relevant to the performance of the organization and its members"[47] in a way that enables organizational learning. OLMs are held to solve the problem of anthropomorphism by relating LIO to LBO:

> On one hand, the approach is embedded in a learning-by conceptualization of organizational learning because the operation of organizational mechanisms, located "outside human heads," describes learning processes that are not mediated by individual learning processes. On the other hand, this approach does not negate organizational learning as LIO because . . . some learning mechanisms are designated to facilitate learning by individual organizational members or to disseminate what individuals learn throughout the organization.

Finally, OLMs are concrete, directly observable organizational systems operated by individual organization members. Thus, OLMs make it possible to attribute to organizations a capacity to learn, without positing hypothetical, unobservable constructs, in a way that is neither paradoxical nor metaphorical.[48]

Organizational learning mechanisms vary in their structural characteristics occurring to the relationship of their members to the larger organization and where the learning takes place relative to organizational tasks—integration/nonintegration and designated learning purpose/dual learning and task accomplishment purpose. An OLM is:

- *integrated,* if its members and clients are identical (i.e., organizational members who are responsible for generating it and those responsible for applying its lessons are identical);

- *nonintegrated,* if members and clients are not identical;

- *designated,* if learning takes place away from task performance; and

- *dual purpose,* if learning is carried out in conjunction with task performance.

Many organizational units such as project teams, task forces, and ad hoc committees are intended to function as organizational learning mechanisms. For HRD professionals these are opportunities for introducing practices that harvest the learning that takes place through the experience of the group in a way that translates learning-in-organization on the part of individuals to learning-by-organization through the processes of team learning previously described, especially the diffusion of the learning beyond the immediate group.

Echoing the findings of Kasl et al. on the importance of team learning conditions, Popper and Lipshitz argue that for OLMs to promote organizational learning, they must be embedded in an organizational culture of shared organizational learning values (SOLVs) that promote productive learning; these values are defined in Box 6.4.

BOX 6.4   Shared Organizational Learning Values

- Transparency—exposing one's thoughts and actions to others in order to receive feedback.

- Inquiry—persisting in a line of inquiry until a satisfactory understanding is achieved.

- Integrity—giving and receiving full and accurate feedback without defending oneself and others.

- Issue orientation—focusing on the relevance of information to the issues, regardless of the social standing (e.g., rank) of recipient or source.

- Accountability—assuming responsibility both for learning and for implementing the lessons learned.

Popper and Lipschitz, Journal of Applied Behavioral Science (vol. 34, issue 2), p. 161–79. Copyright © 1998 by Sage Publications. Reprinted by permission of Sage Publications, Inc.

They add focus to the description by Kasl et al. of learning conditions that are very general and seem to have more to do with group dynamics than with learning per se.

The structural and cultural dimensions of Popper and Lipshitz's model are supplemented by psychological states of safety and commitment on the part of organizational members and by corporate policies that promote these states through demonstrating management's commitment to learning. Such policies include a) tolerating error through, not punishing mistakes, but treating them as learning opportunities, b) de-emphasizing status differences, and, c) promoting safety through job security. Popper and Lipshitz further observe that certain contextual factors, such as the critically of any errors that might occur, rate of change, level of uncertainty in the organization's task environment, and the professionalism of the workforce, play important roles in facilitating organizational learning. The quality of organizational learning will vary in both form and effectiveness across various organizational sub-units, because of organizational need and quality of leadership.

Taken together, the Popper and Lipshitz shared organizational learning values model and the Kasl, Marsick, and Dechant team learning model provide an empirical basis for aligning traditionally OD-oriented interventions, HRD practices, and HRM policies, if organization learning is going to occur. Organizational learning requires individual learning, the establishment of a supportive cultural context, and the incentives that permit learning across organizational boundaries. Team and organizational learning are not ends in themselves but processes for improving performance.

PERFORMANCE IMPROVEMENT MODELS

The emergence of the learning organization as a popular metaphor has extended HRD practice into the realm of team development and organizational-level systems for performance improvement, blurring even more the lines between HRD and OD practice while opening up more inclusive ways of thinking about the role of learning in organizational performance. We now turn to another major body of theory and research that is one of the foundations of HRD practice: performance improvement.

In a comprehensive review, Swanson and Holton[49] identify thirty performance improvement models that have been proposed in the literature. They conclude that performance improvement theories are grounded in a wide range of disciplines, each with its own disciplinary bias, resulting in different perspectives from which performance is defined. Swanson and Holton further conclude that trying to come to a definitive agreement on a single model of performance is probably futile.

Commonalities in Performance Improvement Theories

Regardless of the variety of approaches, there are certain commonalties in contemporary performance improvement theories. The first is that outcomes need to be specified and defined operationally, and matrixes for measuring them must either exist or be developed. From a performance improvement perspective, outcomes anchor discussions around HRD practice. Second, any comprehensive theory of performance improvement defines outcomes for different levels of the organization. Third, a major focus of HRD practice should be to support management in resolving problems in the organization. Finally, training, while a valuable tool in the HRD toolbox of solutions, should not be the primary intervention; rather, some form of root-cause analysis should identify the proper solutions or interventions, some of which may have nothing to do with training per se. These solutions may involve altering systems, changing logistics, or initiating some structural change in the organization.

Performance improvement theory starts with the understanding that a given performance issue may or may not require working by means of what Swanson calls the "human lens."[50] He argues that to work from the frame of reference of performance improvement models, it is necessary to first *define* performance and then proceed to describe the factors that *drive* it. Depending on the situation, this may or may not involve learning interventions. The mental model is to go from "performance to the need for training" rather than from "training to performance."[51]

The key to making this transition to performance improvement thinking is to avoid focusing on a particular performance driver or set of performance drivers, such as training, accounting, team building, and work restructuring, and to begin by focusing on organizational performance. Defining performance as the "valued productive output of a system in the form of goods or services," Swanson proposes the starting point for an analysis of performance improvement as defining units of performance that are "usually *measured* in terms of quantity, time, and quality feature measures."[52]

Kaplan and Norton make the connection between drivers and outcomes explicit while also providing a performance-management tool in their notion of the balanced scorecard.[53] Identifying both outcomes and drivers as elements of performance that must be measured, they argue that having outcome measures that are not linked to drivers fails to communicate how outcomes are going to be accomplished. Conversely, measuring drivers without outcome measures is likely to fail to reveal whether business results, in terms of increased market share and enhanced financial results, have been achieved, regardless of short-term improvements in processes. "A good balanced scorecard should have an appropriate mix of outcomes (lagging indicators) and performance drivers (leading indicators) of the business unit's strategy."[54]

A Systems Approach to Performance Improvement

A defining characteristic of systems approaches to performance improvement is a focus on both drivers and output. Unlike psychology-based models that focus solely on individual performance, an open-systems perspective acknowledges the role of influences in the organization's task environment, the nature and quality of inputs, and process variables, all linked to output.[55] People perform within the context of a broader performance system and processes. The knowledge and competencies that they bring to their task is only one factor in how well they perform on the job.

Rummler and Brache take a holistic system approach (Figure 6.5);[56] they offer a model that describes three levels—the organizational level, the process level, and the

FIGURE 6.5   **Rummler and Brache's Performance Model**

	GOALS	DESIGN	MANAGEMENT
Organization			
Process			
Individual			

From: Improving Performance: How to Manage the White Spaces on the Organization Chart, *G. A. Rummler and A. P. Brache, Copyright © 1995, Jossey-Bass. Reprinted by permission of John Wiley & Sons, Inc.*

individual level—of performance. Each level is impacted by three performance variables—goals (specific standards that reflect customer expectations in terms of quality, quantity, timeliness, and cost); design (structures configured so that goals can be effectively met); and management (practices that keep goals current and ensure their achievement). When the levels are cross-referenced against the variables, they comprise a matrix that can guide thinking about an organization as a system. Swanson incorporates the same three levels of performance, but identifies five performance variables: 1) mission/goal, 2) system design, 3) capacity, 4) motivation, and 5) expertise (Figure 6.6).[57]

Holton has also offered a model that argues for mission, process, critical performance subsystems, and individuals as domains of performance, each with corresponding outcomes and drivers.[58] In all three models, performance outcomes are the starting point for the performance assessment process.

It is important to remember that conceptually the levels in these models do not refer to levels of organizational authority but rather to levels of learning—individual, group process, and organizational learning. For example, the executive level of an organization comprises individuals who must perform certain functions, some of which contribute directly to organizational output (such as servicing customers). Other executive functions focus on creating output for the organization (such as plans and strategies) or for other senior staff (such as counseling the CEO). Carrying out these organizational responsibilities can involve goals, system design, capacity building, motivation, or expertise on the part of individuals.

Performance improvement theory points needs analysis to the possibility that performance issues are not a function of lack of competence on the part of members of the organization, but are attributable to other factors that block performance. Many of these other factors do not fall within the specific domain of HRD, although HRD may have a role in calling attention to these issues and supporting solutions. The idea that HRD may need partners or may need to build alliances with other support functions and disciplines reinforces the importance of the political dimension to the HRD role. HRD's role, as defined by the term "human," is to address barriers to human performance within the organization. As the quality improvement movement in industry demonstrated, this may not involve training people—indeed, people may already know how to do their jobs well, but systems and procedures and various structural impediments may be preventing them from doing so.[59] From this perspective, HRD's

FIGURE 6.6   **Swanson's Performance Matrix**

PERFORMANCE VARIABLES	PERFORMANCE LEVELS		
	ORGANIZATIONAL LEVEL	PROCESS LEVEL	INDIVIDUAL LEVEL
Mission/goal	Does the mission/goal fit the reality of the economic, political, and cultural forces?	Do the process goals enable the organization to meet organization and individual goals?	Are the goals of individuals congruent with those of the organization?
System Design	Does the organizational system and structure support performance?	Are processes designed to work as a system?	Does the individual face obstacles that impede job performance?
Capacity	Does the organization have the leadership, capital, and infrastructure to achieve its goals?	Does the process have the capacity to perform?	Does the individual have the mental, physical, and emotional capacity to perform?
Motivation	Do the policies, culture, and reward systems support the desired performance?	Does the process provide information and human factors required to maintain it?	Does the individual want to perform, no matter what?
Expertise	Does the organization establish and maintain selection and training policies and resources?	Does the process of developing expertise meet changing demands of changing processes?	Does the individual have the knowledge, skills, and experience to perform?

Reprinted with permission of the publisher. Analysis for Improving Performance: Tools for Diagnosing Organizations and Documenting Workplace Expertise, Copyright 1994 by Richard A. Swanson, Berrett-Koehler Publishers, Inc. San Francisco, Calif. All rights reserved. www.bkconnection.com

role is to help the organization manage its human capital, a responsibility very different from straight education. Managing human capital still involves learning, however. Just helping managers realize the limitations of using training as a preferred fix may involve challenging the assumptions held by managers and executives.

LINKING PERFORMANCE IMPROVEMENT AND ORGANIZATIONAL LEARNING

While performance improvement theory increasingly addresses multiple levels of organizational performance, its focus is stronger in specifying the performance linkages at each level than it is in describing the connections among levels. When organizational dilemmas and problems occur at a particular level, they may be symptomatic of problems and issues at other levels of the system. Performance improvement problems are typically linked across the boundaries of the organizational, process (or team), and individual levels. These linkages are complicated by the fact that the levels of performance improvement theory transcend levels of organizational structure. Problems at the strategic level of the organization may reflect learning issues among the individuals occupying senior positions, the inability of the senior group to function as a learning group, or organizational systems that fail to provide proper guidance. Whatever the combination of issues at the root of strategic problems, the consequences cascade down to the middle and operational levels of the organization.

Similarly, performance problems at the middle and operational levels of the HRD pyramid can reflect learning issues at the organizational, team, or individual levels. The challenge for HRD practitioners is to create organizational learning mechanisms that are appropriate for bridging these critical linkages. Some of these OLMs can be created as extraorganizational groupings of employees, who meet specifically to address identified problems (what Popper and Lipshitz call nonintegrated, designated learning units). Often these units will have to comprise people from across hierarchical levels in the organization. In other instances, learning tools and practices can be introduced into existing groupings or teams of employees, converting them into integrated, dual purpose learning mechanisms—learning while performing. Ideally, of course, all work units should have some characteristics of learning groups, so the challenge becomes modifying or redirecting their efforts.

Translating the learning that takes place in these efforts requires putting in place boundary-spanning mechanisms that allow for the transfer of learning to the larger organization, and embedding that learning in practices and systems. There is a political element to this process, since, as a practical matter, such changes often impact people and work units that have benefited from the current configuration of practices. There is also a practical aspect to such changes—what represents improvement for one part of the organization often creates a problem or eliminates an advantage for another part. Organizational learning often involves tradeoffs when it comes to performance improvements—deciding what the balance should be within a balanced scorecard. The implication is that regardless of the focus of an HRD intervention, it requires a system perspective that frames the broader picture of organizational performance within the strategic direction of the organization.

FROM LEARNING TO DEVELOPMENT

Adult development theory and research are closely related to the literature on learning. Learning has to do with acquiring knowledge, competencies, and knowing how to apply them. Development implies growth and progression in one's capacity for learning. Adult development theorists argue that for learners, the ability to respond to many kinds of learning challenges, especially learning challenges requiring increased cognitive complexity, is closely linked to one's level of development.

Writing from an adult development perspective, Kegan distinguishes between what he calls *informational learning* and what he calls *transformational learning*.[60] He characterizes the former as "learning aimed at increasing our fund of knowledge, at increasing our repertoire of skills, at extending already established cognitive capacities into new terrain."[61] This kind of learning, he acknowledges, is important; however, it is "literally in-*form*-ative because it seeks to bring valuable new contents into the existing form of our way of knowing."[62] Transformational learning, in contrast, changes not *what* we know but *how* we know. "Trans-*form*-ative learning" alters the cognitive form within which we learn and involves not just acquiring knowledge but increasing our capacity for learning.[63] By a change in capacity, Kegan means a change in a learner's ability to make meaning out of experience. As in Mezirow's theory of transformational learning, changes in habits of mind and points of view can occur at any phase of the developmental process; however, the qualitative nature of these changes is constrained by an individual's level of development.

The implications of this argument for learning at the strategic, tactical, and operational levels of the HRD pyramid are suggested by William Torbert's seven-stage model of development: 1) opportunist, 2) diplomat, 3) technician, 4) achiever, 5) strategist, 6) magician, and 7) ironist (see Box 6.5).[64] Studies conducted by Torbert and his associates suggest that most first-line supervisors cluster in the diplomat and technician stages of development. Middle managers cluster in the technician and achiever stages, while senior managers, executives, and entrepreneurial professionals spread from the technician to the strategist stage. Only entrepreneurial professionals had significant representation at the strategist stage. Drawing on the research by one of his doctoral students, Hirsch,[65] who studied entrepreneurial professionals (ophthalmologists), Torbert describes the differences in technician, achiever, and strategist mindsets:

> The Technicians—insisting on hands-on participation in every technical phase of their operations—are able to see essentially one patient at a time.

> The Achievers—delegating significant aspects of the operation to their staffs, with oversight—can see essentially three patients at a time.

> The Strategists—able to see critical gaps in services, move into unoccupied niches, and create contracts that motivate partner physicians—are able to create multisite practices and see three times again as many patients.

BOX 6.5   Successive Developmental Stages and their Governing Frames (From Torbert)

STAGE	NAME	GOVERNING FRAME
1	Impulsive	Impulses rule reflexes.
2	Opportunist	Needs and interests rule impulses.
3	Diplomat	Expectations of others rule interests.
4	Technician	Internal craft logic rules expectations.
5	Achiever	System success in environment rules craft logics.
6	Strategist	Principle rules system.
7	Magician	Process (interplay of principle/action) awareness rules principle.
8	Ironist	Intersystemic development awareness rules process.

From: Torbert, The Power of Balance: Transformng Self, Society, and Scientific Inquiry. *Sage Publications (1991). Copyright © W. Torbert. Used by permission of the author.*

Elsewhere, Fisher and Torbert assert that strategists are more likely than achievers to engage in double-loop learning and to make more conscientious efforts at understanding the frames of subordinates and others.[67] When influencing others, they are more likely than achievers to undertake negotiation among diverse frames to create a new shared frame rather than to assert their own view. Bushe and Gibbs, in a study of internal consultants, reported that eleven of them who measured at the strategist stage of development were perceived as more competent by organizational members than were fifty-three other consultants who measured at earlier stages of development.[68] Rooke and Torbert, in a study of ten organizations observed over an average period of just over four years, found that five CEOs at the strategist stage supported a number of progressive and transformative organizational changes, while five who measured at the prestrategist stage supported none and experienced deterioration in indicators of business performance.[69]

For Torbert, as for other development theorists, human development is not a simple matter of goal achievement that can be generated by either "internal motivation" or by "external pressure or opportunity."[70] Rather, transformation to a more inclusive and qualitatively different way of making meaning requires mutuality—reciprocal initiatives among learners who form communities of inquiry and are supported by appropriate structures. These liberating structures are a type of organizing that is productive and at the same time educates its members toward self-correcting awareness.

These kinds of developmental experiences are sometimes found in programs external to the company (the Co-Active Leadership Case in Part III provides examples) since most organizational development events essentially focus on learning congruent with the technician and achiever stage. However, proper internal coaching can also facilitate such experiences, if the coach, whether a manager or an HRD professional, understands the development capabilities that the person possesses already and is able to comprehend the nature of the challenges confronting him or her.

Development cannot be learned; it is facilitated through experience, and it takes place over time. Most often individuals take the initiative to seek out and engage in these kinds of developmental experiences. People must reflect on the challenges that have taken them out of their comfort zone, actively inquire into their response to these challenges, and, perhaps with the help of a skilled coach or mentor, come to a new, more complex way of understanding their relationship to their responsibilities and to others. HRD's role in this process varies, but it most often involves recognizing and suggesting opportunities for development. Action-reflection learning programs and highly experiential leadership development programs can be instrumental to this kind of development.

SUMMARY

This chapter has provided an overview of the connections between three broad areas of theory, each of which provides part of the foundation for HRD practice: learning theory (individual, team, and organization), performance improvement theory, and adult development. The literature in any one of these areas is vast, and we have selected only those models that are most relevant to this text, models that the author has repeatedly used when working in various organizational contexts. For the serious student, the models invite more extensive investigation in those areas most relevant to his or her interest or practice. Learning designs and practices will vary according to the kind of learning that is intended, the performance needs of the organization, and whether the intention is to provide knowledge or skills and competencies, to alter attitudes or frames of reference linked to performance, or to provide more general development that will enhance the capacity of learners to deal with an ever more challenging "hidden curriculum" of life.

Questions for Discussion

1. Think of a situation or challenge that you are currently trying to resolve. What adjustments have you made in your approach to the situation? What have you learned? Are these adjustments examples of single-loop or double-loop learning? Share your experience with a colleague or peer who is familiar with this distinction. Do they agree?

2. As our world has become globally connected, executives and other organizational members have needed to reframe their perspective on the world. Give an example of such learning. Describe what was involved. What factors triggered the learning? How has their (or your) habits of mind or points of view been challenged and reframed? How have organizations attempted to facilitate this reframing?

3. Think of a learning intervention you have recently designed or attended as a participant. Was its focus response learning or situation learning? What were the key elements of the design?

4. Take a challenge or issue you are currently struggling with and work your way around the learning cycle. With which learning style are you most comfortable?

5. In what organizational learning mechanisms have you participated in your organization (if any)? What kinds of learning occurred—learning by individuals or learning by organization? If the latter, what is the evidence for this kind of learning? What opportunities for creating organizational learning mechanisms exist in your organization(s)? How can the existing structures in those organizations focus more on learning?

6. How would you map the performance-improvement system in your organization or an organization in which you participate? To what extent does the Swanson model work in helping you do this? How might you adjust this model to better fit your situation?

End Notes

1. G. Bateson, *Ecology of the Mind* (New York, Balentine, 1972), 283.

2. E. R. Hilgard and G. H. Bower, *Theories of Learning* (New York: Appleton-Century-Crofts, 1966); M. Knowles, *The Adult Learner: A Neglected Species,* 4th ed. (Houston, Tex.: Gulf, 1990).

3. J. B. Quinn, *Intelligent Enterprise* (New York: Free Press, 1992).

4. S. Fox, "From Management Education and Development to the Study of Management Learning," in J. Burgoyne and M. Reynolds, *Management Learning: Integrating Perspectives in Theory and Practice* (London and Thousand Oaks, Calif: Sage, 1997), 30.

5. P. B. Vaill, *Learning as a Way of Being: Strategies for Survival in a World of Permanent White Water* (San Francisco: Jossey-Bass, 1996), 21.

6. W. James, *Pragmatism* (New York: Longmans and Green, 1925).

7. M. Polanyi, *Personal Knowledge* (New York, Harper and Row, 1964).

8. C. Argyris and D.A. Schon, *Theory in Practice: Increasing Professional Effectiveness* (San Francisco: Jossey-Bass, 1982).

9. Bateson, *Ecology.*

10. E. Cell, *Learning to Learn from Experience* (Albany, N.Y.: State University of New York Press, 1984).

11. J. Mezirow, *Transformative Dimensions of Adult Learning* (San Francisco: Jossey-Bass, 1991).

12. Cell, *Learning to Learn,* 60.

13. *ibid.,* 53.

14. J. Habermas, *The Theory of Communicative Action,* vol. 1; *Reason and the Rationalization of Society,* vol 2; *Life-World and System: A Critique of Functionalist Reason,* T. McCarthy, trans. (Boston: Beacon, 1984).

15. J. Mezirow, "Learning to Think like an Adult," In J. Mezirow and Associates, *Learning as Transformation: Critical Perspectives on a Theory in Progress* (San Francisco: Jossey-Bass, 2000), 8.

16. *ibid.,* 5.

17. *ibid.,* 18.

18. Argyris and Schon, *Theory in Practice.*

19. Knowles, *The Adult Learner.*

20. D. A. Kolb, *Experiential Learning: Experience as the Source of Learning and Development* (Englewood Cliffs, N.J.: Prentice-Hall, 1984).

21. A. Mumford, *Learning at the Top* (London and New York: McGraw-Hill, 1995).

22. *ibid.,* xxvii.

23. J. Heron, *Feeling and Personhood: Psychology in Another Key* (London: Sage, 1992), 193.

24. *ibid.,* 194.

25. J. L. Callahan, ed., *Perspectives of Emotion and Organizational Change, Advances in Developing Human Resources,* 4(1). (Thousand Oaks, Calif.: Sage and Academy of Human Resource Development, 2002); D. C. Short and L. Yorks, "Analyzing Training from an Emotions Perspective," in Callahan, (ed). *Perspectives of Emotion,* 80–96; L. Yorks and E. Kasl, "Toward a Theory and Practice for Whole-Person Learning: Reconceptualizing Experience and the Role of Affect," *Adult Education Quarterly,* 52 (2002): 176–92.

26. R. J. Sternberg and J. A. Horvath, *Tacit Knowledge in Professional Practice: Researcher and Practitioner Perspectives* (Mahwah, N.J.: L. Erbaum, 1999).

27. B.S. Bloom, et al., *Taxonomy of Educational Objectives, Handbook I: Cognitive Domain* (New York: McKay, 1956), 7.

28. S. Fineman, "Organizations as Emotional Arenas," in S. Fineman, ed. *Emotion in Organizations* (Thousand Oaks, Calif.: Sage, 1993), 9–35; S. Fineman, *Managing Emotions at Work: Some Political Reflections.* Paper presented at the Academy of Management Conference, Washington, D.C., August, 2001; A. Rafaeli and R. I. Sutton, "Expression of Emotion as Part of the Work Role," *Academy of Management Review,* 12 (1987): 23–37.

29. D. Goleman, R. Boyatzis, and A. McKee, *Primal Leadership: Realizing the Power of Emotional Intelligence* (Boston, Ma.: Harvard Business School Publishing, 2002).

30. M. S. Knowles, E. F. Holton, III, and R. A. Swanson, *The Adult Learner* (Houston, Tex.: Gulf, 1998).

31. D. Boud, R. Cohen, and D. Walker, "Introduction: Understanding Learning from Experience," in D. Boud, R. Cohen, and D. Walker, eds., *Using Experience for Learning* (Buckingham, England: The Society for Research into Higher Education and The Open University Press, 1993), 12–3.

32. Short and Yorks, "Analyzing Training."

33. J. Gozawa, "Cosmic Heroes and the Heart's Desire: Embracing Emotion and Conflict in Transformative Learning," *Proceedings of the Third International Transformative Learning Conference: Challenges of Practice-Transformative Learning in Action.* (New York: Columbia University, Teachers College, The Center for Educational Innovation and Outreach. 2002): 141.

34. V. Vroom and P. Yetton, *Leadership and Decision Making* (Pittsburgh: University of Pittsburgh Press, 1973).

35. R. W. Revans, *The Origin and Growth of Action Learning* (London: Chartwell Bratt, 1982); M. Pedler, *Action Learning for Managers* (London: Lemos & Crane, 1996).

36. A. Edmondson, "Psychological Safety and Learning Behavior in Work Teams," *Administrative Science Quarterly* 44 (1999): 350–83; A. Edmondson, R. Bohmer, and G. Pisano, "Speeding up Team Learning," *Harvard Business Review,* 79 (2001): 125–32; E. Kasl, V. J. Marsick, and K. Dechant, "Teams as Learners: A Research-based Model of Team Learning," *Journal of Applied Behavioral Science,* 33 (1997): 227–46.

37. Kasl, et al., "Terms as Learners."

38. J. R. Hackman, *Groups That Work (And Those That Don't): Creating Conditions for Effective Team Work* (San Francisco: Jossey-Bass, 1990).

39. *ibid.*

40. D. Clutterbuck, "How Teams Learn," *Training and Development* (March, 2002), 67–9.

41. P. M. Senge, *The Fifth Discipline: The Art and Practice of the Learning Organization* (New York: Doubleday/Currency, 1990), 10.

42. Senge, *The Fifth Discipline;* K. Watkins and V. J. Marsick, *Sculpting the Learning Organization: Lessons in the Art and Science of Systemic Change* (San Francisco: Jossey-Bass, 1993).

43. M. C. Fiol and M. A. Lyles, "Organizational Learning," *Academy of Management Review* 10 (1985): 803–13; B. Hedberg, "How Organizations Learn and Unlearn," in P. C. Nystram and W. H. Starbuck, eds., *Handbook of Organizational Design,* vol. 1 (Oxford, UK: Oxford University Press, 1981); J. G March and J. P. Olsen, "Organizational Learning and the Ambiguity of the Past," in J. G. March and J. P. Olsen, eds., *Ambiguity and Choice in Organizations* (Bergen, Norway: Universitetsforlaget, 1976): 54–68; H. A. Simon, "Bounded Rationality and Organizational Learning," *Organization Science* 2 (1991): 125–34; P. Shrivastava, A Typology of Organizational Learning Systems," *Journal of Management Studies* 20 (1983): 7–28.

44. M. Easterby-Smith, M. Crosson, and D. Nicolini, "Organizational Learning: Debates Past, Present, and Future," *Journal of Management Studies* 37 (2000): 783–96. M. Popper and R. Lipshitz, "Organization Learning Mechanisms: A Structural and Cultural Approach to Organizational Learning," *Journal of Applied Behavioral Science,* 34 (1998): 78–98.

45. Fiol and Lyles, "Organizational Learning"; Hedberg, "How Organizations Learn"; Shrivastava, "A Typology."

46. Popper and Lipshitz, "Organizational Learning Mechanisms"; M. Popper, R. Lipshitz, and V. J. Friedman, "A Multifaceted Model of Organizational Learning," *Journal of Applied Behavioral Science* 38 (2002): 78–98.

47. *ibid.,* 170.

48. *ibid.*

49. R. A Swanson and E. F. Holton, III, *Foundations of Human Resource Development* (San Francisco: Berrett-Koehler, 2001).

50. R. A. Swanson, "The Foundations of Performance Improvement for Practice," in *Performance Improvement Theory and Practice,* R. J. Torrraco, ed., *Advances in Developing Human Resources* 1(1) (San Francisco: Berrett-Koehler Communications and Academy of Human Resource Development) Ch. 1, 1–25.

51. *ibid.,* 4.

52. *ibid.,* 5

53. R. S. Kaplan and D. P. Norton, *The Strategy Focused Organization: How Balanced Scorecard Companies Thrive in the New Business Environment* (Boston: Harvard Business School Press, 2001).

54. R. S. Kaplan and D. P. Norton, *The Balanced Scorecard* (Boston: Harvard Business School Press, 1996), 31–2.

55. Swanson, "The Foundations of Performance."

56. G. A. Rummler and A.P. Brache, *Improving Performance: How to Manage the White Space on the Organization Chart,* 2nd ed. (San Francisco: Jossey-Bass, 1995).

57. R. A. Swanson, *Analysis for Improving Performance: Tools for Diagnosing Organizations and Documenting Workplace Expertise* (San Francisco: Berrett-Koehler, 1994).

58. E. F. Holton, III, "Performance Domains and Their Boundaries," in Torraco, *Performance Improvement Theory and Practice,* Ch. 1, 26–46.

59. W. E. Deming, *Out of the Crisis* (Cambridge, Mass.: MIT Press, 1986).

60. R. Kegan, "What Form Transforms? A Constructive-Developmental Approach to Transformative Learning," in J. Mezirow and Associates, *Learning as Transformation: Critical Perspectives on a Theory in Progress* (San Francisco: Jossey-Bass, 2000): 35–69.

61. *ibid.,* 48.

62. *ibid.,* 49.

63. *ibid.*

64. W. R. Torbert, *The Power of Balance: Transforming Self, Society, and Scientific Inquiry* (Newbury Park, Calif.: Sage, 1991).

65. J. Hirsch, *Toward a Cognitive-Developmental Theory of Strategy Formulation Among Practicing Physicians* (Ann Arbor, Mich.: University Microfilms International, 1988).

66. Torbert, *The Power of Balance,* 55.

67. D. Fisher and W. R. Torbert, *Personal and Organizational Transitions: The True Challenge of Generating Continual Quality Improvement* (New York: McGraw-Hill, 1995).

68. G. Bushe and B. Gibbs, "Predicting Organization Development Consulting Competence from the Myers-Briggs Type Indicator and Stage of Ego Development," *Journal of Applied Behavioral Science,* 26 (1990): 337–57.

69. D. Rooke and W. Torbert. "Organizational Transformation as a Function of CEO Development Stage," *Organization Development Journal* 16 (1998): 11–29.

70. Torbert, *The Power of Balance,* 56.

chapter

This chapter

- relates learning design to the learning pyramid;

- differentiates between foundational and supportive learning priorities;

- discusses work-based, program-based, individual, and group learning settings;

- introduces key methods for fostering strategic and tactical generative learning;

- discusses methods of operational training; and

- provides a model for thinking about learning transfer systems and the implications for learning design.

Key terms:

foundational learning	**dialogue**	**near transfer**
supportive learning	**reflection**	**far transfer**
work-based learning	**cognitive mapping**	**stimulus variability**
program-based learning	**harvesting learning**	**distributed application**
individual and group learning designs	**learning window**	**learning-transfer system**
	learning-transfer	

Designing Learning Opportunities

A focus on learning extends the scope of HRD practice significantly beyond designing and administrating training and education programs. While curriculum design remains an important competency, HRD practice involves designing learning into a wide range of experiences, for individual development, team and organizational learning, and performance improvement. This focus on learning, rather than teaching, reaches into classroom settings, such as innovative executive development programs. The challenge is building a learning environment that is relevant to the strategic focus of the organization. For companies who perceive their competitive advantage as knowledge-based or who are confronted with highly dynamic and chaotic environments, this means permeating the organization with a learning culture.

What it means for an organization to have a learning culture is open to debate. But by examining a large number of organizations we can suggest a number of core characteristics, including 1) openness to contradictory views and opinions around important strategic issues; 2) focusing on data (both quantitative and qualitative) for testing attributions and assertions about events and people; 3) careful assessment of experience for purposes of improvement, including double-loop learning through surfacing and chal-

lenging underlying premises; 4) capturing learning through knowledge-management systems and corporate practices; and 5) targeting key people for development. There can be considerable variation, however, in the way that these characteristics manifest themselves within a particular organizational culture. Organizations implementing strategies that place a high value on individualism and competitiveness may manifest learning in ways very different from those whose competitive strategies rest on cooperative teamwork.

Regardless, building learning into the culture of an organization extends beyond the formal classroom and beyond curriculum design. Rather, it reaches into strategy development meetings and it penetrates the knowledge creation process in the organization. Capturing learning in the most useful way for organizational-level learning and knowledge management is another dimension to building learning into the cultural fabric of the organization. More subtle challenges lie in seeking to capture the tacit knowledge of organizational members and converting it into explicit knowledge useful to new members and others; all this in addition to the traditional activities of designing and implementing more formal activities, such as classroom learning, conferences, and increasingly, e-learning (which we discuss in Chapter Eight).

This chapter begins by linking learning design to the HRD pyramid. We then look at various learning delivery methods and the principles of learning design on which they are based. Our focus will be on the design challenges each method presents, along with its advantages or strengths.

---

⑥

LEARNING CHALLENGES EMBEDDED IN THE HRD PYRAMID

Strategy, tactics, and operations define the core levels of the HRD pyramid in conceptualizing how HRD links to the strategic direction and value creation activities of the organization. If, as we have previously argued in Chapter One, the guiding principle of HRD is preparing and continually developing people and learning systems for the highest possible achievable performance to meet our strategic goals, then determining what learning adds value to performance in each of these levels is the core challenge of HRD management. We can describe learning events that specifically link HRD to the levels of the pyramid as *foundational* for performance.

Foundational learning events contribute directly to the formation of strategic direction, its tactical implementation, operational execution in practice, and the development of performance capacity in the organization. Performance capacity at the strategic level means the development of strategic thinking and the strategies that flow from it. At the tactical level, performance capacity involves building the capability of members of the organization to learn from their experience and making adjustments while implementing strategy. As in military action, the players that learn and adjust most quickly usually win. At the operational level, focusing training on those activities that provide the most leverage for effectively executing strategy and orchestrating tactical advantage sets the learning agenda. In today's highly cost-competitive world, training budgets are limited and the time employees have available, even more limited. So targeting training in a way that has a clear connection to operational needs and priorities makes both participation and executive sponsorship more compelling.

Other learning events are *supportive* of the organization's infrastructure and cultural integrity. Supportive learning plays a direct role in organizational maintenance and development and an indirect, or supportive role, in organizational performance. Classifying learning activities as supportive does not mean they are unimportant, only that they are not core to the strategic-value proposition of the organization. Some supportive learning may be required either by regulatory or legal requirements or by changes in technology or processes that make skill training necessary. Other supportive learning events help to integrate individuals into new roles in the organization; examples include orientation programs for new staff; assimilation events, when a new manager takes charge of a work unit; and transition programs for executives preparing to assume their first general management role. The challenge for HRD professionals implementing supportive learning events is to position the events so that their importance is clear and their contribution to organizational well-being is understood. Like foundational learning events, supportive learning has to be selectively targeted and promoted with a clear purpose. The metaphor of a suspension bridge is relevant here: the roadway is foundational for crossing a chasm or river, but the structures that provide support for the roadway are critical to its structural integrity.

Distinguishing between foundational and supportive learning events is a way to organize the conversation with management and HRD staff around priorities, purposes, and expectations to achieve greater clarity as to the purposes, goals, design, and levels of evaluation necessary for various initiatives. Generally speaking, foundational learning events should be linked as a set of learning activities and events to provide clear added value for the strategic agenda of the organization; including results-level assessment and, often, estimated return on investment (see Chapter Nine). Supportive learning initiatives should be sponsored by management and should be carefully targeted at building organizational culture, providing for bench strength, and/or enhancing organizational behavior and practices. Assessment will vary, based on the initiative, but it generally will involve assessing transfer of learning, either immediately or over time. This is the systematic and holistic approach to HRD practice, which integrates purposeful design, management of transfer systems, and assessment. And it enables key stakeholders, including senior line executives, to envision the learning plan as an organized canvas that depicts links to organizational performance and maintenance.

It would be naive to argue that distinguishing between foundational and supportive learning needs will eliminate disagreements about the learning agenda within an organization. If the distinction is clear, the discussion around learning budgets can focus on the expected value to the organization instead of vague and foggy arguments about the budget size and largely undifferentiated training activities. The conversation itself should have an educative impact on line managers, engaging them in making choices among learning options. The links between the strategic agenda of the organization and the demands of the organizational political economy are drawn into the conversation around learning in a concrete and results-oriented way.

PARAMETERS OF DESIGN

The literature on program design in adult education and HRD is diverse.[1] Generally it focuses on steps or phases of the program design process, including analyzing needs, establishing program goals and setting learning objectives, determining content, designing the learning processes, determining methods of evaluation, and, in general, developing curriculum. When adult learning theory is extended beyond the classroom to encompass a number of developmental venues, these program design models become an important, but bounded, piece of the design equation.

Over the years the philosophical foundations of learning theory have served to differentiate training and development practitioners into "schools," such as behaviorists, who focus on very specific competencies and measurable learning objectives, and humanists, who tend to structure learning events around learning objectives that are experiential and oriented toward understanding and sensemaking. As learning theory has evolved, it has crossed the boundaries of these traditions; theory and research now provide a more comprehensive and nuanced understanding of the different kinds of learning. Experienced trainers recognize that program designs both must fit the particular purposes of the training and often require a mixture of approaches. In Chapter Six we presented the theoretical constructs of scholars such as Argyris (single- and double-loop learning),[2] Cell (response learning, situation learning, transsituation learning, and transcendent learning),[3] and Mezirow (instrumental and communicative learning, and transformative learning),[4] who have variously drawn from elements of behaviorism, pragmatism, humanism, and critical theory in developing their ideas. Consequently, the design of learning events should be informed primarily by the kind of learning that is desired in combination with the context of the learning setting.

Varieties of Learning Contexts and the Development of a Learning Architecture

Learning contexts vary along two dimensions: 1) the extent to which they are work-based or program-based, and 2) the extent to which they are focused on the individual or on the group.

Increasingly, organizations are looking to utilize task- and work-based activities as vehicles both for productive outcomes and for learning and development. While there is a long history of using work, such as rotational job assignments, for purposes of staff development, today organizations are paying more attention to intentionally and explicitly harvesting learning. Executive coaches are increasingly bringing tacit learning through experience into learners' conscious awareness, both for knowledge management and to ensure that learners are deriving the right lessons from experience. Alternatively, HRD practitioners are encouraging managers to build learning practices, such as after-action reviews, into their activities in order to formalize informal and incidental learning. More and more participants view meetings as having a learning component, especially when the purpose of the meeting is generative or creative. In all of these instances, a substantial part of the expected learning is developmental or transformative and pointed toward a more complex and inclusive understanding of the business context—in short, building business or functional unit capability through reflection on assumptions, drawing lessons from experience, and generative learning. Meetings designed to draw out the diverse cognitive maps that people are holding in their heads, using methods such as cognitive mapping and future search conferences, are also learning events. Programs that focus explicitly on integrating learning with work are different from formal education and training programs that are packaged as seminars and courses; experiential team building, vestibule training, or simulations, are all delivered either in classrooms or through alternative methods, such as the Web.

Learning events can focus on the individual or the group. Much of the HRD agenda includes the abilities of individual learners, either in terms of developing awareness and understanding, developing skills and competencies, or changing perceptions and attitudes. Learning events may involve group work—for example, case studies, subgroup discussions, and active learning methods such as games and exercises—but the groups are ad hoc, that is, created for purposes of the event, and individuals who may never again interact together carry the learning forward. Other learning events, such as work-unit problem solving teams and team building exercises, involve individual learning, but the objective is to foster learning that is held collectively at the team or organizational level, in terms of either tacit understandings, of group norms and values, or of practices, policies, and/or procedures. The models of team learning and organizational learning that we presented in Chapter Six explore the processes and mechanisms associated with these kinds of learning.[5]

Table 7.1 places examples of various learning settings with which HRD works within the context of the two dimensions we set out at the beginning of this section. The common denominator is that each setting represents space created by HRD for learning within the organization.

The learning settings in Table 7.1 illustrate the expanded scope of HRD practice and point to the differences between traditional training and development thinking—which historically has been program-oriented and largely focused on individual development—and the broader mandate of contemporary HRD. As HRD broadens its practice to include work-based and team and organizational learning issues, the overlap with OD becomes more evident (see Chapter One). One way of framing the expanded learning-design process is by relating the HRD pyramid to the HRD, Training and Development (T&D), and OD processes conceptualized by Swanson and Holton[6] and shown in Table 7.2.

Aside from terminology, at first glance, phases 2, 3, and 4 in the HRD and T&D processes seem essentially the same, but the differences are more than semantic. Training and development is a component of HRD and is a design-oriented practice. Ideally, training outcomes should be determined either as part of an HRD analysis of overall organizational learning needs, or as part of a needs analysis focusing on specific skills or competency sets. In such an ideal situation, learning goals are clear and methods for achieving them are reasonably well-known. Drawing from the lessons of organizational sociology, we can characterize such a situation as requiring what Perrow labels "a routine technology."[7] Cause and effect relationships are reasonably well understood. The design process basically involves the HRD practitioner identifying the client department's learning objectives, which may involve a fairly general description

TABLE 7.1   Two Dimensions of Learning Design

	WORK-BASED LEARNING	PROGRAM-BASED LEARNING
Individual	Action Learning Sets (using Individual Challenges) Coaching On-the-Job-Training	Classroom Training E-Learning
Group	Team Building Action Learning (using intact Group Projects)	Blended Action Learning (Classroom and Projects)

TABLE 7.2   Variations among General HRD, T&D, and OD Processes

	HRD	T&D	OD
Phase 1	Analyze ↓	Analyze ↓	Analyze/Contract ↓
Phase 2	Propose ↓	Design ↓	Diagnose/Feedback ↓
Phase 3	Create ↓	Develop ↓	Plan/Develop ↓
Phase 4	Implement ↓	Implement ↓	Implement ↓
Phase 5	Assess	Evaluate	Evaluate/Institutionalize

of what the organization wants, doing a detailed needs analysis, and taking into account budget constraints. Then the training specialist designs a program and gets the client's approval, as would an engineer or any other design professional.

In designing the program, the HRD specialist can draw on a number of learning methods, such as case studies, lectures, small group discussions, and fish bowl exercises (where a small number of learners engage in a discussion or exercise while other learners observe them; following the discussion, the observers engage those in the "fishbowl" on what the observers heard or saw). These methods are supplemented with design techniques, such as ice-breakers, energizers, reflection, and closing activities.[8] *Methods* are essentially pedagogical processes and delivery mechanisms, while *techniques* are ways of timing and pacing a program to reinforce the pedagogical processes and keep participants engaged. Properly integrated, methods and techniques provide the flow for a training program, integrating the diverse learning styles of the participants with the material. Program designs can be tightened with successive pilot runs of a program so that learning outcomes become reasonably predictable.

When the competency to be developed is itself somewhat vague or subjective in nature or when the means to develop it is not well understood, it becomes more challenging to design a meaningful learning program. Leadership is one example of such a competency; despite a rich and diverse literature, which contains varied definitions of leadership and conflicting approaches to developing it, leadership remains an elusive phenomenon in terms of development. Developing strategic thinking is a similar example. Perrow describes these kinds of development challenges as involving nonroutine technologies, requiring a more creative integration of methods, techniques, and delivery vehicles. The movement toward work-based learning and coaching in part reflects the need for approaches to learning that draw on real experience, and facilitates bringing the resulting informal and incidental learning from experience into the formal knowledge structure of the learner. Here the design process becomes more fluid, less linear, and more generative. As the design challenge becomes less and less routine it also becomes more of an action-research process or action-learning process for the designer, requiring closer collaboration with the client, and the T&D process integrates with the OD process.

T&D is a subprocess of the broader HRD mandate that analyzes the learning needs of the organization as a whole, taking into account both its fundamental and supplemental learning needs. The result is a proposed learning strategy for the organization that includes work-based and program-based learning events as well as individual, team, and organizational learning interventions. This learning strategy proposal should be coordinated with, or linked to, OD initiatives; team learning interventions typically involve OD approaches.

Developing an appropriate array of learning interventions such as action learning, arranging for executive coaching, and building blended e-learning programs (which we will discuss in Chapter Eight) requires a learning architecture that rests on a broad HRD analysis of learning needs, culminating in a proposed learning strategy that may or may not include traditional training. Such architecture is most effective when it is successfully linked to the strategic requirements of the organization and when it garners support from senior executives who understand it as part of their business model.

Figure 7.1 conceptually links the OD, HRD, and T&D processes to the learning pyramid, illustrating the interdependence between HRD and OD in two ways. The first is the need for a strategic architecture that provides a learning context for the entire pyramid—strategic, tactical, and operational, with implications indicated to the far right of the figure. The second linkage calls attention to the need for a connection among learning events at the strategic level. As the learning agenda moves

FIGURE 7.1   **Linking Swanson & Horton's OD, HRD, & T&D Practices (Table 7.2) to the HRD Pyramid**

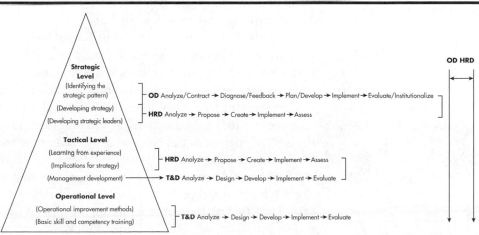

down the pyramid to tactical and operational issues, the focus moves to HRD and T&D interventions within the broader learning architecture of the organization.

Needs Analysis

Regardless of the nature of the learning process, the beginning point is a needs analysis to identify the business case for a program or intervention that links the program to either immediate or long-term business needs. As Wexley and Latham state, "Too often training and development programs get their start in organizations simply because the program was well advertised and marketed, or because 'other organizations are using it.'"[9]

A comprehensive needs analysis strategy integrates *organizational needs* with *individual needs*. Organizational needs analysis considers the entire organization a purposeful performance-focused social system, in interaction with its environment and requiring both a particular mix of human resource capabilities and a culture that is supportive of its strategic objectives.[10] Such an analysis can reveal needs best addressed by organizational development interventions that will align subsystems of the organization and develop more work-cohesive groups. Organizational needs analysis also identifies areas where, because of changes in strategic focus, the organization needs to develop new skills and competencies. Also, past performance may suggest the need for strengthening competencies in certain areas, and reviews of succession plans may suggest that more attention be given to developing managers for future responsibilities. In this way, organizational needs analysis provides a framework for more specific individual-level needs analysis.

Individual needs analysis focuses on the learning needs of particular employees and specific groups of employees.[11] The needs analysis must address the following questions: What learning and development is required for individuals to perform in their current jobs? What development opportunities will prepare them for possible future assignments? In practice, the distinction between the OD and training and education interventions often blur, with some interventions, like team-building and action-learning programs meeting both sets of needs.

A needs analysis strategy can be organized around the HRD pyramid. The chief learning officer can engage the senior executive team in conversations about the organization's needs for strategy creation. At the tactical level, the needs analysis can address the organization's strengths and limitations (in terms of the organizational culture and current mix of employee competencies) for executing its strategy, the lessons it can derive from tactical actions, and its long-term needs for succession planning. At the level of operations the needs analysis becomes more individual and task focused.

There are content and political dimensions to conducting an organizational needs analysis. From a content standpoint, it is important to identify both opportunities for facilitating the development of strategy and the critical factors for successful strategic performance. However, the process through which the needs analysis is conducted can help build alliances with key executives and build commitment for those HRD activities the analysis reveals are necessary. The two dimensions do not conflict if the needs analysis process is approached as a learning intervention in and of itself. The Grace Cocoa case presented in Chapter One is an example of an *emergent needs analysis process* where the future search conference was the first step in solidifying commitment to a global strategy and identifying what needs the organization must address in order to realize its strategic idea in practice. This led to a company-wide organizational task force that consisted of the president of the Chocolate Europe Division and senior managers in the operating companies across the company. The culture survey conducted by the task force identified critical learning factors, in terms of executive and organizational development, for successful strategic change.

The Chubb Study in Part Three of this book provides another example. When Bettina Kelly, the newly recruited head of Chubb Learning and Development Group, was charged by her CEO to develop "a world class training organization," Kelly did not immediately set out to explore best practices in other organizations. Realizing that any meaningful learning architecture would have to be driven by the business owners, Kelly's first move was to take a group of 18 senior executives off-site to develop a multiyear strategy for positioning learning and development as a source of competitive advantage. The group took a "deep dive" into the business by identifying broader strategic trends relative to customers, competitors, industry dynamics, Chubb's "own realities," and the wider business and economic environment. They then identified the enterprise-level learning implications as the basis of the learning strategy. The strategic insights from the meeting provided a compelling business case for building a world-class learning capability. The primary output of the meeting was a global learning strategy focused on six key investment areas: 1) sales skills and culture, 2) leadership and business mastery, 3) technical expertise, 4) technology acumen, 5) learning culture, and 6) learning infrastructure. An executive sponsor was assigned to each "investment area."

In both the Grace Cocoa and Chubb cases, the chief learning officer involved key senior executives in the needs analysis process, building support through educating management while identifying important strategic learning needs. Of course, other times it is necessary for the HRD group to be heavily involved in conducting the needs analysis, interviewing executives throughout the organization and looking at best practices elsewhere. Even so, it is important to engage potential allies in both the interpretation of the data and the proposals for learning initiatives.

Needs analysis at the individual level focuses more on task analysis and performance reviews. Wexley and Latham identify a five-step process for conducting a task-analysis–based needs analysis, 1) review the job description, 2) identify the tasks involved in performing the job, 3) identify key knowledge, skills, and abilities required by the task, 4) set learning objectives, and 5) design the learning intervention.[12]

When conducting a needs analysis in response to an existing problem of poor performance, it is important to determine if the root cause of the problem is, in fact, a learning need. Sometimes the problem is one of motivation, linked to the nature of the work or to the reward and recognition systems in place. Or the cause may be personality differences or the management style and culture in the organization.

These can be challenging issues to resolve, and, too often, managers would like to classify them as "training problems" as a way of delegating them to human resources, rather than confronting them directly. As we discussed in Chapter One, sometimes performance issues are better addressed through other human resource management strategies, such as changing the mix of employees recruited for a particular position. A process for identifying learning needs from other problems is elaborated in Chapter Ten.

Strategic and Tactical Generative Learning Practices within the Learning Architecture

The content of generative, or creative, learning emerges through "learningful" conversations among participants, conversations characterized by data, thoughtfulness, and the building of composite ideas that are rigorously tested by evidence, surfacing premises, and subsequent action. Such conversations need to focus on learning, simultaneously with working toward a "product," in the form of strategic and tactical ideas. Initially, HRD facilitators can design learning practices into the conversation, but as participants experience the value of these practices, the practices will become part of the group's way of working together.

Learningful conversations that are invaluable because they help surface the unquestioned assumptions managers hold, can be structured around five practices: dialogue, structured rational discourse, reflection, cognitive mapping, and harvesting the learning, and we will describe each in more detail in this section. Listening carefully to others and collaboratively testing assumptions frequently reveals how business decisions are being driven by managers' unquestioned assumptions. Managers often improve both their business results and their personal effectiveness by increasing their awareness of assumptions and testing their validity. Generative learning is essentially a relational process—people learn in open exchange with others, understanding and revising various frames of reference and testing data against them.

Dialogue   The first practice is dialogue. Isaacs defines dialogue as "a discipline of collective thinking and inquiry, a process for transforming the quality of conversation and, in particular, the thinking that lies beneath it."[13] Dialogue has become popular for exploring meaning and for facilitating learning.[14]

Dialogue requires careful, active listening, with the listener thinking not about rebuttal but concentrating on what is being said, considering the whole person who is speaking, and being very conscious of his or her own reactions to what is said. Isaacs refers to this last practice as "listening to your listening."[15] Speakers must be willing to explore the assumptions and structures of thinking inherent in their statements. The purpose of dialogue is not to rush to conclusions or to immediately influence others but to share understandings and assess the validity of the thinking of others in the group, committee, or team. Restraint is made possible by the understanding that everyone will have the opportunity of participating.

Dialogue is especially useful when the participants are situated very differently in the organization, each with his or her own compelling perspective on a situation. It is a way for getting all perspectives or lenses into conversation under the ground rules of listening critically and reflectively. This process, or some close variation to it, is especially valuable when dealing with strategic issues where the need is for generative, or transformative, learning and the group has to arrive at an answer that can only be validated by future experience.

During Grace Cocoa's action-learning program, which we described in Chapter One, reflection and dialogue sessions were held periodically throughout the course of each week, typically as the first activity of the morning. The participants, all members of senior management in the operating companies, and the learning coaches sat in a large circle. For approximately ten minutes the group sat in silent reflection while making notes in their journals in response to a focusing question suggested by the coaches. Typically the question had to do with an experience that had taken place during the previous day or with how the group was progressing as a learning community. Following the reflection period the floor was open for dialogue. Individuals would share their thoughts, often triggering new ideas and reactions in others. The only guideline was that people should focus on listening and not engage in exchanges or debate. This kind of dialogue session was used at the close of each week-long session, pulling together the learning in the group.

Reflection and dialogue sessions have often been part of the action-learning designs used by the author. They are structured to take into account the comfort level of the group—sometimes participants remain around a conference table, rather than in the open circle that symbolizes a learning community but makes some executives very uncomfortable. The goals are to share ideas and perceptions and to build a common understanding of where the members of the group are, relative to the task.

Structured Rational Discourse   Mezirow defines rational discourse as "an effort to set aside bias, prejudice, and personal concerns and to do our best to be open and objective in presenting and assessing reasons and reviewing the evidence and arguments for and against the . . . assertion to arrive at a consensus."[16] Elsewhere Mezirow specifies the conditions for rational discourse as:

- accurate as possible information;
- freedom from coercion;
- openness to alternative perspectives;
- a desire to be critically reflective upon presuppositions and assumptions;
- equal opportunity for participation; and
- willingness to accept informed consensus as a measure of validity.[17]

Creating the conditions for this kind of discourse is not easy. While most managers consider themselves rational, it is very easy for them to become personally invested in an issue, especially when it taps into emotionally laden experiences that may even be outside of his or her conscious awareness. The author remembers an incident when a colleague rushed to the doorway of his office, waving an e-mail message regarding a policy issue and declaring, "I am the only person thinking rationally about this." Setting norms that make explicit how members of a group are going to work together can help foster the conditions for rational discourse, as can using the learning practices described below.

Reflection   We saw how the effective use of dialogue is linked to reflection. Schon describes how professionals use reflection-in-action to resolve the challenges and dilemmas that confront them in practice.[18] Reflection on experience has emerged as an important learning practice for translating experience into learning. It is an important element of dialogue—both as reflection on what others are saying and as reflection on one's own assertions and reactions to what is being said.

Reflection takes many forms.[19] *Process reflection* involves reflecting on how the group as been working and on the methods it has used for arriving at consensus. Process reflection requires that participants critique how they are acting and how they are judging things and people. Using previously established norms of group conduct (as we described above) as criteria for structuring a process reflection is one way that such norms can help sustain conditions for productive rational discourse. *Content reflection* focuses on the content of the decisions, on sensemaking, and on the group's actions. *Premise reflection* involves reflecting on the underlying assumptions that are the basis of the group's assertions and actions. Premise reflection is the interplay between individual reflection and group reflection conducted through dialogue that often produces new meaning.

Short breaks for reflection and dialogue are especially useful when a discussion has become heated or disjointed or appears stuck. Each participant reflects either on what is happening in the meeting or on his or her view of the issue. Then each participant shares that reflection with the group under the rules of dialogue—careful, reflective listening and no immediate response or conversation. Once all the reflections have been heard, the group can summarize them and engage in a practical reflection—what steps might be necessary for them to make progress on the issue at hand, either through reframing the problem, changing their process, or making some other change. This slows the action and gets all viewpoints on the table. Often, conversation evolves into divergence in the thinking among group members (which can in itself be very useful). Reflection and dialogue can begin a process of critical convergence, and cycles of divergence and convergence are germane to the process of generative learning.

One way of structuring a reflection and dialogue process is to ask people to reflect on what is in what Argyris calls their "left-hand column,"[20] that is, what people are thinking but not saying during the meeting. Another way of structuring a reflection and dialogue process is to ask participants to reflect on a statement such as "I think we are assuming . . ." This can foster critical reflection on the underlying assumptions that are driving the discussion. Much of the conversation that takes place in organizations involves inferences and attributions that are either untested or based on partial understanding of the "data" on which the inferences are based. Argyris also describes the "ladder of inference" as a way of challenging others to provide data that supports their attributions, to remind them of the need for recognizing and testing inferences.

■ *The first rung of the ladder* is the actual "data"—what we have experienced—descriptively what we have seen, heard, or read.

■ *The second rung of the ladder* is the meaning we have attached to the data—our inference or interpretation.

■ *The third rung of the ladder* is the attribution we make about what caused or is causing "the data."

■ *The fourth rung of the ladder* is any broader generalization we might make about the situation.

For example, conflicting memos about product strategy (first rung), result in the comment that "there is lack of support for the product" (second rung) because of "politics" (third rung), which is how "things always are around here" (fourth rung). The important questions are: "What assumptions are being made?" and "How can we test them?" People should learn to be aware of others' attributions and inferences and then ask, "What's your data for saying . . . ?"

Asking people to give the basis for their attribution and asking them how they can test it are ways of encouraging them to become more data-based in their decision making and actions, which can also lead to double-loop learning. The learning window we described in Chapter Three is another tool for encouraging reflection on attributions to gain clarity around what people know, what they think they know, and what they know they don't know. The window also helps capture and categorize organizational knowledge.

Cognitive Mapping   Cognitive maps capture a person's "personal construct system" and represent their beliefs, values, and embedded understanding. While there are various ways in which cognitive maps can be produced, essentially they all begin by having participants identify the key elements of some aspect of the task environment, in as much detail as possible.[21] Next, participants group individual components that are similar into second-order categories, for example, components of the cognitive maps of Apple Computer or IBM executives engaged in strategic conversations might include corporations, universities and colleges, schools, and government agencies. A second-order grouping might describe these as customers, or market segments. Other second-order groupings might be competitors, investors, and global economic institutions. Components are placed on the map in clusters, based on their grouping. The dynamics among components are then indicated. Individual maps can be tested by using questions from the learning window and then can be merged into a collective map that represents the group's understanding of their task environment.

Cognitive maps can be generated by HRD practitioners who conduct individual interviews, constructing individual maps during the interview, and then combining these initial individual maps into a collective map, which becomes the basis for a group discussion among those interviewed. During this group discussion, participants alter and add to the map and refine it. Alternatively, the entire process can be facilitated as a group exercise. Computer software can help the group structure and refine their map. Cognitive mapping is a skill that needs to be developed through practice with an experienced facilitator. Box 7.1 provides a general summary of key issues in generating a cognitive map through interviewing, and Figure 7.2 is an example of a cognitive map from the work of Eden and Ackermann.

Cognitive maps place the strategic knowledge and thinking of managers into a visual format for reflection; they are also a tool for helping to build common understanding among members of a group about the dynamics of the strategic issues facing the organization. Cognitive maps make explicit the emergent strategy that both has taken place and is taking place, and they can facilitate new ways of looking at events and issues.

Harvesting the Learning   In their book *Built to Last*, Collins and Porras describe the value of building a learning history.[22] One way of doing this is by maintaining

---

BOX 7.1   Building a Cognitive Map (adapted from Eden and Ackermann)

■ Ask the interviewee to discuss the strategic issues facing the organization:
    "What strategic issues are currently impacting the organization?" or, "What strategic issues do you expect to impact the organization during the next couple of years?"

■ Listen carefully, separating out each issue or factor into one phrase, as in the following statement by an interviewee:
    "We need to set out an *electronic office strategy* using products like *Microsoft Office* so that we can *standardize our software.* ("Electronic office strategy," "Microsoft Office," and "standardizing our software," are all separate points.)

■ Also separate statements where more than one action is implied, as in the following statement by an interviewee:
    "We need to *increase* and *improve* our product range. ("Increasing" and "improving" are separate ideas.)

■ Build a hierarchical means–end chain. For example,
    "Use products like Microsoft Office" so that we can "set out an electronic office strategy."

    Set out an electronic office strategy

    ↑

    Use products like Microsoft Office

■ Periodically confirm the emerging map and encourage elaboration, making comments such as:
    "If I understand correctly . . ."
    "There seems to be a theme in your thinking that . . ."

■ Look for final values or goals (good or bad in their own right), and ask,
    "Why is this an important issue?"

■ Look for key strategic issues (those that are broadbased, costly, and/or often irreversible, and those that take time to accomplish).

■ Develop contrasting (opposite) poles in the map. These are identified from key phrases from interviewees, such as "rather than" and "instead of," as in
    "Sustain grants-in-aid rather than government cuts."

■ Give elements of the map a verb to ensure proper meaning through attributed action, as in
    "*Increase* the level of spending," and "*Examine* the level of staffing."

■ Be sure to identify the desired outcomes (this is also an opportunity for elaboration).

■ More generic issues should be superordinate to the "specific" issues that contribute to them.

FIGURE 7.2   A Cognitive Map

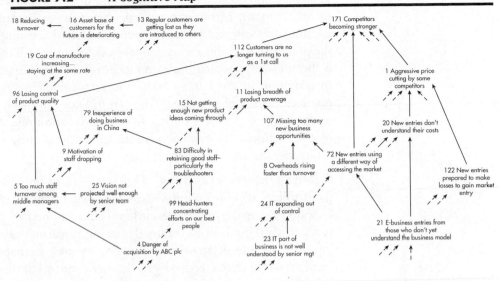
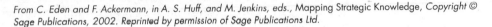

From C. Eden and F. Ackermann, in A. S. Huff, and M. Jenkins, eds., Mapping Strategic Knowledge, Copyright © Sage Publications, 2002. Reprinted by permission of Sage Publications Ltd.

the learning window we described above. Another way is by capturing the reflections of significant events in a learning log or journal. Yet a third way is by having members of a group note the critical events that have occurred over some period of time during a project, writing them on "stick-um" notes and then placing them on a timeline set up on the wall. Once all the notes are in place, the group works its way through the timeline with each person sharing his or her reflections on the event.

Key elements of such an exercise are:

▌ What significant events occurred?

▌ What reflections do you have on the events that have occurred?

▌ What steps do you intend to take in the future based on your experience in the project?

Designing Learning Events That Incorporate the Five Learning Practices

Practices such as the five we have just described assume that people learn while they work on significant organizational challenges that are either strategic or tactical in nature; the line between learning and working is blended. Achieving this blend is itself challenging—task pressures tend to drive out learning as managers seek to work as efficiently as possible. Learning practices must be positioned as facilitating learning that will improve performance going forward, not as ends in themselves.

Incorporating the Five Learning Practices to Design Learning Events   Learning practices can be effectively incorporated into the design of formal learning events in order to both deepen the learning and develop habits of inquiry that go beyond formal content. Introducing practices such as a the ladder of inference and the learning window within the context of a formal learning program can legitimatize the practices by giving learning concrete experience with the practices in a setting that is intentionally focused on learning. Box 7.2 provides an example from a learning intervention in the United States Department of Veterans Affairs. This case also involves transfer of learning on the part of Dan Kowalski, who had been introduced to the learning practices during an extensive action research project funded in part by the National Science Foundation, and subsequently began incorporating them into programs he was designing.

Fostering Informal Learning   One way of positioning learning practices is to subtly introduce them in contexts where they help members of the organization to move forward or to make valuable lessons explicit from their experience as they work. Marsick and Watkins describe informal learning as learning that can take place both during and outside of structured learning events, perhaps intentional or perhaps incidental, but characterized by the learner's control of the learning, which is neither part of any formalized learning objective nor part of a training or education segment.[23] In many settings, such as professional firms and educational institutions, despite required participation in continuing education events, informal learning is the dominant vehicle through which employees develop their professional practices.[24] By positioning themselves to participate in critical conversations and by using learning practices effectively, HRD professionals can introduce what amounts to *facilitated informal learning* into the organization.

Informal and incidental learning can also be facilitated as part of more formal learning events, such as training and education programs. It may appear contradictory to think of harvesting informal and incidental learning from formal learning interventions, yet it is striking how much potential learning is "left on the table" during formal education. Often little effort is expended beyond the formal debrief discussion that reinforces the instructor's intended learning points. Depth and meaning can be added to learning by incorporating learning practices that allow for reflection,

---

BOX 7.2   Incorporating Learning Practices into a Learning Design

I was revising an old lesson plan for an experiential training session on how to deal with employee conduct and performance issues. A client organization had asked me to conduct a four-hour workshop for small groups of supervisors across a multisite health care network. The workshop design included a number of role-play situations in which a supervisor is faced with a highly productive employee who begins to use more sick leave in one quarter than he has used in any previous year. As the role-play situations progress, the supervisor is confronted by this employee whose unscheduled absences are increasing in frequency, and the employee becomes evasive in responding to queries from the supervisor and, at the same time, becomes more and more withdrawn and sullen. In addition, the employee's productivity begins to fall, and other employees begin to talk among themselves of the supervisor's unwillingness to

(continues)

BOX 7.2   Incorporating Learning Practices into a Learning Design [CONTINUED]

address the issue. Finally, the section manager talks to the supervisor about both the declining productivity and the rumors that are circulating about some unspecific problems in the unit.

Generally, the workshop participants who portray the supervisor tend to become more forceful and directive, while those who play the employee become more evasive and deny the impact their absences are having on the work unit. During the final role-play, when anger is generally quite evident in the demeanor of the participants who portray the supervisor, the employee admits to having an untreatable terminal disease. The employee requests complete confidentiality, since he does "not want any pity from the others."

The role-plays are designed to raise a number of important human resource issues:

■ What is the best way to address attendance issues?
■ What policy and contractual issues need to be addressed in this regard?
■ Who can provide assistance to supervisors who are addressing employee issues?
■ How can one balance an employee's privacy concerns with others' perceptions of organizational justice?

For the two years prior to the client's request, I was involved in a large collaborative inquiry project that incorporated a number of learning practices into the reflective action research process. Two practices seemed to offer an opportunity to enrich the course design. The ladder of inference encourages reflection on the personal assumptions that often unconsciously drive action. And the learning window offers a tool to diagnose each role-play.

After I presented an optical illusion as an icebreaker, I introduced the ladder of inference, and I facilitated a discussion about personal filters that are based on our background, education, training, and that often underlie our unconscious assumptions and beliefs.

In the original workshop design, a debriefing session followed each role-play focusing on:

■ What happened?
■ How does the supervisor feel?
■ What could the supervisor have done differently?

With the introduction of the learning window, each role-play debriefing expanded to include:

■ What happened?
■ How does the supervisor feel?
■ What do we know?
■ What do we think we know? How can we be sure?
■ What are the things we do not know?
■ Are there any surprises?
■ What could the supervisor have done differently?

For example, after the second role-play, we know that the employee is using sick leave at a rate exceeding any past period and that the employee does not want to discuss the reasons for this increase. We do not know the reason. During the third role-play, we know that other employees are beginning to talk about the increasing use of sick leave and the employee's declining productivity. In the past, participants began to speculate about the possible reasons for the leave after this role-play. The learning window focuses the participants on what they know, what they think they know, and what they know they don't know; it encourages them to stay low on the ladder of inference; and it stimulates discussion about methods to discover the underlying cause of the change in behavior. The final role-play contains the surprise—news of the terminal illness.

During a reflective evaluation at the end of each session, a number of participants commented that the learning window made them avoid speculating:

"I didn't realize how easy it is to speculate and believe what I made up."

Others commented on how the learning window might be a useful tool in other settings:

"When I talk with an employee about a poor work product, maybe this will help me look at other possible causes—not just assume that the employee was at fault."

"I need to laminate this and carry it in my pocket so I can just pull it out."

Case written by Dan Kowalski, United States Department of Veterans Affairs, 2002.

where learners can make explicit and pool their informal and incidental learning. This is the first step in establishing such practices as a way of learning from experience.

Schon Beechler, Associate Professor and Faculty Director of The Columbia Senior Executive Program, has incorporated several such practices, including devoting a minimum of a half hour at the end of each day for learning groups, where participants engage in this kind of reflective learning practice.

All organizational levels can utilize these opportunities as part of their strategy for embedding learning into the organization's culture—learning that will enhance performance, encourage learning from mistakes, and formalize the lessons learned—both positive and negative—into the organization's continuing process of inquiry.

Action Learning   Alternatively, these practices can be built into formalized programs that explicitly link learning with the resolution of strategic and tactical challenges. One such design that has become widespread is action learning. Action learning has been defined as "an approach to working with and developing people that uses work on an actual project or problem as a way to learn. Participants work in small groups to take action to solve their problem and to learn from that action. Often a learning coach works with the group in order to help the members learn how to balance their work with the learning from that work."[25]

One of the core principles of action learning is that people learn most effectively when they are engaged in activities that are important to them and/or their organization. Another core principle of action learning is that meaningful adult learning is facilitated by the experiential learning cycle (see Chapter Six): having an experience; reflecting on that experience; concluding, or developing a conceptual framework for interpreting that experience; and devising a new action based on this conclusion, which leads to having another experience.[26] One way or another, action-learning programs seek to incorporate these two principles into their design.

There are considerable variations in the ways that action-learning programs are designed. A fundamental design question asks whether the program will be built around group projects or around individual projects. With group designs, a small group (typically five to eight members) work together on a project or issue that is sponsored by a more senior executive. In individual designs, each member of an action learning group (called an "an action learning set" in the action learning literature) brings his or her own challenge or project to the program. Each member of the set is allocated time (called "holding space" in the action learning literature) to discuss his or her project with the other members. The other members of the set ask questions designed to open up the thinking of the space holder around his or her project and the assumptions through which he or she is processing the experience. The group avoids giving advice but, through the use of open questions and other learning practices, such as challenging assumptions, coaches the person holding the space.[27] In both designs, the project or challenge must be one that does not have a possible expert answer. In other words, the problem must be unstructured, meaning it can't be solved through the use of programmed techniques. The solution must be generative in nature.

Other design considerations involve the time and spacing of the meetings that comprise the problem, how the participants are chosen and grouped, and how much formal lecture and other activities are integrated into the program.[28] Increasingly, traditional senior executive programs in companies are integrating executive development classroom designs with action learning projects. Many Executive MBA programs have built in a project component. The success of these integrated efforts at driving learning depends on the extent to which the program operationalizes the two principles identified above—the relevance of the problem to the learning and the design of the learning cycle into the EMBA curriculum.

Additionally, action-learning programs vary in the extent to which they incorporate critical reflection and seek to produce deep learning that challenges organizational norms, learning that is linked to development needs of participants instead of learning that focuses solely on learning that is linked to the business challenge itself. Programs that are designed to foster new thinking—thinking that facilitates major organizational change—are different in many ways from programs that seek to develop capacity for strategic thinking within an existing corporate strategic business model and culture. The Grace Cocoa example we described in Box 1.A (Chapter One) is an example of a program designed to foster a new culture. GE's action-learning programs based out of its Crotonville Executive Development Center are examples of programs designed to develop strategic thinking within the context of a strong existing corporate business culture.[29] Two critical differences separate these two types of programs: the extent to which each uses learning coaches and the extent to which each uses deeply and focused explicit learning practices, such as reflection and dialogue, the ladder of inference, and the learning window.

Work-Based Development   Not all development requires special programs. Challenging work assignments, well–thought-out job rotation programs, and assignments to special task forces are all important ways to develop people. Most executive learning is informal and incidental learning from experience.[30] Here the responsibilities of HRD and broader HRM practices, such as succession planning and talent reviews, coincide. Work-based development is particularly powerful when managers and employees know that senior executives are involved in the process of making assignments, and that they are looking for both development and performance. A. G. Lafley, CEO of Procter and Gamble, devotes most Sunday evenings to meeting with the company's head of human resources and going over the performance of the company's 200 most senior executives. Lafley says about reviewing the performance of one "manager who distinguished himself on one major assignment, but hasn't quite lived up to that since[:] 'We need to get him in a position where we can stretch him.'"[31]

The extent to which such work-based development initiatives become formalized in an organization is a key decision. Coaching has become a popular method for both reinforcing the lessons of experience and producing learning in concert with work itself. From a development standpoint, another way of reinforcing work-based development is to provide managers with tools for working with their people. These kinds of systematic supports can be very effective when they are organized as part of a formal development strategy and supported by senior management and the culture of the organization. The work-experience–based executive development program that Colgate-Palmolive put together, which we described in Chapter One, is an example of a systematic-development approach, centered on development through work and supported by mentoring and coaching systems. The HR executives who organized the program built senior management support and tailored the program to the organization's culture.

The Political Dimension of Generative Learning Events

Creating a safe environment for strategic conversation and innovation is a political act. It needs to be modeled by the most influential and senior members of a group. Accomplishing innovation and change in organizations requires more than the ability to solve technical problems. By definition, strategic questions are more than puzzles; they are unstructured issues, in which the correct answer only becomes known after, rather than before, action is taken. Strategic innovation almost invariability threatens the status quo, and, consequently, organizational innovation is inherently political. This, to a large extent, explains how it is that corporate history is littered with opportunities missed by organizations known for past innovations and populated by very intelligent and experienced problem-solvers who based their opinions on the known science and technology of the day:

> "The telephone has too many shortcomings to be seriously considered as a means of communication." (Western Electric executives, 1876)

> "What the hell is a mouse? You do what with it?" (Xerox executives)

Nor is being in the scientific or engineering community any guarantee of prescience:

> "Heavier than air flying machines are impossible." (Lord Kelvin, President, Royal Society, 1895)

> "Man will never reach the moon regardless of all future scientific advances." (Dr. Lee Forest, "Father of the Television")

Of course these stories, as cute as they are, are instructive in hindsight, and hindsight tends to be 20/20 vision. Not every innovative idea has merit as a valuable strategic product innovation. In fact, many—perhaps most—are just what they seem: interesting, but not feasible. Identifying the winners, while recognizing that following structured technical assessment is likely to let these winners slip away, is at the heart of the innovator's dilemma.[32] It requires the questioning insight we described in Chapter One—what Revans called "Q learning,"[33] which, in turn, often requires the learner to challenge his or her past learning and experience—in effect, to unlearn—in order to reframe a situation to reveal new possibilities and opportunities.

Operational Learning within the Architecture

Many of the methods we have been discussing can be incorporated into operational learning as well. For example, Public Service Electric and Gas in New Jersey used an action-learning design to develop supervisory-level employees as well as managers.

Projects were directed toward resolving operational problems, but required generative thinking, just as in senior-level programs. Additionally, the design emphasized problem-solving tools initially identified in a classroom-based training program in quality management. One motivation for initiating the action-learning program was the lack of transfer on the part of employees in applying the quality tools following the training in quality management.

The quality movement has spurred many learning designs, including problem-solving teams that involve both training components and group or team learning interactions. These activities allow employees to become involved in job design and work process issues, interfacing HRD concerns of individual, team, and organizational learning with various work-engineering and product-design issues.

Beyond these work-based learning activities are classroom-based training programs and e-learning programs, both of which are designed to improve specific skills and competencies. In designing these programs, HRD practitioners look to the various learning methods and techniques available to achieve the intended result. Table 7.3 demonstrates some of the more common links between learning objectives and methods. In practice, there are opportunities for mixing these methods, especially since many programs have more than one type of learning objective. In addition, design involves mixing methods to provide for variety, to maintain learner interest, and to reinforce learning from different perspectives. In addition to the mix of methods, various techniques such as subgroup discussions, open discussion, structured debate, and interactive tests and assessment provide for a more engaging learning experience. However, effective learning often takes the learner outside of his or her comfort zone.

TABLE 7.3   **Learning Objectives, Methods, and Design Considerations**

LEARNING OBJECTIVE	LEARNING METHOD	DESIGN CONSIDERATION
Disseminating information	Lecture with visual aids	Make it interesting by pacing the delivery
	Videos with dramatic vignettes	Make them both entertaining and realistic
Application of information	Practice exercises	Should be realistic, allow time for assessment and feedback
Development of conceptual skill	Case studies	Allow for discussion with feedback
	Business simulations	Should be realistic with debriefing and feedback
Development of interpersonal skill	Combination of lecture, demonstration, and role play	Deliver short lectures, realistic demonstrations, and feedback on role plays
	Experiential exercises	Should be relevant to learning objectives and good debriefing
Physical skills	Simulations or practice	Should have realism
	On-the-job training	Provide proper instruction

The Search for Principles of Design

There are many books on training design that provide menus of methods that can be used for identifying and selecting the components of a training program, seminar, or meeting. Actually selecting from such menus requires combining experience, knowledge of adult learning principles, and understanding of the organizational culture into design decisions. Most of these decisions involve a question of balance among engaging, pacing, challenging, and supporting the learners.

Dainty and Lucas have argued that two critical dimensions of learning design are structure and intensity.[34] Although they present their model in the context of outdoor management development exercises, it has more general application. Beard and McPherson have adapted Dainty and Lucas' dimensions into an interesting framework for thinking about these learning design issues (Table 7.4).[35] The vertical axis measures task structure, which varies from loose to tight. This axis intersects with the horizontal axis, intensity and process reviewing, which varies from low to high to create a four-cell table. Tight structure is required when the skills to be learned are very specific; loose structure is appropriate when the learning task is very broad and less structured. Low process intensity is called for when the learning task involves a very low personal focus, typically on the learning task itself; high intensity is when the learning task calls for significant self- and group-reflection—even critical reflection and feedback.

Some programs are essentially structured within the context of one of the cells. For example, orientation programs or mixers designed to introduce participants to a new product line that is relatively uncomplicated, largely fall into Cell 1. A very specific set of skills, either technical or interpersonal, perhaps spread over time in a distributed learning sequence, would largely fall into Cell 2; developing computer keyboard skills or Web-design skills are examples of programs that might fall into this category. Very broad-based skills, such as negotiation practices, would fall into Cell 3. Critically reflective action-learning programs or assessment centers are examples of programs that fall into Cell 4.

TABLE 7.4   **Design and Sequencing**

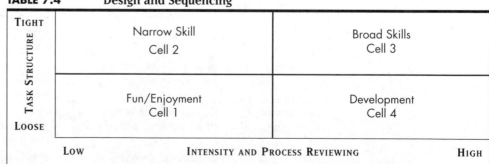

TIGHT	Narrow Skill Cell 2	Broad Skills Cell 3
LOOSE	Fun/Enjoyment Cell 1	Development Cell 4

(Vertical axis: **TASK STRUCTURE**, from **TIGHT** to **LOOSE**)
(Horizontal axis: **LOW** ... **INTENSITY AND PROCESS REVIEWING** ... **HIGH**)

From C. Beard and M. McPherson, "Design and Use of Group-Based Training Methods," in J. P. Wilson, ed., Human Resource Development: Learning and Training for Individuals and Organizations *(London: Kogan Page, 1999), p. 292. Used by permission of the publisher.*

In many cases, development programs will proceed through the cells in sequence. For example, the author taught in an Executive MBA program where the 10-day behavioral science and human resource module began with several experiential ice-breakers that were fun but that also allowed the group to make some relevant observations about group behavior. Much of the subsequent content began with specific sets of skills that were then integrated into broader participatory experiences. As the program progressed, self-reflection and feedback became more personal and focused, building on the trust levels among participants and faculty. In effect, many components of the module cycled through the four cells, with the intensity and overall program cycling through the four cells at a higher level.

Beard and McPherson offer the following design checklist, suggesting that HRD practitioners choose methods that:

- "set the scene and establish climate;
- start from participant levels of skill, knowledge, and attitudes;
- introduce subsidiary essential skills and knowledge;
- allow regular practice after input;
- allow student-directed enquiry and study;
- regularly review the key learning or principles;
- introduce composite/complex skills and knowledge;
- relate/apply the learning to other situations and focus on transfer."[36]

DESIGNING FOR LEARNING TRANSFER

If learning is to add value to the organization, it must translate into improved organizational performance. Performance improvement requires applying what is learned to the work setting—in other words, learning transfer. Facilitating learning transfer has long been the Achilles' heel of HRD. Estimates of wasted training dollars run into the billions of dollars. Transfer is especially problematic in management development because there is "tremendous leeway in what a manager or supervisor needs to know and the contexts in which he or she might apply that knowledge."[37]

Conceptualizing Learning Transfer

The extent to which transfer of learning occurs generally depends on the degree to which the learner outside of a learning program applies changes in knowledge, insight, understanding, meaning, attitudes, competencies, or behaviors. Although this idea is rather straightforward, there are a number of dimensions to the concept of learning transfer. When the purpose of training is to provide the learner with a set of very specific skills, learning transfer means that behaviors or actions learned in the training will be applied in the workplace with little modification. Salomon and Perkins (1989) call this "low road transfer."[38] Examples are computer skills,[39] safety-rule training,[40] legal aspects in company clerical work,[41] and brainstorming and brainwriting for problem solving.[42] In contrast, Salomon and Perkins refer to "high road transfer," where the learner applies a generally known principle to a new situation, and to "forward reaching high road transfer," where "the principle is so well learned . . . as a general principle that it simply suggests itself appropriately on later occasions".[43] Examples include using conflict resolution skills, such as probing for the interests that underlie another person's position or disassociating one's self from the emotion of an encounter. "Backward-reaching high road transfer" has many characteristics of what Butterfield and Nelson conceptualize as "far transfer"—the ability to think and take action in diverse, complex, and uncertain contexts.[44]

Holton and Baldwin build on the notion of transfer distance, describing it as a six-step process: in the first three steps, the learner moves from "knowing that," to know how, to building capability through practice; in the second three steps, involving work-based processes, the learner applies the learning to maintaining and generalizing (far transfer).[45]

Management development and supervisory development programs, in which the intention is the cultivation of cognitive and interpersonal skills, requires high road transfer from the learning event to the job setting. Some customer service training requires this kind of transfer as well. Other forms of supervisory and customer service training, including behaviorally-driven practices designed to keep a conversation on target and away from legal difficulties, want low road transfer. Examples are certain disciplinary conversations in which supervisors learn to use a "broken record" technique to maintain focus on the problem at hand and avoid arguing over difficulties in an employee's life—such as repeating "OK, but what do you need to do in order to get to work on time?" no matter what excuse the employee gives.

The Transfer System

Three streams of research on the factors influencing learning transfer have emerged over the past decade.[46] The first stream focuses on *training design* factors that influence transfer,[47] the second stream focuses on the *organizational context* that impacts learners' abilities to apply what they have learned,[48] and the third research stream focuses on *individual characteristics* that the learner brings to the learning event.[49] Holton and Baldwin have summarized these research streams, adding a temporal dimension to the transfer issue and incorporating them into a model of a *transfer system*,[50] summarized in Figure 7.3.

Holton and Baldwin's model calls attention to the need for incorporating all aspects of the system into the structure of learning events. As a practical matter, some components are easier to influence than others in any given situation. At minimum there can be a concentrated effort toward building visible organizational support, both pre- and post-program. To have impact, this support must go beyond the obligatory introductory talk by a senior manager to include developing a rationale for the training and how it links to organizational performance and future competitive positioning of the organization. An example of this positioning is the Grace

FIGURE 7.3   **Learning Transfer System**

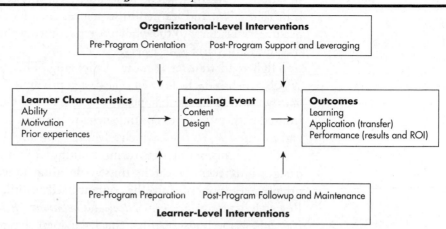

Adapted from E. F. Holton III, and T. T. Baldwin, "Making Transfer Happen: An Action Perspective on Learning Transfer Systems," in E. F. Holton II, T. T. Baldwin, and Sharon S. Naquin, eds., Managing and Changing Learning Transfer Systems: Advances in Developing Human Resources 2 no. 4 (San Francisco: Berrett-Koehler Communications and Academy of Human Resource Development, 2000). Copyright 2000 by Sage Publications. Used by permission of Sage Publications.

Cocoa action-learning program (see Chapter One), which was preceded by a search conference and a culture survey, both of which provided evidence for the need to develop an infrastructure supportive of a strategy of globalization and the executive networks and competencies necessary for supporting the infrastructure. Grace Cocoa's post-program organizational interventions included coaching from line managers on the principles, practices, or skills learned in the program. Post-program assessment is itself a form of organizational post-program support, if the results are used to further reinforce the learning. The concept of a learning system expands the notion of designing learning interventions. The components of the Holton and Baldwin model become conceptual structures for thinking about transfer and for structuring future research.

It is helpful for the HRD practitioner to think of each program he or she conducts as a personal action-learning project providing lessons on how the dynamics of the learning transfer model play out in his or her setting. Answering questions such as "Which learners are the best prepared? How do organizational realities subvert the potential return on investment in the training? What post-program retention strategies work best?" requires thorough program assessment (see Chapter Nine).

Content Design for Transfer

Repetitive practice that simulates the actual job conditions seems to be most effective for developing low road transfer. The goal here is to "embody" the skill or competency in the learner, so that use of the skill becomes a basic response. Where a competency involves a complex sequence of skills that are to be applied in specific situations, "part, then whole" distributed learning designs, in which the competency is broken down and learned in sequence, are effective. Each piece of the sequence becomes subsidiary to the whole. After acquiring the subsidiary skills, practice that integrates the parts is necessary.

High road transfer is more challenging. This requires that general principles as well as behaviors be learned. The design principles applicable here are *stimulus variability*,[51] which holds that positive transfer is enhanced when the learner is confronted with a variety of contingencies to which a general principle is to be applied, and *distributed practice*,[52] which advocates spreading the learning events over time.

These concepts of structuring training content can be useful guideposts for design, but recent research stresses the importance of designing post-program–oriented components into the content itself in order to facilitate learning transfer. Research has examined *goal setting* and *behavior self-management* (relapse prevention training) as methods for enhancing behavioral change following management training programs. In their study of participants in a time management program, Wexley and Baldwin found goal-setting superior to behavior self-management for inducing behavioral change over a two-month period following the training.[53] Gist et al. found a more differentiated effect in their study of the transfer of negotiation skills to novel tasks.[54] In their study, goal-setting trainees used skills more repeatedly than behavioral self-management trainees in novel task situations. Self-management trainees had a higher rate of skill generalization and higher overall performance on the transfer task.

Tziner, Haccoun, and Kadish have identified how both personal and situational characteristics impact learning-transfer strategies.[55] Marx and Burke make the point that it is equally important to prepare learners for transferring their learning through self-management and relapse strategies, and to work to improve the transfer-readiness of the organization by working on the climate, [56] that is, the practices and procedures used in an organization that connote or signal to people what is important. . . . Work units can be characterized by a variety of climates such as a climate for service or a climate for safety."[57] Transfer climate is constituted by how many cues learners receive upon returning from training that support their new skills and knowledge back on the job. Such cues can include reminders from supervisors to use the new skills as well as other influential behaviors from supervisors and peers in support of the learning; the way the work itself is designed; and feedback from others linked to the training—Bates has described the important role managers can play in facilitating learning transfer, including using goal cues to improve transfer and rewards.[58] Marx describes relapse prevention (RP) training as consisting of seven steps: 1) setting a maintenance goal, 2) defining a slip and relapse, 3) explicitly stating the advantages and disadvantages of applying the new skills, 4) learning fourteen specific cognitive and behavioral transfer strategies, 5) predicting the first slip, 6) creating coping skills, and 7) monitoring progress when back on the job.[59]

Burke and Baldwin[60] report on a study by Burke[61] that highlights the importance of the interaction between RP training and transfer climate. Burke's study involved research scientists in a pharmaceutical corporation who were participating in a training program on coaching. The program was conducted six times, with some of the groups getting a full RP module that included all seven steps of the Marx RP framework. This training lasted 75 to 80 minutes. Other groups received a scaled-down RP module, using Marx's steps 4, 5, and 6; this training lasted about an hour. Burke also had a measure of transfer climate. Burke and Baldwin report that the seven-step module was particularly effective in producing transfer outcomes in unsupportive work environments, while the modified RP module produced higher transfer outcomes in supportive climates. They propose that "trainees in favorable transfer climates . . . benefit more from . . . a few simple but useful coping strategies and skills addressing common relapse antecedents. . . . Yet such an elementary arsenal of skills would be insufficient to combat relapse . . . in an unsupportive climate where self-management tools are essential.[63]

Clearly, transfer is a complicated phenomenon. HRD professionals need to carefully assess the potential obstacles to learning-transfer in their own organizations and use a combination of methods to improve the likelihood of effective utilization of learning back on the job. As suggested by the Holton-Baldwin model in Figure 7.3, these methods can include setting the conditions for transfer through careful needs analysis and preparation on the part of both the learner and his or her manager, assessing the climate in the organization, and exploring how to use part of the training time to structure post-program support strategies, some of which might involve follow-up debriefings, coaching linked to 360 feedback results, or other post-program activities. Holton and his colleagues have developed a learning transfer system inventory (LTSI) that can be used for both research and assessment purposes.[64] The product of an ongoing research program, the LTSI is built around a conceptual model with constructs grouped by secondary influences, motivation, environment, outcomes, and ability, providing a comprehensive structure for assessing the factors influencing transfer in a particular organizational setting.

SUMMARY

When designing learning programs and other learning interventions, the HRD professional is engaged in an art that is informed by theory and research. In this sense designing learning events is an exercise is constructing a learning architecture. How much can be accomplished at one time is a function of the extent to which there is a tradition of learning and development in the organization. Regardless, the HRD professional must take into consideration a wide variety of possibilities for designing learning interventions. These possibilities vary; the design may be being work-based or program-based, it may be focused on individual or on collective learning, and it may depend on the degree of structure and intensity of the learning experience. Choosing among these possibilities depends on what kind of learning is intended and on the type of learning-transfer that is required.

A number of specific learning practices can help in both adding depth to the learning experience and beginning to establish habits of learning from experience in the organization. These practices, such as the ladder of inference, the learning window, left-hand column, and reflection and dialogue, are especially useful for making explicit informal and incidental learning. Establishing a context conducive to learning and open discourse is an important part of the HRD professional's responsibility for thinking about learning design. Within these broad considerations, the methods and techniques can be selected and integrated into a learning intervention.

Learning must be applied in the workplace in an effective and sustained manner if there is to be a payoff from the investment in the intervention. Research demonstrates that design of the learning event per se, while important, is only one of the factors impacting on learning transfer. Characteristics of the learning, pre- and post-involvement, and the broader organizational context all significantly impact on learning transfer. Design of learning events needs to take into consideration the learning-transfer system. This requires considering what kind of transfer is necessary for meeting the goals of the program. It also suggests that, when structuring the learning architecture, HRD professionals must consider what organizational-specific factors might inhibit or block transfer.

Questions for Discussion

1. Consider the following topics. Which ones are potentially foundational and which ones are supportive? Assume you are a senior HRD manager. How would you justify your classification, that is, what assumptions are you making?

    Affirmative action training, effective disciplinary action, black-belt certification training, orientation training, work-based learning on our logistics system, pricing strategies

2. What, if anything, would be the value of introducing dialogue and reflection as a regular practice in your class? Why? What would be the impediments to doing so?

3. Select a course from you degree program. Assess its value from a learning design perspective. What changes would you suggest?

4. (For students in the class who currently are or have been employed as professional contributors.) What factors facilitate or inhibit your using what you learn in your degree program in the work world? Are these factors a weakness in your program, or a weakness in your workplace? Explain.

End Notes

1. E. J. Boone, J. Jones, and R.D. Safrit, *Developing Programs in Adult Education: A Conceptual Programming Model,* 2nd ed. (Long Grove, Ill., Waveland Press, 2002); R. S. Caffarella, *Planning Programs for Adult Learners: A Practical Guide for Educators, Trainers, and Staff Developers,* 2nd ed. (San Francisco: Jossey-Bass, 2002); R. M. Cervero, *Planning Responsibly for Adult Education: A Guide to Negotiating Power and Interests* (San Francisco: Jossey-Bass, 1994); M. S. Knowles, *Designs for Adult Learning* (Alexandria, Va.: American Society for Training and Development, 1995).

2. C. Argyris, *Reasoning, Learning and Action* (San Francisco: Jossey-Bass, 1982).

3. E. Cell, *Learning to Learn From Experience* (Albany: State University of New York Press, 1984).

4. J. Mezirow, *Transformative Dimensions of Adult Learning* (San Francisco: Jossey-Bass, 1990).

5. E. Kasl, V. J. Marsick, and K. Dechant, "Teams as Learners: A Research Based Model," *Journal of Applied Behavioral Science,* 33 (1997): 227–46; M. Popper, R. Lipshitz, and V. J. Friedman, "A Multifaceted Model of Organizational Learning," *Journal of Applied Behavioral Science* 38 (2002): 78–98.

6. R. A. Swanson and E. F. Holton, III, *Foundations of Human Resource Development* (San Francisco: Berrett-Koehler, 2001), 210.

7. C. Perrow, *Complex Organizations: A Critical Essay* (Glenview, Ill., Scott Foresman/Addison Wesley, 1979).

8. C. Beard and M. McPherson, "Design and Use of Group-Based Training Methods," in J. P. Wilson, ed., *Human Resource Development: Learning and Training for Individuals and Organizations* (London: Kogan Page, 1999), 285–306.

9. K. N. Wexley and G. P. Latham, *Developing and Training Human Resources in Organizations,* 3rd ed. (Upper Saddle River, N.J.: Pearson Education, Inc., Prentice Hall, 2002), 41.

10. *ibid.,* 42.

11. *ibid.,* 64.

12. *ibid.,* 50.

13. W. N. Isaacs, "Taking Flight: Dialogue, Collective Thinking, and Organization Learning," *Organization Dynamics* 22, 2 (1993): 25.

14. Isaacs, "Taking Flight," 24–39; E. H. Schein, "On Dialogue, Culture, and Organization," *Organization Dynamics,* 22, 2 (1993): 40–51.

15. Schein, "On Dialogue," 35.

16. J. Mezirow, "Transformation Theory of Adult Learning," in M. R. Welton, ed., *In Defense of the Lifeworld* (Albany: State University of New York Press, 1995): 53.

17. Mezirow, *Transformative Dimensions,* 77–8.

18. D. A. Schon, *The Reflective Practitioner: How Professionals Think in Action* (New York: Basic Book, 1983).

19. Mezirow, *Transformative Dimensions.*

20. Argyris, *Reasoning.*

21. C. Eden and F. Ackermann, *Making Strategy: The Journey of Strategic Management* (Thousand Oaks, Calif.: Sage, 1998); A. S. Huff and M. Jenkins, eds., *Mapping Strategic Knowledge* (Thousand Oaks, Calif.: Sage, 2002).

22. J. Collins and J. I. Porres, *Built to Last: Successful Habits of Visionary Companies* (New York: HarperBusiness, 2002).

23. V. J. Marsick and K. Watkins, *Informal and Incidental Learning in the Workplace* (London: Routledge, 1990).

24. V. J. Marsick and M. Volpe, eds., *Informal Learning on the Job. Advances in Developing Human Resources* 1(3) (San Francisco: Berrett-Koehler Communications and Academy of Human Resource Development, 1999).

25. L. Yorks, J. O'Neil, and V. J. Marsick, "Action Learning: Theoretical Bases and Varieties of Practice," in L. Yorks, J. O'Neil, and V. J. Marsick, eds., *Action Learning: Successful Strategies for Individual, Team, and Organizational Development, Advances in Developing Human Resources,* 1(2). (San Francisco: Berrett-Koehler Communications and Academy of Human Resource Development, 1999), 3.

26. D. A. Kolb, *Experiential Learning: Experience as the Source of Learning and Development* (Englewood Cliffs, N.J.: Prentice-Hall, 1984); A. Mumford, *Learning at the Top* (London: McGraw-Hill, 1995).

27. K. Weinstein, *Action Learning: A Journey in Discovery and Development* (New York: HarperCollins, 1995).

28. J. O'Neil and R. L. Dilworth, "Issues in the Design and Implementation of an Action Learning Initiative," in Yorks, O'Neil, and Marsick, eds., *Action Learning*.

29. J. L. Noel and R. Charan, "Leadership Development at GE's Crotonville," *Human Resource Management* 27, (1988): 433–47.

30. M. W. McCall, M. M. Lombardo, and A. M. Morrison, *The Lessons of Experience* (Lexington, Mass.: Lexington Books, 1988).

31. R. Berner, "P & G New and Improved: How A. G. Lafley is Revolutionizing a Bastion of Corporate Conservatism," *Business Week,* 7 July 2003, 52–4.

32. C. M. Christensen, *The Innovator's Dilemma: When New Technologies Cause Great Firms to Fail* (Boston: Harvard Business School Press, 1997).

33. R. Revans, *The Origins and Growth of Action Learning* (London: Chartwell-Bratt, 1982).

34. P. Dainty and D. Lucas, "Clarifying the Confusion: A Practical Framework for Evaluating Outdoor Management Development Programmes for for Managers," *Management Education and Development* 23 (1992): 106–22.

35. Beard and McPherson, "Design and Use," 292.

36. *ibid.,* 293.

37. D. R. Laker, "Dual Dimensionality of Training Transfer," *Human Resource Development Quarterly*, 1 (1990): 219.

38. G. Salomon, and D. N. Perkins, "Rocky Roads to Transfer: Rethinking Mechanisms of a Neglected Phenomenon," *Educational Psychologist,* 24 (1989): 113–42.

39. C. Kontoghiorghes, "Training Trasfer as it Relates to the Instructional System and the Broader Work Environment," in R. J. Torraco, ed., *Academy of Human Resource Development Conference Proceedings* (Baton Rouge, La: Academy of Human Resource Development, 1998): 466–73.

40. R. A Reber and J. A. Wallin, "The Effects of Training, Goal Setting, and Knowledge of Results on Safe Behavior: A Component Analysis," *Academy of Management Journal* 27 (1984): 544–60.

41. E. W. M. Gielen, "Transfer of Training in a Corporate Setting: Testing a Model," in E. Holton, III, ed. *Academy of Human Resource Development Conference Proceedings* (Baton Rouge, La: Academy of Human Resource Development, 1996): 434–41.

42. M. E. Gist, "The Influence of Training Method on Self-Efficacy and Idea Generation Among Managers," *Personnel Psychology* 42 (1989): 787–805.

43. G. Salomon and D. N. Perkins, "Rocky Roads to Transfer: Rethinking Mechanisms of a Neglected Phenomenon," *Educational Psychologist,* 24 (1989): 113–42.

44. E. C. Butterfield and G. D. Nelson, "Theory and Practice of Teaching for Transfer," *Educational Research and Development* 37 (1989): 5-38.

45. E. F. Holton, III, and T. T. Baldwin, "Making Transfer Happen: An Action Perspective on Learning Transfer Systems," in E. F. Holton, III, and T. T. Baldwin, eds., *Learning Transfer in Organizations* (San Francisco: Jossey-Bass, 2003), 3–15.

46. E. F. Holton, III, and T. T. Baldwin, "Making Transfer Happen: An Action Perspective on Learning Transfer Systems," in E. F. Holton, III, T. T. Baldwin, and S. S. Naquin eds., *Managing and Changing Learning Transfer Systems. Advances in Developing Human Resources* 2(4) (San Francisco: Berrett-Koehler Communications and Academy of Human Resource Development, 2000): 1–6.

47. K. Kraiger, E. Salas, and J. A. Cannon-Bowers, "Measuring Knowledge Organization as a Method for Assessing Learning During Training," *Human Factors,* 37 (1995): 804-16; F. G. W. C. Paas, "Training Strategies for Attaining Transfer of Problem-Solving Skill in Statistics: A Cognitive Load Approach," *Journal of Educational Psychology* 84 (1992): 429–34; P. Warr and D. Bunce, "Trainee Characteristics and the Outcomes of Open Learning," *Personnel Psychology,* 48 (1995): 347–75.

48. J. Z. Rouillier and I. L. Goldstein, "The Relationship Between Organizational Transfer Climate and Positive Transfer of Training," *Human Resource Development Quarterly,* 4 (1993): 377–90; J. B. Tracey, S. I. Tannenbaum, and M. J. Kavanaugh, "Applying Trained Skills on the Job: The Importance of the Work Environment," *Journal of Applied Psychology* 64 (1995): 239–52.

49. M. E. Gist, A. G. Bavetta, and C. K. Stevens, "Transfer Training Method: Its Influence on Skill Generalization, Skill Repetition, and Performance Level," *Personnel Psychology* 43 (1990): 501–23; M. G. Gist, C. K. Stevens, and A. G. Bavetta, "Effects of Self-Efficacy and Post-Training Intervention on the Acquisition and Maintenance of Complex Interpersonal Skills," *Personnel Psychology,* 44 (1991): 837–61.

50. E. F. Holton, III, and T. T. Baldwin, "Making Transfer Happen," (2000): 4.

51. H. C. Ellis, *The Transfer of Learning* (New York: McGraw-Hill, 1965).

52. G. E. Briggs and J. C. Naylor, "The Relative Efficiency of Several Training Methods as a Function of Transfer Task Complexity," *Journal of Experimental Psychology,* 56 (1962): 492–500.

53. K. N. Wexley and T. T. Baldwin, "Post-Training Strategies for Facilitating Positive Transfer: An Empirical Exploration," *Academy of Management Journal,* 29 (1986): 503–20.

54. Gist et al., "Transfer Training Method."

55. A. Tziner, R. R. Haccoun, and A. Kadish, "Personal and Situational Characteristics of Transfer of Training Improvement Strategies," *Journal of Occupational Psychology,* 64 (1995): 167–77.

56. R. D. Marx and L. A. Burke, "Transfer is Personal: Equipping Trainees with Self-Management and Relapse Prevention Strategies," in E. F. Holton, III, and T. T. Baldwin eds., *Improving Learning Transfer in Organizations* (San Francisco: Jossey-Bass, 2003): 227–42.

57. J. Z. Rouiller and I. L. Goldstein, *opt, cit.* p. 379. Citing, Schneider

58. R. A. Bates, "Managers as Transfer Agents," in E. F. Holton, III, and T. T. Baldwin, eds., *Learning Transfer in Organizations* (San Francisco: Jossey-Bass, 2003): 243–70.

59. R. D. Marx, "Improving Management Development through Relapse Prevention Strategies," *Journal of Management Development* 5 (1986): 27–40.

60. L. A. Burke and T. T. Baldwin, "Workforce Training Transfer: A Study of the Effect of Relapse Prevention Training and Transfer Climate," *Human Resource Management,* 38 (1999): 227–42.

61. L. A. Burke, "Improving Transfer of Training: A Field Investigation of the Effect of Relapse Prevention and Transfer Climate on Maintenance Outcomes," *Dissertations Abstracts International* 57-04A, Accession no. AAG9627025 (1996): 1725.

62. Burke and Baldwin, "Workforce Training Transfer," 235.

63. *ibid.*

64. E. F. Holton, III, "What's *Really* Wrong: Diagnosis for Learning Transfer System Change," in E. F. Holton, III, and T. T. Baldwin, eds., *Learning Transfer in Organizations* (San Francisco: Jossey-Bass, 2003): 59–79.

This chapter

- provides an introduction to the topic of e-learning;

- presents the definitions and history of distance learning through e-learning;

- proposes a framework for performance through earning;

- discusses benefits and challenges of e-learning;

- addresses the need for e-learning assessment;

- provides examples of e-learning applications; and

- describes future possibilities for e-learning.

Key terms:

asynchronous learning	distributed learning	interactive learning
computer-based training	e-learning	Web-based training
distance learning	facilitated on-line learning	

Web-Based Learning: Distance Learning to E-Learning—From Bland to Blend

BY CAROL GORELICK
PACE UNIVERSITY AND SOLUTIONS FOR
INFORMATION AND MANAGEMENT SERVICES, INC.

Today's business environment of globalization, rapid pace of change, virtual work, emphasis on team work, limited travel budgets, and reduced willingness to travel or spend dedicated time in classrooms means that an effective continuous learning program needs to move beyond traditional classroom training and face-to-face initiatives toward incorporating new pedagogies and delivery platforms for meeting the learning needs of employees. Technology capabilities have increased simultaneously with these challenges, providing viable, cost-effective alternatives to traditional ways of meeting the training and development needs of the organization. While we recognize that technology has not proven to be a panacea and is not able to replace all classroom and other forms of face-to-face learning interventions, it creates many possibilities.

To set the stage with a common language, this chapter begins with definitions and history of distance learning and e-learning. We go on to describe learning technologies, categorizing them by time and place. We integrate short cases with the learning category descriptions to illustrate how the technologies have been applied. We make projections of the e-learning market, and follow with a model that integrates performance and learning, suggesting that learning is a strategic function that can directly impact performance. We discuss issues that should be addressed during an e-learning implementation, and end with a scenario for a future learning environment.

DEFINING E-LEARNING

The phrase "e-learning" conjures up many different images, since students and learners in organizations have had many different kinds of experiences with it, depending on the e-learning formats used by their schools and organizations. Most learners today have participated in some sort of computer or Web-based learning exercise. We start our discussion here by considering various definitions and applications of e-learning and then placing these possibilities within a broader framework of learning technologies.

Definitions of e-learning range from relatively simple applications of technology to highly comprehensive designs that offer an umbrella for education and knowledge creation. Representative examples include

- asynchronous Web-based training (built in HTML or Flash, with little animation and no video or audio);
- real-time Web-based training, where instructors use the Web to extend the reach of the classroom;
- non–real-time Web-based training created in a traditional computer-based training (CBT) authoring system and simply downloaded from the Web so that students take instruction at their leisure;[1]
- the delivery and administration of learning opportunities and support via computer networked and Web-based technology to help individual performance and development;[2] and
- Web-based virtual training that incorporates social interaction and collaborative learning strategies in a self-directed learning environment.[3]

This range of definitions reflects not only the diversity of learning technologies but also the rapid evolution of computer and Web-based technology that is constantly opening up new possibilities for applications. In fact, one challenge of e-learning for organizations is that rapid changes in technology make investment in systems a difficult decision. The definitions we have given also reflect the initial tendency for organizations to simply take information and materials and place them in an electronic format. Effective use of e-learning involves the creative integration of sound learning theory with technology in a way that is both tailored to meet particular learning needs and aligned with HRD theory. To reflect this integration, we define e-learning as *the delivery and administration of learning opportunities and support via computer networked and Web-based technology to help individual performance and development by incorporating social interaction and collaborative learning strategies in a self-directed learning environment.*

A MODEL OF LEARNING TECHNOLOGIES

The term "technology" conjures up images of machines and complex applications of knowledge. However, in sociological terms a technology is any process that provides a method for converting inputs into outputs in the service of some purpose.[4] Essentially, traditional professional and graduate education and corporate training and education are variations of what Thompson describes as an "intensive technology" (one that is designed to affect some change in a person or object; hospitals are one example).[5] The traditional technology employed in learning settings has been the "talking head" at the front of the room, supplemented with some discussion and, perhaps, lab work.

To help us organize our thinking, we can categorize learning technologies using a four-box model (Table 8.1), classifying different technologies according to the dimensions of time and place for learning: same time (synchronous)-different time (asynchronous), and same place-different place. This model makes clear how e-learning is, in some applications, a modification or substitute for a more traditional learning technology and is, in other cases, providing new possibilities. In doing so, the model suggests the pedagogical issues involved in designing a program. We address same time, same place traditional classroom training in this chapter only when it is integrated and blended with electronically delivered distance learning; we will focus primarily on different time, different place electronic delivery tools.

Synchronous: Same Time, Same Place

Electronic meeting support or group decision support systems (GDSS) are meeting rooms equipped with PCs and special software designed to support team activities such as brainstorming, planning, discussions, and decision-making through a voting process. Electronic meeting support sessions are moderated by trained facilitators. Eden and Ackermann provide excellent examples of using this kind of technological arrangement for strategy making.[6] They use computer technology to allow strategy-making groups to engage in real-time cognitive mapping as part of the process of detecting emergent strategy and arriving at strategic intent. Some systems also allow remote (different place) users to participate in the electronic meeting.

TABLE 8.1   **Learning Methods Categorized by Time and Space**

	SAME TIME (SYNCHRONOUS)	DIFFERENT TIME (ASYNCHRONOUS)
Same Place	Traditional classroom Electronic meeting rooms	Learning labs Team rooms
Different Place	Satellite television Chat rooms E-classrooms: audio/video Webcasts	Correspondence courses Computer-based training E-learning Instructor led/facilitated online learning Interactive online learning Web-based training

Adapted from R. Johansen's Four-Box Model, Groupware: Computer Support for Business Teams (The Free Press, 1988).

Synchronous: Same Time, Different Place

Synchronous electronically delivered methods include satellite television, chat rooms, e-classrooms, and audio/video Web conferencing. Satellite television was an early, expensive form of distance learning; it can be used to deliver high-cost expertise. Professors or executives lecture to a large number of students in multiple locations, such as different college campuses or business locations, simultaneously. A large investment in infrastructure and training is required to present material using this medium.

With the broadened acceptance of the Internet, chat rooms have become popular and require a simpler and less-expensive environment. Using the Internet or an Intranet chat room offers the capability for authorized participants to have a conversation by typing interactively on individual PCs simultaneously while at different locations. Training courses have used chat room capabilities to simulate instructor "office hours," for individual conversations, for teamwork, or for an entire class to participate in a case discussion.

E-classroom products are available and used in corporate settings to deliver training. Multiple students in different locations participate using their PCs with an instructor delivering the material and controlling the communication process. Often there is a telephone audio stream, with the text and visual content available through the PC simultaneously. These products require audio and video technologies: telephones, dedicated conference room video equipment, and audio or video feeds delivered through a PC. Students can participate in discussions and ask questions using their PC or a telephone. Tools are incorporated in products that simulate hand raising and that provide white boards for students and instructors to coauthor documents, diagrams, etc. Communication can be public, with the entire class participating, or private, between a student and the instructor. E-classroom products are evolving rapidly and will eventually include video as a standard capability. As of this writing the number of participants in PC videoconferences is limited (ideally, to a maximum of two or three at each location), so it is only viable for a small number of participants.

Webcasts are increasingly used to reach large numbers of people in many locations. Webcasts are an efficient tool for training, education, and knowledge-sharing. VALU (V. A. Learning University), the learning university of the United States Department of Veteran Affairs, uses Webcasts to diffuse learning from various OD initiatives and to meet other information needs. In one such Webcast (called a broadcast) a panel, comprising internal and external people involved in an organizational change effort, took part in a mediated panel discussion, and people in sites around the country could call in and ask questions. Bettina Kelly of Chubb has used Webcasts to economically expose people to business school professors. Her model includes 20 managers who bring their management team to the Webcast. Assuming an average of five or six people per team, around a hundred people (20 managers, plus their teams) can take advantage of the learning at a fraction of what it would cost to assemble the professor and all participants at one place. Participants have certain assignments between the Webcast sessions: the professor describes a process and asks teams to go out and use it. All come back together at a later date, debrief the experience, and get the next process.

The largest Webcast to date was World Jam, IBM's landmark, 72-hour 50,000+ participant event designed to provide a platform where IBM employees could help each other. It was a safe place where all employees could ask for and offer practical solutions to everyday challenges they face as IBMers—whether the challenges were task-related or personally based.[7]

Asynchronous: Same Place, Different Time

Electronically equipped learning labs are examples in this category. A learning lab may be equipped with kiosks or PCs so that individual learners can learn at their own pace. The learning lab is often a central physical resource equipped with expensive or special-purpose equipment or libraries of training materials. Learning labs are commonly used in service centers, such as call centers or factories, where people share workspace and do not have quiet private space.

Team rooms equipped with specialized equipment or materials, e.g., computer aided design equipment for architects or facilities planners are also an example of same place, different time capabilities.

Asynchronous: Different Place, Different Time

There are a variety of asynchronous—different place, different time—learning methodologies (see Table 8.2).

Most recent distance or e-learning literature addresses the asynchronous—different place, different time—category. Items in this category range from low-technology correspondence courses to the most advanced, blended interactive

TABLE 8.2   **Distance Learning Methods**

Category	Delivery Method	Time	Participants
Correspondence Training	Paper, E-mail with attachments	Sequential	Student and instructor
Static ▪ Computer-based training ▪ Web-based training	Floppy disk, CD, DVD, Internet or Intranet	Anytime	Student
Interactive instructor-led; interactive distance learning	Internet or Intranet	Anytime, anyplace, and scheduled sessions	Students, team members, all students, instructor(s), guest speakers
Blended learning	All of the above, integrated with scheduled classroom sessions	Anytime, anyplace, and scheduled sessions	Students, team members, all students, instructor(s), guest speakers

learning. Each method has advantages and disadvantages including cost/benefit, scale, technology availability, development, and implementation requirements.

Interactive distance learning or distributed learning are the most complex forms of e-learning. They are approaches that utilize the computer to facilitate the learning process rather than focus on training for a particular skill. Another label for this kind of learning is "facilitated online learning" emphasizing the role of an instructor as a facilitator in the learning process. Facilitated online learning can include simulations and direct coaching at the individual and team levels. It provides a multimedia vehicle for presenting educational material in a new format.

A BRIEF HISTORY OF THE EVOLUTION OF DISTANCE LEARNING INTO E-LEARNING

Although e-learning and Web-based delivery systems are very much contemporary topics, in a fundamental way their promise is only one point in an evolutionary journey of distance learning. What has really changed is that the technology for delivering learning has progressed to where it can embrace many of the advantages of traditional face-to-face learning systems. Consequently the strategic competitive environment of traditional providers, from universities to consultant firms, has changed. E-learning is an evolving form of traditional distributed or distance learning that has changed the strategic landscape of HRD. Technology can now enhance more traditional modes of learning. A brief history of distance learning, from mail-based correspondence courses through multimedia blended learning, will place e-learning in perspective. Even as e-learning evolves, earlier stops along the journey continue to be used in practice, providing increasing opportunities for mixing learning methods. Each stage we describe ends with a case study example.

From Correspondence Study to Static Computer-Based Training

In seems as if correspondence study, a form of distance education, has been around as long as written language. In the 1800s, correspondence study, since it was conducted through the mail by a school or other qualified institution that kept students and instructors in touch through writing, gained popularity as the postal service became more efficient. Correspondence courses allowed students who were not able to attend classes to receive material from an instructor, prepare a response, and return it to the instructor for feedback and grading.

As media and technology evolved in the 1960s, changes were made to distance education. Instead of relying on the postal system to deliver instructional materials, course information could be delivered via radio and television. Open universities, using multiple media combined with an administrative backbone to support education, began enrolling students.

Since the 1970s computers have been used to deliver training material to individuals using computer-based training (CBT). Initial applications were designed to teach processes and skills related to computer usage within a job function.

Instructional designers created automated workbook material with examples of the screens that a user would use in the process of doing his or her work. Early applications, called "desktop learning," were designed for airline reservation agents and American Express customer service representatives who used online systems. Over time, sophisticated applications of computer-based training were developed for high-volume training. Colgate-Palmolive developed and delivered an advertising course globally to ensure consistency in their corporate message. Holiday Inns developed a simulation to teach managers how to calculate and manage rates for optimum occupancy and revenue. These programs required extensive and expensive development, analogous to making a movie. Interactive elements, high-quality visuals, and assessment capability were all built into the programs. The energy, entertainment, financial services, and pharmaceutical industries were early adopters of computer-based training. Box 8.1 describes one example of a computer-based desktop program.

Enter the Internet

The Web created opportunities to expand desktop learning. In the early 1990s innovative businesses experimented with delivering corporate training, and educators implemented Web-based training (WBT), or distance learning courses. In WBT, as opposed to traditional static CBT delivered through the Web, instructors used the Web to extend the reach of the classroom and the instructors' participation instead of creating material through an authoring system and posting it on the Web for students to download so that they can take the course at their leisure.

BOX 8.1   The Financial World: The Beginning on CD-ROM

Because British Petroleum wanted all professional employees to have basic financial skills, a senior finance person with teaching experience has developed a four-module course. The objective of the first module, called The Financial World—The Beginning, is to get everyone up the skill ladder, to enable them to talk about finance and deal with financial issues. The course developer and several subject-matter experts delivered the training in multiple locations. It quickly became obvious that this small team could not deliver the required volume of training face-to-face. The solution was to videotape the live training sessions and to use the video in a widely distributed computer-based training program that could accommodate different learning styles. Then sections of the live-session video were combined with the related PowerPoint slides on a CD, so a learner could either read the transcript or look at the PowerPoint slides while viewing the video. The viewer could also access frequently asked questions relating to a topic (e.g., debt or equity), while the speaker presented the topic. Occasionally, the video pauses and a message appears:

The video has been paused to allow you to think about your answer to this question:

[A question about the topic appears here.]

Click the play button on the video controller bar when you want to restart the video and hear the audience's replies.

The participant can think about an answer and continue the video when he or she is ready. A quiz, a glossary, and contact details are included on the CD for further learning. The learner can print out, read, or use the text material as a reference at a later time.

In 1992 the New School for Social Research in New York embarked on an innovative program to serve adult students whose geographic locations or lifestyles precluded their attending classes at the university's campus. This program was supported by a Sloan grant and was named Distance Instruction for Adult Learners (DIAL). The program included a mandatory online faculty development workshop and extensive assessments. Students' post-course evaluations and post-course interviews with instructors were primarily positive. These results, similar to classroom evaluations, indicated that student satisfaction depended on instructor skills, commitment, and involvement, as well as the student's level of participation.[8]

As technology has evolved, corporations have become significant players in distance education. As the speed of technology advances and personal computers and Web technologies become abundant, print materials are being replaced by audio/video programs, satellite broadcast, Internet, Intranet, CD-ROM and DVD, all using interactive and prerecorded delivery methods.

By providing instruction via the World-Wide Web or on a CD-ROM/Internet hybrid, even business travelers or students in isolated areas can enjoy interactive virtual classrooms no matter where they are or what time zone they may be in. With the introduction of affordable digital communications and cellular handheld devices, HRD professionals have an abundance of distance learning opportunities to offer anyone, at anytime, anywhere in the world. Newer technologies, like animation and streaming video, combined with other online media provide endless opportunities for instructors to develop training and learning materials.

In the last decade many educational institutions have implemented distance learning programs that range from individual courses to full degree programs. Professional associations (e.g., the American Institute of Certified Public Accountants, AICPA) offer virtual training and grant CEU (continuing education unit) credits. Two examples of electronic distance learning programs, activity-based management and resolving personal issues, are described in Boxes 8.2 and 8.3.

Blended Learning

There is enormous untapped potential in e-learning for transforming an organization's learning and development strategy through blended learning, which combines traditional face-to-face training with electronic delivery. Blended learning includes both traditional instructor-led courses and Internet-enabled tools to create learner-centric education that accelerates performance improvement at all levels.

Creating and implementing a blended learning program is complex and requires a varied skill set. While e-learning typically requires a learning expert partnering with someone with technical systems expertise, sophisticated blended learning programs often require an even more diverse set of skills with competencies in many areas:

▪ Learning strategy—the ability to create a plan that integrates learning design, delivery, and assessment that is aligned with the organizational vision and strategy.

▪ Network integration, or relationship management—the ability to understand all the stakeholders in and contributors to effective learning; develops a team

BOX 8.2   Activity-Based Management—An Interactive Team-Based Training Program

A major accounting firm was moving from cost accounting to activity-based management (ABM) accounting; they designed a distance learning module, using Lotus LearningSpace as the framework for course development, to support their transition. The standard LearningSpace template includes a syllabus, profiles (with pictures of and contact details for all participants), reference material, quizzes, and an interactive discussion forum. The course, *Introduction to Activity-Based Management,* was designed for electronic delivery. Students accessed this basic information when they first logged on to the program:

Introduction to ABM will be offered in a nontraditional way, using a combination of independent study and remote group learning through the Lotus NOTES Learning Network. We expect that it will take three to four hours of your time each week to read the assignment, complete the quiz, and participate in the team exercise. The time can be broken up to work around the demands of your engagement assignments.

Each week's lesson will follow a standard format:

1. Over the weekend, complete the assigned readings for the week.
2. On Monday, complete a quiz on the readings.
3. Monday through Thursday, work in teams to respond to the team project for that week.
4. Thursday evening, submit the project to the instructor.

The course then began with an overview and introduction to the electronic tools and methodology for the course. Students worked in teams using the electronic material over a six-week period. Successful completion of *Introduction to Activity-Based Management* qualified participants for at least 20 CPU credits.

BOX 8.3   Resolving Interpersonal Issues

David Bradford and Allan Cohen created an interactive Web-based program, Resolving Interpersonal Issues, to teach employees basic communication skills. The electronic program has very-high–quality videos and graphics. The vehicle for communicating the content is an engaging story. Interactive models explain concepts, such as transformation or change due to mergers, cultural integration or hypergrowth and retention and recruitment. The program is a standard offering that can be purchased by any organization from a training vendor. The program is available from Ninth House (www.ninthhouse.com.)

of people to design and deliver training programs with diverse content knowledge and skills; the capability of facilitating a vibrant community of practice on the subject of blended learning.

- Project management—having the skills to develop, facilitate, and monitor tasks to implement blended learning programs, and the ability to lead people through influence skills instead of through positional authority.

- Training design—having instructional design skills that integrate learning with performance by creating programs and courses to support individual, team, and organizational learning. For e-learning components, design skills include multimedia delivery and blended learning methodologies.

- Web development—having programming capability, e.g., HTML, to develop interactive electronic courses and tools, e.g., discussion forums and just-in-time learning modules. Computer graphics skills are critical.

HRD professionals implementing complex blended e-learning solutions must be able to manage a diverse team, and it is also important that they be able to address traditional change management issues—the tools, techniques, and processes required to help people move from their current state to their desired state. Process-oriented change models will need to address cultural and human systems, using techniques grounded in behavioral science. This will require attention to managing the people side and the organizational side of the change. To address the people side, the person implementing the change will need to address not only how, when, and how much to communicate about the change within the organization, but also psychological issues related to the transition. The HRD professional should not forget to include him- or herself in the change process, e.g., the HRD professional's transition from performer at the front of the room to online facilitator. On the organizational side of the change, the person implementing the change needs to address the design and structural issues of systemic and long-term change, e.g., rewards and recognition. Examples of successful blended learning programs are Intel's IT Leadership Program (see Box 8.4) and Towards Mastery in Systems Thinking (see Box 8.5).

Box 8.6 provides an example of a blended program at Pace University.

LOOKING AHEAD: BENEFITS, CHALLENGES, AND THE FUTURE OF E-LEARNING

There is no question that e-learning is here to stay, although it is not easy to predict either the extent to which it will be used or the form it will take in the future. The pace and shape of e-learning investments in organizations will be a function of a complex interaction among such factors as its acceptance and use by learners, the possibilities afforded by advances in technology, assessments of its benefits, and the strategic creativity of HRD professionals.

A study conducted in 2001 by ASTD, in collaboration with the MASIE Center revealed that 38 percent of employees polled in seven Fortune 500 companies said they preferred e-learning to classroom experiences; they said that e-learning was faster than classroom training, and they were willing to take additional e-learning

---

BOX 8.4   The Intel IT Leadership Forum

Intel needed to create a forum to accelerate the training of IT leaders. Because Intel is a fast-paced, global company, optimizing training resources, i.e., time and money, was a goal, and to meet this goal, they developed a blended learning program. Since IT is woven into everyone's work life at Intel, it was natural that they develop an IT solution. The course was designed as 66 hours, with three full-day instructor-led sessions and seven half-day virtual (teleconference) sessions, with self-directed homework, small group work, and online asynchronous discussions; each group posted the results of their discussions for the other participants to see. According to Cal Stevens of Intel, "the results at Kirkpatrick level 1 are terrific. The participants themselves say they are learning level 2 (actually learn something). They are in the process of assessing levels 3 and 4, anticipating positive results."

BOX 8.5   Towards Mastery in Systems Thinking

A facilitated online program with a face-to-face component was developed to build mastery in sytems thinking. The program designers were subject-matter experts, aware that students needed coaching and support to become proficient in using systems-thinking techniques after they had attended a face-to-face basic concepts workshop. A three-month blended learning program began with a one-day face-to-face session, for both a practical orientation and the establishment of face-to-face contact among participants. The remainder of the course was conducted online, with each participant allocating a minimum of three to four hours per week.

The program was designed to answer these questions: How do we become skilled in any discipline? How do we become skilled enough to call ourselves competent, proficient, or expert? How do we become skilled enough to use tools and concepts with relative ease, even in challenging and difficult moments?

The program, which mixed learning and application with work on real projects, included

- applications to real-life issues;
- regular practice;
- access to excellent coaching; and
- dialogue with peers who were trying to build the same skills.

Participants were asked to bring their current issues into the program and to take the program elements into their work. The program used online technologies to connect the group of participants weekly (or more often) over a significant period of time, so that "learning" and "doing" were combined in a continuing rhythm to create an optimum combination for increasing capability and mastery.

(Towards Mastery in Systems Thinking was originally developed for British Petroleum by the chapter author, Linda

courses in the future.[9] That same study also looked at how 16 companies (15 of which were also in the Fortune 500) attract learners to mandatory and voluntary e-learning courses. The study found that learners are drawn to courses that blend e-learning with other forms of instruction and courses where they can learn away from their busy desks. This supports the idea of blended learning designs and also points to the tradeoff in providing learning at an employee's desk or work area: it allows for flexibility of access, but can also be fraught with distractions. There are also problems with employee's completing e-learning programs. Especially compared to traditional courses, the noncompletion rate is very high.[10]

A KPMG survey of e-learning implementations in 12 leading global organizations concluded e-learning costs are reported to be 70 percent lower than costs for traditional classroom teaching, and this could rise to 80 percent as the use of e-learning matures.[11] According to The Fletcher Report, which compared multimedia training and equivalent classroom instruction, 30 percent time savings can be achieved by using multimedia training.[12] Other studies suggest employees who participate in multimedia training receive more information in the time spent learning and retain it longer. The average content retention rate for an instructor-led class is 58 percent, whereas e-learning enhances retention by 25 to 60 percent.[13] Currently e-learning is considered excellent for knowledge transfer and procedural training but not for interpersonal skills (e.g., negotiation, sales training, and leadership skills)—skills that require a shared dialogue for comprehension and application. What is required are assessments that are more comprehensive, that look at user satisfaction; at impact, in terms of various kinds of learning; at application; at impact on performance; and

BOX 8.6   Pace University's Interdisciplinary Blended e.MBA Program

Responding to business and student requests for an MBA program for experienced managers and professionals who cannot attend a traditional day or evening program, Pace University designed and offers a problem-centered, team-based blended learning program.

The design principles included: a multi-disciplinary curriculum, balanced theory and practice, contemporary issues, innovative learning model, and a high level of instructional technology.

The program begins with an eight-day residency when students are introduced to the program's six faculty members and the format for the two-year program. The cohort (cycle) of students and faculty work together for the entire program doing nine projects. A faculty member with functional expertise directs each project.

Every 12 weeks the students and faculty meet on campus from Friday through Sunday for a residency. Each residency begins on Friday when the student teams present the results of their project work to a panel of industry experts and the faculty. This is followed by a debrief and celebratory dinner. On Saturday morning the students take an exam related to the academic topic for the project, e.g., operations, marketing, strategy, managerial accounting, organizational behavior. After lunch the project director for the next academic subject introduces the next project. The students are assigned to teams and given a short assignment related to the topic. Each student team has a faculty member as a facilitator. On Sunday the students meet in their assigned teams to create a work plan for the 12 weeks they will devote to this project. Work tasks are distributed and decisions made on how the team members will work together: phone meeting schedules, use of electronic discussion boards, and file-sharing capabilities.

During the 12 weeks between residencies, student teams work online with faculty guidance. Students read related material from assigned textbooks and articles. To respond to the problem or case presented by the project director, students do research on the topic and apply their learning to a specific company or industry. In addition, students do individual learning exercises and contribute to online discussions.

At the first residency the students are introduced to the process through an ungraded orientation project. This is followed by eight interdisciplinary, complex projects. The ninth 12-week period is a capstone simulation as well as an individual student project that is relevant in a work environment (action learning). Students choose, design, and complete the project with one or more faculty members as advisors. The projects are presented at the last residency, followed by graduation.

The program's goal is to provide students with an enhanced ability to transfer learning to their work settings. Students and faculty report applied learning through this integrated (multidiscipline and blended learning technologies), collaborative team learning environment.

at cost-effectiveness—the same kind of comprehensive assessment that is increasingly being asked of other forms of HRD interventions (Chapter Nine).

Despite the hype, e-learning is not a quick fix. Although there are a plethora of suppliers of technology and content, the elements of a complete solution for a complex learning need are often unclear. HRD professionals lack the necessary skills to define requirements for the delivery infrastructure and to assess the current infrastructure, including connectivity limitations; consequently, the e-learning marketplace is vendor-driven. Yet, vendors are not able to support large-scale deployment. Instructors typically lack skills to develop content in the new medium, yet most content needs to be tailored to the organization rather than purchased from catalogs. In fact, experts see custom work becoming more dominant.[14]

Despite these challenges, the projections are for e-learning investments to grow. In 2001 ASTD's State of the Industry Report stated that companies planned to spend between 1.8 and 3.5 percent of their payroll on training and segmented training budgets. Table 8.3 shows an almost 10 percent increase in learning technologies, implying that there is a great opportunity for HRD professionals to positively influence strategy and to develop and implement effective technology enhanced learning programs. A 2001 IDC study concluded, "Corporate E-learning is one of the fastest-growing sectors within the education markets. Since the late 1990's it has grown from a cottage industry to a market with a predicted global value of more than US $23 billion by 2004."[15]

Future Possibilities for E-Learning

Interactive distance learning can combine individual learning with knowledge creation at the individual, team, and organizational levels. HRD professionals are well-positioned to participate in initiatives that have a direct impact on business results. The building blocks are in place for a blended, multimedia learning program. A blended leadership program could be developed using all the components described in this chapter (see Box 8.7).

Is This Realistic Now?

David Bradford, Senior Lecturer in Organizational Behavior, Graduate School of Business at Stanford University describes what he sees as the benefits of e-learning:

> I think that interactive e-learning will determine the future of education—if I were 20 years younger, this is where I would devote my career because it has the promise of revolutionizing—and democratizing—the learning process. I saw a great potential in this medium as we (Allan Cohen and myself) were developing our "Resolving Interpersonal Issues" program. Both of us are excellent teachers, but what I realized is that interactive, computer based instruction has the potential of doing a better job than we could even if we were working directly with students. The technology isn't quite there yet, but it is right over the horizon.
>
> What e-learning can provide (which we can't):
>
> 1. Personalized Learning—Different people have different learning styles. For example, some are inductive and others deductive. It will be possible for a program to reconfigure itself to fit the learner's style.

TABLE 8.3   **Learning Delivery Methods, 1999 and 2002**

Category	1999	Projected 2002
Instructor-led	79.9%	67.5%
Via learning technologies	8.4%	18.2%
Other self-paced sources	8.0%	9.7%
Other	3.7%	4.6%

Data by IDC. Cortona Consulting, a firm that tracks the e-learning market, estimates the e-learning section of the training market to be $50 billion in revenue by the year 2010. E-Marketer, another firm that tracks the e-learning market, estimates that the percentage of training time provided by e-learning in 2004 will be 25 percent, based on studies by ASTD.

BOX 8.7   Blended Learning Leadership Forum Scenario

You are enrolled in a leadership forum that begins with a two-day workshop with 30 senior executives. The program is primarily a social gathering for the entire group to meet, agree on objectives, and form teams. Within the first two days, attendees begin to work in groups, setting up electronic discussion catgories. Each individual goes back to his or her workplace with individual skills and behavior-improvement tasks as well as with an action-research project for his or her group.

For the next six weeks, everyone works on skills and behavior improvement. To accommodate their learning style, people can choose tools from available products, such as self-paced CD-ROM or Web-based training, facilitated online learning with an expert facilitator, multimedia just-in-time learning modules, and help desk learning support 24 hours a day, 7 days a week. Participants simultaneously use electronic team space, video conferencing, and simulations to complete the team project, which is a real business problem. Participants are encouraged to access resources, to learn before and during the project. The-learning specialist assigned to the group is available to provide content and process support when it is requested.

After six weeks, there is a two-day face-to-face meeting for individual and group status updates, coach-ing, and development of new task plans. A significant amount of time during the two days is devoted to socializing.

Individual and team efforts continue at the participant's locations for six additional weeks. The program ends with a two-day event that includes team presentations and retrospects of individual and team performance and culminates in a ritual that is attended by each participant's boss as well as others that have attended the program. The program graduates are invited into the vibrant and growing community of practice comprised of program alumni with discussion boards facilitated by an instructor. Individuals and groups contribute to the electronic knowledge-base that is available for both reference and additional learning by participating in formal "lessons learned" discussion, reflecting on their experience in the training program.

The learnings from the participants are available for HRD professionals to review and take action on. They can change the program and/or provide constructive feedback to participants, based on the results. Participants individually assess the success of the program using criteria they previously defined with the program facilitator and his or her manager before the program began.

That is not something that an instructor can do with a class of 10 or more students.

2. Multiple teaching approaches—Our interactive program has the authors explaining the concepts ("talking heads"), a demonstration/illustration of the concepts, a "story line," which is an entertaining "sitcom" that shows the concepts in actions; "problem-sets" to solve, etc. This is much more variety than even the most creative instructor can provide.

3. Resequencing the material—With our program, the learner can decide what to see first and what later. Do they want a discussion of the concepts? And maybe half-way through they want to see an illustration or try their hand at applying the material to the problem-set. And there is always the "help file" they can turn to if they are confused about a concept. They aren't bound by the instructor's sequence.

4. Learning at one's pace—Some students need more time to assimilate material than others. With e-learning, they can go at their own pace rather than being locked into the classroom hour.

5. Checking on progress—While an instructor could rely on weekly quizzes to see how the students are doing (a cumbersome, annoying process for all), there is now the ability to see how each of the students is performing in real time. Thus help can be given to those who are falling behind before it's too late.[16]

Bradford predicts major changes in education and training methodology; the question is, How long will it take? David, in a conversation with the author, said,

> I would guess that 60 to 80% of what is taught at the university level [and in organizations] can be better taught through e-learning once the technology has been fully developed. This doesn't mean that education will consist of four years in front of a monitor with no student-to-student or student-to-teacher interaction. E-learning can easily lead itself to small self-directed student learning teams. Also, there are things that only a human instructor can do—namely, complex problem-solving. That will be more challenging for the instructor (and few present faculty can do that well—especially since it will require cross-discipline knowledge rather than focusing on our narrow discipline), but for those who can, it will make teaching much more exciting. I think we have seen the future and it is almost here. It will be challenging because it will totally change education and training from grade school through at least the Master's level and training at all levels. Faculty and trainers who don't embrace e-learning will be left behind.[17]

SUMMARY

E-learning comes in many forms, synchronous and asynchronous, noninteractive and interactive, Internet and Intranet, to name but a few. While e-learning and Web-based instruction are the subjects of considerable hype, they are in some ways a technological extension of traditional learning contexts. E-learning also holds great potential for pedagogical designs that are not possible through traditional methods. Among e-learning's benefits are significant cost reductions in delivery, the capacity for reaching a wider audience of learners, and, as many learners report, efficiencies in terms of time spent and retention of material. Still, significant challenges remain, many of which are linked to the need for HRD professionals to develop new competencies relevant to the design and delivery of this kind of learning. There are also technical and social/cultural infrastructure challenges in organizations when new forms of e-learning are introduced.

Questions for Discussion

1. Have you experienced an e-learning training or education program? How valuable was it for you? How do you compare the experience to a classroom program?

2. What knowledge or skills do you believe should be offered as e-learning programs? Are there any subjects that should *not* be delivered electronically or that must be delivered face-to-face in a classroom?

3. If you were asked to develop an e-learning strategy for a company or a department, what would you do? What kind of program do you envision?

4. Think of a learning issue that you are familiar with. You are asked to be the project manager in creating an e-learning solution. Describe the team you would assemble—What skills would people have?

5. If you wanted to become an e-learning specialist within your organization with a goal of designing, implementing, and facilitating e-learning programs, what skills would you acquire? How would you acquire the skills?

End Notes

1. S. Imel, *Web-Based Training Trends and Issues Alerts* (Washington, D. C.: Office of Educational Research and Improvement, 1997).

2. E. Pollard and U. J. Hillage, *Exploring E Learning* (Institute for Employment Studies Sussex England: Sussex University, 2001).

3. Design Strategies for Developing Web-based Training," *International Journal of Educational Technology* 1, No. 1 (1999): 17–21.

4. C. Perrow, *Organizational Analysis: A Sociological View* (Belmont, Calif.: Wadsworth, 1970).

5. J. Thompson, *Organizations in Action* (New York: McGraw-Hill, 1967).

6. C. Eden and F. Ackermann, *Making Strategy: The Journey of Strategic Management* (Thousand Oaks, Calif.: Sage).

7. C. Halverson, J. Newswanger, T. Erickson, T. Wolf, W. A. Kellogg, M. Laff, and P. Malkin, *World Jam: Supporting Talk among 50,000+* (IBM–Social Computing Group paper, 2001).

8. M. F. McCabe, *Online Classrooms: Case Studies of Computer Conferencing in Higher Education* (Unpublished dissertation, Columbia Teachers College, New York, N.Y., 1997).

9. ASTD and The Massie Center, *The Learning Technology Acceptance Study: If We Build It Will They Come?* (Alexandria, Va.: American Society for Training and Development, 2001).

10. E-Learning Brain Trust, *Learning Circuits: ASTD's Online Magazine All About E-Learning* (Alexandria, Va.: American Society for Training and Development, 2003).

11. KPMG Consulting, United Kingdom, a commissioned study "Earning Through Learning: Global Lessons in E-learning" (October, 2001).

12. The Fletcher Report, "Return on Investment and Multimedia Training," *New Media Magazine* (March 11, 1997) cited in KPMG study.

13. W. R. Hambrecht and company, *Corporate E-Learning: Exploring a New Frontier* (March, 2000).

14. E-Learning Brain Trust, *Learning Circuits.*

15. IDC, *Worldwide Corporate E-learning Market Forecast and Analysis 1999–2004,* (February, 2001).

16. D. Bradford, personal e-mail communication, 06/26/02.

17. *ibid.*

This chapter

- provides an introduction to the concept of evaluation;

- presents a model of a comprehensive assessment system;

- presents Kirkpatrick's four-step evaluation taxonomy;

- discusses the positive contributions of Kirkpatrick taxonomy to HRD practice;

- provides a review of critiques and a summary research on the Kirkpatrick taxonomy;

- presents proposed extensions to the Kirkpatrick taxonomy;

- provides an introduction to return-on-investment (ROI) analysis and approaches to costing, converting results into monetary benefits, and isolating the effects of training;

- discusses the Holton evaluation research and measurement model for assessing and researching learning outcomes;

- reviews the inquiry approach to evaluation as the integration of assessment with overall program design and performance; and

- summarizes other approaches to learning assessment.

Key terms:

formative evaluation	costs	confidence estimate
summative evaluation	benefits	isolation factor
Kirkpatrick four-step or four-level taxonomy (Level 1, Level 2, Level 3, and Level 4: assessment, reaction, application, and results)	ROI (return-on-investment)	adjusted improvement value
	estimated value of performance improvement	evaluation model
		evaluative inquiry

Assessing the Effectiveness
of HRD Interventions

If human resource development is to become part of the business, or livelihood, equation of an organization, HRD professionals need to hold themselves accountable for the results they achieve. As support and staff functions come under rising pressure to demonstrate their value-added contributions to the organization, HRD professionals are being challenged to take a more strategic perspective and be business partners in their organization.

Throughout the preceding chapters we have emphasized HRD's role in bringing about learning and change to enhance performance. This role requires HRD to have an impact at both the individual and the organizational level and HRD professionals to collaborate with key operating managers in assessing the impact of HRD interventions. Historically, trainers have invested their energies on the development and delivery of programs and on tracking both attendance and participant satisfaction. Building alliances with senior management requires linking learning interventions to strategy and evaluating their impact across the strategic and operational value chain. How well an HRD program or intervention can measure its impact determines in large part its success in sustaining its viability in the organization. Dilworth, McClernon, and Redding cite a 1997 Conference Board report that named aligning training with business strategy and meeting top management's expectations as the most pressing priorities of

HR and HRD executives.[1] To accomplish these priorities, Dilworth et al. advise both conducting ROI (return-on-investment) analysis of learning programs in order to demonstrate financial returns, and working with senior managers to develop a value-chain analysis in order to identify which HRD factors are directly related to business performance. As organizations find themselves under intensifying pressure to perform, the evaluation or assessment of HRD initiatives take on an imperative beyond justifying the HRD budget, and it becomes increasingly important for HRD professionals to deliver solid analysis that shows which programs and interventions provide real value for the strategic direction of the organization. HRD professionals must become proficient in conducting assessments of their learning interventions. Our discussion of assessing HRD interventions is situated in this context.

In this chapter we use the terms "assessment" and "evaluation" interchangeably to refer to processes of appraising the impact and results of HRD interventions. "Evaluation" is the traditional term and is widely used in the literature. Swanson and Holton explicitly use assessment *as opposed to* evaluation, *pointing out that evaluation is seldom, if ever, found in management books. "Evaluation," they argue, conjures up images of the "schoolhouse" and "grading."[2] The author views assessment as an integrated and continuing process, beginning with a needs analysis. The needs analysis determines the viability of a learning intervention and shapes program content, and then provides the basis for appraising the intervention at critical points, both during its delivery and following its conclusion. This process view is based on the belief that while program development does progress through phases, it should be conceptualized as an integrated and organic process that begins and ends its cycles of delivery linked to the needs of the larger organization, with assessment an integral part of all phases of the cycle. In this chapter we focus on the appraisal phase of this process, on assessing (or evaluating) program impact to providing accountability on the part of the HRD function. Practitioners should use the term for this activity that holds currency and has a clearly understood meaning in their organization.*

⟨6⟩

FRAMING THE ASSESSMENT DISCUSSION

Formal definitions of evaluation vary. Scriven offered one of the first, defining it as "the process of determining the merit, worth, or value of something. . . . the evaluation process normally involves some identification of relevant standards . . . [and] some investigation of the performance . . . on these standards."[3] Phillips (1997) mirrors Scriven's definition, describing evaluation as "a systematic process to determine the worth, value, or meaning of an activity."[4] Boulmetis and Dutwin define evaluation as the "process of collecting and analyzing data in order to determine whether and to what degree objectives have been or are being achieved, for the purpose of informing decisions about the program's efficiency, effectiveness or impact."[5] Patton balances the focus on outcomes with the idea of formative evaluation, defining evaluation as "the systematic collection of information about the activities, characteristics and outcomes of programs to make judgments about the program, improve program effectiveness, and/or inform decisions about future programs."[6] Preskill and Torres take a highly systemic and holistic approach, bringing the organizational learning function of evaluation to the forefront of the process. They define evaluation as "an approach to learning that is fully integrated with an organization's work practices, and as such, it engenders (a) organization members' interest and ability in exploring critical issues using evaluation logic, (b) organization members' involvement in evaluative processes, and (c) the personal and professional growth of individuals within the organization."[7] All of these definitions assume that an evaluation of learning interventions involves assessment against some set of expected outcomes and that the evaluation provides a basis either for making judgments about the value of the program for the organization or for improving the program. These assumptions are embedded in Preskill and Torres' definition, which views evaluation as a highly participative form of inquiry through which the relevant stakeholders as a group define the assessment criteria and interpret the data that is gathered, as opposed to evaluation determined by an external expert. For our purposes the important point is that comprehensive assessment requires a multidimensional approach to evaluation that includes the learning design, the total transfer system, their impact on the learners, the learner's performance, and value added to the organization as a whole.

Much early work on assessment has been framed to focus on improving program design and delivery instead of on the effect of the program and its impact on the organization. When program improvement is the focus of evaluation, assessment can take place throughout the learning event. Scriven has distinguished between *formative* and *summative* evaluation.[8] A formative evaluation is carried out while a program is in process in order to obtain data that permit design changes and other adjustment while the program progresses. It is a feed-forward assessment, allowing for improvement before the conclusion of the program. Summative evaluation is post- or end-of-process assessment, providing feedback on the program's effectiveness after it has been delivered and contributing to adjustments in the next cycle of program delivery. Summative evaluation can also include assessment of the program's impact on the organization. A comprehensive summative evaluation will include all levels of what Kirkpatrick describes as the four levels of evaluation: 1) participant reactions, 2) learning, 3) application, and 4) results. Although numerous approaches to evaluation have been advocated over the years, Kirkpatrick's four-level evaluation model is by far the most widely recognized in the training and development community.[9] We will discuss Kirkpatrick's model in detail below.

While important, simply focusing on summative evaluation is inadequate for meeting the needs of an organization. Rossi, Freeman, and Lipsey categorize evaluations in terms of four general purposes.[10] *Needs assessments* identify the gap between the current and desired states, and the results of needs assessments help establish the goals for a learning intervention. *Impact evaluations* determine whether the program is providing the intended business or organizational benefits and compare outcomes or results against original goals. *Process evaluations*, which are conducted during the program, provide information that is used to redesign or improve the program. *Cost-effectiveness evaluations* study the relationship between cost and outcomes in monetary terms. Needs assessments provide the data that inform the design of the program and link it to the performance needs of the organization. They also provide benchmark measures and indicators that can be used for comparisons in impact and cost-effectiveness evaluations. Process evaluations are formative and provide crucial information to help key decision-makers modify or improve programs, and in so doing they can influence the program outcome. Conversely, impact evaluations and cost-effectiveness studies are summative evaluations and are intended to provide information about the impact and/or value of the program relative to its intended purpose.

Figure 9.1 incorporates these key concepts from the evaluation literature to a comprehensive assessment system. The model suggests the complexity of the relationships between a learning event and its core outcome elements; the reader should keep this complexity in mind for the remainder of the chapter.

Whether the assessment system is applied at the strategic, tactical, or operational level of performance, it begins with a needs analysis that informs program design with expectations that the learning program will lead to improved or enhanced performance at the individual and organizational levels. For this to occur, positive results need to take place all along what can be described as a core learning value

FIGURE 9.1   Comprehensive Assessment System for the Core-Learning Value Chain

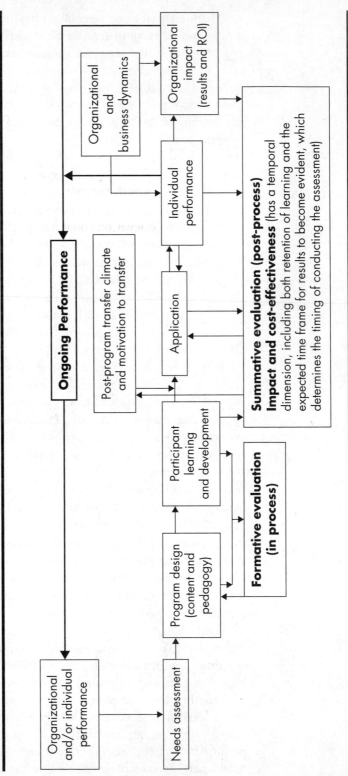

chain: program design produces learning, learning is applied, and its application impacts individual and organization performance; the basic outcome variables defined by Kirkpatrick. During the program, formative evaluation assesses how well both the design seems to unfold and the learning that takes place can lead to opportunities for adjusting the program. Summative evaluation can assess the learning, application, and performance impacts, as well as its cost-effectiveness, providing accountability and informing future delivery of the learning program. Summative evaluation can also become the basis for continuing learning if it is used as a basis for dialogue with learners about their experience in applying their learning. Additionally, summative evaluation should provide feedback into the larger organizational system regarding both the existing transfer climate and opportunities for post-program reinforcement and support. The extent to which this potential is realized depends on the level of collaboration between HRD and management and the climate of evaluative inquiry they have created. Such comprehensive assessment is also time consuming and needs to be targeted toward high-priority learning interventions.

The relationship between Kirkpatrick's learning evaluation levels, while logically antecedent to one another, is neither totally causal nor necessarily linear. As we discussed in Chapter Seven, whether or not learning is applied is a function of the transfer climate in the organization and the motivation of participants to change their behavior or to apply what they have learned. Just as program design should incorporate or take into account the transfer climate, motivational factors must be included in any comprehensive assessment,[11] and can be done systematically through a climate survey or, less obstructively, through follow-up interviews or conversations with learners. As we will discuss in more detail later in this chapter, Alliger and Janak suggest that results can reinforce and perhaps even strengthen the application of learning.[12] Finally, changes in the organization or in the broader business environment may produce large effects in performance. For example, an unanticipated warm winter negatively impacted the performance of store managers in a retail clothing chain. It was impossible to factor out the precise drop in sales attributable to the weather, but comparisons with performance of previous warm winters along with regional managers' observations of the merchandise presentation and store operations led to a consensus that a training program had contributed to more professional behavior from store management.

Two caveats must be mentioned relative to the assessment system model (Figure 9.1). The first is that not every learning program can be expected to directly impact individual and organizational performance. As an example, suppose the organization wishes to develop high-potential staff in order to increase the pool of candidates available for promotion into higher levels of management. In this case, the desired outcome is demonstrated learning and development that could be systematically assessed through a formalized process or through follow-up coaching and assessment by senior management (Figure 9.2).

The second caveat is that the comprehensive system we are describing here is rational, is based on the literature, and is an ideal that HRD professionals working

FIGURE 9.2　　**Assessment System for a Development Program**

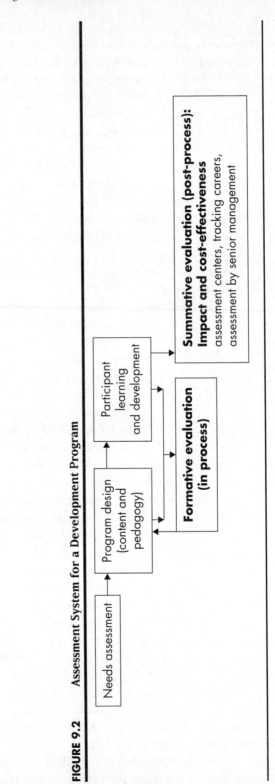

at the strategic level of the organization should strive toward. However, in the world of practice, demand for training and other learning often presents itself in an *ad hoc* fashion, driven by an immediate perceived need. In this situation there is little time for a comprehensive needs analysis, but it is still wise for an HRD professional to vet the request in order to determine whether or not the perceived need can be satisfied by a learning intervention or whether it is either a symptom of a problem with some other aspect of the organization or an HR system problem (issues that we will develop further in Chapter Ten).

For example, at least twice a year, the author is asked to conduct workshops on performance appraisal. When potential clients are asked why the workshops are needed, the answer is often "Because our managers are not doing performance appraisals effectively." It doesn't take long to determine that the problem isn't that managers don't know how to do performance reviews—they have participated in performance management and appraisal training and education programs many times. The real issue is that managers are not motivated to do performance reviews because a) such reviews are often difficult, and b) management doesn't value performance evaluations. As one line manager said "As long as you make your budget you are okay, and no one was ever turned down for promotion around here because they didn't do thorough performance reviews." While the workshop would be lucrative and relatively easy for the trainer (since most attendees, if pressed, could probably run the workshop themselves), it would help neither the participants nor the organization.

Strategically driven HRD requires a comprehensive approach to assessment that is integral to both program development and administration processes. The approach should link, as much as possible, the various kinds of evaluations identified by Rossi et al. into a comprehensive process that not only captures the contribution of the HRD function but also integrates routine evaluations into the organization's approach to learning. This requires that HRD build alliances with operating management to collaborate on identifying the links between strategic drivers of the organization and its learning needs. Galbraith, Sisco, and Guglielmino discuss how effective development of learning programs in organizations use "a collaborative approach which simultaneously taps and develops human resources, both within the organizational system and in relation to other parts of the system."[13] Beginning at the strategic level of the organization, this perspective ascribes to HRD the role of both working to identify needs and outcome indicators that will be valued by operational management and striving to educate them to better comprehend how targeted learning will add value to the organization.

The HR Balanced Scorecard

Reframing training and development into a HRD function whose domain extends beyond the classroom into the workplace to embrace organizational learning has raised more complex questions of accountability beyond program evaluation. Assessment of HRD activities has become more closely intertwined with the wider accountability of the HR function in general. As HR has come under increasing pressure to justify its claims of partnership in the business, various methods for assessing the contributions of HR to the strategic direction of business have been advanced. Linking their work to the balanced scorecard approach of Kaplan and Norton,[14] Becker, Huselid, and Ulrich have advanced the concept of the human resources scorecard, which ties HR initiatives to organizational strategy.[15] High-performance strategically aligned HR systems and processes need to support the behaviors required by the strategic goals of the organization. Learning and growth indicators, such as measures of strategically focused competencies and motivation, are often prerequisites to advances in the other leading indicators of the scorecard—business processes and customer satisfaction.

For example, in the late 1990s a national health care provider, reacting to a trend line of rising costs and slowing growth along with declining customer satisfaction, made a major strategic shift. Improving service and clinical quality were key elements in its strategic plan. This required changed attitudes and a new emphasis on patient service competencies throughout the organization. Action teams were created in selected sites; in a coordinated effort, they helped to refine surveys and develop performance measures. They revised reward and recognition systems and put new organizational communication processes in place. These teams also targeted staff development needs and recommended learning interventions, in the form of workshops that particularly focused on coaching skills for supervisors and clinical directors. Surveys surfaced interpersonal issues linked to both supervisory behavior and peer-to-peer interactions that in turn impacted on service quality and patient satisfaction. Prior to initiating the workshops, the teams fed the data gathered from the surveys back to the employees in their respective sites, soliciting input and interpretative reactions.

Two years later HR measures of overall employee satisfaction, of satisfaction with rewards and communication, and of high-performing work systems all demonstrated improvement, as did measures of service and clinical quality, such as improved waiting times. Initially, cost measures rose, as a function of increased investment in these initiatives, and patient levels continued to decline. However, a year later, profits improved as costs began dropping and, while staffing levels remained constant, patient levels began to grow, reflecting the organization's improving reputation in the marketplace. This is an example HR enablers linked to leading indicators preceding improvement in financial performance, which is a lagging indicator.

Each firm needs to determine the HR enablers that link to leading indicators driving performance. In general, core HR enablers center on recruitment policies and criteria, on support for competencies that are pivotal in supporting the organization's implementation of strategy, and on performance management systems. When enablers in these areas are misaligned, they hinder or defeat strategy. Becker et al. cite the example of a commercial bank that made a strategic shift from service to sales—but whose training programs still focused on service—while it continued to emphasize service-oriented competencies in recruiting and hiring staff and failed to make changes in its performance appraisal and reward systems. Dilworth et al., in their *What Works* report for ASTD, and Donald Kirkpatrick[16] all point out that in companies that have adopted the balanced scorecard approach, developing HR-related measures for the scorecard and using these measures as part of the assessment of HRD initiatives is an effective way of establishing the value of HRD.

OUTCOME ASSESSMENT ACROSS THE CORE-LEARNING VALUE CHAIN

Human capital theory has become a more pronounced influence in HR theory as academics and practitioners strive to find ways to cost human resources and measure the ROI of managing their employees as resources.[17] This work builds on earlier efforts by HR scholars toward constructing accounting measures to capture the value of an organization's human resources.

The focus of the two most widely known models practitioners use to evaluate learning programs are both outcome driven: the Kirkpatrick four-level model of program evaluation and the work of Jack Phillips on measuring ROI. We will examine these models in some detail, both because they provide a foundational framework for any assessment process and because we need to be aware of their limitations. We will also examine more systems-oriented models of assessment.

Outcome Assessment 1: The Four-Level Kirkpatrick Taxonomy of Program Evaluation

Kirkpatrick first advanced his four-step taxonomy of program evaluation in the late 1950s. It has since become common to refer to the steps as "levels." The four levels of the Kirkpatrick framework are

1. participant reaction—measuring participants' satisfaction with the program as well as their stated intentions to take future actions based on what they have learned;

2. participant learning—measuring participants' changes in skills, knowledge, or attitudes;

3. application of participants' learning on the job—measuring changes in participants' behavior or application of practices transferred from the program back to the job setting; and

4. results—measuring the impact of changes resulting from learning in the program in terms of specific organizational results.

Kirkpatrick's framework has several advantages that support its popularity with practitioners. First, the framework is straightforward and easy to understand. Second, it highlights the limitations of program evaluations that are completed by participants immediately at the close of a program (often cynically referred to by trainers as "smile sheets") for assessing the results of a training event. Third—and this is often overlooked—Kirkpatrick opens up thinking about what really constitutes learning and about facilitating learning transfer as an important aspect of the trainer's role.

Fourth, the framework highlights learning as a potential driver of performance. In addition to its widespread acceptance by practitioners, Kirkpatrick's taxonomy has stimulated research in the field of industrial and organizational psychology.[18] The four-level framework also provides the foundation for Jack Phillips,[19] the work of one of the most influential scholar/practitioners in developing approaches for return-on-investment studies in training and development.

Challenges of Putting the Kirkpatrick Framework into Practice

Implementing Kirkpatrick's framework in practice has proven to be very challenging. As one progresses through the four steps, measurement becomes increasingly difficult. Measuring participant reactions is relatively straightforward, although even here in Level 1 the problems of obtaining valid results are often overlooked. Most trainers ask participants to complete brief questionnaires immediately at the conclusion of a program, because once participants leave the program, obtaining responses is difficult; eager to leave the training setting, either to catch up on work that has become backlogged while they were in the training session or because of travel arrangements, participants are likely to give the questions only cursory attention. One advantage of Web-based learning is that learners can more easily align their participation in the training with their work schedules, making it easier for them to complete electronic reaction forms. Even so, participants often view taking the time to complete reaction questions as an inconvenience. The instrument usually relies on numerical scales and includes a request for written comments. Given that participants all have different criteria and standards for ranking, and that the learning groups vary in size, the mean numerical values obtained may not reveal very useful information. The written comments often carry more meaning, although these are often very brief and general. Usually reaction questionnaires, or "smile sheets," are most informative when reaction to the program is at one of two extremes—the reaction indicates a significant problem in the program or the reaction is extraordinarily positive. In both cases, the results generally support what the program coordinator already knows. Participant reaction is most productively gathered during the program, through sensitive observation, through opportunistic conversations with participants, using the emerging data as formative evaluation and, to the extent possible, by adjusting the program as it unfolds.

There has been an important downside to the widespread use of Level 1 assessment. When Dixon evaluated the relationship between trainee responses on reaction instruments and post-test scores, she found that high reaction scores did not correlate highly with actual learning;[20] and she found this to be especially true when the questions on the reaction instrument focused on whether the session was engaging and interesting. The point is not that learning events should not engage participants, but that the reaction sheets reflect training directors' deeper focus on keeping training "fun" in order to minimize resistance to their function. Davis and Davis have labeled this tendency "enter-train-ment."[21] This dynamic has led to the equivalent of a "ratings war" in the training industry. Too often the focus is on what sells rather than what learners need to learn in order to add value to the organization and to their careers. This tendency is especially strong where development directors put forth a wide menu of program offerings and only those programs with repeated high ratings survive. Effective use of participant reactions requires linking them to effective learning strategies for the learning needs at hand.

Level 2, assessment of participant learning, presents challenges that vary according to the kind of learning that is intended by the program. If the intended learning involves job skills training or knowledge acquisition, then the assessment can be integrated into the design of the program through practice exercises. Case analysis and concept tests that are also used for discussion can be part of the evaluation process. More challenging assessments involve learning objectives that involve interpersonal and managerial skills that require competencies beyond mimicking specific behaviors, that draw instead from a set of skills and match their application to various situational contingencies (which we described as situation learning in Chapter Six). Well-constructed role-plays and simulations can provide a basis for assessing how well participants have learned the fundamentals, but only if the instructional staff closely monitors the role-play exercises; often not feasible, given staffing constraints.

Level 2 assessment is more easily built into Web-based programs which require the learner to take tests or make choices in order to progress through the program. Tests are more appropriate in programs where the learning is essentially informational in nature; however, cognitive recognition of behavior choices can also be made part of Web-based learning. The author helped design a supervisory program for an aircraft manufacturing firm that was changing to cellar manufacturing (that is, all the steps in manufacturing a particular product would be done in a self-contained cell rather than moving inventory throughout a large manufacturing site organized on a functional basis). The change would reduce inventory costs by millions of dollars but would also require supervisors to interface with teams of workers. A number of scenarios were presented in video format, followed by possible choices; depending on which choice the participant selected, the next video sequence would play out a different unfolding scenario. The videos were interspersed with instructional commentary. While the design allowed learning to be tracked by recognizing behavioral cues, it didn't assess the participants' abilities to actually execute the behavioral choices that they made in the program when confronted with the same situation in the work setting. A similar Web-based program design for managers that focused on costing decisions, however, was more closely linked to the job setting, since the skills involved were analytical and the problems were workplace-based.

One advantage of building Level 2 evaluation into the design of a program is clear, however. The more a Level 2 assessment is integrated into the learning design itself, the more valuable the assessment is for both the learner and the HRD practitioner, because it provides feedback for the learner and formative assessment for the HRD practitioner. The Level 2 assessment becomes a source of outcome and process evaluation as the facilitator overseeing the program explores the program design factors that are influencing the level of learning taking place.

Senior executive education that covers diverse topics provides an even more compelling challenge for Level 2 assessment. Participants are typically facing a range of issues in their jobs. Their learning, therefore, has more to do with awareness and changes in thinking about the challenges that confront them than it does with specific models or techniques—the intended learning is highly complex situation learning and learning that will further their cognitive development. Assessing such learning requires conversing with the participants to explore how they are shifting their thinking, how they are triggering new ideas, and how they are reframing certain issues. This typically demands structuring reflective learning discussions during the learning event and even structuring post-event interviews.

For Level 3 assessment to be truly valuable, it must go beyond determining how or what learning is being applied and give consideration to what factors are inhibiting or facilitating the transfer of learning. As we stated, one limitation of the Kirkpatrick model is that it assumes that the organizational climate supports the application of the learning back in the job setting.[22] The transfer-of-learning literature demonstrates that the design of the learning event is only one factor influencing the application of learning back on the job (see Chapter Seven). While factors other than program design and delivery undoubtedly influence learning transfer, their effects vary depending what is being learned. These factors include

▪ available opportunities for application;

▪ supervisory styles and support back in the workplace;

▪ incentive and reward systems impacting behavior; and

▪ peer pressure.

How much application occurs clearly relates to the value an organization receives for its investment in training. However, if application of the learning has been identified as crucial to performance improvement and that application is not occurring, part of the value added by HRD is determining what interventions will facilitate transfer. This, of course, runs counter to any notion of training and education as a quick fix for performance problems. Many managers don't want to hear that changes in the work setting are necessary in order for the organization to benefit from learning. This also makes explicit that determining whether or not learning has been applied by the learner is insufficient for understanding the effectiveness of a learning program. The reasons why transfer is or is not occurring must be understood as well.

Assessing application involves a higher level of effort than Levels 1 and 2 because, by definition, it requires that HRD staff extend their involvement beyond the boundaries of a traditionally defined learning event and continue to track their participants' application of their learning. This adds to the demands placed on HRD departments; such demands may stretch the HRD budget. These costs may be bearable, however, if the number of learning programs is targeted to the strategic performance needs of the organization or if Level 3 assessment is limited to high-priority programs.

Like Level 2 assessment, Level 3 evaluation can be designed into the learning process. Follow-up can be part of the learning design if the event is phased, or if subsequent assessment on the part of others, such as supervisors, is built into the program. Follow-up interviews can be conducted with participants who are being coached by HRD staff or consultants. If the overall assessment is conceptualized as a form of evaluative inquiry with all stakeholders agreeing on the strategic or operational importance of a learning program as well as agreeing on the importance of the assessment process that measures the program's effectiveness, Level 3 evaluation can be an exercise in organizational learning, focusing on the learning and development indicators in a balanced scorecard approach and identifying the blocks to effective application of learning back on the job.

Level 4 evaluation requires tracking actual changes in performance results. This is easiest when relevant performance matrixes are specifically tracked within the organization. However, regardless of the measures available there remains the question as to how to isolate the effects of training from other influences on organizational results, some of which can be quite serendipitous. Here the HRD professional requires competencies in quasi-experimental design.

Phillips suggests control groups and trend analysis as two experimental designs that can isolate the effects of the learning intervention from other factors that might be influencing results.[23] Control groups subject to the same general market and business pressures but not involved in the learning event are one way of isolating the effects of a learning event. A matching design would have to be employed if learners come from various units throughout the organization. While a matching design is not as strong as randomly assigning people to experimental and control groups, it is the strongest practical method in most organization situations. Extrapolating a trend line from past business results is an alternative in the absence of such comparison groups. Both control groups and trend analysis designs assume reliable, valid, and uncomplicated measures of performance. In conducting these assessments HRD professionals should be familiar with the general validity threats to such designs.

When the learning focuses on developing very complex and general behaviors such as leadership, simply tracking the changes in participant behavior and decision-making along with performance indicators may be the best way to judge how the learning impacts performance. A consistent track record of participants demonstrating behavior and performance changes can be sufficient for assessing the value of the program. The financial leadership program at AT&T targets new hires into the finance function at the corporation. It is a rotational program that over a period of two years links job changes with periodic course work. In the performance evaluation process, managers assess the changes in analysts' performance as analysts handle cases upon return from the periodic learning events. This part of the assessment is linked to the learning agenda using feedback from peers and managers for both further development of participants and evaluation of the program's effectiveness. A 360 feedback process also includes technical application feedback from peers and managers. This program, designed to develop "bench strength" in the finance function, enjoys the wide support of officers, which enables these kinds of linkages.

Recent studies have attempted to assess the extent to which practitioners in various settings use the Kirkpatrick model.[24] After a thorough review of the available research, Swanson and Holton conclude that, overall, "(1) many organizations use Levels 1 and 2 evaluation for at least some programs, (2) fewer than half the organizations even try Level 4, and (3) only a small percentage of programs receive Level 3 and 4 evaluation."[25] The reasons for this relatively low level of assessment are clear from our discussion and are well known to most HRD professionals; they include high logistical costs and other expenses associated with conducting thorough assessment, difficultly in obtaining responses from participants once they leave the program, political pressures, and the challenges of measuring both learning and results. A comprehensive 4-level assessment is only feasible when learning interventions focus on strategic and operational imperatives and have the support of key organizational stakeholders in management. Building this support, which sees assessment as a process of inquiry into necessary development toward strategic success, is a critical responsibility of HRD executives and staff.

Assessing the Structure of the Kirkpatrick Framework

The Kirkpatrick model has become the standard-bearer for much of the work that practitioners have done around training evaluation. As such, the framework has been the subject of scholarly critique and assessment. Although the need for modifications, extensions, and even alternative models is recognized by HRD scholars, the widespread influence of the framework in both the practitioner and academic communities make it the point of departure for theorizing and research about evaluation criteria.[26]

Alliger and Janak observe that which level of evaluation is most informative depends on the purposes of the learning event and the kind of learning it facilitates. Not every learning event is intended to impact all four levels. In some cases, for example, training is limited to company history or to information about general topics. Such training may be most appropriately evaluated at Level 2, through knowledge acquisition; no changes in behavior or performance indicators are expected. In building "bench strength" at the executive level, the most informative assessment might be enhanced readiness for promotion, not changes in current performance.

Positive reactions may not be associated with learning. Alliger and Janak cite research in educational settings that has found negative a correlation between reaction and learning; that humorous lectures, while liked better by students, do not generate more learning,[27] findings that further reinforce skepticism of the "enter-train-ment" phenomena. Often significant learning requires that learners be put outside their comfort zone; learning is not always a pleasant experience, especially developmental learning, which is often stressful. Yorks, O'Neil, and Marsick, discussing various kinds of action-learning programs, note that programs that challenge the assumptions and premises of participants often produce "noise," initial negative responses from participants as they wrestle with the uncomfortable feeling of critically reflecting on their experience.[28]

That reaction scores may not be good predictors of learning doesn't necessarily mean that they are an unimportant consideration, only that the relationship between reaction scores and learning should not be taken for granted. Further, knowing how participants are reacting to various aspects of the program is of obvious value to a program director and to facilitators.

Despite a common tendency for practitioners to treat the Kirkpatrick levels as hierarchical (as reflected in the level numbers), the relationship among the various levels is potentially complicated and neither linear nor causal. Alliger and Janak argue that behavior changes may be reinforced by results. "In a reverse causality, Level 4, results, should be important to the maintenance of Level 3, behavior, since people will tend to continue behaviors that are perceived to be effective. That is, feedback sustains the behavior-results link."[29] Their point has implications for the interpretation of evaluation data. For example, behavior changes that are not sustained may be a function of the lack of interactivity with results, either real or perceived. Figure 9.3 illustrates the distinction between the causality in the hierarchical model and the alternative suggested by Alliger and Janak.

Alliger et al. conducted a meta-analysis of the relationships among the levels suggested by the Kirkpatrick model using available studies that explored correlations among the evaluation criteria. In carrying out their analysis they augmented Kirkpatrick's taxonomy by making several analytical distinctions within each level, creating constructs that were "less coarse, while maintaining a broad enough framework to facilitate a generalized understanding of training evaluation results."[30] At Level 1, Alliger et al. distinguished between reactions as affect (Level 1a), reactions as utility judgments (Level 1b), and combined reactions (Level 1c). Level 2 was refined as immediate post-training knowledge (Level 2a), knowledge retention (Level 2b), and behavioral demonstration in the training setting (Level 2c). Behavior that is retained and applied in the

FIGURE 9.3   The Traditional Hierarchical and Alternative Models of Causality Among Kirkpatrick's Four Levels of Training Criteria

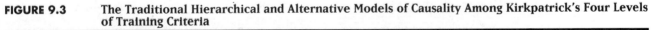

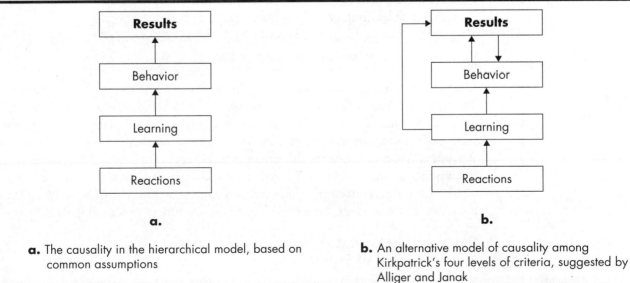

a. The causality in the hierarchical model, based on common assumptions

b. An alternative model of causality among Kirkpatrick's four levels of criteria, suggested by Alliger and Janak

Adapted from G. M. Alliger and E. A. Janak, "Kirkpatrick's Levels of Training Criteria: Thirty Years Later," Personnel Psychology 42 (1989): pp. 331–41. Used by permission of Personnel Psychology, Inc.

workplace was considered transfer (Level 3). They found only three studies providing correlations at Level 4, so they did not include that level in their meta-analysis.

In their analysis, Alliger et al. found that the correlation between affective reactions and immediate learning was almost zero. Utility reactions (Level 2b) were correlated more highly than affective reactions with both immediate learning and on-the-job performance. Although affective reactions are potentially important to the HRD function (negative reactions that are not managed or explained can have an adverse effect), liking does not equate to either learning *or* performing. Utility questions on a questionnaire are a better predictor of these criteria.

Somewhat surprising to the researchers, utility measures had higher correlations with on-the-job performance than did measures of either immediate or retained learning. This may reflect the fact that learners are very familiar with their work context, and this influences how they answer utility questions. By a similar logic, learning may or may not result in learning transfer to the job depending on how favorably the work environment allows demonstrations of new behaviors.[31] As a very senior regional manager from Singapore who was participating in a critical action-learning program reported in an interview to Yorks, "You shouldn't judge how much I learned from what I do later. I have changed a lot inside in how I view things. It may not show in how I choose to act at work," [32] referring to the political context in which she was currently working.

The implications of the theorizing and review of the empirical literature by Alliger and his colleagues point to the need for not oversimplifying the relationships between levels of the Kirkpatrick framework but for thinking carefully about

∎ what kind of evaluation is appropriate for the objectives of the program;

∎ what impact intervening variables, such as learner motivation and the context into which learning is being applied, have on the results obtained; and

∎ avoiding simplistic notions about the superiority of certain levels of data as indicating the value of the learning event.

In a particular situation the interactions among the levels of the model may be more important than the particular outcome measures themselves. Measures of outcomes are indicators of issues for a more in-depth investigation that takes the larger learning architecture of the program into account and treats the assessment process as feedback into the system. We conceptualized this earlier in this chapter as a core learning value chain linking the various components together; the chain itself is part of a more comprehensive learning architecture, which includes contextual factors that research links to the transfer process (see Chapter Six) and to the assessment process (Figure 9.1).

Outcome Assessment 2: Return-on-Investment as a Fifth Level of Evaluation

Rossi et al. distinguish between impact evaluation, which can include improvement in financial results as well as other measures such as behavior changes, reduced turnover, improved job satisfaction indexes and the like, and cost effectiveness evaluation.[33] Perhaps as much as anyone else's work, that of Jack Phillips is familiar to HRD professionals seeking methods of calculating return-on-investment (ROI) in training and performance improvement programs.[34] Phillips positions ROI as a fifth level, building on the previous four levels of the Kirkpatrick framework, that examines results in relationship to investment the same way that earnings-on-capital invested is assessed.

In Phillips' formulation, ROI is calculated as net program benefits divided by program costs × 100. As a formula:

$$ROI(\%) = \text{Net Program Benefits/Program Costs} \times 100$$

The ROI calculation builds on the definitions of results expected on Level 4 of the Kirkpatrick framework. Figure 9.4 illustrates a data collection plan and an ROI analysis plan for a management development program. This figure illustrates the connection between collecting data for a Kirkpatrick Level 4 evaluation and collecting data for an ROI analysis.

Conducting an ROI analysis is not a simple process. However, thinking in terms of demonstrating a credible ROI analysis can lead to better rigor in evaluation practices, even if computing ROI does not prove feasible in particular circumstances. Figure 9.5 presents the Phillips model of the ROI process.

FIGURE 9.4   Data Collection Plan

PROGRAM: _____   RESPONSIBILITY: _____

DATE: _____

EVALUATION PLAN: DATA COLLECTION FOR AN ROI ANALYSIS

LEVEL	OBJECTIVE(S)	EVALUATION METHOD	TIMING	RESPONSIBILITIES
1. Reaction, Satisfaction and Planned Actions	▪ Positive reactions ▪ Completed action plans	▪ Reaction questionnaire	During and at the end of program	Facilitator
2. Learning	▪ Knowledge of motivation models ▪ Knowledge of leadership models ▪ Use of performance feedback skills	▪ Skill practice ▪ Tests	During program	Facilitator
3. Job Application	▪ Use of skills ▪ Monthly goal setting	▪ Questionnaire ▪ Action plan ▪ Follow-up session	Four months after program	Training coordinator
4. Business Results	▪ Improved productivity, quality, turnover, and absenteeism	▪ Performance monitoring ▪ Action plan	Monthly	▪ Routine reports ▪ Training coordinator

From J. J. Phillips, Return on Investment in Training and Performance Improvement Programs (Houston, Tex.: Gulf, 1997) p. 112. Reprinted with permission from Elsevier.

FIGURE 9.5   **Phillips ROI Model**

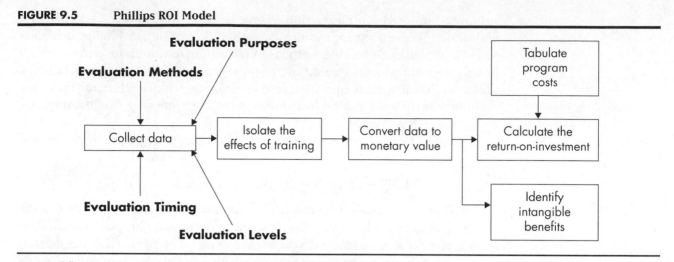

From J. J. Phillips, Return on Investment in Training and Performance Improvement Programs (Houston, Tex.: Gulf, 1997) p. 25. Reprinted with permission from Elsevier.

Key Issues in Conducting an ROI Analysis

Figure 9.5 highlights a number of thorny issues that need to be resolved in order to conduct an ROI analysis of a program or learning intervention. Some issues, such as isolating the impact of the learning event from other contextual factors that influence results measures are common to a Level 4 assessment. Other issues are specific to the ROI analysis: determining program costs and converting results data into monetary benefits. In resolving these ROI issues the best rule of thumb is to always use the most credible and conservative data sources. Also, it is critical to involve management in developing the ROI process since management's judgment about the analysis will determine its credibility. HRD directors embarking on an ROI analysis should view it as a process of organizational learning about the return on the investment the organization is making to execute its strategy, rather than as a campaign for justifying the HRD budget. If the ROI analysis is assessing initiatives that are making a meaningful contribution, the budget argument will be strengthened. However, keeping mind the logic of the balanced scorecard, the value of a particular program can be in enabling other drivers of strategy. Thus, the ROI analysis must be viewed in the context of total contributions to performance.

Costing the Program   In costing the program, prorated costs must be distinguished from direct costs. One-time costs associated with the development of the program are prorated over the anticipated life of the program. For example, if it is anticipated that a program or learning intervention will be conducted three times over the course of a year and it is estimated that the life cycle of the program will be three years before it will require significant updating or revision, then design costs can be prorated by dividing the design costs by nine (three times a year times three years). Overhead costs associated with the design phase can be estimated as total over-head divided by the total number of participant days over the life of the program. A similar logic can be used for any acquisition costs, such as identifying an outside consultant or facilitators and costs associated with ROI assessment. This is because once an ROI analysis has been completed on the initial pilot or pilots, it is not cost effective to continually conduct the analysis every time the program is run. Also, needs analysis costs must be included in the ROI calculation and also must be pro-rated. Part of the needs analysis should be the determination of the measures that will assess learning transfer and results, since these measures will provide a foundation for translating program results into monetary benefits.

Direct costs associated with each individual program are generally calculated as part of the cost of the specific program session being assessed. These include costs associated with delivery, such as facilitators, materials, travel, facilities, and participant salaries and benefits.

This approach is a conservative one, placing costs in traditional accounting categories, and not what Becker et al. refer to as economic-based ROI assessment:

> Fixed costs are economically relevant only if we have to spend money directly on them or if they incur an opportunity cost elsewhere in the organization. . . . [S]uppose your firm wants to determine the ROI of a new training program for midlevel executives. The firm currently owns an executive education center, which is generally booked at 60 percent of capacity. The program you propose will increase capacity another 20 percent. . . . In calculating the ROI . . . should the firm include a charge for the fixed assets associated with the training center? The answer is, it depends. If you want to allocate all of the firm's costs across a set of [conventional accounting] categories . . . then the answer is yes. If, on the other hand, you want to know whether shareholder wealth will increase if the activity is performed, then the answer is no. Note that this situation changes if the training center is running at capacity and additional capital investments would be required to run the new program. . . . This distinction is important, as many firms (often inappropriately) require that new programs cover something called a "fully allocated fixed cost," increasing the costs of the program and lowering the probability that it will have a positive ROI.[35]

Becker et al. argue that if the purpose of the program is to enable results that are related to the economic profit of the business, the "fully allocated fixed cost" approach can distort decision-making about the value created by the program. Phillips leans toward the "fully allocated fixed cost" approach because he believes that this approach will have more credibility. In practice, it is more than a minor issue, and the approach will depend on both the headway HRD has made in establishing itself as a contributor to the strategic thrust of the organization and the extent to which the learning intervention in question is linked to other strategic drivers.

Converting Results to Monetary Benefits   More challenging than costing is determining the monetary benefits of program results. This process begins with deciding on the metric to be used in the calculation, specifically the unit or units, such as sales, response time, quality, or production measures, to arrive at a monetary value for each unit, based either on direct or indirect costs or on average value. After the learning intervention is over, changes in the performance measure have to be calculated and adjustments made to reflect the impact of the intervention versus other factors, such as changes in overall economic conditions. A key decision for this calculation is the time frame, which is subsequently annualized. The final step is determining the annual value (AV) of the improvement by multiplying the annual performance change (P) by the unit value (V), (P × V).[36]

Calculating these benefits is obviously easier when results can be measured in terms of discrete performance units, such as sales, products made, services rendered, or employee turnover. It is more difficult when dealing with data such as customer satisfaction ratings or morale, and it is equally difficult to assess the monetary value of unstructured strategic managerial or executive work. In such cases more subjective estimates of business impact need to be made (see below), taking care to be as conservative as possible. This typically requires talking to a number of stakeholders and getting their estimates of bottom line impact; one such approach would ask them to estimate a range and would then take the low end of the range in their estimate and use the mid-point of average of the combined estimates.

Isolating the Effects of the Learning Intervention   In the best of all possible worlds, isolating the effects of training can be accomplished through quasi-experimental design (Robson offers an excellent discussion of quasi-experimental design issues with "real-world" implications).[37] As we discussed, this kind of design can involve matching control (comparison) groups for purposes of making the evaluation; in the absence of control groups, trend analysis can be used.

Beyond control groups and trend analysis, more subjective methods can estimate the value of performance improvement due to training. Like the calculations for monetary benefits, calculating the value of performance improvement also requires accepting estimates from either managers or the participants themselves. Generally it is best to obtain estimates from both and use either the lower or the average of the estimates of both managers and participants. Since the credibility of any such subjective analysis hinges on the HRD professional being willing to err on the conservative side, whichever estimate gives the lower value should be used.

Phillips' method for calculating subjective estimates involves participants' responses to a series of questions such as those presented in Box 9.1. To arrive at an adjusted value of the training using the questions in Box 9.1, Phillips suggests recording the annual improvement value reported by each participant along with the participant's basis for the arriving at the value. The improvement value is then multiplied by the confidence factor to reduce the amount of the improvement by what is in effect an estimated error factor. The resulting number is further adjusted by the

BOX 9.1   **Questions for Assessing Impact of a Learning Intervention in the Absence of Quasi-Experimental Design**

- How have you changed the way that you do your job as a result of your attending the program?
- What has been the impact of this change in terms of measurable results?
- What is the annualized value of these results?
- How have you arrived at this estimate? (That is, what assumptions and calculations were involved?)
- What level of confidence do you have in your estimate (ranging from 0 to 100 percent)?
- What percentage of this improvement do you directly attribute to the program (compared with other factors that influenced performance)? (Phillips suggests having respondents first list all these factors and then allocate an estimate of the relative impact of each.)
- What level of confidence do you have in your estimates (ranging from 0 to 100 percent)?

Adapted from Return on Investment in training and Performance Improvement Programs, *Jack J. Phillips, p. 99, copyright 1997. With permission from Elsevier.*

isolation factor to arrive at an adjusted improvement value that each participant estimates to be directly attributed to the training. Unrealistic estimates, based on how they either were arrived at or reported are eliminated from the process. Total adjusted value is the estimated value of the program.

Such estimates are highly subjective. Estimates that are based on the active involvement and acceptance of line management can focus attention on the relative contribution that learning makes in supporting organizational performance. Indeed, one of the most important issues is management's acceptance of the measures and process used. Patricia Phillips [38] has published an excellent summary and workbook source for applying ROI analysis to HRD interventions.

Initiating the Human Capital Conversation

Stimulating the human capital conversation with members of management is perhaps as important as the results of the assessment itself, especially if the conversation makes analysis of performance improvement more systematic and focuses management on a realistic assessment of the role that development plays in business performance. As we mentioned in the beginning of this chapter, Becker et al. argue that in the twenty-first century strategic potential of organizations hinges on the role of human and intellectual capital, which in turn hinges on learning. Borrowing from Kaplan and Norton, they frame the value creation process as involving learning and growth, internal business processes, customers, and financial performance, each of which builds on the others.[39]

Although Becker et al. address the human resource function in its entirety, HRD's particular responsibilities are central to their argument that implementation of a firm's competitive strategy requires the development of essential employee competencies and a learning system that facilitates its own employees learning faster than the employees of its competitors. Approaches such as the HR balanced scorecard and ROI analysis provide a metric approach to assessment and it is important that the energies expended in implementing these approaches be directed toward metrics that are meaningful for the organization's strategic direction and that have the acceptance of management.

FROM TAXONOMIES TO MODELS

Holton has taken a strong stand in his critique of the Kirkpatrick framework, arguing that it and, by extension, subsequent taxonomies that build on it are "flawed" because they are not true models (which would specify the variables that impact on or influence measured outcomes).[40] Based on the empirical literature, Holton offers an alternative model that seeks not only to assess outcomes but also to provide assessment of the variables that potentially explain how these outcomes are produced. Although Holton's alternative model is too complex to be used in its entirety by practitioners, it provides an excellent framework for understanding the complexity of assessing learning programs and it maps the factors that impact on the ability of any learning program to improve results. For researchers, Holton provides a testable model that can guide future studies and offers a stronger foundation for practice. The model does not so much negate the value of Kirkpatrick's taxonomy as extend it, incorporating its outcome levels into a larger system of variables and specifying dynamics among the variables. It is a key foundation for the comprehensive assessment system we presented earlier in this chapter (Figure 9.1).

The primary outcome measures in Holton's model (Figure 9.6) are (1) learning, (2) individual performance, and (3) organizational results; a causal relationship extends from the former to the latter. Following Noe,[41] Holton identifies the three primary intervening variables that mediate outcomes as (1) ability, (2) motivation, and (3) environment. Citing the research that found a weak correlation between reactions and learning,[42] Holton positions reaction as another intervening variable, not as a primary outcome. His model also acknowledges the various influences on transfer of learning to the workplace including participants' motivation to transfer their learning and the extent to which factors facilitating transfer are designed into the learning intervention (see Chapter Seven).

Swanson and Holton offer a more practice-friendly approach to results assessment that focuses on three domains: (1) performance results; (2) learning results; and (3) perception results; with two options for assessment under each domain.[43] Performance results can be either *system* results (units of mission-related outputs having value to the organization's customer) or *financial* results (output converted into monetary benefits). Learning results can be either *expertise* (behaviorial), or *knowledge* (mental). Perception results can be obtained from *stakeholders* or *participants*.

FIGURE 9.6   Holton's Evaluation Research and Measurement Model

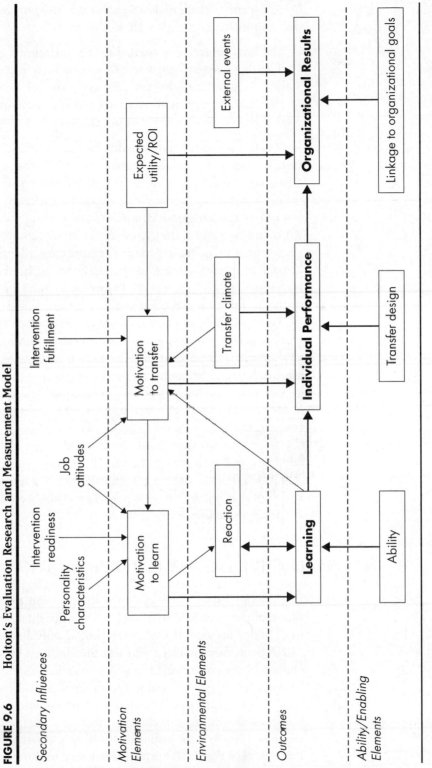

From E. F. Holton, "The Flawed 4-Level Evaluation Model," Human Resource Development Quarterly 7 (1996): pp. 5–26. Copyright 1996 by Wiley Periodicals, Inc. Reprinted by permission of John Wiley & Sons, Inc.

Swanson and Holton make the point that the purpose of assessment is management decision making, not research, noting that

> The level of accuracy needed for organizational decisions is considerably less than that needed for research. Your task is to find the "sweet spot" on the accuracy continuum so that you are buying enough accuracy to exceed management expectations slightly so you earn maximum credibility. If you buy more accuracy than that, you are wasting resources.[44]

This advice seems to contradict Holton's critique of Kirkpatrick by making a distinction between models needed for research that is foundational for practice and frameworks that are useful in the practice setting. The Swanson-Holton assessment model is in many ways a refinement of the Kirkpatrick approach; however, Holton's critique of the Kirkpatrick framework regarding the need for assessing the relationships among various drivers of results in any comprehensive assessment, is valid if assessments are going to generate organizational-level learning about the factors that impact on performance and that facilitate or inhibit the effectiveness of learning interventions. Holton sees the failure to account for these influences as a limitation of the Kirkpatrick and other outcome-oriented approaches.

Perhaps one way of resolving the discrepancy between more elaborate frameworks, such as the Holton evaluation and measurement model, and the rather practical advice contained in the Kirkpatrick and the Swanson and Holton assessment approaches can be found using the metaphor of computer programming. Most consumers of technology want convenience and user-friendly technology, such as Windows. However, effective user-friendly technology rests on the more complex programming that underlies the icons on the screen. Like the sophisticated software designers who provide user-friendly technology, HRD professionals must not only be very comfortable with the underlying empirically-based principles and models that provide them with a sophisticated understanding of the relationships among the variables that impact on their practice but also be able to present their work to their clients in more user-friendly language.

EVALUATIVE INQUIRY FOR ORGANIZATIONAL LEARNING

Preskill and Torres have developed an approach to evaluation that explicitly asserts that evaluation should be a catalyst for individual, group, and organizational learning.[45] They argue that evaluation should only be undertaken when managers and HRD professionals intend to use the findings in the service of change, that is, change in the conceptual framing of issues in the organization or in its knowledge base or change for political purposes. Preskill and Torres' approach is highly participatory, involving the full range of stakeholders in every stage of the evaluation process and striving to incorporate multiple perspectives in the design of the evaluation process. As a sophisticated learning approach to evaluation, evaluative inquiry makes it clear that HRD professionals need to draw on both technical assessment and action research competencies in conducting evaluations—they need to have skills as educators as well competencies in measurement. When conducting a holistic evaluative inquiry, the assessor plays the role of a facilitator, guide, mentor, and consultant throughout the process.

The Preskill and Torres approach to evaluation has objectives that reflect their emphasis on learning:

▌ conducting an evaluation that is understood by and relevant to the full range of stakeholders;

▌ building stakeholders' capacity for doing evaluation work on their own; and

▌ using dialogue to enhance stakeholders' learning throughout the process.

Preskill and Torres acknowledge that evaluation has a political dimension. One potential outcome of their process is evaluations that build support for people in the organization who make use of the evaluations to both improve the learning intervention and foster organizational learning, that creates a sustainable program in a way that more traditional approaches to evaluation do not—especially evaluations where the evaluator functions more as an auditor, apart from organizational members with a stake in the learning process. Their approach provides a framework for inquiry into the forces driving the outcomes highlighted in other evaluation models. Figure 9.7 provides an overview of the evaluative inquiry approach.

The integration of individual, team, and organizational learning with the phases of the evaluation process is key to understanding the evaluative inquiry model. A significant contribution of the approach is its focus on linking evaluation with an overall process of organizational learning that assumes stakeholders will be connected to the entire process and will make a commitment to act on implications of the data that are gathered. While the evaluation literature emphasizes measurement processes, Preskill and Torres place equal emphasis on collaboration in the evaluation process. Accordingly, as seen in Figure 9.7 the same learning practices—such as asking open questions, dialogue, and reflection—that are germane to generative learning process are central to their model.

By framing evaluation as an inquiry process, Preskill and Torres argue for spending time up front, focusing the inquiry through defining evaluative issues, identifying stakeholders, and determining the evaluative questions. Qualitative group-process strategies, such as group model building, open-space technology, and critical incident analysis, focus the inquiry. Group model building involves stakeholders in small groups collaboratively drawing pictures that represent the issue or issues at hand; through a facilitated dialogue, participants then question one another about the various representations, surfacing underlying values and working toward a model that captures their collective thinking and diverse viewpoints. Open-space technology is another way to facilitate dialogue among a large group of people with diverse viewpoints. Participants post themes that concern them on easel sheets hanging on a wall that represents a community bulletin board. Once all the themes are up, people sign up to discuss themes that interest them most. Critical incidents are particularly

FIGURE 9.7   The Evaluative Inquiry Model

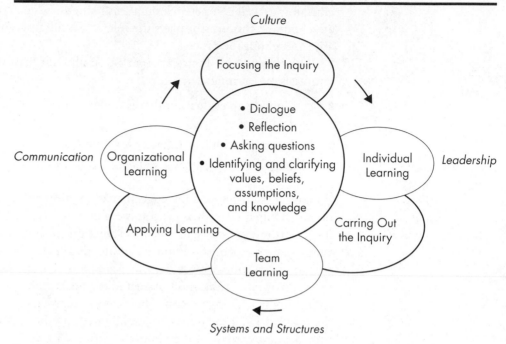

From Hallie S. Preskill and Rosalie T. Torres, Evaluative Inquiry for Learning in Organizations, p. 97. Copyright © 1999 by Sage Publications. Reprinted by permission of Sage Publications.

memorable events related to the issue at hand; people are asked to respond either in written form or orally to a question or series of questions about critical incidents they have experienced relevant to the learning issue at hand. All of these methods are ways of getting diverse viewpoints and issues out on the table so that inquiry incorporates the concerns of all involved and represents a collectively held understanding of the issues; the values, beliefs, and assumptions underlying different perspectives are surfaced and made explicit. This approach avoids using assessment criteria that privileges the values and concerns of powerful stakeholders while ignoring the concerns of less powerful stakeholders and subsequently disfranchising their interests. Creating a climate of open dialogue is critical for the success of this approach; in any case, dialogue is a powerful tool for bridging diverse viewpoints.[46]

Conducting the inquiry involves not only building databases that collect information, but also creating mechanisms for using the data in the service of organizational learning, with consideration given to building on the foundation of involvement that was created during the focusing phase. The overall evaluation design plan should include an implementation plan for taking action. Part of the cycle of organizational learning is to follow through on the meaning and interpretation of the data by engaging the system to apply the learning. In effect, evaluative inquiry is an

OD-oriented approach to conducting assessments that seeks to strengthen the organization as well as to evaluate the learning intervention.

SUMMARY

The literature includes a wide range of approaches to evaluation. The Kirkpatrick and Phillips approaches to outcome assessments are those most widely known to training and development professionals. Although these approaches are limited in their comprehensiveness and difficult to carry out, they are a useful place to begin the conversation with managers about evaluation. As the scope of HRD broadens, more comprehensive models are needed, models that seek to understand the complex relationship between various kinds of results and the factors that produce them. The works of Kaplan and Norton and of Holton have made significant contributions in this regard.

Evaluation models that link assessment to learning are specifically consistent with the core practice of HRD and represent an important balance to the growing emphasis on performance matrixes alone. Using these models requires an organizational setting that has been prepared to understand the dynamics of organizational learning and that is committed to fully integrating assessment into the learning process.

Despite important differences, a consensus emerges among members of the HRD community that

■ assessing outcomes or results is increasingly important for both the profession and the organizations it serves;

■ the measures used in the assessment should be linked to strategic drivers of value creation in organizational goals and objectives;

■ simple reaction questionnaires are woefully inadequate for assessing effectiveness and results;

■ assessment needs to address multiple levels of outcomes;

■ what level of outcome is most important depends on the purpose of the training or development intervention;

■ assessment is linked to broader issues of learning transfer;

■ it is important to measure or identify the variables that influence or impact the outcomes or results in order to ensure their effectiveness; and

■ ultimately, effective evaluation requires a willingness to learn from the findings.

Questions for Discussion

1. What level of evaluation or assessment have you experienced in training or education programs that you have attended? How valuable do you think it was? How could it be made more valuable?

2. How thorough and thoughtful are your responses when you are asked to complete reaction measures?

3. How useful do you find Alliger et al.'s distinction between reactions as affect (Level 1a), reactions as utility judgments (Level 1b), and immediate post-training knowledge (Level 2a), knowledge retention and (Level 2b), behavioral demonstration in the training setting (Level 2c)?

4. Think of a training program you are familiar with. How would you calculate its ROI? What costs would you include? What unit of results measurement would you use? How can the unit of measurement be converted to monetary benefits? How could you isolate the effects of the training from other factors?

5. What do you consider important factors that influence whether learning is transferred back to the workplace?

End Notes

1. R. L. Dilworth, T. R. McClernon, and J. Redding, "No Respect: Bridging the Gap Between HRD Practitioners and Senior Management," *A What Works Report* (September, 2000): 9 (Alexandria, Va.: American Society for Training and Development).

2. R. A. Swanson and E. F. Holton, III, *Results: How to Assess Performance, Learning, and Perceptions in Organizations* (San Francisco: Berrett-Koehler, 1999).

3. M. Scriven, "The Methodology of Evaluation," in R. W. Tyler, R. M. Gagne, and M. Scriven, eds., *Perspectives of Curriculum Evaluation,* American Education Research Association, Monograph Series in Evaluation, No. 1 (Chicago: Rand McNally, 1967) 39–83.

4. J. J. Phillips, *Return on Investment in Training and Performance Improvement Programs* (Houston: Gulf, 1997).

5. J. Boulmetis and P. Dutwin, *The ABC's of Evaluation, 6" × 9"; Timeless Techniques for Program and Project Managers* (San Francisco: Jossey-Bass, 2000).

6. M. Q. Patton, *Qualitative Evaluation* (Newbury Park, Calif.: Sage, 1990).

7. H. Preskill and R. T. Torres, *Evaluative Inquiry for Learning in Organizations* (Thousand Oaks, Calif.: Sage, 1999).

8. Scriven, "The Methodology of Evaluation."

9. D. L. Kirkpatrick, *Evaluating Training Programs: The Four Levels,* 2nd ed. (San Francisco: Berrett-Koehler, 1998).

10. P. H. Rossi, H. E. Freeman, and M. W. Lipsey, *Evaluation: A Systematic Approach* (Thousand Oaks, Calif.: Sage, 1999).

11. J. Z. Rouillier and I. L. Goldstein, "The Relationship between Organizational Transfer Climate and Positive Transfer of Training," *Human Resource Development Quarterly* 4 (1993): 377–90; J. B. Tracey, S. I. Tannenbaum, and M. J. Kavanaugh, "Applying Trained Skills on the Job: The Importance of the Work Environment," *Journal of Applied Psychology,* 64 (1995): 239–52; R. D. Marx and L. A. Burke, "Transfer is Personal: Equipping Trainees with Self-Management and Relapse Prevention Strategies," in E. F. Holton, III, and T. T. Baldwin, eds., *Improving Learning Transfer in Organizations* (San Francisco: Jossey-Bass, 2003): 227–42; E. F. Holton, III, and T. T. Baldwin, "Making Transfer Happen: An Action Perspective on Learning Transfer Systems," in Holton and Baldwin, *Learning Transfer,* 3–15.

12. G. M. Alliger and E. A. Janak, "Kirkpatrick's Levels of Training Criteria: Thirty Years Later," *Personnel Psychology,* 42 (1989): 331–42.

13. M. Galbraith, B. R. Sisco, and L. M. Guglielmino, *Administering Successful Programs for Adults: Promoting Excellence in Adult, Community, and Continuing Education* (Malabar, Fla.: Krieger Publishing Company, 1997).

14. R. S. Kaplan and D. P. Norton, *The Balanced Scorecard* (Boston: Harvard Business School Press, 1996), 31–2.

15. B. E. Becker, M. A. Huselid, and D. Ulrich, *The HR Scorecard: Linking People, Strategy, and Performance* (Boston: Harvard Business School Press, 2001).

16. Dilworth et al. "No Respect"; Kirkpatrick, *Evaluating Training Programs.*

17. W. F. Cascio, "Using Utility Analysis to Assess Training Outcomes," in I L. Goldstein and Associates, eds., *Training and Development in Organizations* (San Francisco: Jossey-Bass, 1989), 63–80; W. F. Cascio, *Costing Human Resources: The Financial Impact of Behavior in Organizations* (Cincinatti: Southwestern, 1991); S. B. Parry, "Measuring Training's ROI," *Training and Development Journal,* 50 (1996): 72–7; Phillips, *Return on Investment;* J. Fitzenz, *ROI of Human Captial: Measuring Economic Value of Employee Performance* (New York: AMACOM, 2000); *The Human Capital Challenge,* A White Paper by The ASTD Public Policy Council (Alexandria, Va: American Society for Training and Development, August, 2003).

18. Alliger and Janak, "Kirkpatrick's Levels"; G. M. Alliger, S. I. Tannenbaum, W. Bennett, H. Trave, and A. Shotland, "A Meta-Analysis of the Relations Among Training Criteria," *Personnel Psychology,* 50 (1997): 341–58.

19. Phillips, "Return on Investment."

20. N. M. Dixon, "The Relationship between Trainee Responses on Participation Reaction Forms and Post-test Scores," *Human Resource Development Quarterly,* 1 (1990): 129–37.

21. J. R. Davis and A. B. Davis, *Effective Training Strategies: A Comprehensive Guide to Maximizing Learning in Organizations* (San Francisco: Berrett-Koehler, 1998).

22. E. F. Holton, "The Flawed 4-Level Evaluation Model," *Human Resource Development Quarterly,* 7 (1996): 5–21.

23. Phillips, "Return on Investment."

24. ASTD Benchmarking Service, 1999; ASTD Leading Edge, 1999; S. Twitchell, E. F. Holton, III, and J. W. Trott, "Technical Training Evaluation Practices in the United States," *Performance Improvement Quarterly* (2000).

25. R. A. Swanson and E. F. Holton, III, *Foundations of Human Resource Development* (San Francisco: Berrett-Koehler, 2001), 363.

26. Alliger and Janak, "Kirkpatrick's Levels."

27. M. Rodin and B. Rodin, "Student Evaluaton of Teachers," *Science,* 177 (1972): 1164–6; R. M. Kaplan and G. C. Pascoe, "Humorous Lectures and Humorous Examples: Some Effects upon Comprehension and Retention." *Journal of Educational Psychology,* 69 (1977): 61–5.

28. L. Yorks, J. O'Neil, and V. J. Marsick, "Action Learning: Theoretical Bases and Varieties of Practice," in L. Yorks, J. O'Neil, and V. J. Marsick, eds., *Advances in Developing Human Resources* 1(2) (San Francisco: Berrett-Koehler Communications and Academy of Human Resource Development, 1999), 1–18.

29. Alliger and Janak, "Kirkpatrick's Levels," 334.

30. Alliger et al., "A Meta-Analysis," 342–3.

31. J. Z. Rouillier and I. L. Goldstein, "The Relationship between Organizational Transfer Climate and Positive Transfer of Training," *Human Resource Development Quarterly* 4 (1993): 377–90; J. B. Tracey, S. I. Tannenbaum, and M. J. Kavanaugh, "Applying Trained Skills on the Job: The Importance of the Work Environment," *Journal of Applied Psychology,* 64 (1995): 239–52.

32. L. Yorks, S. Lamm, and J. O'Neil, "Transfer of Learning from Action Learning Programs to the Organizational Setting," in L. Yorks, J. O'Neil, and V. J. Marsick, eds., *Advances in Developing Human Resources,* 1(2) (San Francisco: Berrett-Koehler Communications and Academy of Human Resource Development, 1999), 57.

33. Rossi et al., "Evaluation."

34. Phillips, "Return on Investment."

35. Becker et al., *The HR Scorecard,* 86.

36. Phillips, "Return on Investment," 118.

37. C. Robson, *Real World Research: A Resource for Social Scientists and Practitioner-Researchers,* 2nd ed. (Oxford, UK and Cambridge, Mass.: Blackwell, 2002).

38. P. P. Phillips, *The Bottomline on ROI: Basics, Benefits, and Barriers to Measuring Training and Performance Improvement* (Atlanta: CEP Press, and Silver Spring, Md.: International Society for Performance Improvement, 2002).

39. Becker et al., *The HR Scorecard.*

40. Holton, "The Flawed 4-Level Evaluation Model," 28–30.

41. R. A. Noe, "Trainee Attributes and Attitudes: Neglected Influences on Training Effectiveness," *Academy of Management Review,* 11 (1986): 736–49; *ibid.* "The Influence of Trainee Attitudes on Training Effectiveness: Test of a Model," *Personnel Psychology,* 39 (1986): 497–523.

42. Dixon, "The Relationship between Trainee Responses"; P. Warr and D. Bunce, "Trainee Characteristics and the Outcomes of Open Learning," *Personnel Psychology,* 48 (1995): 347–75.

43. Swanson and Holton, *Results: How to Assess Performance, Learning, and Perceptions.*

44. *Ibid.,* 49.

45. Preskill and Torres, *Evaluative Inquiry.*

46. W. N. Isaacs, "Taking Flight: Dialogue, Collective Thinking, and Organization Learning," *Organization Dynamics,* 22 (2) (1993): 24–39; E. H. Schein, "On Dialogue, Culture, and Organization," *Organization Dynamics,* 22 (2) (1993): 40–51.

This chapter

- provides a model linking the political economy framework, the strategic learning process, and the HRD pyramid with three areas of HR imperatives for supporting changes in strategic direction;

- describes how the divergent characteristics of strategic learning funnel into a more defined set of learning needs and HR system support;

- describes how organizational core competencies, individual competencies, organizational alignment, and HR systems are interdependent;

- provides an elaborated learning cycle for learning from tactical and operational learning; and

- provides a diagnostic model for addressing performance problems.

Key terms:

gaps	emergent learning needs	symptom
HR imperatives	problematic performance situation	problem
alignment of imperatives		solution

Linking Learning and Performance

HRD practitioners are faced with the challenge of making the linkages between learning and performance explicit in the minds of organization members. Throughout this text we have argued that over time this challenge is best met by selective opportunistic advocacy that targets HRD interventions in order to leverage learning for performance either immediately or by developing people to position them and the organization for strong future performance. Although learning can potentially leverage performance at the strategic, tactical, or operational level of organizational performance, we have considered the challenge as one of building strategic capability as a driver for the HRD function, beginning with strategic learning. In this chapter we pull together the concepts we have presented throughout the text. First we look at strategic learning, and then we provide a diagnostic model for responding to managers who request help in addressing performance problems.

POLITICAL ECONOMY, STRATEGIC CONVERSATIONS, AND THE HRD PYRAMID

HRD interventions at the level of strategic learning can create an overall learning architecture that aligns learning with the performance management system of the organization. As we described it in Chapter Three, strategic learning is a messy process—nonlinear and iterative. Testing ideas as much as possible against the organization's core competencies, internal political realities, and alternative futures, gradually leads to convergence and planning. This process varies from organization to organization, but as we described it in Chapter Three, it involves conversations that converge around a strategy and provide both a basis for framing HR imperatives for enacting strategy and a map to determine where investment in learning is most needed. Figure 10.1 integrates the ideas we discussed in Part One of this book and illustrates the relationship between the organizational political economy, strategic conversation, and the emergence of HR imperatives.

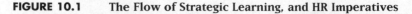

FIGURE 10.1   The Flow of Strategic Learning, and HR Imperatives

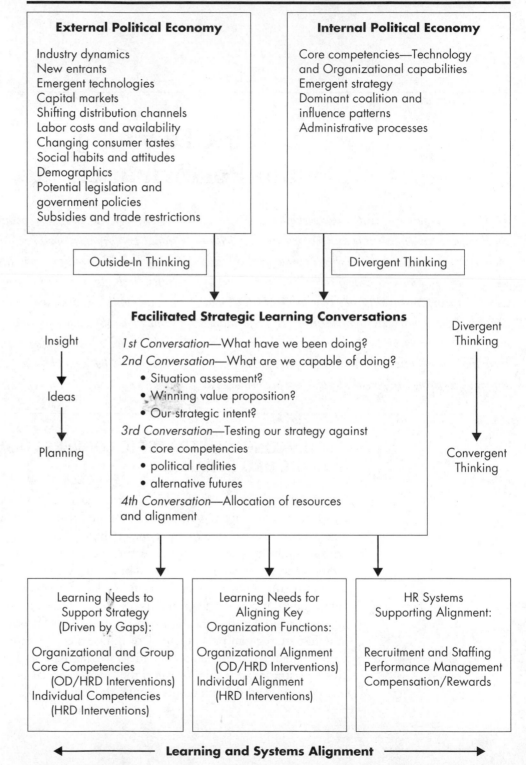

Strategically Driven HR Imperatives at the Tactical and Operational Levels of Performance

From strategic conversations, we can derive three sets of HR-related needs that must be aligned with the strategic direction of the organization: 1) the organizational core competencies and individual competencies necessary for executing the strategy, 2) organizational and individual alignment with the strategic direction, and 3) HR systems in place that position and focus people for performance. Each of these needs can be considered an imperative for positioning people for performance, and each need should be aligned with the others.

Aligning Organizational Core Competencies, Individual Competencies, Organizational Units, and HR Systems

At both the organizational and individual levels, strategic change invariably produces gaps between the organization's capabilities and the competencies it needs for effectively carrying out its strategy. The traditional enabling role of HRD has been to close these gaps.

HRD professionals can directly extend their role in the strategic process by facilitating strategic conversations to identify the gaps. In other cases, HRD involvement begins once the organization has announced a strategic direction, in which case HRD leadership needs to take a proactive role in identifying potential gaps and responding to requests for support from various internal clients. In this situation, HRD plays an indirect role in the successful implementation of strategy, and its leadership has to be highly opportunistic in building alliances that support appropriate learning interventions.

At the organizational level, core competencies and functional alignment often depend highly on one another. Organizational core competencies are embedded in the cultural memory of the organization and become evident in behavioral interactions of organizational members in particular situations. The organizational level transitions that often accompany strategic change are potentially disruptive of existing core competencies; they can involve new work roles and relationships that in turn change the informal working relationships between members of the organization, resulting in organizational systems incongruent with the needs of various organizational units as they strive to realize strategic goals. Strategic shifts are often accompanied by changes in organizational structure that are part of enacting strategy. Organizational changes that relocate critical units of performance may unintentionally create new barriers to cooperation.

For example, the author had a conversation with a design engineer in a General Motors division two years after a major strategic restructuring. "One problem is that now I have to follow the organizational chart," he said. When asked why that was a problem, he said, "It used to be I could directly call over to [technical] . . . and get what I needed; now they don't even exist as a unit any more—they have been absorbed elsewhere. All I can do is follow channels; it takes forever and going back and forth several times to get the information or changes I need." While the engineer didn't understand it this way, as we talked it become clear that the reorganization had disrupted part of the informal organization, and in this case core competencies around product development were embedded in those relationships.

Core competencies, while they are organizational attributes, are built on foundations of individual competencies. Some of these individual competencies are directly related to the exercise of organizational level core competencies and are often learned informally through the socialization process of becoming integrated into the organization. These individual competencies can include collaborative behavior around highly diverse technical issues, and the culture of the organization may naturally support the development of these abilities in new members.

In many new organizations, initial core competencies develop through the informal patterns of interaction that evolve as the business grows and succeeds. The challenge is to maintain these critical capabilities in the face of the increasing organizational formalization that comes with growth and expansion. Maintenance involves awareness of the criticality of these behaviors and interactions, often expressed through stories in the organization. Development of new capabilities represents a significant learning challenge. Key business leaders must be politically aligned in support of an extended focus on learning interventions that will develop the requisite competencies.

Developing core competencies requires intensive interaction over time—often, developing the individual level competencies in concert with establishing the framework within which organizational level core competencies emerge. Examples of these learning interventions include action-learning programs and cross-functional task forces chartered explicitly as task *and* as learning groups.

Seibert, Hall, and Kram describe how 3M, having determined that its strategic competitive performance in Europe was dependent on managing across several distinct but closely interconnected markets, identified "managing transnational businesses" as the critical success factor for its managers.[1] The company created a European management action team with participating members serving a one-year assignment in a European country. The action team served as a learning platform that developed, simultaneously, individual competencies and the requisite organizational core competency.

Another example of such interventions is the Grace Cocoa action-learning program we described in Chapter One. One of the outcomes of that program was the development of a network of informal working relationships necessary for making the globalization strategy workable. These learning-oriented interventions represent what Popper and Lipshitz refer to as "dedicated organizational learning mechanisms" (see Chapter Six). In both the 3M case and the Grace Cocoa case, these mechanisms involve developing individual competencies while simultaneously developing the organizational level core competencies—or, in Popper and Lipshitz's terms, "learning in organization," followed by "learning by organization."[2]

Developing core competencies requires more than HRD-sponsored learning programs. Support from HR systems is necessary for reinforcing the competencies. Reward and performance evaluation systems are critical for both reinforcing desired behavior and sending informal messages about what is considered important. Effective implementation of changes in HR systems often requires learning interventions as well if managers are going to appropriately utilize them in practice. If managers and employees receive insufficient training as to how to use new performance management and appraisal systems, or if assessments show that managers have insufficient work planning and job coaching skills to make the system effective, the systems will fail to impact organizational performance. Simply changing systems does little to alter behavior if managers do not understand the intentions and principles that underlie them and don't have the appropriate skills for using them.

Strategic change often requires changing job profiles for recruiting and staffing, in order to bring new skills and competencies into the organization. However, organizational core competencies must be developed internally once the new personnel have joined the organization. The mix of competencies that are brought into the organization will have changed, but people and work units still need to learn how to work together. Organizational-level learning needs to take place to create the organization's capability for exhibiting core competencies by embedding them in its deep culture.

Gaps in Strategically Critical Individual Skills and Competencies   In addition to building core competencies, the organization may require additional individual skills and competencies from its members that are not linked to organizational level capabilities but are still critical to the success of the strategy. Strategic change often translates into new competency profiles for individuals. These profiles are produced through a systematic process of needs analysis that links skills and competencies to specific performance requirements aligned with strategy. Any significant gaps that are surfaced through the needs analysis have to be closed through HRD initiatives. When one of the prestigious "white shoe" Wall Street investment banks found itself in a changing, highly competitive sales environment, conversations between the bank's senior executives and its HR professionals led to a growing realization that the firm's managing directors and associates would need to develop more skills in "selling." Historically, it had been sufficient that members of the firm play the role of "trusted financial doctor" in a socially stratified industry. Most professional staff had attended prep schools and prestigious universities, then worked for a short time in the firm before continuing on to business school, obtained an MBA, and then returned to the firm. Now a new breed was on the street—more competitive and more aggressive.

With a strategy of relationship-based marketing, any "sales" training had to emphasize principled negotiation and building commitment. Training designed to develop sales skills consistent with the firm's strategy was provided to professional staff, from the managing directors on down, who were in positions of competitive selling.

Emergent Learning Needs through Tactical and Operational Actions

Our discussion has focused on HRD interventions that are driven by skills gaps defined in the context of strategy. Additional learning needs emerge when strategy is enacted by taking tactical and operational actions. Generally, learning from these actions occurs in three ways. First, there is the potential for learning from the action itself. Conducting after-action reviews following any major initiative, such as the introduction of a new marketing program or a sales blitz, while the experience is still fresh in everyone's mind, can surface learning that is important for increasing the effectiveness of future efforts. A second source of potential learning is the periodic review of leading and lagging indicators, from a perspective of learning rather than control. This involves surfacing divergent explanations for what is driving the results, subsequently testing these attributions with others and with additional data, and making adjustments. This learning can be captured for the organization as best practices. The third kind of learning, also from systematic reviews of performance, is the emergence of previously unrecognized skill deficiencies. A learning solution can be proposed when a more systematic needs assessment determines that the performance issues are linked to lack of knowledge and experience.

Surfacing and addressing each of these sources of performance-related learning follows the principles of the learning cycle (see Chapter Six). Whether the process is implicit in the actions of HRD professionals or explicit, it is important to engage members of the organization in a systematic process of inquiry that captures and codifies the learning for the organization and that guides subsequent action. Figure 10.2 provides an elaborated version of the learning cycle.

Box 10.1 tells how a strategically driven tactical reorganization required a complex mix of HRD/OD/HR interventions.

BOX 10.1   Strategically Driven Tactical Change

In the mid-1990s Jim Watson, then president of Thermo King, contemplated how to continue strengthening his company's growing presence as a global competitor. Working with his senior staff after an in-depth cost analysis of Thermo King's operations, he focused on the purchasing organization. Realizing that the buyers, who interfaced with vendors for the company's plants, spent 95 percent of their time expediting, Watson envisioned a more strategic role for purchasing, one that would require a sophisticated set of competencies and that would significantly impact the financial performance of the company, since 70 percent of the company's costs were related to procurement of materials. In Watson's vision, purchasing would work "up-front" as equal partners to sales, engineering, and manufacturing in the strategic planning and decision-making process.

Watson's staff realized that that such a change could not be incremental. Purchasing lacked the structure and stature necessary to drive strategic decisions. Engineering traditionally drove the decision-making process regarding materials, telling purchasing which suppliers they liked and supplying them with specifications. The new strategic mission would require a completely different kind of organization, staffed with highly skilled professionals focused on implementing global procurement strategy. An engineering staff member would come to the supply manager and say, "Here are the specifications. What do you think?" Based on a range of considerations—including price, quality, reliability, and delivery—the supply manager might recommend, "We had better focus on ordering from these suppliers in Europe." The new organization would have to be staffed with people who had world-class negotiating skills as well as strong product and manufacturing knowledge. More specifically, successfully enacting the strategic vision would require

∎ a well-managed redesign of the purchasing organization;

continues

BOX 10.1   Strategically Driven Tactical Change [CONTINUED]

■ effective support for people throughout Thermo King while they learn to interface with the procurement function in a new way;

■ new roles and responsibilities in the manufacturing facilities, where routine activities such as expediting will be carried out;

■ the creation of a fair and effective restaffing process;

■ a redesigned compensation system; and,

■ management of the transition to the new procurement organization.

A cross-functional design team, with members who knew how purchasing impacted the company and who were personally respected and influential in their own departments and across the company, was drawn from marketing, engineering, manufacturing, and purchasing. Its stature would be important in selling the new structure and new purchasing role to the larger company. Following a very fluid, iterative, and creative four-phase process of disassembly and review, analysis, synthesis and reassembly, and structure development the design team created two new positions, supply manager and supply service representative. The supply manager would be the equivalent of a sales manager: supply managers manage vendors, and sales managers manage customers and orders. This new position was given broad authority to develop partnerships with suppliers and to approve vendor prices. The supply service representative would support the supply manager, much like customer service representatives support sales managers. The new structure took the shape of a wheel of tightly knit teams of manager and representatives. Five of the teams each focused on major procurement areas—engines and motors, support team services, metals and fabrications, plastics and nonmetals, electrical and electronics. The other two teams were geographically focused, one on the Pacific Rim and the other on Europe. All the teams reported to a new executive function, Vice President and General Manager of Supply Management.

Working intensively, the design team completed its work in two weeks. With the new design it became apparent that the organization required a new set of competencies. The design team developed new key competencies for each position, including strong negotiation and interpersonal skills, technical and analytical skills, and global commodity knowledge.

Staffing the new organization while the organization kept functioning was especially challenging. Fairness was a critical issue; employees who previously held purchasing positions received first consideration for the new jobs. Some qualified for the new supply manager position, and others were offered the supply service representative position. However, the process was highly selective. It was critical that successful candidates have the right knowledge base and be able to think strategically and tactically. Many previous members of the purchasing organization did not qualify for either position; they were provided with career transitioning training, severance packages, and outplacement support. Some of the positions required unique experience, for example, a mix of plastics and automotive experience. The answer to the question, "Who knows best what we need?" was often found in recruiting from outside the company; in this case, the auto industry.

Because staffing was critical, a behavioral-based interviewing process was designed. Fifteen managers from across the company were trained to use the behavior interview process along with the job profiles and competencies developed by the design team. All candidates for the new positions were interviewed by a two-person team using these methods. This process proved so effective that behavioral-based interviews became standard across the company.

A new broad band compensation salary scale was developed to help attract candidates both from outside and from across the company. This not only brought the supply management salary structure in line with the salary structure of sales and engineering, it also sent a signal to the rest of the company as to supply management's new status.

Once Thermo King had staffed the new organization, a process for providing it with ongoing learning support was put in place. One part of a series of one-day workshops for the members of the new organization was devoted to defining key challenges and obstacles to success. A facilitator worked with the members to produce detailed lists of risk factors that could derail implementation of the strategy and impact performance outcomes. These lists in turn produced a valuable working document that could help the vice president of supply management understand the new organization's

continues

BOX 10.1   Strategically Driven Tactical Change [CONTINUED]

needs. This led to extensive computer system training and testing to ensure the new team was fully capable of using the systems to service the organization as well as to other ongoing investments in learning.

The change in supply management resulted in savings of more than $20 million in procurement costs; in the first year Thermo King delivered a 30 percent increase in operating profits to the parent company on a 21 percent increase in revenue. The following year the company had

a 10 percent increase in operating profits even though economic conditions caused sales volume to decline.

The Thermo King case illustrates a systemic change that involved organizational redesign; the identification of new competencies; staffing; a need for training managers in behavioral interviewing (and transferring this form of interviewing as a best practice throughout the organization); changes in compensation; and subsequent ongoing learning support to the new organization.

FIGURE 10.2   The Elaborated Learning Cycle: Learning from Tactical and Operational Action

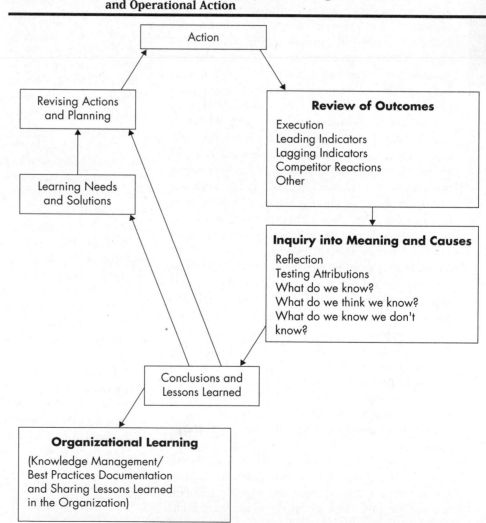

ADDRESSING PERFORMANCE ISSUES

One learning outcome that results from reflecting on the tactical and operational action in the organization is the identification of possible additional gaps or deficiencies in the skills of organizational members. Managers in the organization may also approach the HRD organization for help in addressing performance issues at either the individual or organizational level. In either case it is important for the HRD professional to engage the managers involved in a process of inquiry around the causes of discrepancies between expected and actual performance.

A Framework for Diagnosing Performance Issues

Managers frequently approach HRD professionals and ask them to provide training or education that will address some pressing problem or issue. While training may be the solution, quite often it is not; rather, the manager may see training as the only solution or as a "safe" solution that gives the appearance of the manager taking the responsibility for solving it to the learning and development department.

When the HRD professional either is approached under these circumstances or takes the initiative in addressing some recognized performance problem in the organization, a diagnostic framework will allow him or her to systematically work through the issue and to discuss it with the managers involved.

Such conversations often avoid confusion between symptoms and problems. A symptom is a set of events or behaviors that are associated with poor performance; examples of poor performance are low productivity, poor service response time, late reports, unacceptable error rates or other quality problems, or morale-related issues, such as attendance or general deportment. The poor performance might be manifested at the organizational or group level, or it might be limited to a particular individual or set of individuals. Initial investigation of the situation may reveal deficiencies in communication, planning, organization, or skills. While managers often refer to these kinds of issues as problems, as in, "We have a communication, planning, or organization problem," they are usually symptomatic of more fundamental underlying causes that must be addressed for the poor performance to improve.

The HRD professional's first step is to carefully inquire into the problematic performance situation and to build a diagnostic framework that links the situation, its symptoms, the problem, and ultimately the solution. Figure 10.3 suggests the need for research skills, especially qualitative skills that will provide data linking the stages of the framework. We will return to this issue, but now we direct our attention toward the third step: identifying the underlying problem.

Drawing on the organizational behavior and management literature, we offer six categories of underlying problems, each of which suggests a different kind of intervention or solution.[3] Perhaps not every problematic performance situation can be classified into one or some combination of these categories, but experience suggests most will. The categories are general and intended to structure the HRD manager's thinking and to guide the conversation with managers.

FIGURE 10.3   Building the Diagnostic Framework

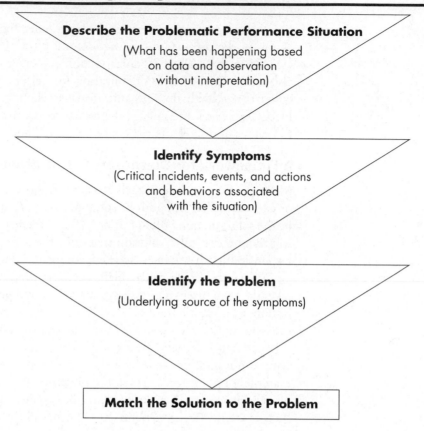

1. *System.* Perhaps the problem doesn't lie with people but with the capacity of the systems and processes with which they work. Deming's assertion, that 80 percent of performance issues are rooted in the capacity of the system, is relevant here and well-understood by most contemporary managers. The current popularity of six sigma reveals the extent to which organizations are aware of system problems.

2. *Others.* The problem may lie with people other than the individual or group associated with the situation and its related symptoms. Coworkers in other departments, an immediate supervisor, or higher management may be causing the symptoms. To take a couple of simple illustrations, poor planning and organization at one level of the organization can be a symptom of inconsistent supervisory or management actions at a higher level of the organization. A lack of delegation on the part of a manager that in turn produces slow response times to customer or client requests can be rooted in defensive behavior on the manager's part against micromanaging on the part of a senior manager. Those employed in assembly line or sequential work processes are well aware that

workers down the line are highly dependent on the performance of individuals and groups whose work precedes theirs.

3. *Knowledge and Experience.* Lack of training, information, or necessary experience for adequately performing certain job requirements can cause poor performance and be reflected in symptoms. For example, perhaps a new manager may not know how to delegate effectively and maintain control.

4. *Motivation.* Motivation is a problem when employees show a lack of interest or an unwillingness to perform. People tend to be motivated by, that is, they direct their energy into, those activities they find interesting (need theory), or those they believe will lead to desired outcomes (expectancy theory). Often, a lack of motivation is really motivation focused away from the job. Employees who do not find their work interesting or the rewards relevant are highly motivated when engaged in other pursuits.

5. *Personality.* Most relevant to individuals, rather than groups, personality problems arise when a person has a trait or quality that is creating difficulties related to his or her job performance. These traits or qualities are personal attributes that comprise the employee's style of interacting with his or her surroundings; cognitive style, habits, and attitudes are all components of personal style. They are all part of an individual's personality and determine in part the degree of fit with the job and organization. While these same personal qualities may be the source of effectiveness in some aspects of the job, they can work against the person in other situations, such as when a very organized person is too inflexible in responding to a quickly changing situation. Everyone has personal characteristics that are strengths in some situations and limitations in others.

6. *Aptitude.* Aptitude refers to a lack of talent or innate ability for doing the job. Again, this problem is most relevant at the individual level of performance, although it can become a work unit problem when organizational restructuring substantially changes the content of jobs.

These six categories of problems can be used to extend Vroom's[4] seminal statement that an individual's performance (P) is a function (f) of ability (A) × motivation (M), that is, $[P = f(A \times M)]$, as follows:

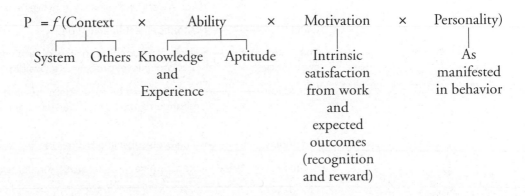

P = f(Context   ×   Ability   ×   Motivation   ×   Personality)

| System | Others | Knowledge and Experience | Aptitude | Intrinsic satisfaction from work and expected outcomes (recognition and reward) | As manifested in behavior |

This extended statement can be applied at both the individual and group level of performance. The nature of the problem provides the logical focus for interventions (see Figure 10.4). A *system* problem requires a change in systems, processes, or the organization. If the problem lies with *others,* an intervention elsewhere than where the problem manifests itself is required, one that involves coaching and corrective action, and perhaps a change in management behavior or actions. A *knowledge and/or experience* problem is appropriately addressed by a well-designed training or education intervention, although whether this involves "classroom," "Web-based," or "work based on the job" learning is a further consideration. *Motivation* problems must be addressed on the job, through some change in either the design of the work[5] or incentives.[6] *Personality* problems require coaching around behavior; the need in this case is for the person to recognize certain reactions, which might be a strength in some situations but in other situations can create problems. If the person can substitute more appropriate behaviors, the problem can be resolved, or at least lessened. *Aptitude* problems might require a staffing change or a change in job responsibilities.

HRD providers can help to resolve several of the above problems, although a traditional training intervention is only relevant when the underlying problem is knowledge and experience. Learning support, such as six sigma, or organizational development interventions, possibly linked to changes in HRM policies, are among the more productive learning components in system problems. When the problem is with others the intervention has to focus away from the symptom and on the source of the problem. This may or may not involve a learning intervention, such as coaching managers who lack the skills to effectively intervene or who need to think through how to approach the source of the problem. In these cases the HRD contribution is indirect, providing necessary skills and support to the person who needs to directly intervene.

FIGURE 10.4   Relationship between Problems and Solutions

Problem	Solution
System	Develop metrics to assess and improve system capability. Work with suppliers and internal functions through task forces, and develop six sigma experts who are "black belts" for system and process improvement.
Others	Management intervention.
Knowledge and Experience	Training, coaching, on-the-job training, education. If a group-level problem, reconsider staffing profiles.
Motivation	Solution must be focused on the workplace. Job redesign, change rewards, consider reassignment.
Personality	Focus on substitute behaviors.
Aptitude	Reassignment, downgrade the content of the job, or tolerate.

If the problem is motivational, then either organizational development—such as work restructuring—or HRM solutions—such as changing incentives, career ladders, and/or staffing practices—are appropriate. Coaching can help with a personality-based issue by focusing on helping people alter their behavior in particular situations. Either an HRD professional trained in job coaching or a manager closely involved in the situation can provide this coaching. Problems with aptitude require HRM-informed solutions, primarily changes in staffing. In all cases, the learning component has to be supported by a realistic set of activities that are designed to ensure learning transfer. Box 10.2 provides a case example where HRD uses the six-category diagnostic model to respond to a request from a senior line executive regarding a performance problem.

INQUIRY FOR PROBLEM IDENTIFICATION

The literature on adult education and HRD offers many models and practices for needs assessment.[7] The most widespread needs assessment procedures have traditionally involved offering training and educational opportunities and then tracking how many participants these offerings attract. Additionally, the needs assessment has emphasized determining both the level of learner interest and the content for particular programs. These processes are highly diagnostic, most commonly treating performance issues as only the tip of an iceberg. The HRD provider must use sound research methods for getting below the surface, first identifying symptoms, then problems, and then using research and inquiry to assess results.

HRD professionals can take the initiative in carefully assessing performance issues that confront their organization, targeting those that are critical for business

---

BOX 10.2   Jacque and Frank—Team Building or Performance Coaching

The director of HRD in a large retail company was approached by Jacque, a member of the executive committee and the vice president for real estate development for the corporation, a job that included oversight of new store construction. Frank, the director of construction projects, was one of Jacque's key subordinates, responsible for a large and complex department. Frank's responsibilities included contracting for all architectural work, for which he had professional qualifications, but these activities were actually to be supervised by Frank's manager of architecture. Another of Frank's subordinates was the manager of facilities layout. For retailers, real estate and store development is a critical tactical performance issue, since the look of "the box," as the store is called, is a key factor in attracting customers.

Frank was out of the office much of the time inspecting projects, meeting with architects, and, generally, heavily involved in the architectural side of his department. His frequent absences from the office prevented Frank from giving direction to his department. Instead of Frank attending meetings with senior executives of the operating divisions, including members of the executive committee, Frank's facilities manager often attended them. While this was not in and of itself a problem, overall, Frank's absences and his lack of oversight of facility layout and development led to a power vacuum, which the facilities manager was more than willing to fill. The situation was leading to various dysfunctional dynamics across the construction department.

continues

BOX 10.2   Jacque and Frank—Team Building or Performance Coaching [CONTINUED]

Jacque's request to HRD was, "I'd like to do some team-building to help these guys get their department under control." Jacque's frustration was evident as he spoke. The HRD director proposed, as the first step, some preliminary interviews with Frank, his managers, and other members of the department. It quickly became evident from the interviews that Frank was immersing himself in the architectural work of his department. He was good at it and, moreover, enjoyed interacting with the architects. His architecture manager was a good architect but had little experience in the retail industry. Although Frank claimed to be developing his architectural manager to accept more responsibility, it was clear Frank reviewed the architects' plans because he enjoyed working with the architects (a motivation problem). It also became clear that Frank had not been getting much direction from Jacque; they had fallen into a pattern of "business as usual" until Jacque's frustration built to the boiling point and he exploded. Frank would absorb the outburst, and then things would again return to normal. If Frank was aware of something seriously amiss in his relationship with Jacque, he hid it well—to Frank, it was just the way things were.

Over lunch, the HRD director told Jacque that neither team-building nor any other indirect third-party intervention was likely to help the situation; in fact, they would probably confuse the situation by failing to address the problem of managerial direction at two levels—Jacque's and Frank's. Instead, Jacque needed to sit down with Frank and, with specific examples, discuss the performance issues and their consequences for the organization. The HRD director suggested to Jacque that he be very specific in having Frank produce a plan for correcting the situation, a plan that would focus on his own behavior and how he was using his time. This plan should be monitored biweekly, along with department performance. There could be no guarantee that Frank's behavior would change, but without such a systematic approach there was no chance of changing the situation.

Jacque reacted with mild disappointment. Somehow he hoped that a third party, perhaps the HRD director or one of his OD staff, would assume the burden of addressing the issue in a more systematic fashion. On the other hand, Jacque recognized the basic truth in the message—that team-building would only be cosmetic. Jacque did ask the HRD director to be present to help facilitate his communication process with Frank. Knowing the people involved, the HRD director judged that this would be helpful rather than inhibiting and agreed to participate if Frank agreed. He also helped Jacque prepare both his comments and how he might respond to Frank's probable assertions that he needed to be out checking on jobs. Meeting with Frank, Jacque gave specific examples of his concerns. He also made it clear that, while he thought Frank was a good manager of architecture, he didn't need him for that job, but instead he needed Frank to manage the construction department. Jacque told Frank he wanted to meet again in a couple of days, and during the intervening period, he wanted Frank to decide whether he truly wanted to continue as director of construction projects and, if he did, to produce a plan that would convince Jacque of his commitment to change. Jacque indicated that he thought it would be difficult for Frank to change his behavior because Frank really wanted to be involved in architecture. Jacque told Frank he needed to decide if he wanted to be the director of store construction rather than an architect.

At their subsequent meeting Frank, presented a detailed plan for changing his approach to the job. He really wanted to stay in his present position. Jacque scheduled specific times to meet with Frank and review how well Frank was executing his plan. After a few months it became clear that Frank was indeed backing up his plans with actions and establishing a new equilibrium. Frank's entire department was operating better, hitting key benchmarks and building supportive relationships with operating division executives. The HRD director also continued coaching Jacque, helping him to reflect on the lessons learned from this experience and how they were relevant to other issues in Jacque's division.

In brief, Frank's behavior was rooted in his own motivation, and only he could decide to make the effort to change. Jacque could, however, change the context of the situation, which he had contributed to by failing to provide consistent direction and which could have worsened had he avoided confronting the situation constructively, but directly.

results, and determining which, if any, can be significantly addressed by a learning intervention. Such inquiries also need to identify what kind and how much support will be necessary to successfully transfer the learning at both the individual and organizational levels. In short, HRD can state, "An intervention is only as important to us as it is to management"; backing up this argument with data and business logic.

The basis for working through the performance, symptom, problem model of Figure 10.3 is the skillful use of both questions and listening to probe beneath the problematic performance situation. This is most effective when done as a process of coinquiry with others associated with the situation, presenting the process as one of problem solving for performance improvement, and not as a process of control or fault-finding.

Agree on a Description of the Performance Situation   A key HRD skill for performance improvement is the ability to describe issues rather than evaluate them. Evaluative statements imply attribution and judgment. They generate defensiveness and, more important, they divert attention away from the real issues by focusing on the evaluation rather than the underlying causes. Many times a manager will approach HRD with an evaluative statement that has embedded within it one of the possible problems such as, "The people in the procurement team aren't motivated to succeed." This statement is an attribution—on the third rung of the ladder of inference, to use the metaphor suggested in Chapter Seven—that must be tested against the facts by first asking the manager for data that supports his or her evaluative attribution, that is, what the manager or others have actually heard or seen. This can lead to a descriptive statement like, "The procurement team has missed its delivery targets in three of the last four months." If all parties can agree that this is a data-based description of the problematic performance situation, they can begin examining the events and actions associated with it.

Skillfully Use Probing Questions to Surface, First, Symptoms and, Then, Underlying Problems   While questions and listening skills have been a staple of supervisory development courses for decades, analysis of actual conversations suggest that performance discussions are often more like debates, with participants making points and counterpoints rather than inquiring systematically. Skillful mixing of open-ended questions (phrased with "how," "what," "where," "when," and "who") with closed-ended questions (phrased with "did," "do," "can," "have," "would," "could," "are," "will," and "is") can be used to essentially coach managers to test their attributions. The guiding principle is that closed-ended questions tend to restrict, constrain, and focus the flow of information, while open-ended questions have the opposite effect. For this reason, early questions generally should be open-ended, to encourage exploration of the issue. Closed-ended questions, asked early in the conversation (other than to confirm agreement), tend to be loaded, putting pressure on the respondents to either agree or disagree. Closed-ended questions are appropriate later, when specifics are needed.

In the actual case we presented in Box 10.2, probing interviews with the team and the manager produced documentation that frequent last-minute changes in both specifications and priorities were causing significant rework on the part of the team. While many of the changes were unavoidable, more realistic adjustment of delivery schedules led to greater cooperation between the team and managers.

SUMMARY

Throughout this text we have argued that the essence of HRD is linking learning to performance improvement. Ideally this begins with creating forums for the creation of strategy and helping management determine the key competencies, both organizational and individual, required to implement that strategy, to build alignment among organizational actors at key interfaces, and to align HR systems to support the strategy.

When responding to requests from management to address performance problems, it is important for HRD practitioners to determine whether the problem requires a training intervention, some other set of learning experiences, or a different kind of solution altogether. Too often symptoms are confused with problems. Long-term credibility rests not on the number of services and interventions provided but on their effectiveness. Careful diagnosis is the key.

Question for Discussion

1. Many students are involved with group projects in their classes. Think of the various issues that emerge as you have tried to complete such projects.

   ▪ What are the issues that have emerged? In the past, how have you characterized these issues to others?

   ▪ Do these characterizations reflect symptoms or problems?

   ▪ What are your data, and how have you tested your assumptions and conclusions?

   ▪ What do you think are the real problems, and what solutions are suggested by the discussion in this chapter?

   ▪ What learning supports might have helped the group avoid these problems?

End Notes

1. K. W. Seibert, D. T. Hall, and K. E. Kram, "Strengthening the Weak Link in Strategic Executive Development: Integrating Individual Development and Global Business Strategy," *Human Resource Management,* 34 (1995): 549–67.

2. M. Popper and R. Lipshitz, "Organization Learning Mechanisms: A Structural and Cultural Approach to Organizational Learning," *Journal of Applied Behavioral Science,* 34 (1998): 78-98.

3. J. Miner, *The Challenge of Managing* (Philadelphia: W. B. Saunders Company, 1975).

4. V. Vroom, *Work and Motivation* (Malabar, Fla.: Robert Krieger Publishing, 1984), 203.

5. J. R. Hackman and G. Oldham, *Work Redesign* (Reading, Mass.: Addison-Wesley, 1980).

6. D. A. Nadler and E. E. Lawler, "Motivation: A Diagnostic Approach," in J. R. Hackman, E. E. Lawler, III, and L. W. Porter, *Perspectives on Behavior in Organizations* 2nd ed. (New York: McGraw-Hill, 1983), 67–78; Vroom, *Work and Motivation.*

7. M. W. Galbraith, B. R. Sisco, and L. M. Guglielmino, *Administering Successful Programs for Adults* (Malabar, Fla.: Krieger Publishing, 1997); T. L. Kowalski, *The Organization and Planning of Adult Education* (Albany: State University of New York, 1988); K. N. Wexley and G. P. Latham, *Developing and Training Human Resources in Organizations,* 3rd ed. (New York: HarperCollins, 2002).

This chapter

- reviews and discusses six critical uncertainties that research suggests will influence the future of HRD practice;

- describes how these six uncertainties might interact with one another;

- discusses the implications of technology and globalization for the HRD role;

- highlights the importance of HRD maintaining a strategic focus on workforce development and changes; and

- describes twelve values that represent a vision for the HRD profession and which emerged from the 2001 ASTD and Academy of Human Resource Development future search conference.

Key terms:

uncertainties	**globalization**	**labor markets**
digital workplace	**lifelong learning**	**workforce development**

Future Directions
in HRD Practice

Prognosticating about future strategies, management practices, or HRD's role in an age of rapid and increasingly discontinuous change is risky business, as those promoting a golden age of technology stocks or a new recessionless economy in the last decade of the twentieth century discovered during the first years of the twenty-first. Nevertheless, future directions must be addressed if for no other reason *than that a profession that seeks to foster strategic learning as a way of bringing a sense of order to uncertainty should not shirk from the challenge of thinking about future demands and opportunities. More importantly, if HRD professionals are going to provide value to their organizations, they must remain at the forefront of practice.*

CRITICAL TRENDS AND UNCERTAINTIES IMPACTING HRD

Chermack, Lynham, and Ruona recently completed an analysis of both socioeconomic trends and trends in other professional disciplines that are either currently or potentially impacting HRD practice.[1] Classifying these trends according to both their probability of impacting HRD and their level of uncertainty, they cite Hodgson and Schwartz in noting that high probability impact and high uncertainty forces and trends are the *critical* uncertainties when thinking about future directions in the field of practice, because we can only speculate about how they will present themselves.[2] Chermack et al. identified six critical uncertainties: 1) competition for the "expertise elite," 2) "globalization," 3) "locus of control—organizational or individual," 4) "marketability of knowledge," 5) "next age," and 6) "technological explosion."

Limiting ourselves for the moment to these six forces, we can speculate on their implications for HRD. Barring the collapse of civilization as we know it, two categories on their list—advancing globalization and increasing rates of technological innovation—are inevitable. What are unpredictable are their consequences, that is, the socioeconomic changes and forces they will unleash and how these changes and forces will shape organizational practices and, by extension, the practice of HRD. Likewise, increasing efficiency in capturing and accessing marketable knowledge is likely to become more important, but the problem lies in identifying that knowledge and in presenting it in a form that doesn't limit creativity. One expects that the phrase "We are not in the knowledge management business" will soon be heard in many organizations; what will be needed by organizations is the ability to access the right knowledge at the right time in order to address a particular problem.

The impact of Chermack et al.'s remaining three categories is even more speculative. What mix of expertise will a given organization need? How quickly will expertise become obsolete as a function of the pace of new knowledge creation? How much development of current staff (as opposed to acquiring new talent) will organizations offer? These are compelling questions. It is interesting to think that perhaps personal qualities, such as aptitude, adaptability, and the capacity for learning quickly, will become more important than any particular type of expertise on the part of employees. As organizations continue to restructure in response to changing strategic opportunities and business conditions—perhaps providing people with ongoing opportunities to develop new competencies and expertise as well as to broaden existing ones will become as important as traditional career ladders for organizations in retaining highly valued contributors. How this development will be provided for—in training rooms, through technology, or providing opportunities for informal and individualized learning—is likely to vary greatly.

Both labor market conditions and the ability of people to move across industries by innovatively repackaging their experience and abilities will influence the extent to which organizations have control over employment contracts. The difference between the late twentieth century, with its talent shortages in many areas, and the early twenty-first century, with its relatively high unemployment, once again drives home the point that things change quickly. The question as to whether the economy has entered a new age remains open and unanswered, for while there exists broad consensus that fundamental changes are taking place in our society, it remains unclear what lens should be used to define it. The "new economy" has turned out to be not so new after all; profits and business models are still important. Paradoxically, while the rate of technological change and knowledge creation accelerates, the scope and pace of adoption and application proceeds more slowly than visionaries predict. It may be more useful to use multiple lenses to think about how our societies are changing, rather than become attached to one label, such as "the information age," or "the knowledge age."

How all six forces interact, blend, or counter one another is at the core of speculating about the future. Will competition among organizations for knowledge and expertise, in interaction with technology, make the content of learning more consumer-driven (individualistic) rather than producer-driven (organization/institutional)? Historically, HRD professionals and various other experts set the learning agenda in their organizations, responding to the learning needs and requirements defined by organizational and professional elites. To what extent will Web access and connectedness become an individualizing and/or a democratizing force altering the supply versus demand balance in the "learning marketplace"? How will this translate into the HRD practice of managing knowledge and making it accessible in tailored forms as opposed to providing prescribed menus of learning? Balancing any individualizing trends will be the need for organizations to create forums that provide for collective integration and alignment of their workforces. Acquiring information is not at the core of the learning process but, rather, is the foundation for making meaning from learning through learning-oriented discussion and dialogue. Not only can technology provide information, it can also provide for more global dialogue and sensemaking through Web-based chat rooms and virtual teleconferences.

How will technology be used to track and control individuals? While it is comforting to view technology as a democratizing force, in and of itself it is neutral. The critical question is, toward what purpose will technology be applied? Historically, technology has been a rationalizing force and workplace rationalization has been accompanied by a shift in power away from employees in general and toward increased centralization and managerial control, even while layers of middle management have been taken out of the organization. For example, senior operating retail executives monitor inventories and operations in local stores without leaving their offices in headquarters. In this context HRD's role is to initiate conversations around the use of the information that technology provides, whether for feedback and development or authoritarian control and micromanagement.

As we have noted, two of the high impact–high uncertainty forces cited by Chermack et al.—technology and globalization—seem certain to intensify in their impact on the workplace and HRD. We saw how the nature of their impact may be uncertain but not their importance as a social dynamic. Indeed, technology and globalization seem to be primary drivers of the other four high impact–high uncertainty forces as they interact upon each other: technology further enables globalization, and increasing globalization enhances the attractiveness of investment in technology.

Innovation in computer sciences, information technologies, and communications continues at an accelerating pace. As a form of socioeconomic infrastructure, the World Wide Web emerged in the late twentieth century, surpassing the establishment of the railways, a century before, and superhighways, in mid-century, and connecting not only the communities of the modern nation-states but also the populations of the globe. In the process, the transformation of multinational corporations into global organizations has become a reality in ways barely imaginable a couple decades ago. Parts and products are now manufactured all over the world for export into high consumer demand countries. Increasingly, professional and white-collar jobs are being globalized. Software development is now a major growth industry in India. Customer service centers for United States companies are locating in countries outside the United States. Investment by high-technology companies has made Malaysia one of the stronger South Asian economies, providing an alternative model for development by encouraging investment rather than reliance on natural resources.

THE IMPACT OF TECHNOLOGY AND GLOBALIZATION ON HRD'S ROLE

In this text, our primary concern is how the technology and globalization drivers will impact on HRD's role. The digital workplace is already here and, as a younger generation, many of whom have taken e-learning courses in their otherwise traditional university programs and familiar with technology and conducting business via technology continues to enter the workforce, receptivity to education delivered by technology is likely to increase even as HRD specialists become more savvy and skillful in their program designs. The impact will increase the complexity of the competencies required of HRD professionals.

Increasing Complexity in the HRD Role

Benson, Johnson, and Kuchinke identify three areas in which HRD will itself be impacted as its own workplace becomes increasingly digitalized: 1) the scope of needs analysis and the design of programs; 2) the relationship between trainers/educators and learners in the learning process; and 3) enhanced opportunities for informal learning.[3]

Broader Scope of Needs Analysis and Program Design   When designing e-learning programs, HRD professionals have to assess both the technology skills of learners and the level of technology that is available to them. HRD professionals will also need skills in technology use and management and will need to increase their competence in media production. Lee, Owens, and Benson note that design involves decisions around what learner-system interface best fits the objectives of the program, whether the design should be outsourced, and what level of instructor and learner technical support will be needed for implementing the system.[4] These decisions require knowledge of both learning theory and technology capability, as well as how various groups of learners experience technology. The net impact of e-learning technology is to add to the competencies required of HRD practitioners, not replace former skills with new ones.

Although HRD professionals will have to become increasingly capable in the application of technology to make the informed decisions described by Lee et al., they will continue to partner closely with technology support experts as technologies evolve. Thus, as we noted in Chapter Eight, more and more HRD work in Web-based learning will involve complex project management skills, integrating the input of content knowledge specialists, instructional designers, and technology and media production experts.

An Expanded Repertoire of Facilitation Skills   In working with learners HRD professionals will have to become skilled in facilitating Web-based discussions, which present different problems and challenges than face-to-face facilitation, especially around contentious issues. Many times learners are more blunt on line than they might be face-to-face. Yet face-to-face presentation and group facilitation competencies will remain an important part of the HRD professional's skill set. Not all learning events will be technology-driven, and blended learning designs are likely to become more widely used as well (see Chapter Eight). While historically a particular HRD professional might have relied on either presentation skills or group facilitation as his or her primary mode of working with learners, paradoxically technology may be creating a environment in which HRD practitioners are required to move among different delivery contexts, often blending them in a design.

Supporting Informal Learning   Benson et al. observe that "the full potential of the Internet to support informal learning is yet to be realized."[5] HRD may not play a central role in this regard, as learners access the Web to obtain needed information on a just-in-time basis. However, Dennen and Wang note two areas in which HRD may have to support those accessing the Web in this manner, especially those who are still relatively new to technology: 1) learning how to conduct efficient searches and 2) learning how to establish the validity of what they access.[6] Providing critical thinking skills that help learners who are accessing the Web to make this kind of validity assessment will be a crucial support function.

Certain kinds of just-in-time information and learning needs are likely to be organization-specific, linking HRD to knowledge management concerns. Some organizations have experienced counterproductive turf battles between HRD and IT groups over the knowledge management domain, when collaboration, with both groups focused on learner needs, is the most useful approach. Organizational members need user-friendly information access and the capacity to conduct meaningful collaboration, either as needed or as part of ongoing collaborative groups.

Although we cannot reliably establish the form and the exact percentage of content that will be delivered in this fashion, it is clear that more and more learning will be somehow mediated by technology. Accordingly, the work of HRD professionals is becoming increasingly complex in terms of coordinating the skill requirements necessary for bringing a sophisticated learning program to fruition.

Globalization

Whether vertically integrated within the organization or dependent on external vendors, the supply chains of a many organizations in the private sector are becoming increasingly globalized. Training programs, whether they use text or multimedia, have to take into account differences in language, contextual interpretations, and cultural assumptions. At a conference on Global Perspectives in HRM, Crawford Beveridge, Executive Vice President of Human Resources at Sun Microsystems, emphasized that creating new institutional arrangements that facilitate the learning of multinational teams in a knowledge-centered workforce is a significant HRD challenge.[7]

How power and group dynamics vary across cultural traditions becomes an important consideration in the design of learning environments. Kim, who has studied the impact of importing North American approaches to a team-based organization into a prominent Korean organization, reports how the effort faltered partly due to the influence of culturally embedded patterns of distributing power according to age and seniority. He concludes that "implementing a team-based structure into an organization in which traditional cultural based hierarchy still determines the patterns of interaction and communication without a strategy for addressing the cultural issues is likely to be a frustrating experience for all key stakeholders."[8] Kim's point, although it addresses a specific form of organizational innovation, carries a more general lesson: when working in the global context, HRD professionals have to be concerned with the learning behaviors embedded in a particular culture, with how cultural factors like power, autonomy, and social distance impact the learning environment, and with how learning is transferred back to the workplace.

In the future, HRD professionals can expect to be asked to provide support in helping global teams to develop their ability to learn and communicate across cultures, often in the virtual format;[9] cultural literacy is becoming an important management and professional competency. An increasing number of managers and professionals are going to need a more sophisticated understanding of how to operate in unfamiliar cultural settings, and HRD professionals themselves will need to be comfortable in preparing learning programs in unfamiliar cultural settings.

MAINTAINING A STRATEGIC PERSPECTIVE ON WORKFORCE

While the exact content of the future role of HRD is somewhat speculative, we have described in broad terms the general trends that are likely to intensify during the next decade. One HRD role that will continue to be especially important is maintaining a focus on the requirements of developing and sustaining a viable workforce, no matter how it is distributed globally. These same trends have potentially important implications for an organization's business prospects. As management's attention becomes increasingly focused on the implications for the organization's strategy in general it becomes important for HR professionals to provide relevant intelligence on the changing dynamics in labor markets and on the implications for the organization's workforce. Capelli, writing in *Harvard Business Review*, has argued that labor markets will ultimately determine the distribution of a company's workforce. This means that HRD professionals must stay abreast of labor markets on a global scale and draw attention to opportunities and threats that emerge.[10] Packer and Sharrar make the point that HRD professionals also need to work with the larger learning system, including high schools, community colleges, and trade schools, to provide opportunities for reskilling and to ensure the availability of a workforce with the literacy requirements and problem-solving skills necessary for employment in the emerging workplace.[11] For HRD professionals, this is a boundary-spanning role that goes beyond working with traditional training vendors.

RESULTS OF A FUTURE SEARCH CONFERENCE ON HRD

In June of 2001, ASTD and the Academy of Human Resource Development sponsored a three-day future search conference; sixty-four people with backgrounds in business, academe, and government were invited to participate.[12] These participants were selected with the goal of including all stakeholder groups that are affected by the future of workplace learning and performance. Conference participants reviewed the past, examined the present, and then focused on constructing ideal future scenarios, finally seeking common ground themes.

Not surprisingly, there were diverse perspectives and differences among the participants. During the third day of the conference, 12 areas of common ground emerged that, for the most part, reflect a set of values that will challenge HRD practice rather than describe role responsibilities or changes: 1) creating synergy between research and practice, 2) leveraging technology without losing the human and social components of learning, 3) striking a balance between work and personal life, 4) striving toward the creation of humane workplaces, 5) acknowledging intellectual capital as the lifeblood or true bottom line of organizations, 6) developing social responsibility, 7) partnering in the changing role of education, 8) developing collaborative partnerships, both inside and outside the organization, 9) embracing globalization and 10) multiculturalism, 11) managing knowledge and learning effectively, and 12) fostering lifelong learning.

Many of these values are open to interpretation as to how they might be operationalized in practice. For example, what constitutes a balance between work and personal life in an organization in which technology allows employees to be always accessible to e-mail or cellular videophone—even on weekends and vacations? During the 1980s, before the emergence of comprehensive wireless communications, one major accounting firm ran ads in the business press featuring one of their professionals working late on Christmas Eve to prepare work for a client. As a company value, and a symbol of what has become a "24/7" professional workplace, what are the tradeoffs, in terms of productivity, time for creative thought, and civic responsibilities, that give meaning to the balance of work and personal life? What is the definition of a humane workplace? This question goes to the heart of working conditions and pay scales in developing countries where factories serve as part of the value chain of larger organizations in the developed economies.

How do these values find expression "on the ground" in profit-driven organizations, and how would this common ground list look if it were constructed from the theories-in-use of CEOs and COOs? While the "total system" was in the room in terms of domains of HRD practice, it is unclear that the system captured the perspective of CEOs in terms of their operational goals. In a very real sense the 12 values capture the dilemmas inherent in the practice of HRD in today's organizations. They represent issues that form the context for HRD practice and where HRD practitioners can, hopefully, foster a continuing conversation in their organization while staying connected to its performance demands.

SUMMARY

During periods of rapid change all workers, including HRD professionals, must be prepared to become lifelong learners. It is clear that strong socioeconomic forces, especially technology and globalization, will continue to drive change in the HRD profession, resulting in continuing challenges around core values in our society and HRD practice.

Participation in professional associations, especially the Academy of Human Resource Development (www.ahrd.org), the American Society for Training and Development (www.astd.org), the International Society for Performance

Improvement (www.ISPI.org), and the Human Resource Planning Society (www.hrps.org), is a way to stay current as the future unfolds. So too is becoming a regular reader of publications like *The Economist, Foreign Affairs,* the *London Financial Times,* and *Business Week,* and staying abreast of new developments in science and technology, both through reading and inquiring of others. HRD professionals hold one advantage in that they have access across the scope of their organizations. They are expected to know "what's new." The one sure thing about the future of HRD is that it is going to be different from what it is today, and the forces shaping it are most likely to first appear outside the more narrow specialized literature of the field.

Questions for Discussion

1. Have you taken a e-learning course in your college or university?

   ■ If yes, what were its advantages and disadvantages when compared to conventional face-to-face classes? What were the core characteristics of the design—i.e., text on line, Web-based discussion, etc.?

   ■ If no, can you talk with someone who has taken online courses and ask them the same questions?

   ■ What do you conclude about the way technology might be better used to foster learning?

2. What can be done to better prepare students to be part of a globalized workforce? How well is the diversity in your school setting or community utilized for this purpose? How can you better leverage learning opportunities to prepare yourself for working in this environment?

3. Consider the 12 points of "common ground" that emerged from the ASTD/Academy of Human Resource future conference. How do you see these issues working out around you—in your job, if you are employed, or in your parents' experience? What tradeoffs are apparent to you?

End Notes

1. T. Chermack, S. A. Lynham, and W. E. A. Ruona, "Critical Uncertainties Confronting Human Resource Development," in D. C. Short and J. W. Bing, eds., *Shaping the Future of HRD: Advances in Developing Human Resources* (August, 2003), 257–71.

2. A. M. Hodgson, "Hexagons for Systems Thinking," *European Journal of Operational Research,* 59 (1992): 220–30; P. Schwartz, *The Art of the Long View* (New York: Doubleday, 1991).

3. A. D. Benson, S. D. Johnson, and K. P. Kuchinke, "The Use of Techonology in the Digital Workplace: A Framework for Human Resource Development," in A. D. Benson and S. D. Johnson, eds., *Information Technologies in Human Resource Development: Advances in Developing Human Resources* (San Francisco: Sage and the Academy Human Resource Development, November, 2002): 392–404.

4. W. W. Lee, D. L. Owens, and A. D. Benson, "Design Considerations for Web-Based Learning Systems," in A. D. Benson and S. D. Johnson, eds., *Information Technologies in Human Resource Development: Advances in Developing Human Resources* (San Francisco: Sage and the Academy Human Resource Development, November, 2002): 405–23.

5. Benson, et al., "The Use of Technology," 397.

6. V. P. Dennen and M. Wang, "The Keyboard-Based Job Coach: Informal Learning via the Internet," in A. D. Benson and S. D. Johnson, eds., *Information Technologies in Human Resource Development: Advances in Developing Human Resources* (San Francisco: Sage and the Academy Human Resource Development, November, 2002): 440–50.

7. Quoted in M. Cseh, "Facilitating Learning in Multicultural Teams," in L. Yorks, ed., *Cross-Cultural Dimensions of Team Learning: Advances in Developing Human Resources* (San Francisco: Sage and the Academy Human Resource Development, February, 2003): 26–40.

8. Y-S. Kim, "Learning One's Way to Implementing Learning Teams in Korea: The Relationship between Team Learning and Power in Organizations," in L. Yorks, ed., *Cross-Cultural Dimensions of Team Learning: Advances in Developing Human Resources* (San Francisco: Sage and the Academy Human Resource Development, February, 2003): 81.

9. M. Marquardt and N. O. Berger, "The Future: Globalization and New Roles for HRD," in D. C. Short and J. W. Bing, eds., *Shaping the Future of HR: Advances in Developing Human Resources,* (August, 2003): 283–95.

10. P. Capelli, "A Market Driven Approach to Retaining Talent," *Harvard Business Review* (January-February, 2000): 103–11.

11. A. H. Packer and G. K. Sharrar, "Linking Lifelong Learning: Corporate Social Responsibility and the Changing Nature of Work," in D. C. Short and J. W. Bing, eds., *Shaping the Future of HRD: Advances in Developing Human Resources* (August, 2003): 332–41.

12. J. D. Dewey and T. J. Carter, "Exploring the Future of HRD: The First Future Search Conference for a Profession," in D. C. Short and J. W. Bing, eds., *Shaping the Future of HRD: Advances in Developing Human Resources* (August, 2003): 245–56.

part 3

From Theory to Practice

Cases

Glossary of Terms

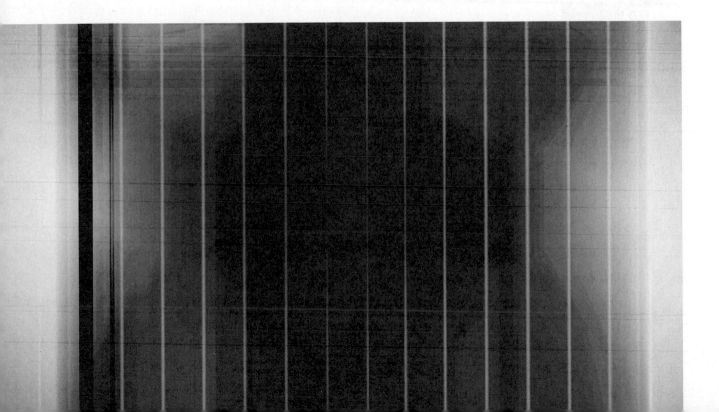

3

part

Cases

The following cases illustrate various applications and configurations of HRD practice. Each case draws on aspects of HRD theory we have presented throughout this text. The cases also represent the diverse settings in which HRD practitioners work. All the cases have been written by practitioners with extensive corporate experience who have worked at senior levels, both inside companies and as external consultants. All these practitioners are also reliable researchers who seek to learn from their engagements and share that learning with others.

Jim Krefft and Lyle Yorks describe performance improvement in a major financial services company that is part of a Fortune Top 50 company with a highly competitive culture. The case involves process analysis linked to HRM issues of selection and competency identification along with the HRD challenges of helping the organization learn. Corporate strategic imperatives drove the project. Christina Luddy demonstrates how principles of action learning were adapted in a highly decentralized global financial firm to create a peer-coaching infrastructure, initially in support of learning transfer but later expanded to support other learning and development needs in the major international company. Stephen Dent, Jim Krefft, and Susan Schaefer describe how
a wireless telecommunication company confronted the organizational changes required to continue its rapid growth in a highly turbulent business context. The transition required that the business address learning issues at the strategic, tactical, and operational levels. Jeff Kuhn chronicles the leadership approach of Bettina Kelly, a senior learning officer at Chubb Insurance, as she revitalized the company's corporate leadership development organization. This case illustrates how building credibility with senior line management by focusing on the strategic needs of the business and by using the metaphor, a corporate university can differentiate the new approach to executive development. Rosa Colon focuses on the development and implementation of a new, Web-based human resource portal for employees. Involving both cultural change and the development of new competencies, the case shows how complex projects require alignment of the traditional focus of OD and HRD, combined with project management issues. Art Shirk describes how learners participating in a highly holistic leadership-development program experience can experience transformative learning. This case provides another example of the diverse contexts in which HRD practitioners can work and the development of socially transformative leaders.

DRIVING PERFORMANCE IMPROVEMENT BY HARD-WIRING PEOPLE TO CORE BUSINESS PROCESSES: A FINANCIAL SERVICES FIRM CASE STUDY

Case Written by James H. Krefft, Partnership Continuum, Inc. www.partneringintelligence.com, and Lyle Yorks

In late 1996 a global financial services firm set a goal to achieve 150 percent revenue growth in five years. The company recognized that to achieve such exponential growth it had to make step-change upgrades in organizational performance, particularly in the production of both its new deal originators and its deal underwriters. In 1997, to accelerate revenue growth the firm built a first-of-its-kind performance improvement system directly linked to core business processes. This case describes an HRD-based approach to performance improvement that resulted in the firm's exceeding its performance goals.

Business Context

In financial services, producing assets often come down to people, a balance sheet, and reputation (brand identity); leveraging of human capital for extraordinary performance may be the only distinct source of long-term competitive advantage. The key to leveraging human capital lies in human resources development (HRD) processes driven by an enterprise's strategic direction and embedded in its core processes. Exceptional performance results from the alignment of purpose, processes, and people. Although both process management and performance management have separately attracted attention, little notice has been paid to how the concrete links that connect people and processes drive performance improvement. These links begin inside process maps and thread their way into four basic HRD tools: competency models, position profiles, performance plans, and development plans. HRD professionals have, for the most part, built these tools based on precedents, anecdotal experience, and expert testimony.

A more integrated approach builds these HRD tools by beginning with the myriad of activities, decisions, and indicators nested in process maps. At the day-to-day operations level, individual process activities and the chorus of human behaviors required for outstanding performance are the same. Using this holistic approach, a global financial services company installed a performance-improvement system hard-wired to its core business processes. Each system component—hiring, performance management, and training and development—was rebuilt based on concrete links to the company's five core (Level 1) business processes: 1) new customer origination, 2) underwriting, 3) closing, 4) account management, and 5) cash management. Under each of these core processes are subprocesses (Levels 2 and 3) that will be illustrated below.

Competencies: The Catalysts

Once an organization has mapped its core business processes in detail, the design of a process-driven performance improvement system begins with defining a set of competencies. A competency model establishes the criteria for filling jobs with the right people and ensures the linkage of individual performance objectives to business goals. Historically, organizations have used either one or both of the following inputs to build selection criteria: empirical data from individual performers and the strategic direction of the organization. The former relies on empirical examples of past performance to delineate competencies (that worked *yesterday*), while the latter looks at business imperatives going forward to determine what behaviors will most likely be required for success *tomorrow*. Missing is a consistent way of determining what is required to perform well *today*. The competencies required by executive core business processes emerge through an analysis of process maps down to the activity level. A holistic competency model can thus be created by using this triangular method involving the perspectives of *yesterday* (empirical data on outstanding performance), *today* (activities and indicators from process maps), and *tomorrow* (strategic directions).

The global financial services company used this triangular approach to define the competencies needed to drive achievement of its aggressive global growth goals. Focus groups were conducted and individual top performers were interviewed to determine what specific behaviors were correlated with outstanding job performance (yesterday). Process maps were analyzed to pinpoint the key behaviors required to execute core business processes (today). Senior executives were interviewed to identify the competencies that were likely to be needed in the future (tomorrow). The data from all three approaches were crosschecked against each other.

A deeper look illustrates how people become "hard-wired" to core processes. One of the company's five core business processes is "new customer origination" (Process 1 at Level 1). Under this Level 1 core process there are three processes, the first of which is "sourcing" (Process 1.1 at Level 2). This Level 2 process in turn has three processes, the third of which is "contacting prospects" (Process 1.1.3 at Level 3). For the entire Level 1 new customer origination process, there are approximately one dozen supporting processes. When added to the other four Level 1 core processes (noted above in the Introduction) and their associated processes, the company ends up with about 50 processes at Levels 1, 2, and 3. For the new customer origination process, the crucial competency was defined as "tenacious about growth." At Level 2 the competency "relationship selling" was judged as essential for "sourcing" new customers. One of the competencies required for "contacting prospects" (Level 3) was determined to be "resilience," comprising behaviors such as "takes initiative to build relationships" and "turns criticism into opportunities for dialogue." This painstaking work produces a competency model that is a powerful, flexible tool for leveraging human capital.

Position Profiles: The DNA

The next step in designing a process-driven performance improvement system is to translate business objectives, process outputs, and competencies into a practical tool that can be used to facilitate definition of jobs and enable selection of the best candidates for those jobs. This step is accomplished by writing position profiles. Position profiles differ from typical job descriptions, which are often drafted to document the *responsibilities* of a job, as well as minimum qualifications (education, certifications, licenses). The main purpose of job descriptions has traditionally been to justify job level and compensation, and as such they have served more as an audit document than as a practical management tool. Position profiles incorporate strategic, process, and competency requirements to link jobs more tightly with operations requirements. Position profiles, in short, are a tool for documenting the validated strengths (competencies) that will drive success both today and tomorrow.

The global financial services company wrote more than 100 position profiles—all grounded in its business objectives, process outputs, and the competencies required to achieve them. Each position profile includes five to seven principal accountabilities (the "what" of a job) and six to eight key competencies (the "how" of a job) described in behavioral statements. Level 1 processes are embedded in the Position Summary section of each position profile. For example, the Position Summary for Vice President Origination in part reads: "Originates deal activity with new and existing customers in assigned market segments." Level 2—and often Level 3—processes are woven throughout the principal accountabilities, especially in position profiles for originators, underwriters, and portfolio support professionals. The number 1 accountability for a vice president origination is to "identify and source customers to achieve origination targets." This accountability is driven by Process 1.1—sourcing, as well as by Process 1.1.3—contact prospects. Process activities help define the evidence for a particular competency in a job. The company now uses these position profiles to staff the organization by matching the "right people" with the "right jobs." It uses structured team behavioral interviewing to choose the best people.

Performance Management: The Engine

The centerpiece of this process-driven performance improvement system is performance management—a subsystem for focusing day-to-day activities on producing outcomes critical to customers and shareholders. Performance management also creates a focus for training and developing employees. In brief, performance management enables managers to

- plan the actions necessary to meet customer and shareholder valid requirements;
- coach employees with a higher degree of credibility, focus, and timeliness;
- develop competencies in a targeted way; and,
- evaluate employee performance based on business and individual performance data.

The two basic tools of performance management are an *annual performance plan* and a *long-term development plan*. The global financial services company built one-page forms that connect directly both to its core business processes and to the position profiles. Working with his or her manager, an individual employee begins performance planning by making sure he or she clearly understands company, division, department, and team goals. Each individual then draws from the principal account-abilities and key competencies in the position profile to come up with individual performance objectives, which are then documented in the annual performance plan. For example, the performance plan for a particular vice president origination documented three key competencies for his job, along with their associated performance objectives and actions. Under "tenacious about growth," for instance, he listed an objective to "generate average annual contributed value of $5 million or more and at least two new deals." To achieve this objective, the vice president listed the following specific actions:

▌ Meet call activity target of 15 per month (check progress by 4/1).

▌ Work through all assigned prospects with follow-up calls by 9/1.

After employees completed the performance planning activity, the organization had documented, in quantifiable terms, how its people would contribute to such critical business goals as income growth, region operating margin, new product deployment, and deal conversion rate.

A process-driven performance improvement system takes coaching performers and developing competencies out of the realm of conjecture and delayed intervention. Since behavioral observations and root-cause performance gap analyses are conducted in an ongoing fashion, performance coaches are positioned to help employees make quick, targeted behavioral adjustments that have a high chance of closing performance gaps. Determining root causes of performance shortfalls is a vital skill, because different performance-problem causes require different responses. If there is a lack of clarity around strategic objectives or disconnects between leadership behavior and values, the problem may lie with managers. Performance problems can also result from broken processes, an antiquated organization design, or inadequate information systems. In such cases, the root cause may not be within the employee's direct control (see Chapter Ten—symptoms vs. problems).

The long-term development plan is used to establish targets for building the competencies that both the individual and the organization will need to succeed in the future. Whether building for the current performance cycle or for the long term, the key to competency development is to establish validated standards against which to observe or obtain data on the actual behavior displayed by an employee in critical situations—how, for example, a sales rep interacts with a customer during a sales presentation. Such data, if not obtained directly through personal observation, can be collected indirectly through behavioral interviews with customers, colleagues, or subordinates. Competency development at the global financial services company encompassed all the activities necessary to develop critical current and future-focused competencies. At a high level, this competency development

▌ draws from core processes, the competency model, and personal career goals to list the competencies required to succeed now and in the future;

▌ uses the position profile to determine which competencies and behaviors are critical to achieving current position accountabilities and to identify competency gaps;

▮ references the position profile of future jobs to determine which competencies will be critical to achieving future accountabilities and to identify areas for improvement; and,

▮ requires a discussion of the gap analysis to confirm that the competencies identified for development will provide the most leverage both in the present job and in the future.

The key to remember in implementing the development process is to focus on only those few competencies that are most critical to the current and future success of the enterprise. The idea is to create development synergy: by building only the most critical competencies, other related competencies will be built in tandem. Paradoxically, focusing on the few, right competencies produces more rapid and long-lasting performance improvement than trying to work on many competencies at the same time.

The final element of performance management is evaluating results—a data-grounded analysis of an individual's performance results relative to the annual performance plan. For performance evaluation to be effective (that is, for it to reinforce productive behaviors, discourage counterproductive behaviors, and serve as a rational basis for compensation), managers must make judgments based on credible performance data, not on untested assertions, guesses, impressions, or hunches—a task that can be challenging, especially when measuring the presence or absence of certain behaviors. This evaluation is more difficult when a subordinate conducts business out of the direct sight of a manager. For example, how is a sales team leader to know what behaviors a sales rep demonstrated during a telephone cold call? Getting timely, accurate performance data in an era of distributed organizations presents an enormous challenge. It is relatively easy to determine whether or not an employee has met each performance objective. If performance is lagging, however, it can be difficult to pinpoint what factors or behaviors are impeding results. Even if a sales rep contacts 100 prospects a month, for instance, how does a sales team leader know that the rep is consistently displaying productive behaviors during these contact sessions? Process-driven performance evaluation addresses such critical questions as: Do we have a replicable way of collecting valid behavioral data by which to evaluate performance? Are performance shortfalls an employee or a management issue (or both)? Do we have the right competencies in place for each job? Do we need to update position profiles and long-term development plans to accelerate performance improvement?

Results

A process-driven performance improvement system gives traditional HRD activities such as hiring, performance management, and training and development new meaning and application. Hard-wiring people to core business processes enables an organization to achieve extraordinary, repeatable business results. The global financial services company has seen promising results: cycle times for external hires have been reduced, managing directors are spending less time interviewing and getting higher quality hires, fees paid to external recruiters have dropped. The company saw performance improvements almost immediately: outside financial analysts noted that new hires were of higher quality, cycle times for external hires shrank, managing directors spent less time interviewing and yet got higher quality hires, fees to external recruiters dropped, and 166 percent more deals were closed in the year after implementation than in the year before. Revenue grew by 175 percent in 3 years, versus the targeted goal of 150 percent over 5 years.

Financial analysts from outside the company have remarked on the high caliber of recent hires. For example, after a one-week risk-analysis session, the instructor, a professor of finance at a major university, turned to the company's HRD manager and asked, "Have you changed something about the way you hire people?" A process-driven performance improvement system is capable of aligning, adjusting, and completely revamping, if necessary, the way people are integrated with strategic requirements and core business processes. Extraordinary results come from customer-focused processes (right processes) enacted by qualified people (right people) using appropriate tools and technologies (right stuff). The global financial services company is making real a new managerial ideal that people and processes require integrated attention to achieve dramatic and sustainable business results.

Questions for Discussion

1. The HRD practitioners in this case were engaged in a strategically driven performance improvement process. The metaphor of "hardwiring" people to core business processes implies a perspective on successful performance improvement projects. What are the implications of this metaphor and for the approach taken?

2. How does this case illustrate the idea of "positioning people for performance" and the links between systems, processes, and learning as part of HRD practice?

3. What are the change management implications of the approach taken in this case?

4. How does a process-driven performance improvement plan facilitate diagnosing performance problems?

BUILDING AN INFORMAL WORK-BASED LEARNING PROCESS IN A GLOBAL FINANCIAL INVESTMENT FIRM

Case Written by Christina Luddy, Entelegy Associates,
www.entelegyassociates.com

Increasingly, corporate leadership development practitioners have been applying action learning to produce individual and organizational learning and to improve organizational performance in the workplace. Foundational to these interventions is the use of managers' "real work" as a vehicle to uncover and examine the underlying assumptions surrounding leadership, management, and organizational practices. Typically, action-learning interventions are formalized, large-scale leadership development initiatives (see the Grace Cocoa case in Chapter One). For organizations with decentralized senior management structures and corresponding decentralized decision-making on leadership development work, such large-scale initiatives present an implementation challenge. These organizations must seek alternative approaches that apply action-learning principles, namely, a focus on using managers' real work to foster personal and organizational transformation in a more informal way. One approach is for organizations to apply the principles of action learning in an informal, small-group setting with managers. The corporate learning and development group in a global financial investment firm adopted such an alternative when they proposed and implemented leadership development interventions they referred to as *leadership forums.* This case study examines the development and establishment of the forums.

Business Context

Global Financial Services (GFS) is a large, international financial services firm, based in the United States. Over the past 15 years, the firm's strong commitment to providing the best market research and innovative, diversified products and services established the firm as a market leader in mutual funds and retirement services.

In early 2000, senior leadership at GFS realized that sustaining organizational performance in the increasingly volatile and competitive financial markets called for a focused emphasis on leadership development. More specifically, they believed that in order for managers to deal effectively with lower rates of growth and consequent margin pressures, technological advances driving system and process changes, and challenges in the area of workforce development and retention, the firm would need to become more innovative, flexible, and adaptive to business conditions and opportunities.

The Development of the Leadership Forums

To support this leadership development agenda, the corporate learning and development group focused on developing products and services which emphasized individual and organizational transformation. The learning framework for each product and service was to engage leaders in reflecting critically on the underlying assumptions, values, and beliefs of their own and others' leadership and management practices. In other words, this learning framework focused on helping managers learn what drives their actions and to realize the ensuing business results are a consequence of those actions. Underlying this approach is the assumption that this kind of critical examination will enable managers to learn why they are successful or not, so that they may either replicate or correct a situation, while they simultaneously develop habits of learning from experience. Additionally, this process of critical reflection will build managers' capacity to challenge conventional wisdom and "think outside the box."

Leadership forums were designed to apply this learning framework to a small-group intervention model for managers, in which managers meet with five to six of their peers to coach one another in addressing specific business and leadership challenges. The leadership forum model is adaptable, designed to meet specific business contexts while still holding the integrity of the learning framework. Figure 1 provides a high-level overview of the leadership forum model. Each leadership forum group surrounds a common learning goal (e.g., leadership roles or development goals), and the content and format for each session vary according to the needs of the group.

Coaching techniques applied in the sessions are drawn from the action-science and action-inquiry practices advocated by social scientists such as Chris Argyris, Donald Schon, and William Torbert (see Chapter Six). These include asking questions, seeking the data for attributions made by others, and left hand/right hand column case studies, all tools to stimulate critical reflection and critical self-reflection. In their work together, managers participating in the forums focus on problem-posing versus problem-solving, helping one another uncover assumptions that underlie their leadership and management actions.

Facilitators from the learning and development group lead an initial orientation session with each leadership forum group. Following this orientation, groups self-facilitate their own half-day sessions, and the learning and development group continues to act as a resource to provide ongoing mentoring and on-demand support for

FIGURE 1   **Leadership Forum Model**

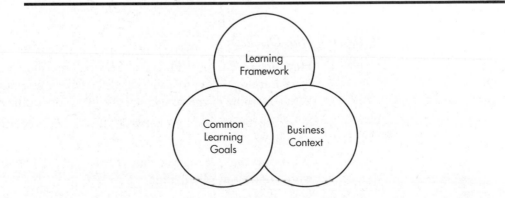

groups. For example, facilitators may be asked periodically to attend sessions and coach group members on refining their application of specific inquiry practices and competencies. It is important to note that this approach, emphasizing self-directed learning, and the application of self-reflective inquiry practices in a forum of peers was a significant departure in a culture oriented toward action and assimilating information provided in traditional delivery formats, such as classroom and electronic messaging. This format was initially implemented to support such traditional learning settings by providing a bridge to facilitate learning transfer from the classroom back to the workplace.

How Leadership Forums Have Been Adapted and Applied

Leadership forums were first used in February 2002 to support a classroom-learning experience developed for directors and vice presidents. The objectives of these forums were to support the transfer of learning from classroom concepts and skills to the managers' work lives and to build cross-company relationships. In each session managers used assignments such as left hand/right hand case studies and business challenge presentations to critically reflect on their leadership and management actions and to develop new strategies and perspectives. Table 1 provides an overview of leadership forums adapted to meet two additional business contexts—a new mentoring program and a new consulting group—and to build informal networks.

Future Research Plans

Early anecdotal information from participants in the pilot leadership forum indicated that the sessions supported the objectives of building cross-company networks and applying classroom learning. Additionally, feedback emphasized that the sessions provided managers with both an open and supportive environment to share real issues and leadership challenges and valuable insights and ideas to address these challenges.

A formal research initiative will be launched during the fourth quarter of 2003 to capture findings from participants. Its goals will be to explore and understand if and how leadership forums contribute to leadership development and cross-company collaboration and how they impact business outcomes.

Questions for Discussion

1. How does the Global Financial Services case illustrate the innovative use of adult learning theory to build self-directed learning capacity among managers? What are some of the core concepts illustrated in the case?

2. What are the connections between the case and the broader design of learning programs?

3. What does the case suggest about the role of HRD practitioners and how their work contexts are changing?

4. What leadership connections would be needed to make this approach work in different organizations?

TABLE 1   **Application of Leadership Forums**

APPLICATIONS	COMMON LEARNING GOALS	OBJECTIVES	BUSINESS SPECIFIC CONTEXT
Leadership Development Program	▪ Application of concepts and skills to real work situations	▪ To transfer classroom learning to the job ▪ To develop an ongoing self-directed community of practice for leaders ▪ To enable leaders to become more self-reflective ▪ To build network relationships across boundaries	▪ Business climate and organizational strategy call for cross-company collaboration and challenging "business as usual" mindset among leaders
Mentoring Group	▪ New mentor role ▪ Cross-functional collaboration	▪ To provide peer-coaching support for managers taking on a mentor role and for their mentees	▪ Focus on building leadership and management bench strength
Human Resource Consulting Organization	▪ Building consulting and coaching skills ▪ Personal development	▪ To build and sustain organizational performance ▪ To strengthen HR consulting capability ▪ To foster cross-functional collaboration and learning	▪ Transition to new service delivery model of HR services
Peer Learning Group in Corporate Learning and Development	▪ Development of peer relationships ▪ Cross-functional collaboration	▪ To provide a forum for directors and managers across the corporate leadership and development organization with a forum for: Practicing what they preach, e.g., leadership learning Candidly sharing feelings, thoughts, and ideas in a safe environment Learning from and growing with each other Focusing on problem exploration Exploring new tools and ideas ▪ To apply inquiry and coaching skills	▪ Virtual and national organization increased need for cross-functional collaboration and learning.

DRIVING GROWTH THROUGH A HOLISTIC STRATEGIC FRAMEWORK: A TELECOMMUNICATIONS COMPANY CASE STUDY

Case Written by Stephen M. Dent, James H. Krefft, Partnership Continuum, Inc. (www.partnershipintelligence.com), and Susan Schaefer, Schaefer Leadership Group (sue@susanschaefer.com)

Growth often results in the need for significant changes in organizational form and culture as well as either rethinking or reaffirming the strategic business model. This case describes one such experience in a wireless communications company, an industry that continues to face a highly turbulent and challenging business environment. Embedded in the case are the HRD implications of transitioning from one phase of business development to another as a consequence of initial success.

Business Context

A wireless division was launched within a large telecommunications company in the late 1990s. Based on a vision that wireless communications could ultimately replace traditional wireline phone service, the division was charged with rapidly building market share for wireless services integrated with other basic telecommunications services. The specific goal was to achieve a number one or two market share position in each of the markets it served within the first three years of business.

Achieving this share would require the company to displace well-entrenched providers, fend off aggressive new entrants, and retain its customers better than other competitors. Organizationally, the overriding challenge was to create an aggressive, entrepreneurial team that would break through the bureaucracy of a firmly established telecommunications company to win in a competitive marketplace.

During the start-up phase, the operation posted strong results. The company had a unique product and quickly established a solid brand reputation. The market also was expanding faster than anyone had imagined. The team was focused on getting things done in ways never conceived of by established companies. By month 18, the company had attained a number two or number three position in most geographic markets. The executive team attributed its success to a superior product and, in part, to individual heroics and the entrepreneurial spirit of the wireless team.

In the third year, challenges began to emerge. Subscriber growth was slowing, and the market was becoming hypercompetitive. Prices were plummeting as each player matched the next in what seemed like a rapidly moving chess game. As it responded to competition, the company's focus blurred, and the lack of operational processes and skills began to strain the organization. In many instances, people were even working at cross-purposes. It was clear that the organization needed to be reenergized so that the same entrepreneurial spirit could be maintained—but within the structure of a more established organization moving out of a start-up mode toward profitability.

Faced with this challenge, the executive team committed to

1. define and communicate the purpose of the organization,
2. implement a process management system to align strategies and tactics, and
3. modify the workforce capability to accommodate the needs of a high-growth operation.

Organizational Challenges

What worked so well during the start-up phase—an entrepreneurial, "get it done" focus—now became the company's biggest obstacle. The organization needed to evolve into a more sophisticated, business-process-oriented team that could scale the business while achieving profitability.

In the start-up mode, the company focused on launching a product that looked and felt like one's regular phone, and it used this feature as its competitive differentiator. As the business grew and operational problems began to emerge, the unifying focus of the business became fractured. Customer service and process failures began driving market "churn," putting heightened pressure on costly customer acquisition to more than make up the difference in revenue shortfalls.

This churn, combined with falling prices, began squeezing margin and, ultimately, the money available for reinvestment into the business. Surveys revealed that employees were confused about strategic direction and operational priorities. Employee pride—experienced in the start-up stage of the business—was turning into frustration and resentment, creating an employee retention issue.

Since the initial objectives were to launch a business and acquire customers, many processes and measurements were not in place. It was becoming increasingly difficult to measure business outcomes and to have the data required to pinpoint the root causes of defects so that those defects could be fixed. As the customer base and operational problems grew, so did the resource requirement for identifying and fixing problems. The venture was now beginning to experience growing pains that threatened the expansion of the business.

Another issue became obvious to management: the employee skill sets needed to start the business, such as product-launch skills, were not necessarily the same as those needed to grow to the next stage of business—that is, operational problem solving skills and collaboration and partnering skills.

Executive leaders recognized danger: the company was starting to lag in its capability to find, sign, and keep subscribers. The president determined that the only way to grow the business was to develop and implement a new organizational infrastructure aimed at operationalizing the business for sustained market leadership and growth.

This organizational infrastructure would address three areas: purpose, processes, and people.

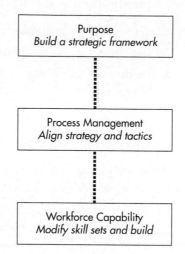

The purpose—the strategic framework—would be the foundation for all strategic and operational activity in the organization. In addition to attracting and retaining key talent, the organization needed a consistent basis for allocating resources, both in the short and long term.

- Processes would be designed to align tactics with the strategic framework through key measurements and process follow-up.

- The people component aimed at strengthening the needed functional skill sets and reinforcing collaboration and continuous improvement.

Purpose

To clarify the organizational purpose, the executive team took the lead in defining and communicating a compelling strategic framework. When the company was small, communications, vision, and objectives were transmitted easily up and down organization lines. However, with growth, the organization was transforming from an agile, focused start-up into a large, process-oriented business needing to provide its growing number of employees with the structure and alignment they needed to do their jobs. The adrenaline-driven growth organization was maturing into a complex company that needed to build employee loyalty while increasing subscriber satisfaction with its products and services. Leaders knew they needed a consistent message, but they did not agree on where the enterprise was going.

During times of strategic learning it is helpful to have a model, or framework, that provides managers and employees with a common lens for addressing issues. The president elected to use the principles found in the strategic framework, "Holistic Organization Model™" (Figure 1), created by Stephen Dent,[1] who was a consultant to the organization's management team. Dent's model integrates two distinct realms—ethereal energies and material outputs—that influence and reflect on each other. The concept of ethereal energies refers to human motivation and potential that powerfully drive organizational performance. Material outputs around products and services result from ethereal energies. This holistic cycle starts with a vision that describes the desired destiny of the organization: not a point on a timeline but, rather, a navigational reference point guiding the business over the long haul. A short compelling description of an altruistic outcome—a vision—reflects the passion of the stakeholders and defines the meaning they place on their enterprise. The vision is buttressed by the values and ethics espoused by the organization's leaders as manifested in the outward behavior they demonstrate towards others.

People watch closely for nonverbal behavioral clues establishing the boundaries of "right" and "wrong." Thus, organizational culture derives directly from the vision and from the values and ethics demonstrated by leadership. Culture defines what, how, when, and why we do what we do, thus becoming a ubiquitous backdrop to organizational performance. The outcome of a business's strategies and tactics are its products and services—tangible reflections on the organization's vision, values, and ethics. The core of the Holistic Organizational Model is the strategic framework; the vision driving the mission, thus linking the ethereal energies to the material outputs in the form of strategies, tactics, and processes. Excellence occurs when alignment between and within these forces happens and people's energies are connected to what they do day by day.

In a series of facilitated sessions, supplemented by subteam meetings and employee focus groups, the executive team developed a vision, a mission, and strategic directions. They rolled out the strategic framework in face-to-face sessions with employees. Employees responded enthusiastically to the strategic framework,

FIGURE 1   **Holistic Organizational Model**

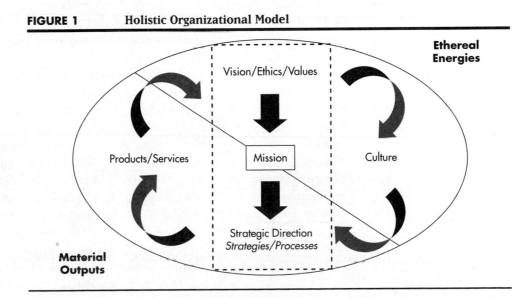

commenting on its simplicity, its power, and its boldness. Managers reacted more cautiously, wondering privately whether the executive team was really serious about building a global wireless communication business.

How the executive team went about creating the strategic framework offers practical learning on organizational dynamics at executive levels. The principal obstacle was getting sufficient time (and energy) from the executive team; it was overcome with a series of facilitated half-day *conversational* meetings with the entire executive team—*only* for general discussions and for decisions. Three-person subteams, guided by a facilitator, met in iterative one-hour sessions to hash out wording for the vision, mission, and strategic directions.

Subteams prepared working drafts for discussion (and decision) that allowed the entire executive team to focus on making sure there was consensus on the big ideas. This kind of multiple, short-burst approach permitted the periods of incubation and testing so crucial for building gut-level ownership of the final document.

Process Management

While participating in the creation of the strategic framework, the marketing and sales executives also implemented a process-management system. Using a SIPOC (supplier-input-process-output-customer) model, process teams documented process flows, mapped marketing and sales processes, identified both process indicators (activity related) and results indicators (output related), and recommended business process improvements. Other teams worked to gather and analyze customer requirement data to better understand what features and benefits were of most value in the marketplace.

Functional silos had been contributing to poor business decisions. For example, as various marketing and sales teams targeted different market segments, the teams drifted apart. Delivering on behalf of one set of customers invariably implied that the needs of other sets of customers would either be only partially met or go unmet. In response, the marketing and sales executive established cross-functional teams as the mandated approach for managing all projects.

Four steps implemented and sustained cross-functional teams. First, people needed to understand the business case for working cross-functionally. For the new venture, the rationale lay in its long-term goal to grow exponentially. Simulating to scale the impact of increasing size on the business would quickly, and dramatically, amplify all the drawbacks of working in silos. Second, executives turned to building the cross-functional project management skills that people would need to work effectively across boundaries. These skills were built through a combination of formal training, one-on-one feedback, and third-party coaching. The third step was to charter several pilot cross-functional teams that could deliver early wins, essential to persuading resistant managers of the value of cross-functional teams in producing solutions that delighted customers. Last, the executive ensured that she and her management team repeatedly told the success stories of these teams to facilitate acceptance of this project-management approach.

Workforce Capability

Employee surveys had shown that employees did not know *how* they were doing. They were unsure of what was expected of them and uncertain about the value of their contribution to company success. Moreover, employees were confused about whether or not they were helping deliver a superior customer experience. Feedback into the organization was needed and the approach used was executive coaching. Results from a 360-degree baselining assessment were used to give each marketing and sales executive a read out on strengths and weaknesses, particularly in the area of coaching and feedback skills. A simple feedback process, a "forced check-in," for facilitating periodic, informal discussions between managers and employees was then implemented. Although initially uncomfortable with getting and giving this kind of performance feedback, managers soon were extending the feedback process on their own, most notably across functional boundaries.

Converting the increased volume of information into actionable business intelligence surfaced as the next major workforce-capability challenge. With the various parts of marketing and sales often working independently of each other during start-up, each manager and team had developed its own approach to problem solving. In some cases these divergent methodologies led to widely differing conclusions drawn from the same raw data, data that itself was often suspect. The marketing and sales executive instituted a consistent problem-solving methodology and had everyone trained in the standardized approach. The common problem-solving steps and nomenclature set a framework for open dialogue about the validity, meaning, and value of the business data put on the table.

The resulting consistency in problem solving further fostered the climate of open communication that had been stimulated by the executive coaching initiative. The problem-solving initiative reduced cross-team friction, diminished discrepancies in interpretation, and helped build consensus on best courses of action. The common approach also coincidentally pointed out deficiencies in how different managers were collecting raw data, thus reducing the problem of suspect data.

The combination of functional silos, lack of feedback, and inconsistent approaches to problem solving had also given rise to adversarial relationships. Competitiveness drove people to act on their own, without appreciation of the interdependence of all parts of the organization. Realizing that a broad intervention was needed to address relationship challenges, the marketing and sales executive established a step-by-step process for building stronger partnerships. The process involved both a task dimension and a relationship dimension. On the task side, partnership development consisted of four stages: assessing the need for a partner, exploring for partners, initiating a pilot activity, and committing to a full partnership.

Success in navigating the form-storm-norm-perform stages of relationship development depends on an individual's personal and a team's collective "Partnering Intelligence."™ Six Partnering Attributes are all learned behaviors: Future Orientation, Comfort with Change, Win-Win Orientation, Comfort with Interdependence, Self-Disclosure and Feedback, and Ability to Trust. Forging durable relationships was important for another reason: long-lasting partnerships with customers would form the foundation of a superior customer experience.

As people learned how to partner, they changed how they interacted with each other. Individuals and teams talked openly about what they needed from one another, immediately clarifying expectations for key business initiatives. Groups that had not yet embraced cross-functional teams moved away from their isolated positions and toward partnering as the way to do business. The partnering process was also used to set the foundation for customer-focused teams, cross-functional teams centered on specific segments of customers. The customer-focused teams comprised not only marketing and sales people but also their colleagues from engineering, customer care, information systems, and finance.

Other Lessons Learned

The wireless telecommunications company learned several lessons during the course of strengthening its organizational capability. Addressing employee concerns in a visible way is a prerequisite for solidifying credibility in the goodwill of the company. Logically, the flow of initiatives is straightforward: purpose shapes processes and structure, processes and structure set specifications for people, and people execute the processes that fulfill the organization's purpose.

This case, however, reconfirms the wisdom of starting where pain is the greatest. The three steps of structuring project management into a cross-functional framework, getting feedback into the organization, and equipping people with a common problem-solving protocol were all aimed at remedying root causes of employee confusion, frustration, and dissatisfaction. Moreover, in that partnerships built within an organization represent a source of unique advantage, factors that threaten to erode or destroy those partnerships must be dealt with forthrightly and speedily. Damaged relationships take extraordinary time and effort to rebuild, time during which competitors are likely to continue to race ahead in the market.

"Start where it hurts the most" is one lesson, but an equally notable learning is that an organization must address each of the components of organizational capability—purpose, processes, and people. Only a holistic approach enables sustainability. Staging various interventions also bears mention as a lesson learned. "Real work," after all, still needs to get done: sign up new customers, get new subscribers installed, respond to billing errors, and the like. Introducing new management processes and tools in a step-by-step way eases the transplanting of personal learnings to workplace applications. Thrusting still more management training on employees who have not yet had the opportunity to succeed in applying previous lessons simply compounds confusion and frustration. On the other hand, waiting until everyone is "on board" holds back early adapters eager to progress. Overlapping of interventions will be required to accommodate the varying paces of individual employee, and team, developmental advancement.

Overlaying these lessons is the rubric that executive management must give these kinds of initiatives enough time to take hold in the organization. The "patience paradox" is that many senior executives have ascended to the top floor in part owing to personal impatience for results. The executive team must thus enter into these kinds of investments with clear, concrete expectations of what success looks like, or else the risk of premature trashing of the initiatives is high. Allowing time for these programs to yield desired business results, however, does not mean abdicating stewardship during the journey. Quick, frequent check-ins (but not hovering) ensure that people understand the magnitude of executive concern and furnish real-time data on successes and on setbacks. Such touch points, moreover, serve to provide early signals that a particular employee may be incapable of getting the results required for business success. Such cases then call for timely executive courage, with compassion, to redirect an employee to another position.

Questions for Discussion

1. This case involves a unit transitioning from an entrepreneurial phase into a much larger business entity. What role can HRD play in helping organizations undergoing this kind of development?

2. The "holistic organizational model" described in this case provided a context for strategic conversations among members of the executive team. A key part of the model is vision. Where does vision come from? If you were an HRD professional working with this or some similar executive team, how would you structure these conversations?

3. There are a number of "learning needs" that needed to be addressed as this organization implemented the organizational changes it needed to make. Which ones stand out for you?

End Note

1. S. M. Dent, *Partnering Intelligence: Creating Value for Your Business by Building Strong Alliances.* (Palo Alto, Calif.: Davies-Black, 1999).

CHUBB GLOBAL UNIVERSITY: FROM TRAINING . . . TO LEARNING . . . TO BUSINESS

Case Written by Jeff Kuhn, Executive Learning Associates (jeff@executivelearning.com)

This case provides an example of how the leadership of Bettina Kelly, manager of Chubb Global University, facilitated the adoption of strategy-based executive learning that transformed Chubb's corporate learning group from a sideline player plagued with a lackluster reputation into a key strategic weapon and source of competitive advantage for the organization.

Business Context

Founded in 1882, the Chubb Corporation is a specialty property and casualty (P&C) insurance carrier with headquarters in Warren, New Jersey. The firm has 12,000 employees serving customers in 134 field offices throughout the Americas, Europe, and Asia. Core offerings include both "off-the-shelf" and customized risk management solutions for middle-market commercial and high-net-worth personal customers.

Property and casualty insurance was a relatively stable industry for most of the 20th century; Depression-era laws barred other financial institutions (e.g., banks) from entering the P&C business. The competitive landscape changed dramatically in the 1990s with the advent of globalization, deregulation, the Internet, multichannel distribution, industry convergence and consolidation, chronic price erosion, and a shift from product-based to knowledge-based competition. As a result, Chubb underwent a series of reinventions to adapt to the new playing field and sustain its industry leadership.

Worldwide Learning and Development: In Search of Value

Traditionally a "promote from within" company, Chubb has enjoyed a longstanding reputation for developing the "best people" in the industry. Responding to organizational demands for greater value, Chubb's worldwide learning and development (WL&D) organization, the corporate learning group, also underwent a series of reinventions throughout the 1990s via a seemingly endless process of focus groups, task forces, special studies, value statements, white papers, and reorganizations.

Everything—the group's name, its mission, roles, reporting relationships, titles, and offices—was in a constant state of change, except for its people, most of whom were self-taught trainers who had worked in line positions before moving into learning and development.

Hidebound by an "inside-out" lens, WL&D failed to make sense of the changing landscape and identify the new drivers of strategic value in the organization. The prevailing learning philosophy (a focus on abstract "soft skills") and methodology ("touchy feely") simply reflected neither the needs of the business nor the complexity and demands of the competitive environment. As a result, the group garnered a spotty reputation, and the WL&D Director position became known as an "ejector seat," given the number of people for whom the position had marked the end of their careers in the company.

The death knell for WL&D (and for most of Chubb's decentralized training organizations) came in 1998 when Chubb embarked on a company-wide activity value analysis (AVA) initiative (a code for cost cutting), which ultimately resulted in massive staff and budget cuts and eliminated all but a handful of people in the WL&D organization.

Kelly, a seasoned leadership development professional, had been recruited by Chubb several months earlier to build a world-class leadership development organization. Unfortunately, learning had entered its darkest hour at Chubb. As Kelly noted, "The organization simply didn't have an appetite for leadership development despite the clear gap between the demands of the competitive environment and the capability of its senior business leaders."

Confident that the situation would eventually self-correct, Kelly opted to ride out the downsizing wave and waited for the eventual opportunity to launch a cycle of renewal—the big question was, "When?"

AVA had apparently cut too deep into the organizational muscle. The "when" was answered in late 1999 when then-CEO Dean O'Hara called and articulated a clear charge to Kelly: "Build me a world-class training organization," he said. "I don't want to leave our industry leadership to chance."

From Training . . . to Learning

With the CEO now actively involved, Kelly moved quickly to launch the transformation of learning at Chubb. Her first move was to take a group of 18 senior executives off-site to develop a multiyear strategy for positioning learning and development as a source of competitive advantage. Other than Kelly, there was only one other learning person in the room. The initiative would have to be driven by the business owners to produce any tangible change.

Using an "outside-in" approach, a significant departure from the "inside-out" framing that had plagued earlier efforts, the group took a deep dive into the business by identifying broader strategic trends relative to customers, competitors, industry dynamics, Chubb's own realities, and the broader environment. They then identified the enterprise-level learning implications as the basis of the learning strategy.

The strategic insights from the meeting provided a compelling business case for building a world-class learning capability. Here are some highlights from their findings:

▌ Our business has become very complex and highly specialized. Our learning and development capability has not kept pace with the demands and complexity of the competitive environment.

▌ Our collective "know how" is a source of competitive advantage that cannot easily be imitated by competitors.

- It's a knowledge game today—the ability to rapidly learn, adapt, and deliver superior customer solutions, is our principle source of competitive advantage. Learning is no longer a choice.
- Leadership plays a crucial role in driving a high-performance learning culture.
- Everyone—including the executive team—is accountable for continuously building their knowledge and skills.
- "Assets have feet"—today's workforce expects high-quality learning and development opportunities as a key component of its relationship with Chubb.

In retrospect, these are rather simple concepts, but they were tantamount to moving mountains, considering the shift of Chubb's inherent mindset from "training as skill building" to "learning as a source of competitive advantage."

The primary output of the meeting was a global learning strategy, which focused on critical resources in the six key investment areas in learning shown below:

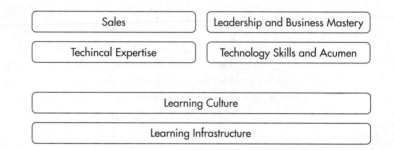

Gaining Traction

Each investment area was assigned an executive sponsor. Chubb's chief operating officer, Kelly's invaluable ally, was the executive sponsor for the Leadership and Business Mastery investment.

Kelly was charged with shepherding the broader global learning strategy until it achieved critical mass and specifically with building a world-class leadership development capability under the aegis of "Chubb Global University," the newly-named corporate center of excellence responsible for the development and delivery of Chubb's corporate leadership and business mastery programs.

She adopted a university metaphor primarily for purposes of branding and segmentation. She explained: "The corporate learning function had a very poor reputation in the organization and needed a clean break with the past. Although most of the prior staff had long left the organization, the 'old brand' was alive and well in the minds of our customers. After examining various models, we decided to go with the university metaphor in name only, to provide an identifiable brand that would be associated with world-class leadership and executive development programs."

It was noteworthy that Chubb had traditionally outsourced executive development by sending high-potential executives to multi-week general management programs offered by top-tier business schools. As such, any internal executive development program would have to deliver a superior learning experience and business impact to compete against the strong brand and professional pedigree of the business schools.

From Learning . . . to Business

Under the umbrella of Chubb Global University, Kelly set out to target Chubb's "top 100" leadership population by creating an internal executive development initiative—the Global Executive Program (GEP).

GEP is a three-session strategy-based executive development program designed to further the business acumen and strategic leadership skills of Chubb's high-potential SVP+ leadership talent worldwide. Program faculty were hand picked from leading business schools and consulting firms around the world.

The program is strategy-based, in that all aspects of the learning experience—content, process, dialogue, and projects—are grounded in the strategic context of the organization. The business impact projects (an action-learning variant) focus on conceptualizing and incubating new businesses and growth engines rather than on the traditional problem-solving action-learning projects found in many programs. Recent projects have included developing a market-entry strategy for China; growing the market for professional liability products in Europe, and creating a business model for capturing the ultra-high–net-worth segment in Chubb's personal lines business.

In addition to delivering strategic value to the organization, GEP has been instrumental in accelerating the transformation of Chubb Global University. Learning is no longer a sideline activity; it is integrated right into the business with the express purpose of building strategic leadership capability at the individual, group, and organizational level. The key shifts inherent in this new model are highlighted below.

The new model required an entirely new mindset and new staff competencies, both of which were largely absent in the HRD field due to a lack of business and strategic acumen among learning professionals. In response, Kelly expanded the

OLD MODEL	NEW MODEL
Sideline activity	⇒ Integrated into the business
Focus on individual development	⇒ Focus on building individual, group, and organizational capability and producing tangible strategic output
Mostly internal faculty	⇒ Mostly external faculty
Mostly developed and delivered internally	⇒ Mostly cocreated and delivered in partnership with external firms
Safe, politically correct, low visibility	⇒ Transformative, high-visibility initiatives that challenge strategic assumptions and mental models
Competency/curriculum-based	⇒ Strategy-based
Senior executive support	⇒ "Hands on" executive sponsorship and involvement

strategic partnership model with several outside firms, complementing her small but highly-skilled internal team of senior learning professionals with as-needed capability and capacity on various initiatives. "Our business model is best described as an outside-in, 'co-creation' model," explained Kelly. "Yes, we are a small team, but we are creative people who don't want to spend our days functioning as vendor managers."

Early on, Kelly noticed a clear shift in business (and sponsor) needs from an "annual offering" model to an emergent, strategy-based approach driven by immediate strategic needs. Kelly explained: "After several years of consistent performance, we [Chubb Global University] are now regarded as the 'go to' source for creating executive learning initiatives that facilitate deep, strategic dialogue around complex business issues facing the organization while at the same time building a cadre of executives with the skills, experiences, and perspective necessary to lead profitable, globally competitive businesses. As a result, our executive learning programs pay for themselves tenfold, considering the economic value created at these sessions. This is a win-win and incredibly engaging model any way you look at it."

Key Insights

Reflecting back on the experience, Kelly noted that she deliberately avoided the widespread HR "we-need-a-seat-at-the-table" entitlement mentality and focused on earning trusted relationships with a number of progressive executives by delivering world-class executive learning programs based on a handful of value drivers: a business-driven design, a world-class faculty, senior executive involvement, and a careful selection of an exciting group of participants with an unwavering commitment to learn and grow as leaders. Kelly shared: "We use a simple free market metric to gauge whether we are creating value—program funding. We are adding value if the phone is ringing and senior executives are allocating critical organizational resources to fund big-ticket strategy-based executive development programs versus looking to alternative solutions."

Chubb's strategy-based executive development programs have been instrumental in driving the broader transformation of Chubb. Participants engage in intense dialogue with the top team, often challenging core strategic assumptions and mental models, and cross every conceivable organizational boundary in the course of the projects.

"The first year was a bit dicey," admitted Kelly. "The boundary-crossing and challenging of assumptions was an entirely new experience for Chubb. As you can imagine, this generated a great deal of strategic noise in the organization." She continued, "The tide clearly turned in the second year, when we incorporated a more entrepreneurial, 'show-me-the-money' element into the projects. The business ventures developed in the program were a real attention grabber in the executive ranks."

The unfreezing of mental models and cross-pollination of ideas around the world has transformed Chubb from a staid, myopic company into an innovative, forward-looking organization with high strategic IQ, said Kelly. "The alumni effect is more powerful than I ever imagined. Graduates of CGU executive development programs now hold many of the top leadership positions in the company and have the entre-preneurial spirit and strategic wherewithal to shape the playing field and maintain Chubb's industry leadership in the years to come."

Questions for Discussion

1. Consider Bettina Kelly's approach to the strategic redesign of the world-wide learning function:

    ▌ How did her approach relate to the broader principles of both strategic learning and political economy?

    ▌ What strikes you about the outcome of the design approach in terms of positioning the learning organization within Chubb?

2. How does the term "Chubb Global University" link political savvy with marketing the learning organization within Chubb?

3. What are implications in terms of the structure of offerings by CGU in the linkage to corporate strategy that has been achieved?

4. Overall, what are the advantages and limitations of the CGU approach?

THE STRATEGIC ROLE OF HRD/OD IN TECHNOLOGY-DRIVEN PROJECTS: THE IMPLEMENTATION OF GLOBAL PHARMACEUTICAL'S HR—EMPLOYEE WEB-PORTAL

Case Written by Rosa Colon Medina

This case describes HRD's strategic role and organizational development initiatives in enabling an HR—employee portal in a company we are calling "Global Pharmaceutical" (GP). The purpose of these initiatives was to ensure that GP's staff willingly adopt the changes resulting from the portal introduction, thereby aligning the organization's expectations and roles. The initiatives were also intended to maximize the opportunity for staff to embrace new technology, associated processes, identifying and developing new behaviors to sustain the new ways of working in the organization.

Organizational Context and Project Goals

With more than 50,000 employees around the world, Global Pharmaceutical faced information-sharing dilemmas, particularly in the human resource employee services area; GP had in place

- over 130 different HR-related Web sites in existence,
- 12 different toll free numbers regarding HR, benefits, and payroll-related information,
- nearly 21,600 HR documents on the various Web sites,
- 122 interfaces between various corporate HR systems, and
- few common HR processes and systems.

Between 1999 and 2001, Global Pharmaceutical implemented an HR—employee portal. There were two main goals for the project: first, to redesign HR business processes in order to dramatically improve performance and to leverage technology in order to achieve competitive superiority by attracting, retaining, and developing top talent; second, to enable the employee portal as the vehicle by which employees have easy access to information and tools needed to optimally manage their benefits, life events, career development, job activities and, in the case of managers, human capital. The HR employee portal was launched in June 2001 to serve more than 27,000 employees in both the United States and Puerto Rico.

What Is an HR Employee Portal?

Jim Holincheck, an analyst at Giga Information Group's Chicago office, gives a serviceable definition of an HR—employee portal: "It's a way to provide an interface to users so they have the resources they need to do their job, linking into a variety of different business transactions, business information and other content and services that might be external or internal." Employee portals are the doorway to all the information a company needs to function. They are generally accessed through an Internet browser via a single sign-on window that in turn leads to a Web page that includes links to all the company's knowledge management and collaboration tools as well as other frequently used Web sites. Higher-end portals such as these can also trawl both internal and external data sources, from Web pages to internal databases, document repositories, and other potential knowledge sources, such as e-mails and office documents. The information found is indexed, categorized, and presented to the user as one set of links in much the same way that Web search engines display their results.

HR portals cut down on the amount of paper that has to be processed, and they give employees round-the-clock access to timely information about their benefits and enrollment information. Using the employee Web-portal, employees can not only enroll in all of the benefits that the employer provides but they can also, throughout the year, take a look and really drill down to find the information associated with their benefits. And just as importantly, as they have life events during the year, the portal will become the means by which they facilitate these transactions.

Project Organization

In the fall of 1998, as part of a strategic HR initiative, Global Pharmaceutical appointed an HR–employee portal team, chartered to design a proof of concept to demonstrate that an HR–employee portal would improve Global Pharmaceutical's HR services by introducing common systems, data, and processes and building a robust advanced technical infrastructure for future HR-related employee needs.

Figure 1 diagrams the project team's organization.

The Senior Vice President (SVP) of HR appointed an HR champion, a vice president (VP) from his senior leadership team, to provide direction from the business side, and sponsor the project. This VP was very clear that the project should be structured to ensure that it would not become technology-driven. The other key leadership role was played by GP's chief information officer (CIO), who would be leading the project from the technology side. The CIO was responsible for the human resources information system (HRIS) team, whose main objective was to help GP achieve competitive superiority in the effectiveness of both its human assets and its HR departments through the strategic application of information technology, including delivery of HR initiatives to employees via technology, in order to provide managers with information and analysis to manage their workforce and enhance the effectiveness of the HR function through maintaining people-related systems companywide.

One of the key challenges of the portal project was to make sure that it was not just another technology-driven project but instead a truly business-, employee-needs, and HR-driven project, but the mechanism to make this happen was still to be defined.

The HRD Challenge: The Need to Address People Issues in the Project—What about Change Management?

By the spring of 1999, the HR champion was concerned that the IT team was taking too much of a technology-focused approach to the project and that its social/organizational elements, which he considered critical for the success of the project,

FIGURE 1   **HR Web-Portal Project Organization**

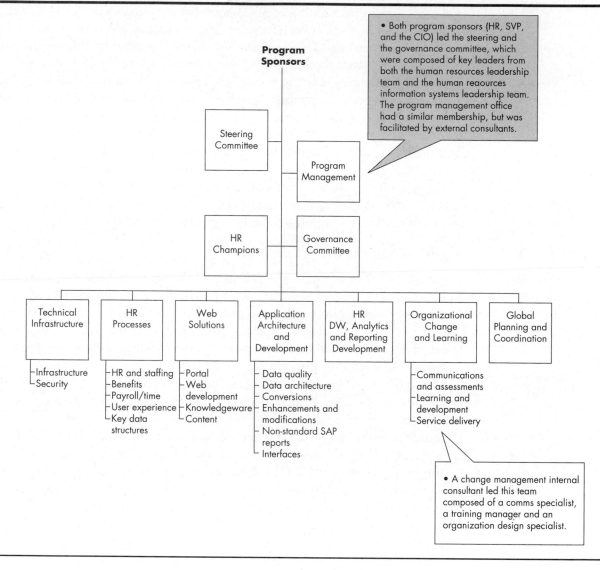

had not been addressed. The HR champion recommended that an internal consultant from change-management (HRD/OD) become a key member of the project management office, but the HRIS leader immediately expressed concern that, normally, change management and/or organizational development practitioners "focus too much on people issues: Because they don't understand technology, it has been difficult for these professionals to add value to IT projects." The HRIS leader's previous experience with change management had shown that its use of complex models or too much theory tended to complicate simple things.

The internal change management consultant saw the need to keep organizational development conversations as simple as possible, by using simple "one-page" models that conveyed the message that the social activities that require attention during any IT project need to be aligned with the IT activities so that the social and IT efforts can be jointly orchestrated. After discussing models, the HRIS leader commented, "This is the first time that I can see change management on a single noncomplex page; this may work." It was then agreed that a full-time change-management internal consultant would join the project with responsibility for designing and implementing strategies for stakeholder management; communications; organization design; performance metrics; and learning and development. A change management team was assembled; it was composed of a communications specialist, a training specialist, and an organizational design specialist.

First Change Intervention: HR Leadership Team Interviews

The first change intervention addressed one of the HR champion's concerns: that the corporate HR leadership team was not fully involved with the project. The HR champion held one-on-one interviews with members of the team in order to know better their business requirements and to document their recommendations for the change management project plan. In this case, the HR champion wanted facts and data that would not only document peer concerns but also demonstrate to the HRIS leader the need for further involvement and clarification of the project vision and objectives. Despite the HRIS team's perception that the HR leadership team had already approved the project and had a good understanding of the project, interviews revealed that this was not the case. They felt disengaged, and, as a team, they fully agreed that there was not a full understanding of how the technology would enable HR to accomplish its vision. The HR leadership team needed to invest more time together to discuss and articulate how the new world would be for HR, whether they had the right skills and competencies, and, if they did not, how to put them in place. The team also recognized its need to fully understand the new HR processes, so that it could make appropriate decisions on the extent to which line managers would be empowered to do HR-related work. These decisions would be a critical, since they would drive new behaviors in both line management and HR, which would have an impact on the existing company culture.

In order to address the concerns and/or recommendations from the HR leadership team, it was agreed that the change-management action plan should include

■ appointment of an HR executive to act as a sponsor of the change-management and organizational design efforts;

■ an organizational design plan to be developed as part of the change-management initiative;

■ HR process workshops, with participation by a subgroup from the HR leadership team, to review processes in detail in order to get process sign-off and final approval;

▪ HR leadership team meetings to get approval of the change-management plan, the communications, learning and development plans, and the deployment plans;

▪ appointment of an HR advisory team, with representation from GP's business units, to act as HR–employee portal champions, validating business requirements, organizational impacts, and deployment plans; and

▪ focus groups, with the participation of employees at all levels in the United States, Europe, Mexico, and Puerto Rico, to ensure that employee needs are considered in the design of the HR–employee portal.

Second Change Intervention: Focus Groups Using Appreciative Inquiry Methodology

The HR leadership team acknowledged that the HR–employee portal represented a significant change in the way HR delivered services to its customers. In order to ensure project success, employees at all levels—employees, members of management, and HR professionals—were involved in focus-group sessions to obtain feedback and reactions to these changes and to the portal prototype. When feasible, the sessions comprised just one segment of the target populations: the majority of the European sessions were conducted with homogenous populations, while the majority of the sessions held in the United States included multiple populations. International focus-group sessions used a survey as part of the feedback collection process; the quantitative data were derived from three participant surveys: one for employees, one for managers, and one for HR staff. Surveys were translated into French, Italian, German, and Spanish to facilitate communication and understanding with international participants. The focus groups followed an appreciative-inquiry format to avoid their starting with negative comments about how difficult it could be to adapt to new technology.

Conversations about the introduction of a new system can easily begin on a very negative note. But conversations that begin with an unconditional positive question, such as how technology can improve processes and procedures, can open the door to an immense number of great possibilities. In addition to such questions, the HR leadership team demonstrated a mock-up, or picture, of the HR–employee portal and then gathered the participants' reactions and opinions. (See Table 1.)

Ninety-seven percent of participants agreed with the project's vision and purpose and liked the new way HR services would be delivered. Some HR professionals expressed concern about the new way that HR services would be delivered and some confusion about their role going forward. Managers also expressed concerns about the future role of HR. Employees wanted reassurance that face-to-face interaction with HR would still be available for things like employee relations. Almost all participants recognized that there would be a complete philosophical change in HR. Some participants felt strongly that nonnative language would be difficult for some employees and could decrease use and acceptance of the portal. Although participants said the portal looked easy to use, they still wanted to receive

TABLE 1   **Appreciative Inquiry Questions**

DISCOVERY: APPRECIATING THE BEST	DREAM: WHAT ARE THE POSSIBILITIES?
▪ What Web sites do you most frequently visit? ▪ What internal or external sites do you visit that assist you in performing your job? ▪ Are there sites you visit for HR information or to perform HR transactions? ▪ Think of a time in your entire experience with computers and the Internet when you felt most excited, most engaged, and most productive. What elements made it a great experience? ▪ What made you visit the site in the first place?	▪ What kind of information will you value the most on a company Web portal? ▪ Work, non–work-related
DESIGN: WHAT SHOULD IT BE?	**DESTINY: WHAT WILL IT BE?**
▪ What specific content would you expect to see in an HR portal? ▪ What other information or online application would help you perform your job? ▪ What are your initial thoughts and reactions to the demonstration?	▪ What kind of support do you think we might need to effectively use this site? ▪ What will motivate people to use the portal? ▪ What would you recommend for communications and training to support the implementation?

training, and they acknowledged that this effort would require changes in behavior and work practices. This was expressed across all three groups: employees, managers, and HR.

Third Change Intervention: OD-IT Change-Management Model, Aligning Technology with People's Needs

The focus groups and the HR leadership team interviews provided enough insight to guide the development of a change-management approach. The HR leadership team identified the following steps as critical factors to success in enabling the alignment of change management and IT professionals' needs:

Step 1: Preliminary Project Planning—Not only IT experts but also business management needs to become involved early in order to articulate project needs and benefits.

Step 2: Project Start-Up—A stakeholder management component needs to set clear expectations at the executive level, to decide how success will be measured, and to envisage how the organization might change.

Step 3: Project Study Analysis—Instead of using the software to drive process changes, business management should document the ideal process and then the technology to find ways to enable the ideal vision. During this step it is critical to analyze organizational impacts and to identify both how responsibilities might shift and any new roles that may be needed to support the new vision.

Step 4: Implementation Planning—Organizational design needs to identify how roles will change, the new roles that may be needed to support the new processes, and the new skills and competencies these processes will require; a performance-measurement strategy will also be needed.

Step 5: Implementation—The design component should include the development of an organization transition plan that implements shifting responsibilities (identified in Step 3) and also creates the new roles and/or functions (identified in Step 4).

Step 6: Performance Measures—A set of measures needs to be introduced and communicated so that key stakeholders can monitor progress and so that the IT-OD project team can continuously improve.

Fourth Change Intervention: Establishment of an HR Advisors/Champions Team to Support the Change Process

As part of the stakeholder management and communications strategy, the change-management team worked with the HR champion to identify and appoint HR representatives, one from each of the company's business units, to join a team of HR business area advisors (HR advisors). The objective of this team was to establish a partnership with the HR business unit heads to provide guidance and direction, define new processes, and develop local implementation plans. The HR advisor role was to act as the primary vehicle for structured communications; proactively disseminate critical information to key clients; be a liaison between the business unit and project teams; interact with the service delivery, process, change-management, and security teams to support strategy validation and implementation; and understand business HR needs and strategies, adjusting business unit needs/wants to the scope of the project and supporting the training of end-users. Over the course of several meetings, the HR advisors made several key recommendations to ensure that both HR and its customers understand the new HR processes and buy-in. GP was constructing a new world—the one in which the HR processes would be executed—with participation not only from the HR–employee portal team members, but also from key stakeholders, who would be living in this new HR world.

Fifth Change Intervention: Performance Measurement—Portal Post-Implementation Survey

The HR–employee portal was launched in the summer of 2001 to approximately 17,000 employees in the United States. After six months, the HR leadership team designed and conducted a post-implementation survey that assessed not only user satisfaction with technology and with the new HR service delivery, but also nonusers' perceptions. The survey showed that

- seventy-three percent of users that participated in the survey felt comfortable with the Internet;
- fifty-one percent agreed that the communication provided for the launch of the portal was adequate;
- the majority of the participants (between 60 and 72 percent) agreed that the information provided in the portal was useful and easy to understand. Sixty-four percent agreed that the information was easy to find, and 51 percent found the portal easy to navigate;
- sixty-four percent of users were satisfied with the functionality of the portal. They most liked the convenience of having access to information 24 hours a day, 7 days a week;
- users who did not frequently use the portal recommended a more robust search engine, marketing reminders, and also an index page to facilitate easy identification of available information.

Questions for Discussion

1. How does this case illustrate the blending of traditional HRD and OD competencies?
2. What opportunities does this case present for aligning HR, HRD/OD, and corporate performance objectives? How might HRD leadership take advantage of these opportunities?
3. What other competencies does this case suggest?
4. What are the implications of this case for the implementation of e-learning initiatives? What common issues are likely to arise with the introduction of e-learning programs and knowledge management efforts into an organization?
5. What are the broader implications for any initiative that requires a significant change in organizational culture?

COACTIVE LEADERSHIP DEVELOPMENT: FOSTERING TRANSFORMATIVE LEARNING THROUGH HOLISTIC EXPERIENTIAL LEARNING

Case Written by Art Shirk, The Lantoga Group (www.Lantoga.com)

Many HRD professionals work as consultants and providers of learning experiences to both private individuals and organizations. Coactive leadership is a program designed to develop the leadership capabilities of individuals who are engaged in a process of self-development. The facilitators are experienced leadership development coaches who themselves participated in the program and then continued on to program leadership roles. In addition to their involvement with the coactive leadership program, the facilitators have private practices working with executives in a wide range of for profit and nonprofit organizations. The coactive leadership program is an example of how deep personal change is involved in the growth of transformative leadership. The focus of this case is on the experience of the learner, which is appropriate because fostering personal change and growing authentic leadership requires a learner focus.

Introducing Sonia

Today Sonia Sinisterra works with political and community leaders of her state in Colombia, South America on a quest to create social transformation. It is her life's ambition to see life change in her homeland, a country fraught with violence, terror, and oppression. This was not an easy choice to make—just a year or so ago she lived a comfortable life with her family outside of Washington, D.C. working as an organizational development consultant in corporate America, her teenage children in public school. Amidst the comforts of her life she felt a growing outrage toward the conditions in Colombia, accompanied by an increasingly loud inner voice calling her to return home and direct her energy and talent to constructive social change. After several years of soul searching and active engagement in processes of ongoing learning, Sonia and her family packed up and returned to the home they had left behind years ago. It was a bold step, requiring courage and a willingness to step into an uncertain future for herself and family.

What was it that enabled Sonia to muster the courage to take this step into the unknown? She responds by saying that there were many factors—it was a time in her life when "change was brewing from the inside out." In part, her decision was catalyzed by participation in an intensive learning experience called "Coactive Leadership." Sonia's learning occurred on multiple levels: on one level, the program fostered specific leadership skills in creating learning and rallying groups toward action; on another level, the learning was personally transformative and freeing, creating more expansive ways for Sonia to view possibilities for how she might live her life.

Format and Focus of the Coactive Leadership Program

The Coactive Leadership Program is a year-long intensive program designed to foster learning in personal leadership. Four five-day learning sessions conducted in a residential retreat setting in Northern California are spread throughout the course of the year and provide the cornerstones of the program. The four sessions focus on increasingly complex levels of leadership capability:

1. personal leadership: discovering, practicing, and enhancing individual capacities to lead;

2. leading with others: building awareness and strength in leading in collaborative and mutual (coactive) partnership with others;

3. leading from nothing: fine-tuning our sense on multiple levels—emotional, physical, and intuitive—of the entire dynamic of our environment and group; and

4. leading from everything: drawing on all levels (emotional, physical, and intuitive) to lead with intention toward meaningful purpose and having desired impact in a chaotic world.

You won't encounter many flip-charts, conceptual models to be learned, or instructors delivering lectures. The program integrates aspects of experiential learning, critical reflection and dialogue and action learning, with the momentum created through a closely-knit, highly motivated community of learners working collaboratively. On one level the program builds capability in specific leadership skills through practice, reflection, and feedback. On another level the program fosters emancipitory shifts in meaning perspectives as described by Jack Mezirow (see Chapter Six).

Sonia's Transformative Experience

"The experience up in those redwood trees really altered my perspective—my trust in myself, my ability to take risks, and my capacity to work coactively with others will never be the same," Sonia recalls from her experience on several high and low ropes courses that are part of the program. The creation of experience—whether undertaking a challenge on a high ropes course or engaging in a simulation—provides a basis for reflection on the learning that has taken place—what changes occurred on physical, emotional, or cognitive levels. Experience feeds learning that can be transformative in nature, where underlying perspectives become apparent and the subject of scrutiny, potentially replaced with frames of reference that enable new ways of approaching life.

For Sonia, one aspect of the program with the most impact was the continual shifting between action and reflection in the learning process. Following each formal retreat, learners return to their regular lives for several months and are challenged to put new learning into practice via a specific project as well as in daily life. During these periods, Sonia worked with a learning coach who helped her to reflect on her experience and to continually translate learning into concrete action. In one of these "in between assignments," Sonia and a partner designed a workshop for Colombian immigrants residing in the United States to support them in reconstructing productive lives in a new country. For Sonia, the experience was a stepping stone toward embracing the bigger challenges that awaited her return to her country. Learning from action helped her to hone and refine new skills and, more importantly, to build a new base of confidence and sense of herself as a leader.

The instrumental learning that Sonia experienced as she built and practiced new skills in group leadership was useful, but not the most significant aspect of the program. She describes this period of her life as transformational, and the coactive leadership experience as one component of a larger developmental shift that she underwent during that time. "Looking back, I can see that the way I experience myself and the world has changed. The impact that I have does not so much come from the things that I do, but, rather, from the person that I am and the way that I engage with others and the world."

Sonia's view of the world today appears more developmentally complex. She describes a sense of connectedness with others and a trust in her intuitive sense of the world that didn't exist previously. She cites an ability to step forward into action even when outcomes are ambiguous and uncertain. "I no longer feel that I must have answers and solutions to problems to move forward—life is complex, and I know that together we can find the right answers." Her sense of purpose has expanded and seems to come from a different source. "I now have the experience that I am following a path that is genuinely my own and at the same time connected to a purpose that is fundamentally human and connected to others. What has changed is that I am no longer defining the direction of my life based on expectations or obligations that seem artificial or obligatory to me."

Reflections on the Process

These shifts are developmental in nature and provide glimpses that suggest movement more fully into a self-authoring self and sense of interdependence, aspects of the latter developmental stages defined by Kegan and Torbert (see Chapter Six). Was this developmental growth actually caused by participation in the coactive leadership program? We don't know, but Sonia's view is that her learning experience was an integral part of an important period of life transition and growth. The learning program was one structure in her life that "continually pushed the developmental buttons—prompting the right kinds of reflection and learning at the right times."

At the crossroads of our lives, structures that support constructive learning can be pivotal to positive growth and change. The path Sonia has followed hasn't been an easy one—the transition has been difficult for her husband and two teenage boys, as well as challenging for herself. Her efforts, though, are beginning to take root. Recently, her work with the governor of her state has included leadership development and team building for a cadre of community leaders. This is the start for her broader vision of creating local transformative social change that can in turn create larger change in a world in crisis.

Questions for Discussion

1. How does this case illustrate the power of the learning perspective on HRD work?

2. What connections do you make between this case and adult learning and development theory we described in Chapter Six?

3. What are the implications of this case for fostering leadership development in organizational settings?

Glossary of Terms

A

Achiever—A mid-level stage in William Torbert's (1991) model of personal development in which needs of system success are seen as taking precedence or rule of craft logic and technical logic.

Action-Learning (AL)—An approach to working with and developing people that uses work on an actual project, challenge, or problem as the way to learn. Working in small groups and often with a learning coach participants engage in cycles of action and reflection to both make progress on the task and learn.

Affective Learning—Engaging feelings and emotions, and intuition as part of the learning process.

Alliance Building—Creating allies among managers who come to see the interests of their functional areas aligned with the proposals of HRD professionals

Analyzers—A construct from the strategic typology of Miles and Snow (1978). A form of organizational strategy combining stable and changing product lines with a particular competence in product or technology imitation and improvement on innovations pioneered by other organizations, seeking to be second to market with improved products, effectively transferring the efficiencies of production.

Asynchronous—Digital communication between computers in which there is no timing requirement. People can communicate with each other from any place at any time.

B

Black Belts—Used for training in six sigma (see below) to refer to highly trained experts who serve as internal consultants or change agents and apply rigorous process improvement methods to enhance the performance of an organization's production and administrative processes. The analogy to black belts in judo and karate is deliberate.

Blended Learning—Integrating face-to-face learning or training events with electronic tools, e.g., computer-based training.

C

Challenging Assumptions—The process of asking questions, presenting scenarios, asking for supporting data and facts, or otherwise clarifying and testing the assumptions that underlie proposed decisions or courses of action.

Cognitive Mapping—Cognitive maps capture a person's "personal construct system" and represent their beliefs, values, and embedded understanding.

Computer-Based Training—Nonclassroom training delivered through a computer; self-paced training, where the participant interacts with a computer

Control-Oriented HR System—Human resource practices that emphasize cost control, including simplifying and systematizing jobs to reduce the costs of training and development and to minimize the skill levels of employees required by the firm (and therefore keeping wages relatively low). Typically employee compliance with work rules and procedures, rather active participation is sought by the organization.

Corporate Oversight—Exists when responsibility for the administration of programs and policies is located with centralized headquarters staff. In the realm of HRD these are learning initiatives that are seen as needing to be consistent across the entire organization.

Corporate Signature Programs—A term sometimes used to denote programs that have corporate oversight and are administered by headquarter staff.

Credibility Path—The series of interpersonal relationships among people who respect the opinions of one another creating a possible path for influencing critical and powerful decision-makers. Basically the idea is that the messenger is as important as the message when trying to influence someone with whom we have little credibility on an important issue.

Cultural Superstructure—The deep organizational culture that supports and stabilizes the exchanges that take place in the organization, rendering life somewhat predictable. The embedded values and beliefs are taken-for-granted by members of organization and largely operate outside of their awareness.

Defenders—A construct from the strategic typology of Miles and Snow (1978). Defenders maintain a limited, stable product line, competing through a particular core competence in cost efficiency achieved by economies of scale. Their focus is on protecting their strategic niche.

Dialogue—Isaacs defines dialogue as a "discipline of collective thinking and inquiry, a process of for transforming the quality of conversation and, in particular, the thinking that lies beneath it." Dialogue requires careful listening, with each party not thinking about rebuttal, but concentrating on what is being said, and being very conscious of one's reaction's to what is being said.

Digital Workplace—Business conducted via the internet and web-based technology.

Distance Learning—Learning that takes place with electronic media linking instructors and students who are not together in a classroom.

Distributed Application—A principle of learning program design that holds that having practice and application take place at points throughout a program results in higher retention than massed or concentrated practice. Argues for spacing a learning event over a period of time—perhaps a modular design.

Double-Loop Learning—Involves questioning the assumptions, or "governing variables" which guide our actions and informs how we frame or interpret a situation.

E

E-Learning—Any electronically assisted process that is used to acquire data, information, skills, or knowledge.

Experience Curve—Originally called the "learning curve" by the Boston Consulting Group (BCG) in the 1970s. BCG's model was based on research that demonstrated a predicable and exponential inverse relationship between costs and a company's experience producing a particular product. The model postulates that this "economy of experience" provides a significant competitive advantage to any company with a new product line that can establish itself as the early market leader because of the superior ability to control pricing and margins based on experience.

F

Future Search Conference—A large-group planning meeting that brings a "whole system" (i.e., representatives of all functions or levels of an organization, including customers, suppliers, etc.) into a room to work on a task focused agenda exploring possible alternative futures. Often described as learning laboratories, future search conferences typically take place over a period of two days and seek to arrive at common ground at a future direction for action.

Far Transfer—The ability to think and take action that transfers learning occurred in one context to other diverse, complex, and uncertain contexts.

Foundational Learning—Learning that directly contributes to the formation of an organization's strategic direction, the tactical implementation of strategy, operational execution in practice, and the development of performance capacity in the organization.

G

Generative Learning—The creation of new knowledge and meaning perspectives that change how people view or understand their world and creates a mental model for taking action. In business,

generative learning may involve a new way of thinking about an organization's markets or a new strategic application of an organization's core competence.

Globalization—A very generalized concept that refers to the increasing interconnectedness and integration of markets, organizational work processes, and communication links that transcend nation states.

Group Learning Designs—Learning designs that engage groups of people and rest on the premise of learning through active engagement with others.

Growth Share Matrix—Popularized the portfolio-analysis approach to corporate strategy treating the various businesses of a diversified company as a portfolio of business units. The dimensions of the matrix are 1) relative competitive position against the market leader and 2) industry attractiveness, expressed as the business growth rate. Based on an assessment of each business in the organization's portfolio, businesses are placed in one of four cells: Stars, Cash Cows, Question Marks, Dogs.

H

Harvesting Learning—Any process through which a group or individual can engage in a comprehensive review of a process or complex set of actions and through reflection bringing into conscious awareness what has been learned.

High-Commitment HR System—Refers to what has been variously called high commitment, high involvement HR practices, or high performance work practices consisting of a comprehensive set of policies and methods that include employee requirement and selection, incentive compensation and reward systems, extensive employee involvement, and investment in training and development to improve the knowledge, skills and abilities of current and potential employees. The intent is to maximize motivation and retention of quality employees while encouraging non-performers to leave the company.

Human Resource Management (HRM)—The processes of managing employees based on the assumption that they are an important source of competitive advantage for a business and significant contributors to its organizational performance. Broadly defined, human resource management includes all aspects of recruiting, selecting, training, compensating, and administering employees. More specifically defined, HRM functions are the administrative elements of managing people within the organization.

I

Ideological Consensus—The degree of agreement among managers and employees regarding the lifestyle and values which are appropriate for the organization. This consensus justifies the strategy and practices that implement it.

Imaginal Learning—Learning that is based on the use of imagery and uses metaphor, stories, and artistic expression and symbolism to arrive at insight and vision.

Incidental Learning—Unintentional learning that occurs while pursuing other tasks or formal learning objectives. Incidental learning is a subcategory of informal learning.

Individual Learning Designs—Learning designs that focus on individual practice and involvement.

Informal Learning—Learning that takes place outside of a formally structured learning event. Self-directed learning projects that are being pursued without participating in a continuing education program would be one example of informal learning.

K

Kiosk—A structure with one or more open sides that is used to provide products (newspapers) or services (a computer-equipped learning station in a library).

Kirkpatrick's Four-Step Taxonomy—A framework for evaluating training programs that consists of 1) participant reactions, 2) learning, 3) application, and 4) results. Although numerous approaches to evaluation have been advocated over the years, Kirkpatrick's four-level evaluation model is by far the most widely recognized in the training and development community.

L

Labor Markets—Defined by the relative supply and demand for workers who are available and activity seeking employment in various industries. The balance between available workers and available work opportunities has a strong influence on the cost of labor.

Learning Cycle—A model describing the process through which adults learn from experience. Although different versions exist, the primary elements of the cycle are having an experience through taking action, reflecting on the experience, making sense of the experience, and developing a theory or mental model about the experience, and taking further action through experimentation with alternative courses of action, based on the theory or mental model.

Learning Transfer System Inventory (LTSI)—A research instrument developed by Elwood Holton, III and his associates that is built around a conceptual model with constructs grouped by secondary influences, motivation, environment, outcomes, and ability, providing a comprehensive structure for assessing the factors influencing transfer in a particular organizational setting.

Learning Transfer—Applying what is learned in one context to another, such as using skills learned in a classroom back in the actual work setting.

Learning Window—A tool for encouraging reflection on attributions to gain clarity around what people know, what they think they know, and what they know they don't know. The window also helps capture and categorize organizational knowledge.

Learning-Transfer System—A comprehensive framework that considers all the factors that influence the degree to which learning transfer from a learning event occurs, including learner characteristics, organizational context, the design of the learning event itself, and pre-event preparation and post event maintenance activities.

Leveraging of Human Resources—Targeting where and how the development of people will most effectively add value to the performance capability of the organization.

Lifelong Learning—A concept in adult education that refers to the fact that learning, including formal learning opportunities, will occur throughout a person's lifetime as opposed to being front-loaded in the first two or three decades of the life span.

Low-Cost Strategy—The strategy of being the lowest cost producer or provider in a particular industry or market.

M

Magician—One of the most advanced stages in William Torbert's (1991) model of personal development. Magicians are preeminently attuned to creating contexts for inquiry into and across the organizational territories of purpose, strategy, operations, and environmental impact. Highly intuitive, process awareness (the interplay of principle and action) takes precedence over and rules principle.

Mid-Level Development—Learning and development targeted toward the basic professional and managerial competencies needed by people as they assume middle management positions or critical levels of professional responsibility in the organization.

N

Near Transfer—The transfer of learning from a learning event to a context very similar to, or the same as, the context in which the original learning occurs.

Need Teory—Based on people's tendency to direct their energy into those activities they find interesting. Various need theories have been formulated over the years focusing on needs such as achievement, belongingness, physical, and psychological growth needs. Organizational behaviorists classify these theories as "content" theories (compared to theories that focus on the "processes" through which people pursue satisfying their needs).

O

Organizational Development (OD)—Broadly defined, organizational development is a process of planned systemic change in an organization's culture. Organizational development practice has traditionally been based on strongly valuing increasing employee participation and empowerment as fundamental to organizational health and sustained competitive advantage.

Organizational Learning Mechanism—Institutional structural and procedural arrangements that allow organizations to systematically collect, analyze, store, disseminate, and use information relevant to the performance of the organization and its members.

Organizational Power Practices (OPPs)—OPPs are the taken-for-granted practices that "serve to position individuals in relation to other organizational members . . . that are most central to . . . sustaining and perpetuation of various—frequently unnoticed—hierarchies" and sets of power relations (Voronov and Coleman, 2003).

P

Performance Domains—Areas or aspects of an organizational system within which performance levels or outcomes might be measured. In his taxonomy Elwood Holton, III (1999) identifies mission, process(es), critical performance subsystems, and individual(s) as performance domains.

Performance Levels—Results realized from taking action compared against a set of goals, objectives, standards, or some other set of expected outcomes.

Political Advocacy—The process of advocating for programs, practices, strategies, and practices with a high awareness of the political power dynamics in the organization, building alliances through trading resources and currencies, aligning interests, and following the credibility path.

Polity—Consists of the patterned use of power and influence within the organization, the structures and mechanisms that reinforce these patterns, and the patterns of influence between the organization and other social institutions in its task environment that sustain its economic form.

Porter's Five-Forces Model of Strategic Positioning—Porter posits five competitive forces that shape competitive strategy: 1) industry competitors, 2) suppliers, 3) buyers, 4) potential new competitive entrants, and 5) substitute products. These five structural forces interact with one another to comprise a framework for analyzing the strategic position and opportunities for a company. Porter advocates using the framework to rapidly identify and focus management's attention on the forces that determine the nature of competition in an industry.

Portfolio Analysis—The process applying the growth share matrix to classify products or business units of an organization in terms of their potential and current contribution to the corporation. Based on an assessment of each business in the organization's portfolio, businesses are placed in one of four cells: Stars, Cash Cows, Question Marks, Dogs. This analysis becomes an important part of the strategic decision making process and determining how resources are allocated across the various business and product lines.

Portfolio Management—The process of making strategic decisions based on portfolio analysis. Senior management treats various products and business units as pieces of an investment portfolio, transferring assets and resources from one business or product line to another, and buying and selling off businesses.

Positive Evaluation—The judgments workers make about the value of their work and the work of others.

Program-Based Learning—Learning that takes place within a formally planned and organized situation.

Prospectors—A construct from the strategic typology of Miles and Snow (1978). Prospectors have a broad, changing product line and seek to be first to market with new products and technologies. Their strategic focus in on innovation.

R

Reflection—The process of turning thought back onto the content, processes, and premises of actions that have been taken for purposes of learning and testing their validity.

Response Learning—A change in the way we are prepared to respond in a particular situation (Cell, 1984). Response learning is studied by behaviorists in psychology and includes rote learning and what Skinner has called "operant conditioning."

S

Scenario Planning—A learning process that engages participants in thinking about multiple and distinctly different possible alternative futures. Scenarios focus less on predicting outcomes and more on understanding the forces and trends that will eventually produce those outcomes and on understanding the probabilities of which outcomes might actually occur. Scenario planning seeks to generate insight into possibilities. Stories and computer simulations can be used in scenario planning. Scenarios can be tested as to how well different strategies hold up against them.

Self-Authoring Mind—A phase in Robert Kegan's constructive-developmental approach characterized by self-regulation, self-formation, autonomy and individuation. Provides the capacity for arriving at beliefs and values through one's own internal authority, rather that accepting the values espoused by others and social institutions as truth based on an awareness that values are inherently assumptive.

Sensemaking—The process through which people construct sensible meaning out of the events they experience. This involves the psychological process of interpreting experience through existing frames of reference. As a social process of critical reflection and dialogue with others, sensemaking may generate new interpretations. We engage in sensemaking when unexpected events occur or when our experience significantly diverges from our expectations or projected plans.

Shared Organizational Learning Values—Cultural values which are supportive of organizational learning such as inquiry, integrity, issue orientation, and accountability.

Shared Services—A way of organizing the learning staff at the corporate level to avoid duplication of resources among various business units. The centralized staff is shared by the operating units who contribute to the cost of maintaining the staff resources.

Single-Loop Learning—Occurs when we detect error; our actions fail to produce the results we desire, and we adjust our tactics or strategies without challenging the assumptions that frame our understanding of the situation.

Situation Learning—Involves a change in how a person organizes his or her understanding of a situation; a "change in ability to do response learning." (Cell, 1984)

Six Sigma—"Six sigma" quality means the design tolerance for a product or service should be ±3.4 defects per million opportunities. Defects per million is now the global standard for quality measurement, and companies have been conducting training programs to teach process improvement methods for achieving this standard.

Socialized-Mind—A phase in Robert Kegan's constructive developmental approach characterized by role consciousness and mutual reciprocity. The person uncritically and unawarely identifies with external sources of ideas, and is unable to question or weigh the validity of these ideas.

Stimulus Variability—Holds that positive transfer is enhanced when the learner is confronted with a variety of contingencies to which a general principle is to be applied.

Strategic Learning—Strategic learning brings the strategy development process into alignment with learning theory, specifically with the learning cycle. A strategic-learning perspective views strategy development as a continuous process of renewal.

Strategic Learning Cycle—A model describing the process of making strategy, implementing it, and assessing it as a cycle of organizational learning.

Strategist—An advanced stage in William Torbert's (1991) model of personal development where one moves beyond adhering to a belief in objective reality to a synthetic, post objective theory that coordinates multiple realities. Principles take precedence over the rules of the system.

Streaming Video—Distributing video so it can be viewed on a PC. Streaming video can be live, directly from the camera, or on-demand from stored video.

Supportive Learning—Plays a direct role in organizational maintenance and development and an indirect, or supportive, role in organizational performance. Corporate citizenship issues are examples of potential content for supportive learning.

Synchronous—Digital communication between computers at the same time.

T

Tacit Knowledge—The capacity for effectively performing tasks without being able to explicitly describe all of the skills and abilities involved. Tacit knowledge is grounded in personal experience. Gilbert Ryle's classic comment, "we know more than we can say," captures the essence of tacit knowledge.

Team Learning Modes—The products of the effective functioning of team learning processes—1) fragmented [individual learning that is not shared with or by the group], 2) pooled learning [individuals share information and perspectives and small groups learn together, but the group as a whole does not learn], 3) synergistic [the group as a whole creates knowledge mutually, integrating divergent perspectives in new ways], 4) Continuous learning [synergistic learning in the group becomes habitual]. (Kasl, Marsick, & Dechant, 1997).

Team Learning Processes—The learning processes through which individual learning is converted to learning by the group or organization; such as problem or question framing, experimentation, reframing, and boundary crossing. These learning processes have parallels in how individuals learn and the effectiveness of how well group members enact these processes is causal to the emergence of distinct team learning modes. (Kasl, Marsick, & Dechant, 1997).

Technician—A stage in William Torbert's (1991) model of individual development in which internal craft logic rules expectations.

TQM (Total Quality Management)—A phrase adopted by the quality movement in industry to capture company-wide efforts to define and improve quality. These efforts involve a variety of coordinated programs and organizational forms, but typically include such practices as statistical process control, process mapping, special tasks forces, various kinds of employee involvement practices, and training in quality "tools" and practices. What these efforts share in common are a philosophical orientation towards involving people in the quality improvement process and a systems perspective for analyzing organizational processes.

Transcendant Learning—Modification of or creation of new concepts to open new kinds of interpretations. (Cell, 1984).

Transformative Learning—The process of adopting new meaning schemes or new meaning perspectives through a revision of the premises that frame a person's point-of-view or habits-of-mind.

Transsituation Learning—Learning how to change one's interpretations of a situation through reflection on one's acts of interpretation (learning to learn through reflexivity on one's learning processes) (Cell, 1984).

V

Value Added—A concept that refers to enhancements made by various organizational and individual actors in the value chain that add to the total value of a product or service.

Value Chain—A strategic concept that refers to the integrated system involved in the design, production, and distribution of a product or service, where each organizational entity of the system adds economic or market value to the product or service. It is a way of thinking about an organization's strategic position in the overall process and about the opportunities and threats or limitations that it potentially faces. An organization's position in the value chain determines its power and dependency relative to other organizations in the chain and provides a basis for assessing value added.

W

Web-Based Training—Training that is accessed via a computer with a Web browser, i.e., Internet Explorer.

Webcast—An event or meeting accessed through PCs by participants at different locations.

whole person learning—Occurs when the learner is engaged both cognitively and affectively with the learning experience, utilizing all of their capabilities, rational, imaginal, intuitive, and feeling and emotion.

Work Coordination—Collaborative or cooperative beliefs that facilitate interdependent work effort among employees.

Work-Based Learning—Using real work experience for purposes of learning and development, facilitating the resulting informal and incidental learning from experience into the formal knowledge structure of the learner.

Workforce development—The systematic acquisition and development of talent through the application of recruiting, learning and development, and management strategies to insure an organization has the human resource talent necessary for effective performance and sustaining competitive advantage.

Index